NEVER
SURRENDER

NEVER SURRENDER

LOST VOICES OF A GENERATION AT WAR

ROBERT KERSHAW

HODDER &
STOUGHTON

First published in Great Britain in 2009 by Hodder & Stoughton
An Hachette UK company

1

Copyright © Robert Kershaw 2009

The right of Robert Kershaw to be identified as the
Author of the Work has been asserted by him in accordance
with the Copyright, Designs and Patents Act 1988.

A CIP catalogue record for this title is available from the British Library

Hardback ISBN 978 0 340 96202 2
Trade Paperback ISBN 978 0 340 96262 6

Typeset in Bembo by Hewer Text UK Ltd, Edinburgh
Printed and bound in the UK by CPI Mackays, Chatham ME5 8TD

Hodder & Stoughton policy is to use papers that are natural, renewable
and recyclable products and made from wood grown in sustainable
forests. The logging and manufacturing processes are expected to
conform to the environmental regulations of the country of origin.

Hodder & Stoughton Ltd
338 Euston Road
London NW1 3BH

www.hodder.co.uk

To my mother and father

CONTENTS

INTRODUCTION

When my father landed at D–Day he was one of the youngest soldiers, at barely eighteen, in his regiment. He had joined the Home Guard as a young lad, saw the troop trains steam back from the south coast after the Dunkirk evacuation and viewed masses of German bombers pass over his home en route for London in 1940. Having fought his way through Normandy and north-west Europe, he 'liberated' my mother, a young German girl, and married her in the ruins of Hamburg's suburbs. I was always curious about how previous enemies, who did not speak the same language, could marry, bear children and still be together after sixty years. My father says it all transpired from a single meeting where he admits, 'I struggled with my German and she with her English, so the conversation lasted a while.'

Now he is reluctant to request help from the state, despite my mother's disability. 'Making do with less' and saving for a 'rainy day' stem from his underlying view that governments rarely appreciate individual needs – something he saw vividly in wartime. Like many Second World War veterans I have interviewed for books, he modestly understates his contribution. 'You should understand that the world was a more moral place then. People were more patriotic and had a greater sense of responsibility to each other.' Whether his observations are correct or not I will leave you to judge from this book.

As a long-serving Parachute Regiment officer I have been involved in the organisation and conduct of many Second World War com-memorations in Normandy and Arnhem. After the fortieth, fiftieth and sixtieth milestones the media invariably claimed this would be the 'last' occasion because fewer veterans survive. Yet every year the interest grows, motivated less by the veterans and more by their families and others with an apparently insatiable appetite to find out about a war they never experienced. I've heard people express a sneaking suspicion that the Second World War generation had a more fulfilling life spiritually than many today, who by comparison have – materially – everything. Of course, this fulfilment came at a high price as so many did not survive to enjoy the benefits of their sacrifice.

This book is not a social history of the Second World War, nor is it a story of battles and campaigns. It is a selection of vignettes designed to illustrate the experience of war portrayed through interviews, letters, diaries and personal accounts. I have used 'snapshots' to focus on individuals in selected scenarios. What was it like to witness the fall of France and wait on the beaches at Dunkirk? What did people feel about the prospect of invasion watching German bombers overfly during the Battle of Britain and the Blitz? What were the burdens undertaken in desert and jungle defending the Empire in the Middle and Far East? What did it feel like on an Atlantic convoy; in a bomber over Germany; storming ashore during a Commando raid in Norway or occupied France or wading through an obstacle-strewn surf under fire at Normandy on D-Day? These scenes from the Second World War have been freeze-framed to display the unique characteristics of this wartime generation.

When Winston Churchill was appointed Prime Minister at a low point in the war, he felt he could only offer 'blood, toil, tears and sweat'. This is what I have tried to reflect in seeking to illuminate why this generation, soon to leave us, is so unique. It has also helped me to better understand my father and mother, why they are so different from me and why I should feel so grateful that they are able to pass on some of their characteristics to their grandchildren.

I have spoken to a wide cross-section of soldiers and civilians, men and women, and have used their personal accounts, letters, diaries and spoken word to relive their wartime moments. The best way to bring such moments to life is by describing their thoughts and feelings on a typical day or following their progress through a sequence of related events. So we see the development of a typical day on the beaches at Dunkirk in 1940 or the nerve-wracking build up of briefing through to execution of a RAF bombing raid over Germany in 1943. What happened after boarding an aircraft up to the point of jumping into night skies over Normandy on 6 June 1944?

The youngest of these veterans are now in their eighties; and many of their comrades have passed away. TV documentaries are already having to interview their children to gain these insights.

Now is our last chance to hear this generation's voice before it is gone forever.

1

THE WORLD THEY LEFT BEHIND

Holiday-makers at Shoreham-on-Sea and along the south coast nearby heard an ominous droning from inland. It broke the idyll of that pale blue summer afternoon on Saturday 2 September 1939. Some 142 aircraft rose from bases inland, flew south to the coast and swept over the sea at Shoreham. Formations of Battle bombers flickered shadowy silhouettes across upturned faces reflecting the tension of past weeks as they flew overhead. Holiday crowds gazed intently at their progress as each successive wave roared over, shrinking into minute dots that disappeared into the direction of the north of France.

Flight Lieutenant Bill Simpson RAF, piloting Battle bomber 'V' for Victor, recalled the wing commander had assembled them the day before saying: 'Well, the balloon's going up at last. We are to take off for France tomorrow after lunch.' The Royal Air Force was making its first war deployment, sending the Advanced Air Striking Force on its way to France.

Dazzled by the hypnotic reflection of the sun on calm water, Simpson looked about. 'Everyone of us had his eyes skinned, looking around keenly for any signs of German fighters – not that there was much chance of being intercepted by Messerschmitt so far from bases in Germany.' They were accustomed to practising dummy attacks from their own fighters. Watching out for black crosses on hostile aircraft 'was new and real'. War was not yet formally declared. 'What a relief to pent-up feelings and worn nerves that now, at last, something definite was happening.' Excitement and curiosity at what conflict might bring was intense, but misgivings were few. He dwelt on the final mess party the night before: 'smoke, beer, excitable chatter of the officers and girls – genuine hilarity of a few, forced cheerfulness of the majority'. Last minute packing and letter-writing continued into the early hours of the morning. His worst memory was having to leave his wife behind ill in hospital – 'leaving Hope when she needed me most'.

Down below the holiday-makers settled back into deck-chairs. Fly-pasts were interesting rather than unusual. Large scale air manoeuvres were occurring throughout the summer months over the south and south-east coastlines testing air defences. Tomorrow the Prime Minister would speak to the nation, because the day before Hitler had invaded Poland.

The outcome of the Munich Agreement had left a poor taste in many British mouths. Moyra Charlton living in Essex felt opinion was turning against Chamberlain, 'I must say it does seem a short-sighted policy to give in to Germany over Czechoslovakia.' Tommy Woo-droffe, a BBC reporter, broadcast the tumultuously noisy and enthu-siastic crowd outside Downing Street when Chamberlain returned from Munich. The Prime Minister's quietly spoken announcement of 'Peace in our time' was drowned out by the cheering. 'I should never have said that,' he later confided to his wife. Charlton commented in her diary that 'his devoted sincerity and tact speak for themselves, but has he really done the best thing?' Ironically war was regarded less likely in 1939 than the year before. Nella Last observed on the fateful day that 'the dazed look on many faces' indicated 'that I had not been alone in my belief that *something* would turn up to prevent war'.

Sunday 3 September dawned, a beautiful clear early autumn day; by 1000 it was already hot. Early church services were packed with worshippers, greater congregations than normally seen. Alexander Cadogan, the Permanent Under-Secretary of State at the Foreign Office and a diplomat of thirty-one years service, reflected on yet another intense political crisis in Europe. Intimately involved in the succession of pre-war emergencies preceding this day, he wearily reflected 'these crises really are too tiresome. We can't go on living like this in Europe. There's no point in it.'

'The atmosphere during the latter part of that [previous] August was electric with uncertainty' remembered Territorial Army (TA) soldier Wilf Saunders having joined a signals unit six months before. News of the Polish invasion 'was in a very real sense a relief to most of us, when we knew the die was cast'. So far as he was concerned, 'this meant we were at war' because 'our country had said crystal clear that we would take up arms if Poland's frontier were violated, and now this had happened.'

People arriving at church that morning were at peace when they went in and the country was at war when they came out. If the polls were to be believed, it appeared war was less likely than had been anticipated during the Munich crisis the previous year. At a quarter past eleven Prime Minister Neville Chamberlain began speaking carefully and deliberately through wireless sets in parlours, kitchens and drawing rooms throughout Britain. Mrs Gladys Cox listened 'with bated breath – the whole world was on a tiptoe of expectancy this morning'. Chamberlain immediately came to the point:

> This morning the British Ambassador in Berlin handed the German Government a final note, stating that, unless the British Government heard from them by 11 o'clock that they were prepared at once to withdraw their troops from Poland, a state of war would exist between us.

'We knew it was coming,' remembered John Colville, a newly installed private secretary to the Prime Minister, sitting listening to the radio at his desk in Whitehall. 'All the same Chamberlain's broadcast, made with slow, solemn dignity, induced numbness.'

> I have to tell you that no such undertaking has been received, and that consequently this country is at war with Germany.

'I shall never forget the thrill of his closing words,' remembered middle-aged Gladys Cox living in West Hampstead.

> Now, may God bless you all. May he defend the right. It is the evil things we shall be fighting against – brute force, bad faith, injustice, oppression and persecution. And, against them, I am certain that the right will prevail.

The speech was followed by the playing of the National Anthem. Mrs Cox recalled, 'I rose and remained standing until it was finished.'

Interrupting church services was not undertaken lightly but soon brief flurries of activity began to occur within congregations, heightening the sense of momentum and unreality. At St Johns-sub-Castro in the East Sussex village of Lewes, Miss H Sandles the parish clerk hurried into church to give the Reverend H Langhorne the news, which he gravely announced from the pulpit. All over England similar scenes took place, a whisper to the vicar, the fading of hymns and a still congregation until the awful announcement. An audible gasp came from the congregation, remembered the wife of a Cambridge-shire vicar and matins was abandoned for a short improvised service of prayers and hymns to enable everyone to get home early. One Birmingham woman remarked she felt sorry for Chamberlain. 'Fancy,' she said, 'it's the same time Armistice was declared [in 1918]. Fancy declaring war on Sunday.'

Everyone appears able to picture what they were doing at the precise moment Chamberlain announced the declaration of war that Sunday. Feelings were mixed, after weeks and months of uncertainty there was intense relief – it was over – closure to interminable diplomatic crises. Some felt positively nauseous, anticipating horrors that likely lay ahead, others were simply numb. The only certainty was uncertainty. 'I can see the day now,' reflected one man, 'a glorious, golden September day, September morning and the French windows were open', sitting listening to the radio with the dog on the rug. 'Although the sun was shining the day was not so bright. I can see it now, much too nice a day to start a war.'

All about were the sights and smells of a typical Sunday. 'You could hear church bells,' remembered one woman, 'and you could hear Sunday sounds, mowing of grass and all this sort of thing and a lot of people lay in late and so there were late breakfast smells.' The declaration of war to another woman would be forever associated with the homely smell of cooking. 'I can just smell it now,' she chuckled, 'so every Sunday lunch smell I am immediately taken back to that Sunday morning.' Josephine Pearce, a nurse organising evacuees, standing on a rural bridge admiring trout through bright sunlight-reflecting water, was enjoying the stillness. An idyllic scene until 'I heard somebody's wireless, through one of their cottage windows, when Chamberlain was announcing that war was declared' and 'the whole bottom fell out of one's life'.

The doleful whine of an air-raid siren sounded out in London and Kent and other parts of the country within minutes of Chamberlain's broadcast. John Colville sitting at his Whitehall desk started out of a daze, 'rudely revived by the sirens moaning out the war's first air raid warning'. It was widely assumed London would be reduced to rubble within minutes of war opening, a perception heightened by distressing Spanish Civil War newsreels dwelling on the horrors inflicted on the civilian populations of Madrid or Chinese cities in the Sino-Japanese War. Immediate consternation was visible to Joseph Kennedy, the American ambassador to Britain, who saw the nervous anticipation of 'quite a few white faces among the men'. 'He didn't wait long,' he heard. 'Isn't that like Hitler to hop in minutes after war was declared?' Ellen Harris, a thirty-seven-year-old Reuter's parliamentary correspondent, jumped off a bus alongside all the other passengers in Islington. 'So now, here was the first warning, your mind immediately flew to the worst of everything,' she thought. People did not know what to expect. They scrambled into the nearest air-raid shelter, mothers carrying babies, 'even little babies with their gas masks on'. Clattering down the stairs, they heard unsettling warnings from air-raid wardens calling out 'mind the live wires' because the shelter had not been finished. 'That to me was the first shock,' she declared. 'I thought, what a terrible thing, I wonder if this has happened all over the country.' It had in many parts. 'They'd seen something off the coast and this alarm was given, put the wind up everybody but there was no raid.' False alarms did little to uphold the dignity of air-raid precaution staff who in the lead up to war were maligned as being an unnecessary and expensive nuisance to an ever discerning and ready to comment British public. 'Where is this 'ere war?' one old chap asked ARP warden William Holl, with one eye cocked upwards, as he lit his pipe and passed on.

Gladys Cox, likewise startled by the false alarm, was nervous, startled and bewildered, 'glimpsing dimly that all my known world was toppling about my ears'. Things would not be the same again. 'Chamberlain had a most profound effect on me,' admitted one man. 'I remember him saying "we are now at war with Germany" and he almost cried at the implications it meant to himself and everyone in the country.' Nella Last, a forty-nine-year-old housewife living at Barrow-in-Furness, grasped what it meant for her two sons, both of military age. Observing the profusion of sailors at Portsmouth while on holiday at Southsea two months before, she noticed the 'slightly brooding faraway look' on their faces. 'They all had it – even the jolly-looking boys – and I felt I wanted to rush up and ask them what they could see that I could not.' War was fast threatening their security at sea. 'And now I know,' she reflected. The man listening to Chamberlain's broadcast continued with the same realisation.

> I felt pretty low I tell you. We were just starting out our life. We were just getting our home together. We were newly married and I knew full well, I should have to go.

Like the rest of the male population of England, his circumstances had to be radically revised.

> Our life was going to be completely and utterly changed. The first thing, I was going to be parted from my wife. The first and most important thing. The second was I'd got to give up my home and my job had to go. I felt absolutely, completely and utterly shattered.

The BBC broadcast a feature on turning civilians into soldiers, reporting on bayonet training at a Tidworth army camp. An enthusiastic army NCO instructor was recorded singing out in a rising and falling staccato about the fundamentals of bayonet fighting. It was a light-hearted introduction to a world the sensitive would consider positively surreal. 'This is known as the *throat*, this is the *left breast* and this is the *right breast* and this is the *stomick*! Turn about! Now these are the *kid-er-neys*. Those are the places where you kill a man! So I want you now to do what I tell you. First rank behind the dummies – Move!'

Nella Last had confided to her diary the look on her son's face 'when someone mentioned *bayonet charging*'. 'He has never hurt a thing in his life: even as a little boy, at the age when most children are unthinkingly cruel, he brought sick or hurt animals home for me to doctor.' He would join the army and would be trained to kill. The instructor advised his bayonet-wielding recruits in the BBC broadcast: 'You're not on Buckingham Palace Guard! Now! Three good points: at the right groin, at the stomach, at the throat. Point! Not with your finger! Get in there and kill 'im!'

Nella thought of her son Cliff. 'It's dreadful to think of him having to kill boys like himself – to hurt and be hurt. It breaks my heart to think of all the senseless, formless cruelty.' It was her last day with her son at home.

Bella Keyzer from Dundee also appreciated: 'We knew Hitler was evil and we knew that Fascism had to be destroyed. But it was with mixed feelings that you looked at your brother and thought, he is the one who is going to have to go and fight.'

Tommy McSorley from Glasgow recalled his father kissing him on the forehead at about nine o'clock the day war was declared. 'Well, son,' he said, 'that's me away to the sodgers.' He didn't see him again for two and a half years.

Three days later on Wednesday at 0650 the radar station at Southend plotted what appeared to be 200 aircraft approaching the River Thames estuary from the east. Alexander Korda's recent film of *Things to Come* (1936) was a fictional dramatisation of world war breaking out at Christmas 1940, with 'Everytown' – a pseudonym for London – massively bombed to rubble and reduced to panic after bat-like swarms of aircraft fly in from across the white cliffs of Dover. Mass German raids were likewise fearfully anticipated.

RAF Bomber and Coastal Command reported they had no friendly aircraft operating in the area. Fighter Command labelled the approaching armada 'hostile'. Air-raid sirens howled across London again even as anti-aircraft guns began to bang away at fighter aircraft engaged in combat. A Hurricane squadron tore into the twin-engine 'hostiles' and the first RAF twin-engine Blenheim fighter spun into the ground. A technical radar fault caused Fighter Command to swarm in to intercept their own aircraft. Two Hurricane fighter squadrons engaged each other in the spiralling dog-fight and two aircraft belching flame and smoke spun into the ground, killing one of the pilots. The 'Battle of Barking Creek', fought over Essex amid swirling aircraft and puffs of anti-aircraft fire, provided an ignominious start to the air war.

Part of the world left behind on 3 September had been fear of war, which changed once it became an irreversible actuality. There was an instinctive dread of war based on the experience of 1914–18 and certainty that a more modern one would be worse. Alec

Douglas-Home, Chamberlain's private secretary recalled the extent to which:

> The shock to the national system of the First World War had really gone very, very deep. It is almost impossible now, looking back to see how deep it had gone. The trench warfare of the last four years of the First World War had really bitten into everybody's soul. You will remember of course, there was to be no more war, it was the war to end all wars.

Every family had anguished memories, even children. 'Hadn't I heard all about my uncle Tom who, in the First World War, had been gassed, blinded and wounded?' declared schoolgirl Elizabeth Aynsley, about to be evacuated. 'Hadn't I heard how, after a time in hospital, he had been returned to the front where he had been blown to pieces?' Thirty-nine-year-old Madge Kershaw lost all her male classmates. Asked why she never married, her indignant response was: 'Young man – there *were* no young men!' An attractive Miss G M Hodges left school in 1920 'pitched into a world bereft of my pre-war boyfriends and my father having died in 1915, three days after my thirteenth birthday'. His last birthday gift had been a topaz stone mounted in a hand-wrought gold wire brooch. She lost it on a western front pilgrimage 'in the midst of those days and days of experiencing those acres and acres of small wooden crosses'. It was the last straw. Gazing hopelessly over the vista of crosses she accepted it would never be retrieved and broke down and wept. 'It was really such a horrible war,' declared Nance Satterthwaite, whose mother lost both brothers, the youngest at nineteen. 'They would never have another war,' she declared, 'people did not want it.'

Rearming and resurgent Germany had replaced the perfidious French of Napoleonic times as the traditional British arch-enemy in the twentieth century. Feelings about them were ambivalent. 'I find that conversation at dinner tables, drifts inevitably to Germany and the Germans,' recalled journalist Phillip Gibbs, referring to the talking point at society soirées. ' " Personally I like the Germans," said the lady at my left elbow. "I believe Hitler means peace when he says peace.

Why don't we take him at his word? After all, the Germans are the best organized people in the world."'

Press comment was raking over scandalous innuendos about an apparent relationship between Unity Mitford, the daughter of Lord Redesdale, and Adolf Hitler. Her sister Diana was married to Sir Oswald Moseley, the leader of the British Union of Fascists. Upon the declaration of war, Unity sensationally attempted to commit suicide in Berlin.

Middle-class opinion was often felt to be too compromising to the 'Nastys' − 'Nazi' was a difficult pronunciation for the less well-informed. Joan Thorp in London complained to the left-leaning *Picture Post* magazine about 'people ignorant enough to spend a fortnight as tourists in Nazi Germany, and return full of the atmosphere of peace and plenty, lack of panic and general friendliness of the Nazis'. The majority of people visiting Nazi Germany thought otherwise. 'There can be no compromise with these people,' declared journalist Robert Byron after viewing the final Nuremburg 1938 Nazi Rally with Unity Mitford. 'There is no room in the world for them and me, and one has got to go. I trust it may be them.' Without compromising ideals he was lost at sea in 1941 due to enemy action.

Britain's working class were under no illusion who the enemy was. W J Cooksey wrote: 'I am an ordinary working man, which in my part of Great Britain means an unemployed man.' A veteran of the Great War, he admitted: 'I suppose I shall fight in the war that is expected now.' Munich was a 'let down' he declared, so he was not going to fight for Chamberlain, rather against Hitler and Mussolini, and not for the 'callous selfish holders-on to privilege, who are ready to betray me and mine, those people whom they know so little about'.

With one in five of the working population unemployed during the 1930s the immediate problem was not a resurgent Germany, but the economy. Attention focused on economic and social survival, not developing crises in Europe. 'I'm not talking starving in the sense of people in South Africa,' explained Labour youth activist Ted Willis, 'but I've known hunger pangs and not known where the next meal was coming from.' Their domestic situation was fragile. 'I'd seen desperation on my mother's face,' he admitted, having to feed five children and his father. Even so, there existed a basic moral decency in local societies at this time based on shared hardship. Ted Willis recalled frustration on returning famished after school to see his mother on her way out to deliver their stew to a more deserving family. 'But I'm hungry!' he remonstrated, prompting an immediate face slap in response. 'You're hungry,' his mother jabbed at him, 'but they're *starving*!'

Nevertheless, the threat of emerging Nazi Germany was to eclipse even social problems at home. 'I can't describe to you our feelings about Chamberlain adequately,' Ted Willis explained, 'he was regarded as *the* arch-enemy.' Munich was the catalyst. 'We felt he had betrayed the country, he made war more inevitable, not less inevitable.' Even apolitical travellers to Germany were detecting signs of menace. 'I was not thinking seriously about anything except enjoying myself,' said twenty-nine-year-old nurse Mary Lloyd on a ski trip near Munich in 1938. 'I was a youngster on the first big holiday I ever had.' All around she saw swastikas, which in hindsight exuded menace. 'People periodically listened to their wireless in the shops, there was a lot of excitement,' she recalled.

Sixteen-year-old Tony Hibbert was learning German in Bavaria to prepare for entry into the family wine trade. 'Everyone was in uniform around me,' he recalled. He studied alongside two Hitler Youth members, who trained to be motor-cyclists in their spare time. This was oddly militaristic because they drove a circuit with bogus signposts 'declaring so and so many kilometres to Paris'. Taking tea with the two family sisters he boarded with he heard complaints that two-thirds of their family had been lost in the Great War and 'that bloody little man Hitler was going to make it happen again'. Hibbert returned to England and decided against the wine trade and opted for a commission at Sandhurst in 1938 instead, 'because there was going to be a war in two years time anyway'.

'The fear was there ticking away like a bomb,' explained Labour youth member Ted Willis. An IRA bomb explosion in Coventry in August coincided with a RAF bomber flying overhead on air manoeuvres and caused some panic. Eleven million Peace Petition signatories accompanied by marches with demands to the government to form a pact with Russia had come to nought. Indeed, Hitler's Non-Aggression Pact with Russia the same month was a diplomatic coup that confounded all in its cynical effect. 'In our hearts I think that there was realization that the machinery was in motion, it couldn't be stopped,' reflected Willis, 'that the bomb was going to explode one day.'

People looked to BBC radio for news. 'My knowledge of the crisis comes from the wireless,' declared Miss French in a Mass Observer report, 'for I never miss any news bulletins that I can possibly have.' When the BBC merged its national and regional services on 1 September it signalled both the scale of the emergency and the thoroughness of preparations to meet it; this made uncomfortable listening. Gas warnings, the radio announced, would be relayed by the sound of hand rattles. Such an incongruous mix of familiar football match devices alongside the creeping horror of Great War trenches caused uneasiness and confusion. Clipped and urbane BBC upper-class accents accentuated the unreality of some transmissions:

> Yesterday we broadcast a reminder of the proper way to look after the gas masks that have been distributed and a warning against strange misuses such as testing the masks in gas ovens and by the exhaust pipes of motor cars. Today . . . the public are warned against this highly dangerous practice. The government respirators are not designed to give any protection against ordinary domestic gas, which would not be used in war.

Gwyneth Thomas, a nurse working at Highgate hospital, recalled the panic-stricken rush to fit masks during the false air-raid alert that sounded in London immediately after Chamberlain's radio speech declaring war. Consultants rushed into the wards to ensure every patient put one on. Pandemonium ensued when the nurses realised 'we couldn't, the patients couldn't breathe' and soon 'they were terrified, crying and pleading not to make them put them on – well, I didn't make them wear one,' declared Gwyneth.

Four-year-old Len Lewis in Portsmouth wore the colourful small child's 'Micky Mouse' mask version. It had a rubber vent 'and this made a rude noise every time you breathed through it,' he remembered. 'Most of the boys would see who could blow the loudest raspberry sound.' Circumstances, however, were not always funny. Baby gas masks were a grander version of the adult mask, a mini-chamber that was laced up with the baby inside. Len recalled how distressing it was to see his baby brother crammed inside while his mother and next door neighbour tried to work out how to lace him up. 'The thing was laid out on the dining table and I could see him through the gas mask window bawling his eyes out. He was obviously very frightened. I started crying too, because I thought he could not breathe.'

Kate Phipps, a nurse involved in supporting ARP work, remarked how 'some people are getting jittery, and expecting to be annihilated at any moment by bombers that cross the coast unannounced'. Her experience of training and preparation thus far lead her to hope 'if that happens that one will cop a nice clean hit, and not linger on badly injured or having to clear up the mess with inadequate help'. ARP women volunteers were issued with unflattering blue shirts and dark blue trousers but often kept their inappropriate and coloured civilian shoes, looking distinctly non-martial with up-turned soup-plate tin helmets. This incongruous uniform seemed to reflect their preparedness to face the anticipated intense air-raids. There are 'great arguments as to where wounded gas casualties are to be treated', she observed. 'Does one treat wounds first or gas? At what point are they removed from contaminated stretchers? Are the contaminated dead to be decontaminated or kept separate from the "clean corpses"? If it wasn't so serious it would be ludicrous.'

'Patriotism,' remembered Stanley Tress, 'ran like a thread through everything, through your school, family, through society. We thought that the Empire was a force for good in the world, a benign force.' This emotion would be largely unrecognised today. Empire Day was held on Queen Victoria's birthday. Children were bombarded with imperial propaganda, which was an important part of the school curriculum. In Bolton schools were asked to identify the 'Empire's Heroes' through projects and essays. Twelve and a half million visitors attended the 1938 Empire Exhibition hosted at Glasgow. As Tress commented: 'we thought that the British were a little better than most people.' Nobody could have foreseen the extent to which the Empire's sun had already set. Britain was still a superpower, her flag flew over one-fifth of the globe and beneath it was one quarter of the world's population.

'Even working men at that time, many of whom had a rather poor standard of life, were nevertheless intensely patriotic,' assessed Stanley Tress, 'and thought generally that the "British" was better than ten foreigners.' This war was to bring even more political and social change than the Great War that preceded it.

There was less patriotic fervour in the Dominions than in 1914. Britain's declaration of war was accepted and followed, but often with some misgiving. There were few formal military agreements. Military support had to be negotiated. Many within the Dominions had the feeling it was 'not our war'. British politicians had blundered in, it was up to them to blunder out. Moreover this underlying feeling was not unique to the Dominions and colonies.

'It is difficult to describe the mood and attitude of ordinary folk during the early years of the war,' declared Barbara Davies, who aspired to be a nurse but was to be driven by force of circumstance to become an aircraft factory worker. 'It may sound trite but we were all eager to do our bit. We young ones were as idealistic as the youngsters of today. The war seemed to heighten the emotions. We blamed "the old fools" in Parliament for this country's predicament. We, the next generation, had to do something about it.'

Part of the world-changing in Britain was an intangible appreciation that somehow their betters had let them down. British politicians appeared to have failed to handle a series of crises, suggesting control and a deft hand was found wanting. Gunnar Hagglof, a Swedish diplomat reflecting on events, asked, 'has British foreign policy ever been so mishandled?' The British public was starting to believe their betters may not be as reliable as inter-war social hierarchy so comfortably assumed.

Even the declaration of war was mismanaged. Exasperated TA soldier Wilf Saunders commented: 'to us, the deferment until Sunday 3rd September of the official declaration of war was no more than a rather strangely delayed formality.' To begin with Chamberlain had proposed Parliament adjourn for a two-month summer holiday in August when even the most optimistic had recognised war was imminent. The Prime Minister next indulged in a fish-and-line holiday while his staunch critic, Churchill, not in government, visited French troops on the Maginot Line. The bombshell of a Nazi–Soviet Non-Aggression Pact burst on the scene amid half-hearted British and French diplomatic representations to do the same. War – embarrassingly – was not declared on 1 September, when the German invasion of Poland clearly demonstrated violation of the ultimatum, because the French were not ready, delayed by mobilisation unpreparedness, to agree the joint declaration sought. 'What's the Prime Minister about?' was the background to the cheers the Deputy Leader of the Opposition attracted from both sides of the House of Commons when he asked Chamberlain, despite more German bombing in Poland, 'I wonder how long we are prepared to vacillate?'

One government plan at least was well conceived and executed and this was the evacuation of schoolchildren, which began the day Hitler invaded Poland. Movement was based on the premise that 600,000 civilians would die and one and a quarter million likely wounded in the first two months of any war. By early September three and three-quarter million individuals participated in an exodus involving nearly 4,000 special trains and seventy-two London transport stations alone. Red London buses carried 230,000 passengers to London stations and wartime homes.

'Aren't we going to stay here always?' asked one seven-year-old boy, eyes brimming with tears. 'I saw the look on the mother's face,' described Nella Last during one such initial parting, 'and my heart ached as I thought how I would have felt if my family had been scattered.' Increased mobility was one of the primary dynamics producing the changes that left the world of the 1930s behind. Evacuation presaged some 60 million changes of address from a population of 38 million in England and Wales during six years of war. To have seven or eight homes during the coming war, none of them permanent, was not uncommon. Parting was the most emotional part of the initial process. Richard Reeve left his weeping mother surrounded by other tearful parents and children the day after his ninth birthday. 'I wanted to cry, but being a boy, I forced on that stiff upper lip. It may have quivered a little though.'

Parting was followed by the journey, often by train. Richard Reeve's little world began to crumble because 'I had always believed that Mum and Dad ran my world and protected me'. Tommy McSorley's train puffing out of Glasgow was 'the start of a great adventure. Everything was magic. When the train left you could hear the cheers.' New could however be strange and disconcerting. Peering out of the train window half an hour later: 'All I could see was the white things. The place was full of them. I was terrified in case all these white animals should all gang up on us and eventually attack the whole train. It was only later on that I actually discovered they were sheep.'

When the masses of children began to arrive at their destinations the migration revealed at a glance what decades of static hierarchical living had never meaningfully shown before. The nation had an inward glimpse at itself which revealed the abyss between rich and poor. Many on both sides would never be the same again. J D Bones, assisting at a selection centre in a Colchester school, thought he was poor until the arrival of mothers and babies from the East End of London. He was horrified: 'I remember some poor little girl tripped and fell in the hall and I saw that she was naked under her thin cotton frock. Well, I had always a pair of pants, they may have been a bit ragged but I had some.'

The pain of the billeting process became even more pronounced when cultural and economic gulfs opened up. Quite often children were lined up in village halls and schools where householders would come and take their pick. The latter became disgruntled missing out on earlier choices while it was upsetting for the children who remained lingering. 'My mother said "they must be together" remembered Elizabeth Aynsley, standing forlornly alone with her little brother. 'I looked out of the window saying fiercely to myself, "I don't care if no one wants me, I don't care." I had never felt so unwanted in all my life.'

Goodwill soon evaporated when householders were given obviously verminous children or if bed-wetting occurred. One young girl described living with an old lady who 'frightened the life out of me and I proceeded to bed-wet practically every night, which must have been rather nasty for her'. Official estimates of the number of children so afflicted varied from 4 to 30 per cent but, whatever the number, it represented a serious burden to many a housewife. 'Instead of treating this in a nice or gentle manner, she used to come in about 11 o'clock,'

'I was a civilian soldier not a professional one', remarked one conscript called up in June 1939. Saying goodbye prior to embarking for France.

'Does one treat wounds first or gas?', asked one ARP nurse. Civil defence exercises, practising casualty treatment after air-raids, were taken seriously.

Around the crying little boy's neck is a label with his name and address. He refuses his gas mask. 'Aren't we going to stay here always?', asked one little boy faced with the dismal prospect of evacuation.

continued the girl, 'yank me out of the bed and insist I went to spend a penny.' Of course this did not work. 'After she'd left the room, I'd wet like mad, much to the horror of my elder sister who used to try and dry the bed before morning.' 'Dear Mum,' began one postcard to a parent, 'I don't like the man's face. I don't like the lady's face much. Perhaps it will look better in daylight. I like the dog's face best.'

Both sides of the class divide had subsequently to learn to live with or alongside each other. Most homes with rooms to spare were middle-class, while a significant proportion of evacuees were from working-class backgrounds. Despite negative aspects, the nation's mothers revealed a warmth and good nature towards other people's children during those early September days that have endured in relationships to this day.

Many of the children glimpsing these new surroundings would forever leave the norms of 1930s life behind them. Helen Jackson remembered the impact upon her young charges in rural Scotland. 'There were no chip shops. There was no cinema. They were appalled at what they found in the country, and they thought that we were primitive. And we thought they were . . . oh dear! It was a complete clash of cultures.'

Glasgow boy Tommy McSorley indignantly rejected the farm-owner lady's offer of milk from the cow she was milking. 'No, there is no way I am going to drink that stuff. Cow's urine! I couldn't possibly drink that.' Some youngsters meanwhile projected a maturity way beyond their years. One small Oxford boy aston-ished the two respectable ladies who took him in by offering to put himself to bed after supper 'so you two old geezers can get off to the boozer'.

Evacuation seemed the only government success and even this was swiftly transcended by the total lack of enemy air activity that followed it, trivialising the emotional cost of the great migration. Many returned home by Christmas because 'Phoney War' had broken out. New York journalist Mollie Panter-Downes called it 'the curious twenty-five percent warfare', describing how 'the war of nerves has degenerated into a war of yawns'. Everyone was slightly fed up with something or another and it reflected on the government: the Ministry of Information did not inform, the BBC was depressing, and worse, verging on boredom. There was even misguided exasperation that the bombs were not yet dropping. Until they did, it was universally thought that ARP workers paid £2.10s a week did little except wait around playing cards. Housewife Nella Last described the veil of depression settling over many after one month of inactivity: 'I think people are beginning to feel the war – blackouts and restrictions – for a gloom seems over us all. I've shaken off my fit of the uglies, but I felt I'd just crawl into a hole – and pull the hole in after me.'

Flight Lieutenant Peter Townsend RAF, flying with 43 Squadron, observed a final peacetime scene from his Hurricane fighter flying the last sector reconnaissance from Tangmere just before the outbreak of war. 'It was the last time we should see the friendly lights of Horsham, Brighton and Portsmouth spread out below.' The next time he would do it 'would be in the inky darkness of the blackout'. Nella Last called it 'the City of Dreadful Night' which had a 'strangeness that appalled me'. Blackout was universally detested and is difficult for anyone today to appreciate the sense of isolation verging on panic that could afflict those who often lost their way in the dark. Solitary men were often heard swearing aloud groping in the darkness, while many women admit to being reduced to tears. 'Once the lights went out,' said one man, 'it was a matter of putting your feet and feeling if there was anything there before you put your weight on it.' It was a habit that had to be developed in wartime, 'and it was a work of art putting your feet along, yet maintaining a steady pace'. One woman crossing the street in pitch darkness recalled blundering 'against something I couldn't identify at all, which frightened me to death'. A man shone a torch revealing the ghostly outline of a troop of elephants making their way from the circus to their stables. 'It gave me quite a fright coming up against this monstrous thing,' she later laughed. About 20 per cent of the population was to sustain some sort of injury on Britain's darkened streets during the war, giving vent to the criticism that the government were doing more deadly work than the clearly absent Luftwaffe.

The Phoney War was one with all holds barred. It smacked of the appeasement desire of the government not to go to war and was totally out of kilter with the general public's desire to 'get it done'. War did not appear to be taken seriously as if 'someone' was looking for a reasonable solution. Waiting for something to happen made it a queer and sinister time. Krupp's armament factories in the Ruhr were not allegedly bombed because they were private companies. RAF pilots risked lives dropping leaflets instead of high explosives. One was admonished for dropping them in bundles: 'Good God, man, you might have killed somebody!' he was told. Another, back late from an operation, explained the delay: 'he'd been as quick as possible pushing them under people's doors.' The Royal Navy provided the main headlines during the Phoney War. TA soldier Wilf Saunders recalled 'the sinking of the *Royal Oak* in mid October [at Scapa Flow] created a stir' and 'spirits soared with the sinking of the *Graf Spee*' in December. But in England, the severe winter of 1940 appeared to cause more surprises with the freeze and subsequent floods than the course of the war.

The army, the 'Cinderella of the Services', was not ready for war. Unpreparedness and the sudden mass dilution by TA and conscripts completely changed its ethos, size and structure, so that the small regular force that characterised the inter-war years soon formed yet another element of a world left behind in 1939. Julian Ridsdale, a subaltern in the Royal Norfolk Regiment, recalled the state of the 1st Division, the force that might have been called upon to resist Hitler's remilitarisation of the Rhineland in 1936. The Wehrmacht marched in with only three battalions.

> We had the same machine guns that we had finished the 14–18 war with, the Lewis gun. We had flags for men. My platoon that should have been 45 to 50 men had three or four. We were essentially a cadre for reinforcing the Indian Army and our forces in India, not a cadre for an expeditionary force in France. We relied on the French to do that.

German conscription, begun the previous year, had already trained two or three mass waves of manpower sufficient for scores of divisions well before England's belated change of course announced in April 1939. Only three years prior to war, General Edmund Ironside, the Eastern Command GOC, confided his opinion on the rearmament paper he had just received. 'It is truly the most appalling reading,' he wrote, 'how we have come to this state is beyond believing.' Virtually no resources had been devoted to tank development and Britain had slipped from lead place in the early 1930s to fourth by 1939. Ironside suggested 'no foreign nation would believe it if they were told'.

Watching the departure for France of the initial four regular divisions of the British Expeditionary Force (BEF) was not unlike viewing the re-run of a 1914 newsreel, the soldiers were even dressed alike. Albert Gaskin, a twenty-three-year-old bugler with the Kings Shropshire Light Infantry, recalled crowds waving them off.

> Soon the decks were crowded with khaki-clad soldiers, some very silent, wondering perhaps the same as I. Would this be the same as Dad's war? Fix bayonets, over the top, barbed wire, mud and blood? As the troop ships nosed their way to the channel a friend of mine had brought along his long silver trumpet and he stood at the bows of the ship and played 'Auld Lang's Syne'. Looking around me on the deck I watched some of the troops for their reaction, and like me many were gulping and some were weeping, as I was unashamedly.

All R H Medley's five major-company commanders in the 2nd Battalion the Bedfordshire and Hertfordshire Regiment were 1914–18 veterans and Military Cross holders, which meant that, though experienced, they were quite old. 'Age differences between ranks were sufficient alone,' he commented, 'to create barriers even without the very formal atmosphere which existed in the officer's mess at that time.' The average age of brigadiers and division commanders left behind in England was fifty-six, with some as old as sixty. During the Munich crisis the TA and Air Defence (AA gunners) had been called out and found wanting. With conflict imminent, an overtaxed War Office had to belatedly tackle four major projects, each overwhelming even in isolation. Fear of air attack required the expansion of Air Defence from five to seven AA Divisions. At the same time conscription was introduced and the TA was doubled, competing for the same man-power pool, and the first major expeditionary force to revisit France since 1918 required immediate despatch. Shortages, compromises and confusion were the unsurprising result. The exasperated Army Chief of

Staff, Lieutenant General Sir Henry Pownall, confided to his diary 'it is a proper Granny's knitting that has been handed out to us to unravel' by the politicians.

In stark contrast to the Wehrmacht facing it, the BEF and French Army conducted precious little training on arrival, even though conflict was anticipated in the spring. Flight Lieutenant Bill Simpson's Battle bomber squadron's experience was typical. On landing in France the afternoon before war was declared two refuelling pumps broke, delaying the rest of the squadron's refuelling until well after dark. Two 'decrepit old buses' then picked them up but 'practically nothing had been arranged about our billets'. Village accommodation was not found until two o'clock in the morning. Champagne was available but no food, neither did they have francs to buy any. 'Our presence was accepted with nonchalance,' he remembered, 'there was no enthusiasm.' Simpson's Phoney War 'was spent moping about the aerodrome, getting thoroughly browned-off and hoping against hope for some real action'. The excitement of arrival quickly wore off and 'was replaced by a feeling of anti-climax and of frustration'. Two things now dominated their miserable existence: leave and conjuring up amusement.

'They were firing mortars across the river somewhere,' recalled twenty-seven-year-old David Howarth, a BBC war correspondent observing the Germans 150 yards away across the Rhine, 'but anything warlike is done with an air of apology, one feels.' The Germans called it *Sitzkrieg*. Unteroffizier Max Lachner manning German defences on the Upper Rhine recalled 'our weeks flowed by peacefully' until one morning they were surprised by a sudden barrage from the French bunkers across the river. 'My people came out of the water and bushes naked and half-naked, jumped into uniform and manned their defence positions and we waited – nothing happened.' Soon a French soldier emerged with a huge white sheet gesticulating at the area behind his bunker. The penny dropped. Lachner and his men appreciated they were the victims of a visiting French general 'who had instructed the poor machine gunner to give the Boche a good going over with the gun'. Whenever the white sheet appeared, the German soldiers took cover. Coming from the Alsace (a province that had historically changed hands following Franco-German conflicts), 'we realised that the fellows on the other side were our age', recalled Lachner, 'and endured the same unfortunate school time as us'. BBC reporter Howarth saw exactly what was going on. 'There were a couple of German soldiers wandering about which didn't seem to worry the French – one gathered it wasn't worthwhile to shoot at the Germans because a lot of other Germans would shoot back.'

'I was a civilian soldier not a professional one,' remarked conscript Jack Brunton called up in June 1939. He described the diverse elements the rapidly expanded BEF needed to incorporate before anticipated operations in the spring. 'There's three types of soldier: there's the regular soldier who's joined up to do the type of work they were meant to do, there's the part-time Territorial who played at soldiers at week-ends for the fun of it; then there's the civilian soldiers – the militia.'

Brunton saw himself in the last category. His three-year course of study to qualify as an architect required him to work in the building trade by day to pay for evening classes at night. But he was conscripted. 'The whole pattern of my life was changed from that moment,' he bitterly recalled. 'Seven years of our youth were taken from us, which I have never recovered from.' Deprived of his education and earning potential, he found 'by the time the war finished, I was married and had to make a living'.

The BEF was a reluctant army, patriotic and prepared to do its bit, but wrankling at perceived 'Colonel Blimps' and the bureaucratic muddle that appeared to characterise Phoney War. There were shortages of everything. Although the TA was embodied into the regular army, the character of their formations remained the same. This was often described as the TA having an inflated opinion of their prowess alongside the regulars' penchant to regard their capabilities as worse than they actually were. Attempts were made through cross-posting of individuals and units to share experience where practical. Training was stymied by the appalling winter weather, false invasion alarms and the bureaucratic inertia of guarding key static locations, which might soak up as much as 25 per cent of a division or 3,000 men. In France there was confusion over accommodation, training areas and operation plans. One indication of the parlous state of training was the 23 Division order directing 'no man should be placed on guard at a Vital Point who has not fired a rifle'.

The BEF appeared not to be preparing for modern mobile war. Irritatingly it felt it was not told enough. 'Gentlemen, tonight you leave this country for an unknown destination,' recalled an infantry officer when the assembled battalion was addressed by the CO. 'Later I hope to be able to tell you where it is, but at the moment I don't know myself.' Everyone had worked out it was France. 'Keep your nob down and knock the Liebfraumilch out of the bastards,' sang out one of the disingenuous sentries, as they made their way to the boat train. On arrival in France, all they appeared to do was mend roads and dig. Platoon commander R H Smedley remembered one of his sections took eight weeks to dig a position, whereupon they moved on. Another infantry officer caustically remarked:

> During those eight months [of the Phoney War] I don't think I took part in one field exercise, though I did construct a railway station yard, build a road and turn a stream into an anti-tank obstacle. When it was half-finished we left it to build the road. Again I'm wrong; we half-finished the road and left it to construct the railway yard.

Soldiers in the new Expeditionary Force had a less trusting and more cynical attitude towards authority than their predecessors of 1914–18. The Depression had hit hard. Social deference towards officers was weakening but still in evidence. The upper echelons of society were still producing a disproportionate number of officers but public school was recognising that grammar school may have to be accommodated. Christopher Mayhew, a Territorial gunner in France, wrote home:

> All I'm saying is, I loathe it. I loathe being told exactly when to get up, exactly what to wear, exactly how to fold my bed clothes and overcoat. I loathe people looking me up and down on parade, commenting on my boots, perhaps, or telling me I haven't shaved enough. I loathe being marched to my meals, my games, and even to my prayers.

He was totally exasperated at the 'army's mania for uniformity'.

The soldiers in the BEF, like all other servicemen and women, reflected a microcosm of the society from which they were drawn. This society would be left behind after 1939. Increased mobility occasioned by evacuations and the priorities of service life meant that previously polarised classes not only saw each other for the first time, they had to live together. It was not always comfortable viewing. Newly joined soldier Ken Tout's first barrack task was to teach another lad how to lace up his boots. 'That 18-year old from the poverty stricken Gorbals had never before in his life been properly shod,' he remembered. Eighteen-year-old Muriel Gane Pushman joined the WAAF from an upper-class family that celebrated her decision by toasting her with 'bubbly'. She was then introduced to service lingerie: navy-blue knee-length knickers known as 'blackouts', just one glimpse of a foreign world, which had its own unique language. 'What an extraordinary phrase I thought – "'effin off".' Her new streetwise companions stifled their giggles at such naivety. When one girl, proffering advice about rapacious men, confided the origin of her expertise, the confused Muriel enquired: 'Er, what "game" was that Rosie?' She had not associated prostitution with Kipling's description of high-level imperial intelligence on the North-West Frontier.

'Hundreds of boys just like me from the hard times,' recalled nineteen-year-old Coldstream Guardsman Bill Weeks in France. He had joined because of the Depression. 'They talk about the good old days,' he remarked, 'I don't think they were – bloody awful really.' Soldiers joined not necessarily to fight for lofty ideals like 'democracy', signaller Wilf Saunders explained: 'many young people of my age were getting pretty fed up with Hitler's antics.'

War at this stage remained an adventure. 'I was only 19 at the time and the others were only slightly older,' recalled signaller Private Clive Tonry. 'It was all rather marvellous actually – the adventure – sky-larking schoolboys!' 'French drinks, at the equivalent of about two pence a glass seemed unbelievably cheap to men brought up in a stern land where the cost of living was around a shilling a pint,' remembered Wilf Saunders. So, on a night out 'we quickly resolved to try every bottle on the Café's display shelf'. Guardsman Bill Weeks, out with two mates, came across a mystery queue and, on enquiring, joined when told 'Fish and Chips'. 'When we got there we found it was a brothel!' he laughingly confided. 'It was – honest! So of course us boys did a runner and got out of it! Don't forget we were only 19!'

At this time the German 18th Infantry Division, earmarked for future operations in France, was conducting route marches of up to forty to fifty kilometres per day. It had been severely bloodied during the twenty-seven-day Polish campaign, losing 12 per cent of its strength. Commanders and men had few illusions of what lay ahead. No time was lost in preparation. General Guderian commanding a new panzer corps drummed into his tank crews the necessity during training was to reach the River Meuse on the French-Belgium border in three days. The French General Staff assessed the very earliest it might be achieved was nine days. By contrast seventeen-year-old TA gunner William Seeney with 53 Brigade in the BEF felt that, despite being taught how to fire their artillery pieces, 'we'd never been taught to be soldiers'. More to the point: 'We'd never been trained to kill people. I mean just think, we were soldiers we'd never heard of a killing ground, and as for being killed yourself, blimey, that was the last thing you thought about.'

The young age of some of these soldiers was attracting occasional comment in the press at home. One First World War veteran voiced some prescient misgivings about the call up. 'I do oppose the young ones going to the front,' he wrote. 'I speak from experience. No young fellow under 22 can stand up to the front line and live a normal life afterwards.' He had been despatched to the front in 1914 aged eighteen. 'The things I saw there – and did – I'll never forget.' His bitter commentary was: 'A lad of 18 is little more than a schoolboy. If he can't stick it, then his spirit is broken, he's failed before his fellows, he's dubbed a coward henceforward. If he does stick it, he becomes either a hard callous man, or a poor ditherer full of repressions.'

Many were soon to experience this dilemma. Despite the fact that conflict was anticipated in the spring, the men of the BEF had not transitioned to the practical realities a real shooting war would bring. Conscript Jack Brunton's heart was not in the coming fight. 'My generation were born just after the first war,' he said, 'and everyone was still recovering from it; then there was the General Strike in the 'twenties, then in the 'thirties, the Depression. Then, before we could get turned around, the second war started.'

'The way of living became quite easy,' admitted Lance Bombardier William Seeney with the BEF in France, 'The spring came along, the weather became pleasant and we settled down to a nice easy war; we also had a few days leave back in the UK and the war generally was almost forgotten.'

But it was not. Even Seeney noticed: 'all the time those people in their recce planes above were busy day in, day out.'

THE BLITZKRIEG EXPERIENCE

NAKED SOLDIERS: NORWAY, APRIL 1940

Shadowy sleek destroyers, larger cruisers and pocket battleships as-sembled at 0200 on the 7 April 1940 in the murk of the North Sea near lightship 'F', off the mouth of the River Weser. Ships glided in from Wilhelmshaven, Cuxhaven and Bremerhaven. Packed aboard each destroyer and filling every available space were up to 200 Gebirgsjäger, German mountain troops and other infantry with heavy weapons, equipment and light vehicles. Many had de-trained in total secrecy the night before near the Kaiser Lock at the mouth of the River Weser. Shipping was halted on the river to avoid unauthorised prying eyes. The gathering fleet turned northward and ran into the teeth of a force seven south-westerly gale with rising winds. Hitler was launching Operation Weserübung, a five-pronged assault upon the Norwegian coastline. It was the first air-land-sea operation in history, an enterprise typically as risky as his pre-war diplomatic forays.

The Kriegsmarine, or German Navy, carried 8,850 men following in the wake of seven Trojan Horse merchant ships laden with troops that left Hamburg three days before. This was the initial wave of two mountain and five infantry divisions that would follow by sea or air. Fliegerkorps X was to fly in 8,000 troops with 500 JU 52 transport aircraft supported by 345 bombers, fighters and other aircraft. On land they anticipated opposing 40,000 to 50,000 Norwegian troops. Hitler characteristically insisted in his 1 March Directive that 'numerical weakness must be compensated for by astute handling and the use of surprise'. The objective was to secure the passage of vitally needed iron ore supplies along the Norwegian coastline to Germany and secure the northern flank for future operations. By 1635 hours on departure day the first man was washed overboard from the destroyer *Erich Koeller* and left behind. 'No rescue attempts were made,' noted Kapitänleutnant (Lieutenant Commander) Heinrich Gerlach, the Narvik Gruppe operations officer. 'On no account was there to be any interruption of the time schedule.'

Gerd Böttger, a correspondent on board, recalled 'rain gradually changing into thick driving snow and huge mountains of water smashed against the front of the ship reaching the bridge'. The sea was wild, sweeping destroyers from astern, making them yaw so badly they could barely be held on course. Maintaining the scheduled speed of 26 knots caused some destroyers to roll 50 degrees, narrowly avoiding broaching. On 8 April the gale increased and with it came momentary contact with a British destroyer. The weather, having scattered the German flotilla, was more dangerous than the foe. When Kapitänleutnant Kurt Rechel increased the speed of the *Bernd von Arnim* to engage HMS *Gloworm* his bows dived under water at 30 knots, burying the forecastle and washing two men overboard. Rechel only righted his destroyer by decreasing speed. The heavy cruiser *Hipper* smashed *Gloworm* at point blank range after being rammed by the intrepid little ship, taking in 500 tons of sea water through the rent in the process. Only thirty-eight of the British destroyer's crew were picked up in heavy seas while the German flotillas ploughed on.

The stormy water was 'glass green' remembered Gerd Böttger and 'everything not nailed down tightly, tied down two or three times, went overboard'. Sea states for the flotilla heading for Narvik reached force ten and the ships low in fuel rode high on the water and were battered even more. Edmund Hubert, the first mate of the destroyer *Anton Schmitt*, recalled the 'dreadful voyage' in the teeth of hurricane winds, 'seas rolled over the length of the ship, ripping off everything not properly fastened'. Down below deck seasick vomiting Gebirgsjäger filled every conceivable corner. 'They were so sick that all that came up was bitter bile.' The relentless pace was maintained. 'We had to maintain speed,' Hubert recalled, 'to achieve the scheduled time for our arrival at Narvik.'

Operation Weserübung, the combined invasion of Denmark and Norway, burst upon an unsuspecting Europe like a thunderclap on

9 April because all eyes were on France, where an attack in the spring was expected. 'The blow fell on me personally at 5.50 in the morning when I was still in bed in my Copenhagen flat,' recalled Anthony Mann. 'We were wakened by a mighty roar of engines, wave after wave of bombers almost at rooftop height. Handfuls of pale green leaflets burst from each plane and floated lazily down to the almost deserted street. They informed the Danish people that Germany had forestalled an attack on Norway and Denmark by Churchill.'

This was not necessarily untrue. British Prime Minister Neville Chamberlain had agreed with the French to mine Norwegian waters to block the transit of iron ore and landings were envisaged at four locations to enforce this. An ironic scenario had developed whereby two sides at war with each other planned to invade a neutral bystander at the same time to protect it from the other. Denmark capitulated on the same day, Norway was to prove different.

As the German assault Gruppe began to approach Norway's 1,550-mile coastline, their objectives: Narvik, Trondheim, Bergen, Kristiansand and the capital Oslo seemed almost impossibly dispersed. Ships were mercifully becalmed as they slipped in out of the gales, entered the narrow fjords breaking up the coastline and stealthily approached their objectives. All were in German hands within twelve hours, taken via a mixture of surprise, bluff and ruthless aggression when forestalled. Not one initial landing exceeded 2,000 men and, despite some small hard fought naval actions, opposition was suppressed and follow-on units landed. 'Am putting in with permission of Norwegian government. Escorting officer on board,' signalled the cruiser heavy group entering the Oslo fjord. As they picked their way between the forts guarding the final approach to the capital the newly commissioned German cruiser *Blücher* was mortally struck by two enormous – ironically Krupp-manufactured – 280mm coastal guns at the narrow strait and finished off with shore-mounted torpedoes. She capsized, but the remainder of the force disembarked before the narrows and proceeded to Oslo by train. Among *Blücher*'s 800 crew and 1,500 strong landing party was the Gestapo contingent earmarked to police the capital. Over 300 men perished during the freezing swim to nearby shore.

Fog dispersed the initial parachute assault at Oslo's Fornebu airport and most aircraft had to turn back to Denmark to refuel. Two JU 52s were shot down by Norwegian Gladiator bi-planes and the German Fallschirmjäger (parachute) first wave airlift commander was killed as his aircraft came in to land. It flew on to Denmark. First one and then later more JU 52 transport planes landed beyond the range of the airport's intermittent defensive fire until the entire first wave returned from Denmark and landed in clearer weather. Aided by confusion and intimidating low-level Luftwaffe over-flights, the Germans bluffed the Oslo garrison into surrender.

Most of the troops preceded by a military band that marched into Oslo had flown into the airport. 'Norway's capital in every quarter was a scene of dazed disorganization completely without leadership,' reported an American correspondent at the scene. A city of nearly 300,000 inhabitants was being occupied by only 1,500 troops he observed. 'It was a thin, unbelievably short column' that 'required only six or seven minutes to march past', incongruously escorted by Norwegian policemen. Bluff, intimidation and audacious tactical skill supported by efficient organisation carried the day. The reporter felt the sinister intent of the column passing by: 'They were hard-muscled stony-faced men. They marched with rifles on shoulders with beautiful precision. Mostly they stared straight ahead, but some could not restrain triumphant smiles in the direction of the onlookers.'

Prime Minister Chamberlain could not believe reports that the Germans had already captured Narvik, 600 miles from Oslo. It was incomprehensible, Norway was 1,100 miles long, the same north–south distance by which the United States separated Mexico from Canada. He announced to the House of Commons that the reports must be referring to Larvik, a small port just outside Oslo Fjord. The efficient execution of this joint air–land–sea operation crossed thresholds of scale that dwarfed previously accepted military experience.

An undercurrent of British opinion began to develop suggesting the Scandinavian landings appeared easy for the Germans but difficult for the Allies. Denmark fell at the cost of twelve dead and twenty-three wounded Danes for twenty-three German casualties. German infantry simply walked ashore from merchant ships tied up in Norway, while Allied countermeasures 'missed the bus', as Chamberlain originally claimed of Hitler. Subsequent British experience in Norway was to confirm this sneaking perception. Norwegian forces resisted from the north of the country and were reinforced by British and French troops who landed at Namsos, Aandalsnes and Narvik between 14 and 19 April. A French–Polish Expeditionary Corps arrived by late April and early May. Ten German destroyers were sunk by the Royal Navy at a cost of two outside Narvik, during two naval battles on 10 and 13 April, but by then five German columns were already pressing northward from Oslo. The aim was to link up with the footholds already established on the coast, joining up a country-wide occupation like oil spots on water.

The Norwegian experience began for British soldiers with the seeming absence of any coherent plan, before and during the campaign. General Edmund Ironside despaired of Chamberlain's war cabinet from the very first when initial planning for an occupation of Norway was considered in March. 'A more unmilitary show I have never seen,' he concluded after a series of pointless technical questions ended with Chamberlain poring earnestly over a map of Norway and then asking about its scale. 'The Cabinet presented the picture of a bewildered flock of sheep faced by a problem they have consistently refused to consider,' claimed Ironside, suspecting the plethora of hypothetical formulas being put forward was to 'shy off' decisions. 'I came away disgusted with them all,' he confided to his diary.

Private Joseph Kynoch, a TA Leicestershire Regiment soldier with 148 Brigade based near Rosyth, thought they were going to assist the Finns against the Russians. His battalion was embarked on the destroyer *Afridi* and then told they were going to Norway. 'There was to be as many orders and counter orders as would fool not only the enemy but everyone else associated with the move, including ourselves,' he complained. 'To add to the chaos, most of our movements were carried out in the black-out,' he added. Maps were issued 'but were on such a large scale as to be fairly useless and also they were completely out of date and were collected up later on'. Like many embarking troops they found themselves on the wrong ship and re-embarked on the cruiser *Devonshire*. She in turn was summoned to resist the unexpected German invasion and troops were off-loaded again. 'In the general mêlée that followed, some of our equipment was damaged as it was swung ashore willy-nilly in nets and dropped onto the quayside.' Vital signalling equipment and ammunition 'were left behind in the heat of the moment' as the hastily formed naval group steamed off into the North Sea.

Five days later they re-embarked on the *Orion*, sailing on 14 April, only to return to the Forth again that night. 'There is nothing more frustrating and nerve racking for a soldier than stop-go attempts to get at the enemy.' When they got back there was 'much invective on board and much muttering about ourselves and Fred Carno's army.' Kynoch's brigadier, Harold de Riemer Morgan, received his fifth plan of action on the 17 April while at sea en route to Norway, which changed his landing from Namsos to Aandalsnes. Stores from Kynoch's ship *Orion* were transferred to *Cederbank* and she was sunk by a German U-boat en route. 'All of our kit was on that boat, lorries, bren carriers, rations and ammo,' grumbled 'Crusty' Curtis from the same battalion. It was a considerable blow. 'We now had only our rifles, one or two anti-tank gun rifles and bren guns to face the enemy with,' observed Joseph Kynoch gloomily, 'and the clothes we stood up in.' This was not the way to start a campaign. Snow blizzards enveloped the boat as they neared Norway. The weather reflected the prevailing mood. 'We were naked soldiers now in more ways than one,' reflected Kynoch, 'as we shivered in the sub-arctic morning.' They landed several days after the rest of their battalion, which had been split in two halves to serve the administrative rather than tactical imperatives of the mission.

Norway was a land of fjords and few roads, with the midnight sun bleakly reflecting over the rough terrain of 1,800 metre peaks. Twenty-one-year-old George Parsons with 5 Independent Company 'landed at this place Mojöen, and imagine how we felt when we saw a towering ice-capped mountain in front of us standing about 2,000 feet high'. It was completely outside the experience of the British soldier. 'We south London boys, we had never seen a mountain before, most of us had never been to sea before.' Lieutenant Patrick Dalzel-Job, one of very few Norwegian speakers, was embarked with the Expeditionary Force staff and two companies of the Scots Guards on the cruiser *Southhampton*. He recalled the dearth of knowledge about the land over which they were to fight. 'None of the other officers on board, from the General downwards, knew anything about the country where they were supposed to operate, no arrangements had been made for landing troops there, and none of the officers or men had any knowledge of winter warfare.'

Norway was a strange little known land of which 69 per cent was bare mountainous country, completely open to air observation and attack except for the defiles, passes and valley bottoms through which the few roads passed. This was the terrain that characterised the Narvik area encountered by the British. Twenty-three per cent of the remainder was forest and lay within the zone being contested by the German Army in central and south-east Norway. Very little, only 3 per cent was cultivated, primarily around the settled areas and the remaining 5 per cent was rivers and lakes. 'When I said that there would be deep snow on the north Norway coast at that time of year,' which was spring time in England, 'at first I was not believed,' recalled Dalzel-Job. 'There was consternation' among the staff because the Expeditionary Force had brought motor cars and bicycles but 'there were no skis, or snowshoes – nor any men trained to use them – and there was no white camouflage'. Ominously, there were also no anti-aircraft guns, which might well prove a problem. Londoner George Parsons had already noticed the ambient hue that never left the sky at night. 'We saw dusk when we left Scapa [Flow] and we never saw any darkness after that.' They were completely exposed to aircraft.

In comparison to these shortfalls, the British 146 Brigade, landing further south at Namsos, were ironically issued the full range of arctic stores and equipment. 'What's all this lot?' asked Tom Carroll who had joined the Irish Guards earlier that year. They had extra shirts, vests, thick long pants and twelve pairs of knee-high woollen socks, supplemented by balaclavas, jerseys, gloves and 'a wacking great big coat with snap fasteners on and fur hats'. Understandably they assumed 'well, we must be going to some sub-zero place'. It was Harstad, a small fishing village in northern Norway. The winter clothing was so heavy and bulky that according to the jaundiced eye of their Force Commander, General Sir Adrian Carton de Wiart, they were reduced to the status of 'paralysed polar bears' being 'scarcely able to move at all'.

In Norway the British soldier went to war against the elements first, the Germans came a close second. Private Joseph Kynoch, the TA soldier with the 1/5th Leicestershire Regiment, recalled that even simple manoeuvres were difficult in a country 'alien to British troops surrounded as they were on all sides by densely forested heights, frozen lakes and the ever present snow'. It was bitterly cold and their unit had no arctic equipment. Indeed as Territorial part-time soldiers they were unused to basic field soldiering in even immoderate British weather conditions. To the dismay of their Norwegian allies they could not operate off roads, the only firm going underfoot because their footwear was unsuited to wet and freezing conditions. 'By day in April the snow is like a bog to walk through, but when night comes it again freezes solid,' remembered Kynoch; trench-foot — a familiar First World War affliction — and frostbite were the result. One Norwegian officer thought the seemingly unmartial Territorials looked like 'untrained steel workers from the Midlands'. Digging defensive positions down was virtually impossible, so rock sangars, piles of stones, had to be built upwards. All this was learned through a painful process of trial and error. Greatcoats kept the cold out during the hastily snatched hour or two during short nights but were restrictive by day. Excessive sweat built up in the heat of day chilled and froze damp bodies at night. The climate and conditions proved a bitter adversary, as a more sympathetic Norwegian liaison officer Colonel Jensen commented: 'A difficult job in a strange land, in frost and snow with dark thick forest on all sides. It might be difficult enough for us who are used to these conditions, but for them it must be sheer hell.'

When climate and enemy coincided, little went well for the British soldier in Norway. The Germans pushed two battle groups up country: Gruppe Oslo North-West with 163 Infantry Division reinforced by elements from two others, and Gruppe Oslo North, spearheaded by 196 Infantry Division. By 18 April they were advancing on a five-column front 120 kilometres beyond Oslo. Mobility on both sides was restricted to the few roads and railways that followed valley bottoms. Luftwaffe air supremacy enabled German reconnaissance to accurately pin-point British blocking positions in advance, whereas the British had to constantly react to unexpected engagements. Lone roads were shot free of any moving traffic by aircraft and suspected pockets of resistance in villages ruthlessly bombed. 'Where the hell's the RAF?' was the question after incessant air-raids. 'Where are all our Spitfires and Hurricanes?' 'No one answered the question' recalled Joseph Kynoch, 'no one could.'

This was the first war in history during which air power would play a decisive role. Its one-sided application against British soldiers rudely disabused commanders who had previously assumed the difficulty of moving artillery forward in mountainous terrain would confer some defensive advantage. Air-raids were a brutal psychological and physical shock, typically initiated by the sudden appearance of bombers. They could rarely be discerned early enough due to limited vision from steep-sided forested valley bottoms. 'Get down,' was the only warning Kynoch received: 'The high pitched scream of the falling bombs gradually fell down the scale and ended abruptly with a dull crump and a crack of an explosion which made the ground beneath our bodies heave and tremble. Then the debris began to fall and shrapnel howled and hissed all around us and we were thankful for our steel helmets.'

Immediately following behind were Messerschmitt ME 109 fighters flying and strafing so low that pilots could clearly be seen squinting through Perspex cockpits. The experience was terrifying and many veterans testify to the utter helplessness of their situation with no anti-aircraft protection. Infantry sections could lie in a line and attempt volley fire, aiming just in front of the propeller. Kynoch's section succeeded on one rare occasion in winging a fighter that subsequently crashed. More men were wounded than killed and each casualty tied up four others who had to carry him. Bombers dropped incendiaries on forested valley sides to burn out and force the abandonment of prepared positions.

The momentum of the German advance along difficult roads, swiftly overcoming road blocks in concert with the flying artillery of the Luftwaffe, was maintained by advance detachments of a platoon of two or three light Panzer I tanks accompanied by infantry on bicycles. Light though these 'Krupps sports cars', as the Germans nicknamed them, were, they remained impervious to British or Norwegian anti-tank fire. Heavier lorry-borne forces of infantry on captured or sequestered civilian Norwegian vehicles followed with horse-drawn artillery. They came across fragmented and hastily established defence positions. Shortages of equipment prompted the British commander of 'Maurice Force' operating alongside the 5th Norwegian Division near Trondheim to declare there was 'very little point in remaining in that part of Norway sitting out like rabbits in the snow'. He recommended evacuation. Under-equipped British troops were road-bound to valley bottoms while their Norwegian allies were better equipped to hold valley sides. Coordination, however, was not good because, as Lieutenant Patrick Dalzel-Job explained, 'I never met a British or French officer in Norway who could pronounce Norwegian place-names, and mistakes and delays owing to errors in Allied signals were the rule rather than the exception.' Once fighting began, chaos reigned.

Gebirgsjäger, or German mountain troops, often spearheaded German advances. French Chasseurs, similarly trained, had joined the Allies but were immobile, having left crucial ski straps, snow-shoes and all their white camouflage suits behind at their base in Brest. Not all German equipment had arrived, but every Norwegian family could ski, and the Germans helped themselves to what was needed from shops or the civilian population. Once Allied positions were identified by the Luftwaffe they were reconnoitred from valley sides by mountain ski patrols.

British troops manning defensive positions could only expose themselves for limited periods in the bitterly cold Norwegian climate. They were not equipped to deal with rapidly alternating temperature ranges which might vary from +2°C to −20°C to 30°C if the wind direction shifted from the milder south-west to pitiless eastern winds blowing in from Russia across Finland. In any case 1940 had a particularly severe winter. Excessive cold induces lethargy that erodes fighting power at the expense of the need to shelter to survive when temperatures drop to −15°C or more. Soldiers struggled on little realising that cold disguises the need to increase fluid intake. Surrounded by snow and frozen water, there was not enough fuel to transform the required seventeen-times volume of snow for one of water. Unnatural hazards ensnared the inexperienced. Snow blindness became common place, as also fume poisoning when men huddled together in unsanitary conditions for warmth. Constipation came from insufficient water and reluctance to face the discomfort of defecating in freezing conditions. Physical health rapidly deteriorated, making soldiers vulnerable to pneumonia, frostbite and equally debilitating trench-foot, caused by constant immersion in deep wet snow and slush as rock sangars or trenches were constructed on valley sides.

Private Joseph Kynoch recalled the nights were worse: 'My hands and feet were covered in chilblains due to the cold and melting snow during the day penetrating our boots and socks, then freezing again at night. Even gloves would have helped. Most of us suffered from chilblains causing fingers to swell and break into sores.'

This was the state of the defence prior to attempts to block the German advance on Tretten near Lillehammer in late April.

The Germans soon appreciated that Allied blocking positions were relatively immobile beyond valley floors. Artillery and mortars were brought forward to fix the defence in the valley bottom in frontal feint attacks while light forces manoeuvred across seemingly impassable mountains to the flank or rear. Merchant ships and even sea-planes landed soldiers further along the coastline and paratroopers dropped in the Dombas Valley. German infantry division advances stretched over a hundred kilometres while light *vorausabteilung*, or advance guards, fought roads clear. One action fought in mid-May by the 2nd Gebirgsjäger Division at Stien on the approach to Narvik demonstrated the methodology. At a road block bitterly contested by the Scots Guards German ski troops marked and prepared an epic flank march of sixteen to twenty kilometres. The battalion traversed 800-meter climbs and roped and sledged its way across deep, then thawing, snow overlooking the Sorfjord while a German attack, heavily supported by artillery, was mounted along the valley floor.

Private George Parsons, resisting with 5 Independent Company, remembered 'the alarm came in that they were coming round the back over the top round behind us', which was a shock, 'because we just didn't know what to do'. There was little alternative but to fall back. Parson's unit, about to be enveloped in the German pincer, was directed to get ahead to Mojöen before the engineers blew a bridge.

Parsons, a recently joined TA soldier reflected: 'Well, this was the first time I had ever done a speed march, it was really quite hectic, it was desperate, I mean we were sort of fighting for our lives really.'

They barely made it in time. 'And all I can remember there, I was so gasping for something to drink and I had nothing.'

These rapid reverses made the British soldiers feel outclassed by apparently superior German tactics and equipment. 'It's sheer bloody slaughter,' declared a corporal in the 1/8th Sherwood Foresters fighting near Lillehammer. 'You can't see the bleeding Jerries for trees, then before you can even cock your rifle, they're on top of you and they've all got automatic weapons that spray you with bullets.' These were inexperienced TA troops but regular troops were also afflicted by equipment shortcomings. Deep snow made barbed wire defences useless and Bren-gun bipods and mortars sank in it unless they were stabilised on *pulks* or sledges and prepared surfaces that only veteran winter-war soldiers could identify, practical guidance which was unavailable. 'Some silly bastard wanted to dig trenches and put up barbed wire,' complained the corporal. 'Can you imagine it? They'd have got round it, over or through it with the kit they've got.' Light tanks could not be effectively fought. 'We tried to stop their tanks with road blocks of tree trunks but they just shove them out of the way.' Mortared and strafed by low flying aircraft, he cynically concluded: 'It's bloody hopeless trying to stop them with rifles and bren guns – we might as well have used pea-shooters; and cold at night – might just as well be in our birthday suits as in our own gear.'

The pitfalls of the equipment chaos exposed their nakedness. 'We could almost hear the Jerries laughing,' declared the corporal. 'Honestly, Fred Carno's Army just isn't in it!'

The shock of intense fighting was often the final straw for soldiers convinced they were badly led, equipped and outmanoeuvred. George Parsons' first battle started innocuously enough with an advance by German soldiers on bicycles. Motor-cycle combinations with machine-guns followed and then the main body. 'Then all hell broke loose' during a thirty-minute engagement. 'I think I went into that first half hour a young lad of 19 and finished up by the end of it a man,' he recalled, 'very experienced because, for the first time you realise you're playing for keeps.' Almost immediately he saw a man blown apart by an anti-tank round. Nothing went right. 'It got rather alarming because we were very inexperienced and we hadn't quite realised that behind all this there were their ski troopers', experienced mountain troops.

Weapons could often be adversely affected by the cold and the men were not practically astute enough to appreciate the consequences. Muzzle velocities tailed off with poor cordite burn on firing, while the pronounced expansion and contraction of barrels also impaired accuracy. Brittle metal cracked in the cold, adding to breakdowns, and oil made viscous by freezing temperatures clogged what should have been dry-cleaned working parts. Ice fog and blown snow from weapon reports gave away their firing positions. 'The proximity of the mountains and woods combined to play the strangest tricks with the hearing,' explained Private Kynoch, while all the time they were constantly assailed by the unsettling cry of: 'Look-out – they're behind us!' The blocking action fought at Tretten by Kynoch's 148 Brigade on 21 April was a shattering reverse. 'Out of nearly 2,000 men,' he recalled, 'the Foresters and Leicesters were now reduced to some 300 men and nine officers between them.' It took only three light panzers to crack the position. Now the retreat began.

'We marched for over 24 hours non-stop and covered something like about 60 kilometres,' remembered Private Tom Carroll with the Irish Guards. They were heading for Bodö. 'In that part of Norway there were only mountains with roads running around their bases or round the coastline.' They marched to the accompaniment of monotonous sonorous booms behind, which echoed around the mountain tops and valleys as the Royal Engineers blew every bridge. Carroll counted eighteen before they reached the port. Even as the ship was pulling away from the harbour the Germans drove up on motor-cycle combinations with mounted machine-guns. Carroll marvelled at the speed with which the German engineers must have negotiated the demolitions. Machine-gun fire was splattering against the metal hull as they pulled out into the main channel.

After their mauling at Tretten the Leicesters faced a sixty-mile march from the railway station at Dombas to Aandalsnes. Lieutenant Hugh

Guy, the battalion intelligence officer, remembered 'walking through the dark pine woods with the red glow of burning farmhouses on our left'. There was constant apprehension during 'a most tiring march through sludge and snow and the perpetual expectation of having Germans jumping on us from the woods flanking the road'. Some of the soldiers walking the sleepers of the railway line began to falter after fours hours tramping through the night painfully measuring each sleeper-bound step. 'Some of our comrades began to crack up,' recalled Private Kynoch, 'and it was understandable enough. By this time we had begun to suffer from the effects of lack of food and unsuitable clothing.' Greatcoats, too hot to wear by day, snagged their legs due to their frock length by night when 'the sub arctic temperatures penetrated them easily'. Without food for the past week, 'we didn't realise it at first, we just didn't have the energy for a sustained march; our physical batteries were flat.' Men began to throw down tin hats, greatcoats, even rifles and cries came from the snaking column. 'For Christ's sake stop – the bloody man's a maniac – I'm not going any further – the bloody Jerries can't be any worse than this bastard!' Men dropped out, some quietly and without fuss, 'others with curses and threats as to what they would say and do when they got back home'. Many did not make it.

Aandalsnes was no longer the picturesque little town they had seen on arrival. Sub-Lieutenant John Adams, observing offshore from the destroyer HMS *Walker*, saw that it 'was in indescribable ruins, not a wall standing and fires everywhere. The German Air Force certainly knew their stuff.' The destroyer took off 578 troops. 'They were in a completely demoralised state,' Adams recalled, 'and had been machine-gunned and bombed the whole day by three Heinkels who had come all the way from Hamburg.' The dismal scene shocked him into the realisation that 'we don't seem to be doing too well in Norway!' Only 120 men stepped aboard from the 1,200 Sherwood Foresters who had disembarked 'and they had only been ashore a week!'

With the approaching dawn ships were anxious to move to avoid being caught in the narrow confines of the fjord. 'German planes were due any moment now,' wrote Adams early on 1 May. They left in a hurry, producing a huge bow wave on the calm fjord waters, heading at speed for the open sea. Consternation mixed with relief that the Luftwaffe was apparently not about was interrupted by the rat-tat-tat of machine-gun fire as a bomber dived at them above the mainmast, anticipating the destroyer's difficulty elevating its heavy armament. 'One could see the tracer bullets coming at the bridge,' recalled Adams, 'but the range was too far and they fell into the sea astern.' As they sped to the fjord entrance another bomber came from ahead. 'I could see the bombs coming the whole way – and at first I thought it was going to be a hit.' Water geysers shot up forty yards away abreast of the bridge as they sailed clear through the spray.

'My mouth felt as though it was full of sawdust,' remembered Private Joseph Kynoch, now beyond hunger. 'The thought of food made not the slightest impression on my salivary glands.' But it was his legs and feet that puzzled him. 'They felt so heavy and it seemed as though they were weighted down by leaden weights similar to the boots worn by deep sea divers.' He was strafed and bombed from the air for another two days before being taken off with the rearguard by the cruiser HMS *Sheffield*. He felt fortunate glancing back 'for one last look at the place where we landed such a short time ago. No pretty houses now, only black chimney stacks standing erect like ghostly fingers pointing upwards accusingly at its destroyers.'

A pall of smoke rose into the air spilling into the Romsdal fjord like a black smudge as *Sheffield* departed soon after 0200. By the time she reached the open sea thirty-six miles away the swastika flag flew from the ruins of Aandalsnes. The evacuated troops were bitter. Mortars had arrived without base plates and could in any case only fire smoke bombs. There had been no bullets for rifles and only 'pathetic' anti-tank rifles that could not penetrate panzers. Artillery and air support had been non-existent. 'Most important of all,' remarked Kynoch dryly, 'our officers were equipped with walking canes, not automatic rifles like the enemy.'

General Ironside, the Commander-in-Chief, addressed his unit in Glasgow on return. 'You were in no sense driven out of Norway,' he told them amid much appreciation. 'You were ordered out.' The *Daily Mirror* columnist Cassandra responded laconically the following day: 'Who by – The Germans?'

Defeat had been total.

RUNNING THE GAUNTLET: FRANCE, MAY 1940

It was still dark when the force of forty-two JU 52 transport aircraft took off from Cologne-Wahn airport on 10 May 1940. Eleven towing gliders circled steadily, climbing to 8,200 feet over Germany before turning west, following a navigational trail of incandescent searchlights. On board were 193 Fallschirmjäger from the Stürmabteilung Koch. These men had been confined to barracks since the previous November when not training, secured by barbed wire and guards. Tension among the Fallschirmjäger sitting in groups of ten inside the draughty DFS 230 gliders was high. The gliders had been secretly delivered to the airbase in furniture vans. Wrapped in blankets to ward off the cold, an officer recalled, 'our chances of success lay clearly and absolutely on surprise, because in every case we would have to fight against superior forces'. Within thirty-five minutes they began to land among the sleeping Belgian garrison at Fort Eben-Emael, assessed by the Belgians and Allies to be the most modern and formidable in the world. It commanded three vital bridges the Germans needed to cross the Albert Canal.

One of the popular toys on sale at Hamley's store in Regent Street was a Build Your Own Maginot Line set complete with toy soldiers, lorries and even a barrage balloon. Writer George Beardmore reflected 'all right, it's only a toy' but it prompted him to consider that 'historically purely defensive positions have never held out for long'. Had not the French General Staff ever read Plutarch? The German assault through the Low Countries was to outflank the French Maginot Line to the north, but to do so they needed to penetrate the complex of Belgian forts around Liège to clear a path for the approaching 4th Panzer Division.

Oberleutnant Witzig's assault engineer group assaulted 'Granite' one of the Eben-Emael strongpoints. Despite two gliders crashing and Witzig's casting off in the wrong place, the remainder achieved textbook landings. One glider even snagged a Belgian machine-gun, dragging it from its emplacement on touchdown. Witzig's fifty-five assault engineers quickly blew in the fortress exits with explosive satchel charges. A superior force of 700 Belgians was trapped

Troops in Norway issued with over-bulky kit looked like, 'paralysed polar bears' remarked a senior officer, 'being scarcely able to move at all'. It epitomised the British response to German Blitzkrieg tactics.

'The Belgians loved us . . . it was flowers all the way in!', announced one BEF soldier. A roadside welcome.

'You tell me who could be that cruel?', declared one British soldier watching refugees strafed on clogged roads alongside the retreating BEF. Civilians and soldiers share a ditch during a raid.

impotent inside their casemates, while the small company of Fall-schirmjäger disabled fourteen guns with prepared hollow-charge explosives and flame-throwers. At daybreak Koch's men paused to view swarms of aircraft crossing the Dutch–German border. Some 580 JU 52 transport planes alone, laden with paratroopers and air-land troops, were heading for Rotterdam and The Hague. The German Army Group B was bypassing the Maginot Line. The war in the West had begun.

The much anticipated conflict in the spring of 1940 was still a shock to the Allies when it arrived. Radio added to the immediacy of events back in England. French and British forces moved their mobile units forward to the line of the River Dyle in Belgium, hinging their right flank on the Ardennes Forest region, which was considered impassable to tanks. 'I'm here standing on the Franco-Belgian frontier watching long columns of British troops and transport and supplies coming through France from France into Belgium,' was the on-the-spot BBC commentary from Bernard Stubbs. 'The frontier posts are now open,' he dramatically announced. 'As I am speaking to you I can see the columns coming up – here's another!' Such actuality recordings suggesting the situation was well in hand reassured listeners in England. Cheering could be heard above the background roar and drone of moving traffic in the metallic recording. 'This is a day of great beauty,' announced J L Hodson, another BBC commentator, 'and if the occasion were not so grave, one could enjoy it thoroughly.' The war was off to a good start in beautiful spring weather.

'The welcome being given by the Belgian people is really tremendous,' reported Bernard Stubbs, shouting above background cries of 'Vive la France!' 'Ee, I'm havin' a terrible time,' announced a Lancashire Tommy smothered by kisses from half a dozen girls. Hodson regarded his BBC car, already partially filled with tulips and narcissi. Belgian villagers, drawn to their doorsteps by all the activity, sat on chairs and watched the cavalcade drive by. 'I don't know how many passed this way yesterday,' Hodson commented, 'but the numbers today are colossal.'

'Going into Belgium was a wonderful experience,' remembered John Carter with the 7th Battalion the Worcester Regiment. 'The

Belgians loved us and we were going to save them from the Boche. It was flowers all the way in!' The British Expeditionary Force (BEF) went to war confident in their capabilities, even though the main effort during the Phoney War had been about assimilating reservists and Territorials; an organisational rather than training success. Three of the twelve divisions had arrived in the rear areas barely two weeks before, with reduced scales of transport and signallers and no artillery. They were brought across the Channel to utilise their labour – digging – rather than military competence. Only four soldiers were killed in action in France by the beginning of 1940. Nobody had got the measure of the German soldier. 'German troops look at you across the Rhine in No-Man's-land with no more threatening expressions than the drivers of other cars,' recalled an unimpressed David Howarth reporting for the BBC. Bill Crossan, serving with the 51st Highland Division, had a similar view: 'We were only young lads. We thought ach, Germans. We'll beat them nae bother. We never thought for a minute they'd ever bloomin' beat us! Never for a minute.'

War ran within clearly defined traffic lines during those early hours in Belgium, as if, reported BBC reporter JL Hodson, one was being efficiently directed to the annual Aldershot Military Tattoo. All went to plan. The French and the BEF would block the German advance into Belgium and throw it out. 'Occasional gunfire thuds heavily like someone beating a carpet a long way off,' Hodson recalled. 'From time to time a shrill air-raid siren blows, but the procession does not stop.' As the lorry columns moved up the first refugees were spilling on to the roads leading back.

The BEF advanced sixty-five miles to its predetermined Dyle River line, with the Belgians to their left and two French Armies (the 1st and 9th) to the right. Even as they started to dig in the Dutch Army, left of the Belgians, surrendered on 14 May, exposing the north-west flank. Likewise the first major tank battle in history began at the Gembloux Gap to the south and right of the BEF with 415 French tanks clashing with 623 panzers. Within days the bulk of the French armoured divisions were badly mauled or destroyed. Both flanks of the BEF became vulnerable. James Bradley, a twenty-nine-year-old artillery gunner, recalled they had 'dashed into Belgium where there were no prepared positions for us', exposing the irony of pointless digging throughout the Phoney War period. 'It was mobile war after that; it was fight and move, fight and move.'

Deep inside the forested and hilly Ardennes region clouds of dust and intermittent gunfire heralded the advance of the totally unexpected German Army Group A. It was spearheaded by the Panzergruppe Kleist, an undetected panzer army. Utilising mobile engineer teams and astute General Staff planning, columns of panzer and motorised troops appeared at the River Meuse on 12 May. Behind them was the biggest traffic jam ever seen in Europe. Over 41,000 vehicles stretched back 250 kilometres across France, Belgium, and Luxembourg as they were still leaving Germany. 'In three days to the Meuse – on the forth day *across* the Meuse!' was the rhyming ditty that one of the panzer corps commanders, Schnelle ('Speedy') Heinz Guderian, had drummed into his tank crews during training. Two panzer and a motorised infantry corps, complete with supporting arms-carrying 134,000 men, emerged from the 'impenetrable' Ardennes forests. Backed by 3,200 aircraft, against an inferior 1,800 Allied, two German Army Groups remorselessly ground by either side of the BEF. By the seventh day of the campaign a forty-kilometer gap had been torn in the Allied line to the right of the British, in the 9th and 1st French Army sectors.

Twenty-nine-year-old Staff Captain James Hill, serving with General Gort, the BEF Commander, recalled: 'we hadn't quite envisaged them going right, through the north and going around the flank like that.' The command post was taken aback. 'We hadn't imagined that at all.' Panzergruppen clattered off in swift unstoppable columns north-west toward the Channel coast which they reached on 21 May. Despite holding the line on their sector the British were obliged to withdraw fifteen miles on 20 May, defend, then withdraw a further twenty miles to defend again. Such deployments meant even greater distances from the divisions, forced to extend lines and react to threatened flanks.

The British were, in effect, running a gauntlet under fire, the essence of the British soldier's Blitzkrieg experience. 'Everybody was safeguarding the Maginot Line,' explained Coldstream Guardsman Bill Weeks, 'never get past that – and what do they do? They went round it and attacked *us*!' But for the fact the BEF was a well equipped lorry-borne force, it may well not have kept ahead. The 3rd British Division was attacked for nine days and retreated for seven during the three-week campaign. Other divisions fought less but moved more with as many as nine days retreating. 'They moved fast,' recalled Weeks, referring to the pursuing Germans, 'we weren't ready, not ready for this.' As in Norway, Blitzkrieg was to prove a painful formative experience for the British Army. 'We had five rounds of ammunition for each rifle,' claimed Weeks, 'which was quite ludicrous really, but that's the way it was.'

The first shock of contact was borne by the Royal Air Force, flung at the Meuse River bridgehead to stem the advancing flow. Seventy airfields were attacked on the opening day of the campaign and the Luftwaffe quickly established air supremacy. Thirteen of thirty-two Fairy Battles of the Advanced British Air Striking Force were shot down on this day and all the reminder damaged. 'After just a few days of combat,' RAF Pilot Officer David Looker recalled, 'most of us were living on our nerves.'

Flight Lieutenant Bill Simpson, who had been in France since the declaration of war, was tasked on the afternoon of 10 May to attack a large German column reported moving through Luxembourg from Germany. Two Fairy Battles loaded with four 250 lb bombs made a 210 mph hedge-hopping approach to strike the column. Crippled by low-level flak, Simpson was sprayed with glycol in a cockpit reeking of petrol when 'suddenly there was a heavy thud' and flames poured from his engine. 'There was a series of sickening crunches,' he recalled as he belly-landed the aircraft, 'and we stopped.' Petrol vapour inside the cockpit ignited with a tremendous 'whoof' and 'great sheets of searing flames rushed between my legs and up to thirty feet above me'. He was unable to disentangle his straps because his scorched hands 'were completely useless' and pinned to his seat 'a tremendous white heat enveloped me'. Bizarrely he retained consciousness. 'It was impossible for me to escape from my trap by my own efforts, I let my hands drop on to my knees and curled myself up, waiting for the release of death. My whole mind was full of a blood-curdling scream; but no sound came. If it had it might have relieved the shock.'

As he involuntarily slumped in his seat waiting to die he recalled the irony of his electronic klaxon sounding off, reminding him to lower his wheels on landing. Mercifully his crew appeared through the flames, tugging at harness straps that had already burned through. Sergeant Al Odell, his navigator, and Corporal Tomlinson, his gunner, hauled him out, burned half naked, scorching their hands on his red-hot parachute release box. They involuntary gasped at his hideous appearance. Simpson felt 'a peculiar drawn feeling about my face; the left side of my nose and my right eye felt completely distorted – as indeed they were.' As the Fairy Battle disintegrated in a series of fiery explosions and plumes of black smoke, he sat on the grass in shock. 'I shivered in the cool evening air,' he recalled as his charred body stiffened up. His pain was endurable but future consequences flashed before him as he regarded his hands – what might his wife say? 'I stared at them with an unbelieving terror . . . The skin hung from them like long icicles. The fingers were curled and pointed, like the claws of a great wild bird – distorted, pointed at the ends like talons, ghostly thin. What would I do now? What use would these paralysed talons be to me for the rest of my life if I *did* live?'

The air war was going badly. 'From the Royal Air Force point of view, the battle for France was a complete and utter shambles,' complained Flight Lieutenant Frederick Rosier. Intelligence and communications were poor and 'everything appeared to be ad-hoc'. Many quickly appreciated they were outclassed, as Flying Officer Richard Gaynor confessed: 'Terror and exhaustion dominate my recollections of that period over France and Belgium – terror because of all the bloody Huns. There were many more of them than of us, and they were better at it than we were. They liked war and most of us didn't like war at all.'

Squadron losses such as seven of nine and five of twelve became commonplace. Flying support came out from bases in southern England. Pilot Officer 'Birdie' Bird Wilson recalled 'the wives of the men who were missing came to the mess every day to see if there was news of their husbands'. Invariably there was not and it made a marked impression on the survivors. 'It was a lesson for the rest of us to delay marriage and to try and keep our families out of such things.' The army never saw the dog-fights conducted out of their sight. 'Where are they? Where the hell are they? Why aren't they helping us out?' complained Sapper Sid Crockett indignantly. 'This was all wrong. They had left us on our own. They just didn't care! This was what the attitude to the RAF was.'

The BEF was every bit as pressed as the RAF. From the moment they closed with the Germans it appeared they were falling back. 'I say this quite honestly,' declared TA gunner Harry Garrett, 'I'm going to Heaven when I die because I have been through hell.' The infantry took the initial impact. 'There was a terrific fight took place with rifles and bren guns, with us fighting the Germans,' remembered Martin McLane, fighting forward with the Durham Light Infantry. 'But once the tanks started making an appearance, the men lose heart, because they've got nothing to stop tanks.' Only fifty-seven of their 700 fighting men got away. Artillery gunners positioned to the rear had more opportunity to break clean. Harry Garrett recalled: 'we got this move to get up the road. It was very demoralising for us to have to run away from the fight all the time.' Bob Brooks, another TA gunner, explained: 'we were in action on and off for the next fortnight. Only once did we go forward, all the other times unfortunately we were going backwards.'

The infantry fought a war of counter-attack and rearguard, constantly seeking to protect the rear of the army as it retired. Coldstream Guardsman Bill Weeks described the pandemonium when 'the stuff started flying about, you sort of laid down, move out, dig in, move out – until you get into the action yourself.' They always seemed to contest high ground. 'Take the high ground!' but 'you couldn't even get up,' he caustically remembered.

> Not only were you crying, you were probably sick as well and you had probably messed yourself as well with sheer fright! It was unbelievable! You can't explain it really – you're petrified. Bang! Crash! This stuff whistling all around you and you're thinking 'What's going on here?' Then someone shouts 'Lay down! Dig in! – all this sort of carry-on.'

German advance guards initiated the fighting preceded by motor-cycle infantry with machine-guns mounted on sidecar combinations. They conducted reconnaissance. The Vorausabteilung, or advance guard, that followed fought with light armoured cars and lorry-borne infantry with anti-tank guns and mortar support. This is what most British units encountered. Behind came the main force, marching infantry regiments. These infantry divisions were the killing formations, able to embrace opposition with mass foot infantry and pulverising artillery, including Corps and Army formation support. Panzer units advanced with light tanks, mixed with assault engineer units at the head. Main force medium and heavy panzers, mixed in company and battalion-size groups, drove down parallel roads in column at best speed. The main weight of the panzers bypassed the British on their left retreating flank, heading for the Channel.

Leutnant Hans Steinbrecher wrote an exuberant diary account of his advance with the 2nd Panzer Division. 'We drove the whole day,' he wrote on 11 May as the BEF moved forward into the 'sack' prepared for them by the German operational plan. 'If that continues we will soon find ourselves in England.' Although the strongest enemy was the French, they watched out for the British, 'burning to catch them up'. On the third day he reflected on the 'huge tank battle' that lay behind them in the area of the Meuse River that 'was simply dreadful.' Then on 15 May he reports: 'finally the English! We were let loose like hunting dogs on the British.' It was his final idealistic diary entry, the same day he was killed driving forward with the advance reconnaissance force.

British units were sacrificed during the headlong retreat running the gauntlet to the coast. Sergeant L D Pexton fought in a rearguard action in the Cambrai-Arras area. 'Afraid we shall have to retire soon,' he wrote in his diary. 'Can't hold tanks with rifles or bren guns,' he dismally pointed out. 'We have to hold on till 8 pm and then retire. Roll on 8 pm.' After retreating a further leg his unit was overrun in a village. 'Germans came from nowhere. Properly surprised us. Got down to it in the open and fought for all we knew how. Getting wiped out this time all right . . . Remember the order "Cease Fire" and that the time was 12 o'clock. Stood up and put my hands up. My God how few of us stood up.'

Only 425 of his unit of 1,400 men were left. 'I expected my last moments had come and lit a fag. Everyone expected to be shot there and then.'

'The first man I killed,' recalled twenty-year-old Private Desmond Thorogood with the Coldstream Guards awaiting the onslaught, 'was when we heard voices – that's a German voice,' he thought, 'and sure enough it was.' Gazing out from his position he detected the German private who was shouting and shot him. 'I didn't boast about it, you don't . . . killing a human being, it was my job,' he reflected. 'If I hadn't he would have killed me.'

Death, mutilation and loss now began to permeate their daily lives. Bill Weeks remembered his friend Ernie Costa, a local 'who came from Governments Lane' and died in his arms. 'He was smoking when he got hit and the cigarette was dangling from his lip and it was burning all his flesh.' These indelible images preyed on the mind. 'It didn't seem to worry him all that much, you know.' Gunner James Bradley lost his close friend and thought, 'he can't be dead, and you pat his face and say, "Come on, don't fool around" and you see all the blood running down and so forth and by God – you know he's dead.' Men lost friends they had joined with, had intimately shared their lives with for months. Bradley recalled with anguish: 'He's a chappie with whom I laughed and played football with and now he's lying in a bit of boggy ground. His mother would die of shame if she saw her lovely baby being dropped [for burial] like this . . . If these parents could see them, like that, in a corner of a foreign field. They must never know.'

Fighting was all-encompassing and primal, emotion came with reflection after the event. Thorogood was troubled by shooting the German. 'It made me feel as though I was a criminal,' he confessed. 'It was different from what most men do.' But like most veterans, he put it emotionally to one side and rationalised: 'I had to shoot – and I shot.' Captain James Hill with the hindsight of later hard and distinguished active service felt able to succinctly express what was required of the combat soldier: 'You can only ask people to die if it's in a worthy cause, and you can only ask people to die if you are prepared to die as well as them. If you have got these two, you are in business. It's as easy as that.'

The BEF, unlike the Wehrmacht, now into its second campaign after Poland, came to terms with this unassailable logic. Guardsman Bill Weeks remembered 'the only thing that bothered me were bits of flesh, arms and legs that had been hit by shell fire and sort of disintegrated'. He feared an anonymous 'missing in action' label. 'That's why you wear your dog-tags,' he explained: 'You have got your name and rank and number – who you are – on a metallic dog tag. He may have been decapitated, but its still around his neck.'

The lack of situational awareness made a deep impression upon British soldiers. Bill Weeks' fear of disappearing without trace represented a concern permeating all ranks of the BEF. Not being informed about what was going on suggested they were not important enough to know. 'You do begin to worry a little bit and get a little concerned,' claimed James Bradley, 'because they are saying you're in a position here or dug in there, this is really the place to be.' Then unexpectedly they had to hook up the guns and pull back yet again, to where nobody knew. At which point he confessed, 'you were really getting a bit of an up and down hill feeling, weren't you?'

'What's going on, Sarge?' George Wagstaff a Bren-gun-carrier driver with the Oxfordshire and Buckinghamshire infantry asked, like everyone else. 'You'll know soon enough,' was the reply. 'Of course we never did learn what it was all about,' he recalled. 'The ordinary soldier, the ordinary Jock, doesn't know what's happening,' agreed Donald MacLean with the Black Watch in the 51st Highland Division. 'He's told to be here, be there, do this, do that. They don't know the ins and outs of where this or that company is. As far as I was concerned we were in a cornfield in France.'

It was irritating and unsettling. Driver George Bowers with the 50th Northumbrian Division worked it out for himself. 'In retrospect we realised that the civilians already knew something that we didn't – that the Germans were coming and the Allies were retreating.' 'Of course the top brass were in a right state,' declared George Wagstaff. 'But not us, because we didn't know a blind thing about it.' Retreat, he pointed out, had never been practised in any of their exercises, only attack, if they were not digging holes. 'Retreat was never mentioned,' emphasised Wagstaff, moreover 'the mechanised army had had only two years of life; before that it had been as it was in 1918, with horses and limbers and lots of trenches.'

Confusion was compounded by the constant strafing and bombing as the retreat was conducted in the teeth of seemingly absolute Luftwaffe air superiority. 'There was bitterness towards the RAF,' remarked E Newbould with the KOSB, and it would be manifested in inter-service fist fights on return. 'Their absence was because they were frightened to come out and fight.' Lieutenant Henry de la Falaise with the 12th Lancer armoured cars was strafed and bombed or observed air attacks nearby every day bar one of the twenty-two days he was in action during this campaign. On seven of these he was attacked more than once and personally strafed by low-level fighters twice. Germany had mobilised three-quarters of its potential against only one quarter flying for the French. The net result was 2,589 German aircraft pitted against 1,453 Allied. 'They stunt over our heads as if in a peace-time air-show,' de la Falaise complained, 'they have been practically unmolested.'

'Breaking clean' from contact with the enemy is one of the most difficult phases of war. It requires pre-planned rendezvous (RV) or meeting points to be set up behind retreating units through which they slip away. Methodically passing through such RVs establishes control and enables the missing to be identified en route. The difficulty was explained by one infantry sergeant major who claimed, 'it's not like any other fighting I've never known before.' Constant air attacks broke up the process. 'When we've lost some ground, and we're digging ourselves in to make a stand, they're suddenly all behind us – this happened again and again' like in Norway. The very control sought in withdrawing was denied by the Luftwaffe.

Fred Page drew up outside one such RV outside Armentières under intermittent shell fire and bombing. He anxiously asked his lieutenant when they were going to get moving. 'God knows,' was the response, 'I suppose when we get told where to go.' Eventually they cleared the gates of the chateau checkpoint and were stopped by two military policemen (MPs) on motor-cycles. 'Where are you going?' they asked. 'So and so,' was the response – but 'Not now' they were informed. 'Pull forward so you can see.' Armentières, through which they had to drive, was in flames with all the bridges down. 'Turn left, first turn left, and go like hell!' the MP shouted urgently. 'You haven't any time!'

The BEF withdrew another twenty miles on 22 May and set up yet another defensive line north of Ypres and along the Lys Canal. 'It was get back,' declared Guardsman Bill Weeks. 'You don't retreat in the Brigade of Guards, it's "Strategic Withdrawal", sort of fall-back, fall-back.'

Air attacks added to the perception that they were running a gauntlet of fire as, despite the dearth of information, soldiers grasped their dismal predicament, as did also the civilians. Reg Rymer, a nineteen-year-old machine-gunner in the Cheshire Regiment retreating through Brussels, was reminded of the flower-bedecked advance. 'As we came through the city they were throwing bricks, never mind sweets at us,' he chuckled, 'the booing was something terrible.' TA signaller Wilf Saunders discerned from signals traffic that 'our force held out in Belgium as spearhead, but the French and Belgians on our flanks retreated, and to avoid being cut off we had to go back too'. The radio set became his eyes and ears: 'Important messages passed. German tanks broken through the French. 80 armoured cars about 5 miles away. Everyone in pent up state of preparedness.'

'I could have cried my eyes out,' remembered one infantry officer ordered to withdraw after repelling German advance guards. 'The men were in fine fettle,' having 'pasted the Hun', but once on the move the Stukas sought them out. Common to many veteran accounts of Stuka attacks was a very human conviction the victim was personally in the centre of the pilots aiming sight.

> I thought *I* was their target, and nothing they did in any way dispelled that feeling. Down, *Down*, DOWN they screamed, straight at me . . . Big black lumps fell out from under their bellies and these came straight for *me*. Tracer-like bullets, like little flying glow-worms, came from their noses, and those came straight for *me*.

He saw the pilot passing overhead at about fifty feet. 'His head strained back against gravity, eyes shut and mouth wide open, and he seemed to be laughing at *me*.' Guardsman Bill Weeks was likewise intimidated. 'The worse thing of all was the Stukas as they came straight out of the skies,' he remembered. 'They used to scream, they had sirens on their wings – terrible!' Signaller Wilf Saunders found the raids surreal. 'I supposed the bombs would come down so quickly you wouldn't see them,' which was not the case. 'You could see them and it was extraordinary! You feel it's for you personally.'

Clogging the roads alongside the BEF were the refugees. Veteran accounts are permeated with the anguish felt for their plight. Private

Reg Rymer retreating with the Cheshire Regiment was caught by a
Stuka raid on a refugee-packed road:

> They do their normal circle around and one after the other they dive
> down. And I thought they must be blind, they're not going after us.
> The next thing is that they let their things go in among the refugees.
> Now these are old people, young people, young people, babies – to
> see them blown to pieces, and not one bomb anywhere along the
> army convoy. You tell me who could be that cruel? We were there
> and being paid and supposed to be doing a job so you can expect it.
> But that? You see baby's legs and all kinds being thrown up in the air!

Refugees painfully reminded them of their own families back home,
who but for circumstances might well have been in the same predicament. There was a class system in evidence even here. The wealthy had
cars with mattresses tied on top for pathetic air-raid protection, while
the poor pushed carts piled high with their possessions. Most of the
soldiers had been civilians themselves only months before. Arthur
Gunn, an ambulance driver, saw roads leading into France from
Belgium littered with dead innocents. One 'poignant memory was
of a young mother dead with a baby still suckling her breast'. They
passed the infant to another young woman with a child 'but one never
knew'. TA gunner Tom Jones with 68 Field Regiment, assisting in
clearing roads after raids, saw 'children and babies, old and young'
strewn about, 'some so badly injured that French medics were putting
them out of their agony with half their bodies blown away and with
terrible injuries'. He was only twenty and had never seen a dead person
in his life. 'This stuck in my memory and will do to the end of my days,'
he admitted.

One British soldier retreating westward noticed an old lady sitting in
a chair next to a middle-aged woman handing out water to the
exhausted marching soldiers. She wept silently. Her grand-daughter
explained she was going to see the German Army for the third time.
'The old lady could not only recall the '14–18 war, but she could recall
as a young girl, the Franco-Prussian of 1870,' recalled the soldier who
'found that quite poignant'. She was about to see it all again. Another
soldier pausing between rearguards observed a four- or five-year-old

toddler stumbling between the pram handles of a mother pushing a baby with possessions. 'Every now and again this child would be dragged and the mother would grab it up, lift it up again and the child never fell on the floor.' Stepping over to help, he saw 'she'd actually tied the kiddie's wrists' to prevent the child from falling as she pushed. 'All its wrists were cut and bleeding and I thought – well what could you do? There were thousands and thousands of them.'

It could just as easily be in England.

Fred Clapham with the Durham Light Infantry was barely five months in the army and easily identified with the mass of humanity streaming past. Farm carts were stacked with possessions, with one bizarrely topped with a double mattress with 'an aged granny' tied on. 'How terrifying,' he reflected, 'for these old bodies when they were being dived bombed or machine-gunned.' Sapper Reg Bazeley damned the Luftwaffe because 'I will never believe that they were mistaken in their target.' The miscellany of carts, wheelbarrows, prams, mules and donkeys – 'all but the kitchen sink' – were obvious. Tasked with keeping the roads clear, he never forgot the appalling stench from explosives, eviscerated animals and human beings. 'On one grisly occasion the Sergeant with seeming callousness, kicked the severed limb of a child into a ditch, all the accompanying family having been wiped out.'

Extreme fatigue is what veterans remember most about the retreat. Tired and disillusioned men lost all recollection of time and days. Normal rational deductions took twice as long, if they were achievable at all. Nine days after the start of the campaign Lieutenant Robin Medley began to appreciate the cumulative drag of physical efforts conducted under constant threat and mental strain. At company orders at 2300 he remembered 'heads were nodding, and memory played tricks early next morning'. Three days later they were retreating on foot. 'The long march back became more exhausting as the East Surrey territorial battalion ahead of us were dead beat and the pace became slower and slower. One of their soldiers shot himself in sheer desperation at about 0200 hours.'

Bernard Fergusson with the Black Watch recalled being on a long thirty-mile trudge 'with men falling asleep almost as they walked'. They stumbled into a carpet factory on the French frontier on leaving

Belgium, only to learn from the BBC 'that the Germans were already in Boulogne'. TA signaller Wilf Saunders was 'absolutely physically whacked' by the eighth day of the campaign. 'The electrician fitter of our party has not slept since Tuesday and it's now Saturday.' He calculated that he and his co-operator Clive had only achieved five and a half hours' sleep in the previous seventy-seven and a half hours. 'Infantry I saw were absolutely played out – fatigued as I have never seen men fatigued. Christ, if this is war I don't know how long any of us will last.'

Fatigue, refugees, roadside scenes of destruction and the nervous tension of running the gauntlet of enemy preventative measures from above and the flanks took its toll. They were not only outmanoeuvred, they felt outclassed. 'We didn't realise how poorly equipped we were until we came up against the Germans,' declared Murdo MacCuish with the Cameron Highlanders: 'The equipment we had was what they stopped using in 1918. Just one machine gun, no tommy guns. The anti-tank guns we had were just like pea-shooters. They told us we were the best equipped army that had ever left Britain. We were soon disillusioned about that.'

Lieutenant Tony Hibbert's ack-ack battery was equipped with guns that had been removed from a Russian cruiser in 1917 'and mounted on what looked like farm-carts'. They still had Russian Cyrillic inscriptions on the block and 'they were absolutely useless'. Each gun had only a hundred rounds of shrapnel shells designed for use against enemy infantry, not aircraft. 'Unbelievably they worked,' Hibbert claimed, but only because they set the fuses to one instead of five seconds, enabling them to fire twelve rounds a minute. They were intimidating rather than effective, producing a shotgun effect. 'We only knocked down two aircraft in the entire campaign,' he lamented.

Many units of the BEF were only semi-effective nineteen days into the campaign when the surrender of the Belgians on 28 May triggered another defensive withdrawal of up to twelve miles. As the columns trudged north and westward toward the coast they were able to follow the navigational aid of a huge pillar of smoke rising above the blazing oil refineries at Dunkirk. One soldier described it as an omen: 'the pillar of smoke by day and pillar of fire by night which guided the Israelites, guided the BEF as well.'

With their backs to the sea the British established a perimeter around the coast near Dunkirk. Twenty-year-old Ronald Mott with the Queen's Regiment had arrived in France barely six weeks before the German invasion. His whole world and that of the BEF had been turned upside down.

It seemed to me that the whole world had suddenly gone mad. We had been bombed, shelled, marched off our feet, been in action umpteen times. I cannot remember when we had last eaten. Then with chin on ground we heard General Gort giving the order 'every man back to Dunkirk'. It seemed then that the orderly withdrawal was no longer orderly.

But where would they go beyond the coast? 'Only to the sea,' concluded signaller Wilf Saunders. 'I suppose what we shall do if we do fall back is defend the port of Dunkirk like blazes.' There seemed to be little hope of success. 'They seem to be all around us,' he wrote in his diary, 'what a life!'

3

DELIVERANCE AT DUNKIRK

FROM THE PERIMETER TO THE BEACHES

A subdued hum emanated from rows of well-dressed people, four to five deep, snaking away from the Westminster Abbey entrance on to Parliament Square. Hats and Sunday-best were in abundance for the all-denomination service on 26 May that included newly appointed Prime Minister Winston Churchill, who turned up with top-hat, stick and incongruous gas mask container. His Majesty King George VI and a host of dignitaries listened intently as the Archbishop of Canterbury addressed the congregation in a tremulous voice. 'Let us pray,' he enjoined, 'for our soldiers in dire peril in France.'

For several days wives, sweethearts and families had asked about what was happening to their menfolk in France. These 240,000 soldiers and servicemen had family links with perhaps 24 million people from a civilian population of 38 million. Virtually everyone knew of or was related to a serviceman in France. Disappointing progress in Norway in the teeth of optimistic BBC reporting created apprehension among people in Scotland and the Orkneys who realised the war was not far from their doorstep. Norway remained a distant vista of mountains and fjords to the rest of the country until the Germans invaded the Low Countries when the war became everyone's business. Two days after the Westminster service a Birmingham working-class housewife wrote:

A BLACK DAY. We need all our prayers now, and they won't have to be ordered. The 1 o'clock news has made me feel sick . . . I don't think France will give in, but neither did I think Belgium would. We *must* win – we *must* win, I could not live beneath a brutal power. I said to my husband Sunday, I would die fighting rather than live the life of a slave!

Clara Milburn, living at Burleigh near Coventry, switched on her wireless set beginning at 8 am, then at intervals at 10.30 am, 12 noon, 1 pm, 4.15 pm, 6 pm, and finally 9 pm. News was increasingly grave. 'The Germans have turned the salient into a bulge on the western front and great strength will be needed to flatten it,' she wrote in her diary on 17 May. Four days later: 'the German thrust penetrated unexpectedly and blunders had been made' – a 'startling revelation' and 'a black day indeed' because she had no news of her son Alan serving somewhere in France. Housewife Nella Last in Barrow noticed people she met when the German offensive began 'seemed as stunned as we all did last September' when war was declared.

Mass Observation reports noted that the media – and government – desire to report fast moving events in a positive way created false expectations. These were dashed when Hitler was seen to be delivering yet another masterful stroke. Women who were so worried and depressed at coming to terms with the unthinkable simply switched off their wireless sets. 'Yesterday I felt I never wanted to hear an announcer's voice again,' Nella Last confided in her diary after the Dutch surrender; 'and yet the feeling of "must hear the latest" is stronger'. It was even worse twelve days later. 'A dreadful coldness seemed to grip me when I heard the one o'clock news,' she wrote. 'I'd got to that stage when to talk of Belgium's capitulation would have sent me *howling*.' Thoughts focused immediately on the vulnerability of the BEF and for Clara Milburn, her son. 'The thought of Alan being with them in Belgium is almost more than one can bear tonight,' she confided to her diary. She correctly deduced 'our men of the BEF are now exposed on another flank to the enemy' and condemned the Belgians for a 'treacherous act'. Nella Last observed the increasing concern. 'So many mothers in the WVS [Women's Voluntary Service] Centre have boys in France or on the sea, and I know their hearts are heavy.' Even level-headed and rational people were reduced to poring over news bulletins, vainly attempting to pick out an encouraging remark. No news heightened suspense, while that available was invariably alarming. 'Mrs B was telling me that when the Belgians gave in she felt *terrible*,' commented a Mass Observation diary extract, 'she felt like sitting down and weeping her heart out.'

News was inconsolably bad and the Service of Deliverance at Westminster was the first official recognition that it would likely affect everybody. For those in the know, monitoring events, the implications were even worse. 'I'm rather ashamed to say it put the fear of God into me!' confessed twenty-five-year-old Elizabeth Quayle with the Women's Auxiliary Air Force (WAAF), running the one phone line from Portsmouth into Dunkirk. 'Because every time you came on duty, we knew where the Huns were, we had maps with pins in, and they seemed to be advancing very fast.' She heard of units retreating on foot out of control, abandoning guns and vehicles and sheltering in buildings being bombed along the shoreline. It did not look good. 'We had no idea they were going to be rescued; it seemed the whole army was going to be bottled up there and the whole army was going to be captured.'

G M Hodges, a WAAF driver based at St Margaret's Bay near Dover, drove regularly to RAF Hawkinge, the Hurricane fighter base nearby. They were sending fighter sweeps across the Channel in support of the BEF and she soon appreciated 'how far west Jerry tanks had penetrated'. Fighter pilot reports 'always placed the tanks so much further west than any news appearing in the National Press'. 'Calais was in flames for five whole days and nights' she could see from the Dover signal station 'before Churchill told the world'.

> At night, with field glasses, the harbour gantries could be seen silhouetted against a wall of flame, which itself was reflected in a calm sea. By day it was all smothered by a moving pall of heavy smoke; and when the wind blew southerly it all came over to us, the scent and flavour of it getting into everything.

Admiral Sir Bertram Ramsay, Flag Officer Dover, was presented with a hypothesis on 20 May that the BEF *may* have to be evacuated. During the next six days he quietly laid down sea routes, organised control staffs and concentrated shipping. Only a select few knew what was going on until Operation Dynamo, the evacuation plan, was launched on 26 May, when the Admiralty were told the crisis moment had arrived.

Captain Bill Tennant was appointed Senior Naval Officer Dunkirk, and crossed the Channel with twelve officers and 160 ratings as communications staff that night.

Aircraftswoman Hodges, like many onlookers at Dover harbour, noticed 'refugee' ships and small craft gathering off the quays, doubtless to transport more unfortunates fleeing over the Channel. Dover harbour was completely deserted, however, when she peeked from her cliff edge on 27 May. 'All the ships were gone,' she recalled, 'not one left.' Hawkinge fighter base orderlies told her the 'refugee' craft had joined hundreds of others from points along the south coast as far west as Dorset and up to the Wash on the east coast. 'They had gone off in the night to attempt the rescue of our armies,' she heard, 'from the dunes between Calais and Dunkirk.' Looking further afield from her clifftop vantage point on St Margaret's Bay, she saw the Channel was full of small ships that evening, with 'fast small units of the Royal Navy darting here and there, yapping like sheepdogs herding their flock'. She could even hear the 'drubbing pulse of the multiple throb of light engines' as the fleet rolled its way gently in slow motion through the golden haze of a setting sun. 'All we could do was to stay put and keep our fingers crossed,' she recalled, 'for there was less than a fifty-fifty chance that they would succeed.'

When Captain Bill Tennant arrived he found BEF units disorganised and dispersed across ten miles of beach seafront from Malo-les-Bains eastward past Bray Dunes to the front at La Panne just across the Belgian border. Soldiers were drinking wine because there was no water. One of the destroyers took eight hours to load 400 men with inadequate twenty-five-man whalers. Some 45,000 men were expected to arrive at the beaches in the next thirty-six hours and a further 293,000 Allied soldiers were anticipated behind them. There was even some dispute over who might arrive first, the BEF or the Germans. Sub-Lieutenant John Rutherford Crosby RNVR flippantly asked one bedraggled soldier clambering aboard his boat what all the hurry was. 'Christ alive!' he croaked, 'he's only two miles down the road,' vaguely indicating the enemy with his arm, 'and he'll be on the beach by midday.' Crosby recalled, 'my jaw must have dropped with dismay at that.' Survival was dependent on the ability of a tenuously established perimeter to keep the enemy at bay.

'We were told that we were going to hold up the German Army as best we could, to the last man to the last round,' remembered twenty-year-old Second Lieutenant Julian Fane of the Gloucestershire Regiment at Cassel. 'I thought oh dear, I didn't think I was going to be losing so soon in my military career.' German momentum had to be slowed to establish a perimeter. Cassel became a momentary strongpoint on the west side of the collapsing sacklike outline of the retreating BEF line being squeezed from the west, south and east as it made its tortuous way to the coast. The town lay atop the same hill the 'Grand Old Duke of York' had marched up and down again at the end of the eighteenth century, an earlier British expeditionary debacle.

A rectangular-shaped enclave, twenty miles around and six miles deep, coalesced along the concentric canal and waterway systems immediately west of Dunkirk and east to Furness and Nieuport on the Belgian border. These water obstacles hindered the panzers. The French held the west side, including the small medieval fortified town of Bergues, with its Vauban-shaped walls and narrow winding streets. The British defended the east side. Bergues, at the centre, was the linchpin connecting both sides of the perimeter. It took just over an hour to drive its outline by vehicle.

The experience of the British soldier fighting on the east side was to get men to dig, stand and fight after running a sixteen-day gauntlet under fire. They were hemmed in on three sides with their backs to the sea in an apparently hopeless situation. 'By now we have lost the Guards Brigade, we didn't know where they are or what they were doing,' recalled nineteen-year-old Private Reg Rymer with the Cheshire Regiment. 'So we have got to take orders from whatever, and that's the way it was.' As they moved back, selected units began digging hastily improvised positions on the canal line, while the remainder fell back to the beaches. 'Going back, taking up positions, firing, doing what we had to do,' said Rymer, 'and in the meantime getting hammered, and unfortunately we're losing men.'

Positions were unprepared. There was little water, only that beneath slimy scum-covered canals, which was too brackish to swallow. 'Most of us rinsed our mouths out with it only, for the taste made one want to retch,' remembered Patrick Mace a gunner with 52 Heavy Regiment.

Food was scarce, only what could be foraged locally, and soon ran out. Ammunition was the primary commodity brought forward.

Soldiers dug to survive, beginning with knee-high shell scrapes, but these filled with water as they went beneath the high water table. The British sector behind the canal zone was virtually devoid of cover. Positions soon disfigured the rich green pasture land like so many molehills among the stagnant watercourses. Private Bill Cordrey, with B Company of the Royal Warwickshire Regiment, recalled the isolation of these widely dispersed and thinly held positions, but 'we had excellent fields of fire'.

'Look, Corporal! Right in front!' and there about seven or eight hundred yards away and coming towards us, was a long line of figures. Sticking the sights up to 800, I fired a long burst – and within seconds, the sections on my right joined in. We must have been scoring hits, because gradually the line started to break up into small groups.

Initial meeting engagements were conducted at distance, impersonal exchanges of fire. No longer committed to the vagaries of mobile war, British units held fast, relishing the opportunity to return fire at last, without peering over their shoulders for panzers. 'There was no cover for them,' Bill Cordrey remembered, firing Bren bursts at the infantry to his front, 'and we had them pinned down before they had moved a hundred yards.' The Germans attempted to advance in small rushes, 'but at last they gave it up as a bad job'. Attacks were persistent and determined but 'they must have been losing far too many men'. Cordrey satisfactorily recalled stalling the assault, 'but I must admit they had guts'.

Ten German infantry divisions constricted the perimeter from the east and south, hinged on panzer divisions temporarily halted to the west. Such divisions were more lethal than the panzers, able to close with their opposite numbers in strength and, more significantly, able to bring a far heavier weight of artillery to bear. Open British positions were easily detected from numerous church steeples projecting from villages around the perimeter. Grass-covered mounds and earth-stained holes could be picked out in the flat featureless landscape from these loftily sited artillery observation posts. 'It wasn't long,' Bill Cordrey remarked, 'before we were getting our fair share of Jerry shells.'

Vernon Scannell with the 70th Argyll Battalion in France described the impact of his first artillery barrage:

> I had never heard that before and it really is a terrifying noise, a tremendous din . . . To be under a barrage, you feel that you are the personal target, that all this red hot, white hot metal that is screaming through the air and landing around you with extraordinary force is actually out to get you. When one's crouching in one's slit trench, and has one's hands down protecting one's genitalia because that is what you're most afraid of losing. It is absolutely instinctive.

After the multiple bursts of explosions an unearthly silence reigned, punctuated by the wounded shouting. Scannell felt the cries of 'stretcher-bearer' when intelligible were pathetic enough, but the calls for help from a badly hit hard-bitten sergeant affected him deeply. He cried for his mother. 'To hear this man who I'd always regarded as a hard case, wailing and moaning for his mummy – that was one of the things that no amount of preparation and training prepares you for.'

As the Germans closed in fighting became bitter. German reporter Christhof von Imhoff recalled desperate British resistance in gardens and buildings from well camouflaged positions on the perimeter at the end of May, 'defending their strong positions to the last man'. This was uncomfortable for those German infantry divisions, who until now had enjoyed a virtual 'walk' across much of Belgium and France. 'Hard fighting continued into nightfall,' reported von Imhoff. 'The courage and weapons proficiency of the English demonstrated we were up against an extraordinarily bitter foe this day.' SS units, enraged and taken aback at the ferocity of resistance, reacted. On 27 May, ninety-nine members from the 2nd Battalion the Norfolk Regiment were massacred by SS Regiment 2 from the Totenkopf (Deaths-head) Division at Le Paradis, west of Béthune. Major Hans Riederer von Paar driving nearby saw '89 dead Englishmen shot-up by the SS people – a dreadful picture'. His regiment had lost 450 men the day before.

Resistance from Bill Cordrey's Warwickshire battalion near Wormhout pinned down elements from the II SS Battalion Leibstandarte Adolf Hitler, killing twelve and wounding twenty-nine. Until then the Leibstandarte had encountered scant resistance crossing Holland, which changed on meeting the British at the Dunkirk perimeter. Frustrated by their biggest casualties in the war so far, they grenaded and shot some fifty helpless Warwicks and other British POWs in a barn at Wormhout, a bitterly contested village on the road between Cassel and Dunkirk. Two days later they lost twice their previous worst figure of dead.

It did not improve. Gefreiter (Corporal) Lachman with the German 18th Infantry Division marching by night toward the Dunkirk perimeter observed 'the fiery sun that slowly set beneath smoke and cordite covering the horizon'. With misgiving he reflected it was to be a night 'that was likely to bring little peace'. They were heading for an assembly area prior to attacking the town of Bergues, the linchpin strongpoint of the perimeter 'where the enemy had resolved to fight to the last'. German soldiers were as uncomfortable and nervous as their opponents. 'The flat terrain offered little protection against enemy fire,' described the Grossdeutschland Regiment official report. 'After three or four spadefuls of earth' to avoid it 'the soldiers struck ground water'. Grenadier Wolfgang Müller in the 7th Kompanie recalled observing the perimeter where 'a fine Flemish drizzle sprinkled on our helmets'. They were suddenly spooked by the sound of rattling equipment and hushed voices: 'Hans, man they're coming! Hans said to take it easy. We both stared into the darkness. We couldn't see a thing . . . But Hans had heard the noise too. Should we fire? Don't drive the whole front crazy! If we see something, we'll fire.'

Thinking they had likely won the war in the West, the German soldier was reluctant, unlike his desperate adversary, to risk his life on the verge of an Armistice. Hitler halted the panzers on 23 May, which was not viewed as particularly auspicious at the time. Tank crews and machines were clearly exhausted, would be required for the next decisive phase of the final battle for France and were in any case unsuited for operations over canals and the inundated marshy terrain. The BEF, with its back to the sea, was going nowhere apart from POW camps. With the collapse of the Belgians the greater and more immediate danger was from the mass of German infantry divisions marching up from the south and east of the perimeter. Three directions of advance meant detailed coordination was required to avoid own casualties and enable the ten divisions to edge forward to position their artillery before beginning the final assault. As German forces drew breath the British and French consolidated their grip on the perimeter defence.

Although situation maps displayed little movement, fighting around the Dunkirk perimeter was characterised by frequent adjustments to a porous line. It did not appear or feel secure for the British. 'News of tanks in the village next to us,' signaller Wilf Saunders heard on the net, and recorded in his diary on 28 May. 'Village is on the other side of the road from the chateau [where they were operating] – about 150 yards away. Woe is us!' Gunner James Bradley recalled 'there were roads that you couldn't go down, it was just impossible – absolute chaos reigning'. 'Still keep fighting wherever you go,' instructed their commanding officer. 'You're a British soldier, keep fighting, don't give in, don't put your hands up.'

Second Lieutenant Julian Fane with the Gloucester Regiment was caught up in one of the many adjustments in the line, exfiltrating from Cassel after it was overrun. He was ambushed with survivors at the edge of a field. 'The whole hedgerow opened up – we were easy targets.' A grenade explosion knocked his helmet askew and shrapnel peppered his shoulder and arm. 'Oh dear,' he thought, 'what was happening now?' One of his fellow platoon commanders was mortally wounded in the chest alongside him. 'The next thing the Quartermaster Sergeant was hit and killed and so I moved my way along, really crawling over these people who had been killed.' He gathered together fourteen people who were left and they started to laboriously crawl south through ditches to gain the perimeter. 'If you are a hunted animal and put yourself in the same position, you escape as best you can,' he remembered. 'You're driven by fear really, of not being captured.'

The nearer escaping units got to Dunkirk the greater the frequency of air attacks. Charlie Brown in the Royal Army Service Corps recalled the trepidation accompanying the now familiar Stuka attacks. 'They'd do acrobatics for about five minutes', setting themselves up for an attack and then down they would remorselessly dive: 'You're in a ditch if you can find one and you are saying to yourself: "For God's sake! Drop them and get it over!" They'd come down one after the other and whistling – a frightening noise. And if anybody said he wasn't frightened when the Stukas were around, he was a liar – anybody.'

British units entered the perimeter from the French hinterland to the south or from Belgium to the east. Ted Stonard with 286 Battery Royal Artillery recalled 'passing through the outer perimeter of the first defence line where British infantry were dug in. We exchanged banter and insults in the typical British manner and threaded our way through barbed wire and road blocks.'

Just inside the perimeter were the immobilisation areas where all heavy equipments and vehicles had to be abandoned. Reg Rymer, retreating with the Cheshires, recalled it was at the four-mile point from Dunkirk. They were halted by MPs who said, 'Right that's it, unload, shove the trucks into the field and set fire to them.' As signaller Wilf Saunders came through he observed 'whole mobile workshops, beautiful huge things, probably worth a couple of millions of pounds these days' all consigned to the junk heap. It made the point 'we were in full retreat, there was no question about that'. Staff Officer Captain James Hill considered it a professionally painful experience. 'If you are a soldier, you cannot imagine what it must feel like to see all your equipment being thrown away, dumped – handed over to the opposition if you would like to put it that way – dreadful.' The immobilisation areas dashed any illusions soldiers may have been harbouring about their predicament. One artilleryman recalled their brigadier addressing the formed up remnants of their defeated unit:

> Chaps, I'm afraid to tell you the worst has happened, we are almost totally surrounded and we are going to try and fight our way back with a rear guard action to the sea. We are going to be evacuated from Dunkirk. I must tell you the worst, we expect that 1 in 10 will be able to get back home,' and he wished us all the best.

They then proceeded to immobilise their equipment 'and presently there was so much smashed vehicles etc in the canal that you could walk over them'. The significance of this self-imposed destruction was apparent to all. Captain James Hill moving toward the beaches reflected: 'We knew then we were a completely defeated army.' Nobody wanted to be captured after what they had endured. Gunner

Stanley Dilley from the Devon Heavy Regiment voiced this apprehension, never far beneath the surface, when he observed: 'Not only
did we have the fighters and bombers to put up with, but you could
hear the rear guard getting nearer and nearer every day as the perimeter
they were holding shrank.'

FROM THE BEACHES TO THE BOATS

Once troops moved away from the immobilisation area or broke clean
from the perimeter defensive lines, they made their way on foot to the
beaches. Signaller Wilf Saunders declared on arrival, 'never dreamed
we had so many troops in the area – can't see why we are retreating.'
The first glimpse of the ten-mile long beach was a stunning sight for
most. On crossing the sand dunes at La Panne on the Belgian border it
was just possible to pick out Dunkirk in the distance, obvious from its
column of smoke and flak signature, with aircraft buzzing around it like
gnats. Bray Dunes in between, bordered by less obstructive sand dunes,
had immensely wide flat beaches. Dunkirk was more easily visible from
here with Malo-les-Bains, the picturesque seaside town alongside it, in
the bay formed by the harbour mole.

Dennis Avon with a Field Park Company recalled, 'the beach was
just black with troops, from the harbour as far as you could see, it was
just troops.' Over 300,000 soldiers were to pass over it. At any one time
during the height of the evacuation the equivalent of the whole
modern British Army (just over 100,000) could be seen spread over
its ten-mile expanse. Three times the numbers of the present army were
to be evacuated across it. Two-thirds of them were taken off in the first
week at the rate of about 400 per destroyer, varying from eight hours to
load at first to eventually thirty-five minutes at the height of the
evacuation. It was a gigantic undertaking, thousands upon thousands of
men stretching into the distance as far as the eye could see. The
enormous spread offered some dispersion against air attack but certainly
complicated the administrative efforts required to sustain the process.

When Reg Rymer emerged on to the beach with survivors from the
Cheshire Regiment 'my first impression was panic, seeing that lot!' he
confessed. 'Honestly, they were strewn all over the place, some dead,

'*A Black Day*. We need all our prayers now', confided one housewife to her diary. Crowds patiently wait to gain entry to Westminster Abbey for an all-denominational service of Deliverance held during the Dunkirk evacuation.

'To us sailors it was a saddening sight, cor, to see the British Army – you know – defeated! They were all running about in groups'. The beach under fire viewed from the ships.

Dunkirk survivors disembark in England. One civilian observer soberly remarked, 'the troops were in a terrible state', as they disembarked, something had gone badly wrong.

some dying and I suppose some wounded.' He was at La Panne where 'there were hundreds and hundreds of soldiers in the sand there'. Ships, he saw, were attempting to pick them up. 'But there were so many that I thought, how are we going to get these people off here?' Wilf Saunders was similarly dismayed at his first view of crowds of exhausted men. 'I had to lay down,' he admitted. 'This is it I thought, I can't get away from this place. I more or less gave up.'

Whatever the emotional state of the troops stumbling onto the beaches, it could not be denied they witnessed an amazing spectacle. Royal Engineer officer John Woollett from 23 Field Company emerged on to Bray Dunes with his driver, a seasoned 'old sapper'. They gazed about: 'A lovely fine day. There were Stukas attacking the ships. There were Hurricanes attacking the Stukas in turn and there was anti-aircraft fire going up, and he [his driver] looked around and said to me: '*Cor Sir* − it's better than a fucking football match!'

Men shuffling onto the beaches had been in action on and off for about twenty-one days, having failed on average to hold up to six defensive positions, involving advancing sixty-five miles and then retreating about eighty. Divisions were on the retreat between four to nine days and only a few were effective on reaching the perimeter. Those that were became the rearguards. All three of the second-line divisions, which only had hand-held weapons and no artillery, were badly rattled. Not one second-line brigade survived its first serious contact with the enemy, the severity of punishment depending on whether it was caught on the move or in the open by the panzers. Many of their soldiers were captured.

Large numbers of the soldiers on the beach were TA or newly conscripted and consequently could be quite old. They were shaken, as one 'old campaigner', a sergeant major admitted: 'It's not like any other fighting I've ever known before. When we've lost some ground, and we're digging ourselves in to make a stand, they're suddenly all behind us; this happened again and again; and ten-to-one they're laughing at us with kids' voices.'

Soldiers were also often shell-shocked. 'It was called the planned evacuation, but it was a whole army collapsed really,' commented Dr Patrick de Mare, who worked in a field dressing station. 'It was around that time that they decided not to shoot deserters − well, they couldn't shoot the whole army, could they?' William Sargant, a civilian psychiatrist, recalled treating a soldier who came across his own brother lying by the roadside with a severe abdominal wound. He pleaded with him to cut short his suffering, which he did, dragging him into a field and ending it with a rifle shot. From that moment on the soldier's right hand, the one that administered the coup de grâce was paralysed.

Men moving on to the Dunkirk beaches had been exposed to acute physical and mental stress. Twenty days of continuous physical exertion with insufficient sleep and constantly recurring air-raids exacted a toll. They had lost friends, killed and mutilated holding defensive positions, and had seen the miserable plight of the refugees on the roads without being able to do anything about it; their own families could well be next. For at least one-third of the three-week campaign they had run a gauntlet of enemy attempts to cut them off from reaching the coast. Sapper Charlie Brown recalled his state of mind as being 'completely shattered, hungry and tired. We'd got no interest in anything – I couldn't have cared what happened.' The emotional experience of Dunkirk was to prove a formative experience for the entire army.

Running for days on end suddenly transitioned to waiting, with the anxiety of possible capture at the last moment after all. 'For mile upon mile between La Panne and along the stretch of sand at Bray Dunes we could see what appeared to be lines and lines of ant-like figures, and the lines stretched from the dunes to the sea,' recalled Sapper Reg Bazeley. At sea there was 'a regatta' of ships. 'Ants were being loaded into boats taking them willy-nilly out of the water.' Bazeley eventually appreciated 'they were *men* not ants, and that they were *our* men'. There was no option except join the queues and hope to get away. Veterans recall it was mainly the NCOs who organised the zig-zag lines across the beaches to the small boats trying to get them off. 'We helped one another as best we could, standing for hours in water up to our chests,' recalled Frank Shearmen in the Ordnance Corps. 'We were cold, wet, hungry and tired – my rifle was tied around my neck and my tin hat never left my head.'

'We were given a serial number and only when that number was called out would we move,' recalled Reg Bazeley. But these were no ordinary queues. 'Can you imagine standing in single file, in water, being periodically shelled and machine-gunned, and waiting for a boat?' asked Fred Durham waiting with the Durham Light Infantry. 'Each time I got anywhere near the head of the queue,' declared Private Percy McDonald with the Royal Army Service Corps, 'it seemed an enemy plane warning would be given which caused a mad 200-yard dash back to the sand dunes, and so I lost my position in the queue!' Following several attempts he gave up and flopped down amid the relative safety of the sand dunes. Waiting might last days.

Simply getting down to the water's edge through ankle-deep sand was an effort. Exhausted men found it difficult to maintain contact with comrades or units, especially in the dark when so many little groups looking very much alike became separated among the masses. Captain Richard Austin with 204 Field Regiment found 'if you stopped for a few seconds to look behind you, the chances were you attached yourself to some entirely different unit'.

Men waiting in the queues fed off rumour. 'Yes we were scared,' admitted Arthur Gunn at La Panne, 'it could be seen on the faces of the men.' Leaflets were dropped, interspersed with bombing raids, according to Reg Bazeley, urging them to 'give up because you have no RAF left, and all the Generals have gone home'. Generally the response was a ribald oath coupled with satisfaction that paper was at last available for more earthy purposes, but pessimism did occur. Doubts were quite widespread, Bazeley claimed, and comments such as 'we will never get back' and 'they have deserted us' became pronounced as the numbers of small boats became fewer day by day. He observed one young officer who cracked jumping into a small boat that was loading. When he refused to get out he was shot 'to stop the panic that could well have followed'. Heroes and cowards were in abundance. Gunner James Bradley recalled the 'most magnificent bit of British discipline' at the water's edge. 'They went down and they stood in the water and the tide came in, and it went up to here [indicating his upper chest] and the tide went out and then it came back. I was there I remember three tides, and staying there at night – and it was so terribly British!'

John Graves, a RNVR sub-lieutenant, observed in the first faint light of dawn, as the paddle steamer *Medway Queen* nosed into a point a half mile out from the beach:

Long lines of men standing still like human piers stretching out into the water – knee, waist and even neck high in it, standing so patiently there in full equipment, boots, rifles, packs, tin helmets and all with Sergeants passing or rather swirling their way up and down the lines with a word of encouragement here and a command there.

Reg Bazeley conversely witnessed 'the nerves of many men gave way, leading to queue jumping, hustling others in front of them to scramble into boats that were already overloaded, or claiming it was their turn before somebody else'. This was background to another rumour, that there was to be a surrender, 'that we had already asked for terms'. Although it was not true, Bazeley recalled 'at the time it seemed to have some credence'.

Clambering into boats was a physical ordeal for soldiers weighted down with khaki-serge heavy cloth uniforms and equipment. Wilf Saunders tried to get on one boat that had too many men on board which sank when it was turned broadside-on into heavy waves. He tried another lifeboat, which suffered the same fate, and staggered exhausted back to shore and collapsed.

Heavy wet clothes and full kit, less rifle dropped when the first boat turned over had reduced me to such a state that I didn't care if I did die. Continued wading into a heavy sea had also sapped my strength, and at the end of that three weeks – I decided it was impossible to get a boat and for the third successive day gave myself up as finished.

Sailors, being shrewd judges of human character, employed every ruse to encourage or cajole exhausted soldiers into their boats. Delays increased the risks to themselves. Captain Richard Austin RE described what it was like to be on the receiving end of sometimes rough handling. In his sodden state he found 'it was practically impossible to move even from one foot to another' weighted down by clothing and equipment. He momentarily panicked when after standing for hours in waist-deep water he had to suddenly galvanise limbs locked by the cold to climb aboard, while his feet were 'fixed, immovable, as though chained' beneath mud and sand. The navy seemed to judge the moment perfectly. If kindness had no effect, then rough words, threats or bullying were employed to spark anger to snap limbs or minds out of their paralysed state. 'Come on, you bastards,' they were cajoled, 'get a move on, dopey!' Austin was irritated into producing the required effort, and received scant comfort when he was safely hauled in. 'Come on, you bastard. Get up and help the others in.'

Saunders, depressed at missing what he suspected was the last destroyer, noticed three small boats in a line. 'As a last final effort I started wading.' Two boats refused him, promising they would come back and directed him back to shore. 'But hundreds of men were there all waiting for the boat.' Thankfully, the third boat waited. 'I was weighed down by the wet equipment and I had managed to get a leg up the side of the boat, but I simply could not get in. I was helped in for the last bit by someone already in the boat and then we had to row the thing.'

Surf on this day made the handling of whalers almost impossible. Men were directed to the mole, the sole surviving jetty in Dunkirk harbour where ships could still enter and tie up. It was a fifteen-foot wide wooden plank construction stretching nearly two-thirds of a mile, supported by timber palisades over rock. To get there might involve an eight- to ten-mile trek through sand for those at La Panne or Bray Dunes. It was not a particularly inviting prospect as its significance was beginning to attract enemy attention. Artillery Captain Richard Austin had assessed its length: 'The great black wall of the Mole stretched from the beach far out into the sea, the end of it almost invisible to us. The Mole had an astounding, terrifying background of giant flames leaping a hundred feet into the air from blazing oil tanks.'

Soldiers were reluctant to approach it, as at the shore end 'high explosive shells burst around it with monotonous regularity'. Most of the men evacuated were in fact taken from this hazardous jetty, which became the primary focus of the air-sea battle.

FROM BOATS TO HOME

Tugboats towed groups of twenty or more motor pleasure launches four abreast along the River Thames past Westminster heading down-stream to the Channel. It was a fine day and Francis Codd, a thirty-year-old Auxiliary Fire Brigade member was summoned by bell during lunch with seventy others to the Blackfriars landing. They included the crew of the *Massey Shaw*, a shallow draught Thames fire-fighting ship. 'A message from Lambeth Headquarters,' the station office solemnly announced, 'the *Massey Shaw* is going to Dunkirk.' 'Oh, everyone gasped,' suspecting the deployment had to do with fire-fighting. 'Someone suggested the whole sea would be a mass of flame and we'd have to guide the *Massey Shaw* through acres of flaming sea,' Codd recalled. Nobody actually knew what was required, but 'with that awful vision' the station officer asked for volunteers. Codd was picked and they left Ramsgate in the afternoon and 'the sea was like a mill pond – quite exceptional'. After an hour, with no coastline visible, they spotted a huge black cloud of smoke ten miles away. 'And as we got nearer and nearer this seemed more menacing,' remembered Codd, 'it became an enormous black menace.' As they approached, the whole of Dunkirk appeared alight and burning.

Commander Brian Deane, captaining the destroyer HMS *Sabre*, read the tense signal from the Admiralty on the evening of 27 May: 'From Vice-Admiral, Dover. The last chance of saving the BEF is tonight. You are to proceed with all despatch to beaches two or three miles east of Dunkirk and embark troops in your own boats.'

He could return at his own discretion, but before it got light. 'So it had come to that,' he reflected. 'Gosh, things must be worse than we had thought!' There was no time to meditate, within minutes they were heading out to sea, creating a huge bow wave at 28 knots, heading for the green light buoy off Calais. Commander Cyril Ross was abruptly summoned from the minesweeper *Gossamer* on the Tyne and 'shown in to a very old and tired Admiral' and thought, 'had I known all that he knew then no doubt I should have looked old and tired too.' He was to sail to Dunkirk. 'Minesweeping?' Ross legitimately asked, 'No,' was the almost inaudible response. He stepped nearer and murmured, 'Evacuation?' and got a silent nod in response.

Crews received the news almost by innuendo. Thomas Russell on the paddle steamer *Medway Queen* pressed into minesweeping service only realised something was up when the rest of the flotilla were not out on their daily sweep. Instead a naval barge was alongside unloading more food supplies than they could ever use. News eventually filtered out they were heading for Dunkirk. Lorries pulled up alongside other vessels and began to unload mountains of life-jackets. An armada of 222 naval vessels including forty-one destroyers and 665 civilian boats began to make their way across the Channel. Two-thirds of them were privately owned trawlers, coasters, tugboats, seaside pleasure craft and gentleman's cruisers requisitioned from the moorings of England's south coast and the River Thames. Most were skippered by naval personnel but others were taken by their owners. Ordinary people were becoming part of this war for the first time. As one Fleet Air Arm officer described it: 'Men who owned boats put down their fountain pens, or their tools of trade, hung up their bowler hats, kissed their wives goodbye, and then sailed to one of the two Kentish harbours.'

Charles Lightoller, the surviving second officer of the ill-fated *Titanic*, skippered a cruiser called *Sundowner*. As the name suggested, 'she was what a gin palace would have looked like in the 1930s,' commented John Watkins who maintained the boat for Ramsgate Maritime Museum. 'On her tours of Mediterranean and Baltic ports, she could take up to 15 family and friends in comfort.' Lightoller, assisted by his son, was to pack 130 soldiers aboard at Dunkirk. Jimmy Christmas, a nineteen-year-old naval conscript, sailed the *Minotaur*, a former naval training pinnace, across to Dunkirk. Accompanying him was a new recruit called Alfie and the First Mortlake Sea Scouts master and a Rover sea scout as crew. During the evacuation the boat was up-ended by a near-miss bomb and Christmas remembered, 'I never saw Alfie again. I only knew him for a day. I didn't even know his surname.'

Crossing the Channel was an ordeal in itself, because all the lighted buoys and lightships were blacked out and the waters heavily mined. The navy only swept three lanes – X, Y and Z – through the treacherous shoals and sandbanks off the coast between Calais and La Panne. Route X required a dash under heavy German guns already set up on the outskirts of Calais. Sub-Lieutenant Charles Lamb viewed the awesome spectacle of traffic commuting between Dunkirk and Dover and Ramsgate from his Swordfish torpedo bomber. 'It looked as though it would be possible to use them as stepping-stones and walk across the Channel,' he recalled. A pattern emerged whereby home-coming ships stayed in the centre columns during the forty mile crossing and outgoing ships protected their flanks. Destroyers surged along with huge wakes at 28 to 30 knots while the little ships meandered at best speed. Charles Lightoller on *Sundowner* came across his first burning casualty in mid-Channel at about 2.25 pm, the twenty-five-foot *Westerley*, broken down 'and badly on fire'. It was an omen for what lay ahead. 'Soon we were passing many other vessels including tugs towing clusters of naval whalers and cutters,' recalled seaman Frank Pattrick on an excursion steamer the *Crested Eagle*, one of the fastest paddle steamers on the Thames. Many of the soldiers due to be picked up had enjoyed holiday trips on these steamers with their wives and families.

As the vessels approached the beaches those on board were shocked and perplexed as the true situation became apparent. Francis Codd on the fire-fighting ship *Massey Shaw* saw buildings take shape in the distance and a beach with water so calm the background was reflected upon it. 'Dark shapes on the sand' were discernible, shelving in lines down to the water and they were distinguished as men. 'It was an extraordinary sight,' he remembered, 'nothing seemed to be happening.' Hundreds of thousands of men stretched back to the houses behind the beach. 'They didn't seem to be moving in any organized way, not marching.' Standing and sitting rows of men spread from the beach out into the sea. 'We didn't understand what this was at first', but clearly they were not needed to fight fires. 'It suddenly occurred to us that these were columns of men waiting to be picked up.' The *Massey Shaw* drifted in slowly, 'not knowing quite what we were supposed to do. But we knew we would have no instructions.' They began to ferry men from the beach with an improvised rope ferry.

'When we arrived off the beaches,' remarked a seaman, 'to us sailors it was a saddening sight, *cor*, to see the British Army – *you know* – *defeated!*' It was a sobering sight. 'They were all running about in groups, they were waddling out into the water, up to their neck, looking for some boat to pick them up.' 'There were thousands on the beach – *thousands!*' exclaimed another crew man: 'Stuff was coming over and you would literally see platoons of men walking along the beach when all of a sudden they weren't there. You'd see legs and arms up in the air, terrible it was, and there was racing horses, dogs of all shapes and sizes, rushing about the beach, seemingly mad. It was a terrible sight.'

Commander Trevor Crick, approaching Dunkirk more slowly in a commandeered Dutch barge, also felt apprehensive during the final approach. He realised with trepidation 'that what I thought was thunder clouds was in reality smoke drifting away from Dunkirk'. It hung in the sky, a menacing ominous pall 2,000 feet above the sea. Glancing to the west Crick saw blue sky, and realised with amazement 'it was in reality the beginning of a perfect day'.

Good weather brought the dive-bombers. 'They'd aim for one ship, which was obviously moving and zig-zagging to get away,' recalled Dennis Avon with a Field Park Company, observing from the beach. 'There'd be one Stuka that would peel off and then two – three – four – five – six – seven – eight. Well, the ship wouldn't stand a chance' as it took desperate evasive action 'and many ships got hit'. More than anything else it was the noise that was the most intimidating. 'And there was the scream from the engine,' described Avon, 'and the falling bombs as well.' 'You've got to remember,' Private Reg Rymer with the Cheshire regiment pointed out, 'we're running across the beach and you're jumping over blokes dodging and diving because they're coming down machine-gunning you and everything else.' It was pandemonium. 'You're trying to keep an eye on there,' he indicated in one direction, 'and there's another one coming that way', pointing in the opposite direction.

'The Germans came in as low as they possibly could strafing everyone including the wounded as they laid helpless,' declared Tom Jones with 68 Field Regiment Royal Artillery. They could only respond with rifle volley fire. 'I remember the bellies of the planes seemed to be nearly skimming the sand.' Ack-ack gunner Norman Hammond was strafed in the dunes to the east of Dunkirk. 'The first man bought it with shrapnel through his side – I know because the blood spattered over us.' One of his officers had his foot blown off and Hammond is left with an indelible image of the foot, still in the boot, lying in the sand. Lawrence Bennett with the Lancashire Fusiliers recalled 'we put one chap on a bren gun' in the anti-aircraft role, mounted on a tripod, but it made little difference. 'They split him down the middle more or less, killed him instantly when they fired at him.'

Feldmarschall Hermann Goering brashly offered the Luftwaffe to Hitler as a means of finishing off the BEF. German operational planners had excelled on land because they were essentially a land power. They had little comprehension of the Royal Navy's competence as a sea power to conduct an evacuation of such magnitude. Despite intelligence reports indicating otherwise, German planners did not believe what their eyes saw. Even the most cynical German staff officer felt there was an outside chance the Luftwaffe might succeed, bearing in mind their Blitzkrieg accomplishments thus far. But the Luftwaffe had to switch from a land to sea main point of effort with no notice. They were short of bombs effective against ships, aircraft crews were tired and machines badly in need of servicing. Casualties of men and aircraft were high. Low cloud and smoke from the very refineries they had bombed obscured targets in and around Dunkirk for six and a half days of the BEF's nine-day evacuation ordeal. Even so, twenty-eight ships were lost in five days and thirty-one major vessels sunk by the end of the month with eleven out of action. It became no longer feasible to expose major ships by day.

The long vulnerable jetty line of the mole became the focus. Destroyers and transports pulled alongside and hurriedly loaded troops under a torrent of shell fire and aerial bombing. 'It's hard to imagine as it was then,' explained Jack Saunders with the East Lancashire Regiment. 'Nobody would believe it unless you were actually there.' A lottery of chance was played out on and around the mole. 'We were just waiting for the boats and hoping for the best and hoping you'd get through alive and get back to England.' Men virtually queued under fire or ran a gauntlet along its two-thirds of a mile length. Sapper Sid Crockett was ordered by Captain Tennant to 'run as fast as you possibly can, because the more you run the more we can get off'. When he arrived breathless at the end, 'this big sailor, he grabbed my rifle in one hand and me in the other and dumped me on the deck.'

'There was some high-ranking British officer and he said to us – *run!*' recalled Dennis Avon, a Field Park Company soldier: 'So we ran and a pal I know, one of the chaps lying there, grabbed his ankle. He was near the boat and he heard "please – help me!" He was hailed by the sailors "Get on the boat, mate!" and he left him. He never forgot it, it used to haunt him.'

Moving down the mole was laborious enough without the distractions caused by enemy action because holes and gaps were opened by bombing and shelling. Charlie Brown with the Service Corps remembered 'we had to go down in the middle on two builder's planks, about that wide', he indicated with hands narrowly apart. 'If you looked down,' he grinned, 'you had vertigo.' Fifteen-foot tidal ranges meant a formidable jump on to a deck or a rope ladder at low tide. Artillery gunner James Bradley recalled apprehensively considering the man behind him 'must be mad, because he had his tin hat on, a rifle and everything of his equipment'. He would have no chance if he went into the water and sure enough 'as he went to step he fell into the water and I shouted to him.' The image was to remain with him for the rest of his life. 'I saw him going down like this,' he demonstrated raising his arms up in a plaintive gesture to the sky, 'and all the bubbles coming up and he's still got a tin hat and rifle around him.'

Boats did not pause for individuals who fell overboard. Private Clive Tonry jumped for a scramble net which several exhausted soldiers missed and fell into the water. 'The ship wouldn't stop,' he recalled, 'it went very slowly, but it wouldn't stop to pick them up — it just left them.' Boats were at their most vulnerable alongside the makeshift jetty. 'Get on the deck, get down on the deck!' Bradley was ordered. 'We are going to take off as soon as possible.' This was the culminating point for men who had retreated for three weeks. The next few moments would decide whether they escaped, died or were captured. As individuals they were no longer in control. 'All I can remember,' said Bradley, 'was the humming of aeroplanes coming, Stukas are coming.'

The consequences of being struck by a bomb within the narrow confines of the Dunkirk basin were horrific. When the old Thames paddle steamer *Crested Eagle* was hit onlookers saw 'men on fire from head to toe, dancing like dervishes, their faces contorted, leap screaming into the sea'. When the crippled boat was beached west of Bray beach beyond the harbour 200 survivors were heavily machine-gunned from the air, threshing in the water while rescue ships were bombed. Few could ever forget such an experience. Dr Ann Dally, a psychiatrist student, treated one such patient rescued from a sea of blazing oil at Dunkirk. Given carbon dioxide 'or something to release his memories he would then act as if he was in a sea of boiling oil, shouting and screaming and leaping all about the place'. Perhaps the most disturbing part of Tom Corteen's experience, as mate aboard the Isle of Man packet *Manxman*, was steaming through bodies kept afloat by their cork life-jackets, which 'bobbed up and down with the swell like huge shoals of jelly fish'.

After clearing the harbour or beaches, ships had to get under way and the main impediment to achieving this came from the skies. Commander Ross described the difficulty of picking out the main channel buoy exiting Dunkirk with 'that horrid swarm of dive bombers overhead – a great circus of them, Junkers 87s, great bent-winged gnat-like creatures'. Survival required adroit seamanship because there was little room for evasive action in the shoals which also made it difficult to speed up. The unwary grounded themselves on sandbanks, creating even more obstacles to dodge. 'Enough water to turn?' Ross asked his yeoman, "Yes, sir, just high water" – trust him to know,' Ross thankfully thought and put the wheel hard over. Evasive action required seamanship matched with instinctive steering. 'I judged each case on its merits and conned the ship clear of the bombs,' he recalled. High diving aircraft could not be engaged by heavy-calibre guns unable to reach the steep elevation needed. Perceiving this, German aircrews flew a vertical line down the mast. 'Aircraft after aircraft screamed down at us: salvo after salvo fell in the sea close by – then a pause – then a terrific *Bloompf* as they burst under water.'

After eight aircraft, he briefly sailed a steady course utilising the pause before 'seven more came at us'. One of these proved especially persistent, Ross recalled, and 'did a sort of little dance high up in the sky, then came down almost vertically'. The ship swung round so slowly that Ross was convinced, 'I think they've got us this time', to which his yeoman phlegmatically confirmed, 'Afraid so, sir.' But with a 'Whish! Woompf! Missed!' Suddenly the sky was clear. 'Just two rounds left,' came the metallic report from the foremost gun and Ross confessed, 'I felt a little sick, and sat down.'

'The bombardment of Dunkirk from the air,' recalled Stuka Staffelkapitän Dietrich Peltz, 'was so concentrated that a pilot had literally to watch out that he did not get a bomb in the neck from his comrades flying above him.' His squadron – I/Stuka 76 – conducted eight bombing attacks on Dunkirk harbour. Despite cloud coverage over the target, he claimed 'anti-aircraft shell bursts could invariably be seen above the clouds at a point where the town ought to lie'. He described the Stuka attack technique upon a heavily armed transport which 'starts to zig-zag' even before he begins his nose-dive, 'the foam in its wake wriggles like a twisted tail'. The whole squadron was directed at one key ship. Each pilot picked an object on the deck, such as a heavy-calibre gun, as aiming point and continued the dive until the last possible moment. 'Now for it' – the release point, Peltz explained, when 'according to all human calculation, the bomb must hit it'. As the pilot pulled out of the dive 'once more centrifugal force with its giant fist thrusts him back on his seat'. This could be so severe pilots might momentarily black out. Wings were then lightly banked to observe the effect of the strike.

One problem for Luftwaffe pilots penetrating the cloud was a tendency to be overwhelmed by the target-rich environment. Peltz tended to direct his squadron against the larger units, but direction was loose. 'And now the small fry are for it!' he declared, machine-gunning 'motor boats, yachts and fishing cutters – craft of every description'. Time on target and the attendant images were fleeting. 'These small craft also try to escape by zig-zagging but it doesn't help much.' So dominant was the Luftwaffe off Dunkirk that gunner signaller Stanley Dilley, watching a large ship on fire with sailors diving from it, declared, 'I can remember a plane doing a victory roll over it.'

Luftwaffe air attacks were, however, indecisive. Rather than attempting specifically to block the port, they harassed and attacked ships off shore. Coordination over target was lacking and in particular the significance of the mole – the linchpin to the British evacuation – appears to have been missed. Attacks were directed at ships and not the jetty, which was exceedingly thin viewed from the air and difficult to hit. Ships were a different proposition from weakly defended static targets on land, not only did they move, they fired back. The Royal Air Force had also put in an appearance and was making its presence felt.

Soldiers on the beaches may have felt the 'Brylcreem Boys' had let them down but Sergeant Pilot Bernard Jennings explained, 'what we tried to do was intercept the Germans inland, before they could get to the beaches.' It cost them eighty pilots and a hundred aircraft. Air Chief

Marshal Sir Hugh Dowding, the Commander in Chief Fighter Command, wanted to conserve RAF fighter strength for the inevitable coming battle over the UK mainland. Three hundred and twenty pilots were killed in France, a hundred pilots lost as prisoners and almost 1,000 aircraft destroyed. 'The soldiers thought we had let them down,' reflected Sergeant Jennings. 'We didn't. It was no use flying over the beaches at Dunkirk. By that time the Germans would have been there to drop their bombs on the men below.'

Air fighting moved from low to high level as battling pilots increasingly sought the advantage of height. Few men on the ground saw what was going on. 'It was funny weather over Dunkirk,' explained Flight Lieutenant Brian Kingcome. 'A lot of the time there you saw nothing but aircraft because you were sandwiched between layers of cloud.' Fighting was fleeting. 'An aircraft would suddenly appear and disappear.' Kingcome explained, 'you didn't have time to follow up on an attack. You fired at something which disappeared, perhaps with some smoke coming out of it.' Motivating them throughout was the spectacle on the beaches, momentarily visible through cloud breaks. 'The thousands of troops on the beaches was a fantastic sight,' observed Pilot Officer Wally Wallens. 'You weren't long over Dunkirk,' remembered Brian Kingcome. It took an hour and a quarter to cross the Channel by the time they were up and rendezvoused with another squadron, then 'you had maybe ten or fifteen minutes of fighting time before you had to hightail it home again'.

Veteran German accounts from troops on the ground testify how uncomfortable these ten minutes could be. 'We took losses and the troops were calling for help,' admitted a VIII Fliegerkorps War Diary report on 25 May. Conditions around Dunkirk were changing: 'They are very sensitive to air activity as they are hardly ever used to being attacked out of the air,' the report confided. German soldiers used to Luftwaffe dominance did not appreciate the temporary role reversal. 'Our own troops will do nothing without air cover,' the report complained. The SS Leibstandarte Adolf Hitler reported 'active enemy flying' on 29 May, losing one man killed and another wounded when their column was attacked by Blenheim bombers. 'Persistent British air attacks forced the troops to keep their heads down,' complained the Grossdeutschland Regiment fighting around Bergues on the Dunkirk perimeter the same day. The German Fourth Army admitted they had lost air superiority six days before closing in on the perimeter, 'something new in this campaign' they gloomily commented.

The price exacted to achieve this was expressed in fighter pilot Flight Lieutenant R D G Wight's letter to his mother written during the Dunkirk evacuation. 'Well another day is gone and with it a lot of grand blokes,' he wrote. 'Got another brace of 109s today but the whole Luftwaffe seems to leap on us – we are hopelessly outnumbered.' Wight was aware that BEF troops were booing the RAF in Dover as they disembarked. 'Tell them,' he said to his mother, 'we only wish we could do more.' Wight attacked more than eighty German Me 109 fighters escorting twelve Stuka dive-bombers while 'practically out of ammunition and juice'. Pilots complained about the lack of armour in Spitfire cockpits, poor tactics and realised they were up against a crafty and competent foe. 'Every day, a few less of our men come back from over Dunkirk,' observed Flying Officer John Bisdee. But Wight assured his mother, 'don't worry – we are going to win this war even if we have only one aeroplane and one pilot left.' British pilots began to perceive, despite the humiliating reverses in France, that fighting nearer home made them an increasing match for the opposition. 'The Boche could produce the whole Luftwaffe and you would see the one pilot and the one aeroplane go into combat.' Wight matched his tenacious prose with action. Two months later he was killed leading three Hurricanes against sixty Messerschmitt 110 fighters at the height of the Battle of Britain.

Unpredictable weather was the primary impediment to cross–Channel traffic this time of year. People living in the south coast ports now realised what was going on. Anxiety about the outcome was matched by wonder at the extraordinary calm weather that appeared to mythically protect the evacuation. For almost nine days a sluggish southerly air flow covered the British Isles and France. At the end of May the sea was so calm it was like a mirror. Some isolated thunder-showers came with a weak frontal trough which produced a brief spell of choppy water but this was swiftly replaced by a large high-pressure system generating only light winds and slight seas during the first four days of

June. Veterans recall a Mediterranean-like opaque hue to the sea, which was beautiful but enabled German bombers to track ships along sparklingly luminous homeward wakes. Second Lieutenant Tony Hibbert recalled wading out to boats in water 'that rippled as if on fire with the flames reflected from the blazing oil tanks'. Explosions spraying up from the water around possessed the same phosphorescent hue, 'like ducks and drakes spinning across the water' after the flash of the impact. 'I had never seen anything so beautiful,' he remarked with total irony. Calm waters amid the Dunkirk carnage was the genesis of the feel-good factor that was to later coalesce into the so-called 'spirit of Dunkirk'. One woman, who watched Dunkirk burn from the south coast, claimed, 'you could see it clearly.' 'You know – it was marvellous! The sea was like a mill-pond. It looked like God was there and he was watching over us, and there wasn't a wave! As if God was watching over us and I believe it today, that we was going to win the war because of that'.

Ships moved back across the Channel at best speed to avoid marauding German bombers. These became less committed to pressing home attacks over such a wide expanse of water, when engine failure might be less forgiving than over land. The *Princess Elizabeth* paddled home at her best speed of 10 knots. Signalman Les Mallows on board recalled apprehension at 'various crumps and bangs heard at intervals somewhere over the horizon'. They were not home yet and 'this was to remain a frequent occurrence, and we could only gaze around with a wild surmise'. They disembarked their troops at Margate Pier, which some of the troops had visited on holiday with families along the south coast before.

Most of the troops slept on ship. Common to all on-board accounts was dehydration and the insatiable hunger of men who had not eaten for days. Thomas Russell, the cook on the paddle steamer *Medway Queen*, remembered:

> Suddenly there was a crush at each galley door, with innumerable khaki-clad arms – many dripping wet – waving billy-cans, mugs and mess tins at us. The hub-bub of voices was clamorous and insistent. These were not 'peckish' men. These were starving animals, most of them too desperately hungry and thirsty to be polite.

Evacuation ships were pitched into an exhausting routine of prepare for the next pick-up, the voyage across, the anxiety of plucking troops off beaches in the teeth of air attacks and looking after the desperately hungry and exhausted men on board. These had then to be disembarked and the ship cleaned up and made ready for the next crossing. Tom Russell recalled: 'days merged and became like one. Torpor took over. My actions became automatic.' Later, after no sleep for seventy-two hours he ladled stew all over the bandage drooping into a mess tin held before him. Looking up, he saw it was connected to a soldier with a head wound, 'his young face pinched and white under a blood-soaked field dressing'. 'Our eyes met as, reaching out, he removed the bandage and then heartily sucked off the gravy before tucking the end of it back into place. It was a savage gesture and I wondered when he had eaten last. He grinned as if it hurt his lips to stretch them saying: "Thanks mate, tastes smashing." '

Rescue on board ship meant normal life might yet beckon ahead. 'I sat there and I thought what happens now?' recalled sapper Sid Crockett. A sailor offered him a packet of Woodbine cigarettes and a cup of tea. 'It was the first decent drink I'd had for days and I drank that and I fell asleep.' Tired out, like many others, he was completely impervious to what was going on around him. 'They could have bombed the ship and I wouldn't have known and the next thing I knew I was in Dover.' Humphrey Bredin, a company commander with the Royal Ulster Rifles, collapsed exhausted on to the deck of a cross-Channel ferry. Asked by a steward whether he could bring him anything, Bredin responded, 'Yes thanks, a beer', only to be advised that alcohol could only be served beyond the three-mile limit. 'That,' he recalled, 'convinced me we would win the war.'

'I shall never forget my first glimpse of Margate as we peered through the haze of that hot day in June,' wrote another veteran. 'It was paradise compared with the hell that we had left.' This letter resides in a poignant glass cabinet in the local museum, its author appreciating he was living on borrowed time. 'We have always spent our holidays in Margate as we feel that the town was partly responsible for our chance to spend our lives together again.'

On Sunday night 2 June the navy released the signal 'BEF evacuated', ships were returning half-empty. About 338,000 soldiers, including 112,500 French, were taken off. French troops had manned the perimeter line as the British rearguards had disengaged. In recognition of this Admiral Ramsay prepared a final hazardous lift on Monday night with capacity to get off the 30,000 strong French rearguard. But as ships stealthily berthed alongside the mole for the last time they were overwhelmed by a rush of an estimated 40,000 soldiers who came out of the cellars and ruins of Dunkirk, undetected by the French Military Command and their Military Police. Although 26,175 soldiers were taken off, pitifully few of them were from the courageous rearguard, for whom the operation was intended. It encapsulated the heart-rending totality of the French collapse.

In Dover harbour there were often sixteen to twenty ships at eight berths, moored in tiers two or three deep and all handled by tugs. Soldier Brian Bishop came ashore from the paddle steamer *Medway Queen* immediately spotting a girl of about sixteen with a big tray of sandwiches. Ravenous, he asked for one. 'Looking back I must have been a frightful sight to her, unwashed, unshaven, uniform torn, blood and dirt everywhere.' He looked back after moving on but could not see her 'only the soldiers surrounding her and grabbing sandwiches'.

At the new customs shed at the Marine Station the dead were sorted from the living, where a makeshift mortuary was established. The living proceeded to the old customs shed where men who had arrived practically naked or in tattered rags, received clothing. One man left the Ramsgate clothing store kitted out with a college blazer, striped city trousers and white plimsolls.

Civilian onlookers were getting their first glimpse of the war. Eric Martin an eighteen-year-old apprentice electrician saw a destroyer at the Ramsgate pierhead disgorging soldiers. 'It was packed with troops and that was the first time we knew that something was going on and had gone badly wrong.' He noticed 'the troops were in a terrible state'. All along the south coast civilians sobered by the sight of soldiers coming ashore began to react. 'Soon people from the town were coming down,' Eric Martin recalled, 'to give assistance handing out food and cigarettes and anything they could lay their hands on.'

Soldiers were moved on to the railway platforms adjoining the harbours and countless trains began to depart, hissing steam and smoke. Some 327 trains moved 180,982 men from Dover, the rest were in eighty-two trains from Ramsgate, sixty-four from Folkestone, seventy-five at Margate and seventeen from Sheerness.

Staff Captain James Hill took his sandwiches on board, and 'the train set off and we didn't know where we were going'. Second Lieutenant Julian Fane from the Gloucestershire Regiment was shuttled with the other wounded on to ambulance trains. As he lay there, regarding his extra-ordinarily changed circumstances, peering through the train window, he felt quite emotional: 'I was absolutely amazed, coming from the hell of Dunkirk and seeing people in white blouses and shorts. You can imagine the effect, quite extraordinary, quite extraordinary. It looked in effect as if one had gone to hell and then gone to heaven you know.'

'Across the main road the dear old British public were queuing for the cinema, as though nothing had happened,' recalled Ernest Lang, an artilleryman, who landed at Margate Pier. 'It was just wonderful to be back in Blighty, alive in one piece.'

The fair-haired Stuka pilot crossing the gangplank from the paddle steamer HMS *Sandown* grinned broadly. He too was happy to be alive. Wrapped in a blanket, he may not have epitomised the might of the Luftwaffe, but gazing at the myriad of English soldiers in similar attire disembarking at Dover, he could be forgiven for feeling similarly optimistic. It should not be too long before he would be joined by his colleagues even now preparing forward airfields facing the British south coast. The front line had become the Channel, 'Churchill's Moat', as it would be called.

Gazing across that divide was German officer Eberhard Dennerlein. He stood on a beach littered with equipment and vehicles. Waves lapped gently over a torpedo washed ashore.

There was a deathly silence. No soldiers could be seen, only what they left behind. It was a macabre scene – a British Army that vanishes into thin air, even though it had been fighting extremely hard beforehand. They were the bravest compared to the others we were up against. They had retreated step by step until the moment that they suddenly vanished into thin air.

The British Army had escaped. What did it matter? 'Sure, we had some second thoughts at the end of the Western campaign in 1940, when we let the British get away,' remarked SS officer Otto Kumm, 'but these didn't last long.' The British Army was completely beleaguered, so why the doubts? 'They were superficial and didn't cause us to question Hitler or his genius.'

4

CHURCHILL'S MOAT: OPERATION SEA LION

THE BELEAGUERED ARMY

Schoolboy Leslie Kershaw had never seen so many steam trains crossing the embankment opposite his home at Swanley, Kent. They were passing at the rate of one every fifteen minutes, one after the other. 'We used to stand against a rail and wave at the soldiers, looking scruffy and dishevelled, as they went by,' he recalled, 'long trains, absolutely packed with troops.' Southern Railways employed nearly 2,000 locomotives and carriages to move 319,056 troops from 27 May until 4 June; running 620 special trains. Normal services for commuters to London ran remarkably to time, another triumph of improvisation.

'I shall never forget the troop trains,' remembered locomotive driver Jack Hewett on the Southern Eastern and Chatham Railway. 'Out of every compartment the soldiers' clothes were hanging from the windows to dry.' Many boarded dripping wet from the evacuation. 'Another thing I remember well is the number of people on each station platform and beside the track, to see if they could spot their relatives and friends.'

Joan Morgan recalled the trains clattering through Newport station, when scraps of paper and cigarette packets would be ejected from the windows like confetti. 'As soon as the station was clear, railway personnel got down on the line and collected every scrap.' These were taken to the stationmaster's office and carefully read, names and addresses deciphered and sent on so that 'every person was notified and told that their loved ones were safe and had passed through Newport'.

Civilians compassionately responded to the needs of their returning army. Train after train paused at the small station at Headcorn in Kent, where 145,000 troops briefly stopped for an average of eight minutes.

Forty to fifty local women worked eight-hour shifts for nine days and nights cutting up 2,500 loaves for sandwiches each day, while nineteen stoves were producing tea and coffee. Forty soldiers handed out 5,000 meat pies, with 5,000 sausages, 5,000 rolls and 5,000 eggs, all consumed in less than twenty-four hours. Thirteen-year-old Joan Launders peeled a bathload of boiled eggs, shells into a bucket and eggs into a big bowl. 'I tell you,' she recalled, 'I couldn't eat a hard-boiled egg for years after that!' She was intrigued to be asked by soldiers to pick flowers. 'I was much older before I realised that the sight of an English schoolgirl complete with panama hat and blazer, and the lovely summer flowers must have made them feel wonderful after all the horror they had been through.' As the trains pulled into the station she recalled the mixed attitudes of soldiers: 'some cheerful, some so sound asleep we didn't rouse them, others just sitting with blank staring faces.' Smart soldiers with bearing contrasted with others wrapped in blankets, 'but all had the strained look around the eyes that shows when anyone has been through a bad time'. As each train puffed out a cry of 'sling them out' produced a shower of cans clattering on to the platform, hurriedly gathered up to be washed for fresh tea before the next train due in fifteen minutes.

The beleaguered army was stunned at its reception. 'Although we were happy to be back in England, we thought we had let England down, we'd lost the war for them,' recalled an anxious sapper, Sid Crockett, gazing from his train window. Returning soldiers were apprehensive. 'What are people going to think of us now, because we have come back?' Sid Crockett's concerns were allayed as his train clattered by a big factory wall splashed with whitewashed graffiti proclaiming *Welcome Home the Dunkirk Veterans!* 'We never thought we would see that, never!' Crockett remembered. 'We thought we would be disgraced because we had given in.' Second Lieutenant Robin Medley was travelling with survivors from the 2nd Battalion the Bedfordshire and Hertfordshire Regiment and spotted banners as the train weaved through London's outer suburbs: *Welcome Home Boys!* and *Well Done Boys!* They were acutely embarrassed 'and felt these tributes were undeserved'. Signaller Wilf Saunders had got back and reflected: 'the Dunkirk evacuation generated in Britain an intensity of national emotion the like of which has probably never been known before or since', the genesis of a Dunkirk spirit. Saunders recalled, 'the anxiety, the relief, the general state of emotion, communicated itself to us the moment we set foot on shore, and likewise at every railway station, full of cheering crowds, that our packed troop trains passed.' Vital emotional therapy for a defeated army that had still to fight.

The Dunkirk spirit was an ambivalent concept applied like a therapeutic balm to a troubled army. Housewife Nella Last read newspaper reports about the Dunkirk evacuation and 'felt as if deep inside me was a harp that vibrated and sang'. She was inspired. 'The story made me feel part of something that was undying and never old.' Like many of her contemporaries, Nella Last had had an ordinary and hum-drum life up to this point, but now she 'felt everything to be worthwhile' at a time of universally perceived national danger: 'I felt glad I was of the same race as the rescuers and rescued.' 'People cheered us as if we were the victors,' mused Coldstream Guardsman Desmond Thorogood, 'but what had we done?' The BEF had lost 68,111 men killed, wounded, missing, and taken prisoner. None of its 2,472 guns and 63,879 motor vehicles made it back and only twenty-five of 704 tanks. Six destroyers were among 243 ships and boats sunk off the beaches and 474 aircraft were lost. As Winston Churchill warned the day the last ship departed Dunkirk: 'we must be very careful not to assign to this deliverance the attributes of a victory. Wars are not won by evacuations.' Clara Milburn's son Alan missed the boats. She became depressed at continually having to respond with 'no news' to the string of well-wisher enquiries. 'Always one is thinking of him, wondering whether he still lives and, if so, whether he is well, where he is, what he does all day, what discomforts he is suffering. If . . . If . . . And so the days go by.'

Blitzkrieg in France and Norway had a profound psychological impact on the British Expeditionary Forces involved. As Dunkirk fell the last of the Allied expeditionary force was being disembarked from Norway. Narvik was ironically recaptured at the beginning of the Dunkirk evacuation and had to be given up again by the end. On 14 June the Germans entered Paris, followed eight days later by French acceptance of an Armistice. Britain was alone. 'When France withdrew from the war, my feeling was of sheer and utter relief,' confessed Pilot Officer Christopher Currant with the RAF. 'We didn't have to depend on anybody. We felt that now we could really tackle this thing without any hassle, without any political nonsense.' The RAF suspected its strength was frittered away needlessly in Europe and Air Chief Marshal Sir Hugh Dowding echoed the sentiment: 'thank God we are now alone,' he professed. Even George VI wrote to his mother: 'I feel happier now that we have no allies to be polite to and to pamper.'

Whereas the RAF and Royal Navy had endured punishment, the BEF was in effect shattered. When Prime Minister Winston Churchill announced, 'the Battle of France is over. I expect that the Battle of Britain is about to begin', he was not simply referring to the air force, but the intimidating nature of the totality of the struggle that lay ahead. 'The whole fury and might of the enemy must very soon be turned upon us,' he stated. Next time, the newly beleaguered army might be battling the Wehrmacht on the beaches of southern England. 'Hitler knows,' Churchill sombrely announced, 'that he will have to break us on this island or lose the war.' The morale of returning troops was therefore of some consequence. 'I had no feeling of failure,' claimed Gunner James Bradley, who had rejoined his artillery unit, 'we had fought to the last with the greatest effect we could bring to bear.' They had simply been outclassed. 'You've only got a rifle and you're on your own and that sort of thing,' he reasoned, 'well, the regiment was just about destroyed really.'

What had been a sobering defeat for soldiers was acutely worrying to civilians who observed their bedraggled return. 'The first time the war seemed really menacing,' admitted Mrs Irene Thomas, was when she saw an old friend, 'a boy who had been a couple of forms above me at school.' They met in the high street as the boy was walking home; forty-eight hours before he had been on the Dunkirk beaches:

He was a weird sight, his battledress stained with sea water, old plimsolls instead of boots, no forage cap, and all his kit gone except his knife and fork sticking out of his top pocket. He was still shaking, and stared past me as I chatted on about how good it was to see him and how pleased his parents would be. Maybe it was just as well that I didn't think of offering sympathy, he looked near to tears as it was.

There was psychological trauma. 'Bomb–happy' sailors denied sleep for sixty hours started to behave oddly after the action was over. On HMS *Hussar*, according to a medical report after the evacuation, 'men became hyper-emotional and broke down and wept when given an order'. Publicly the Dunkirk spirit was vigorously communicated. In hindsight it has become associated with courage in the face of over-whelming odds and with the traditional obduracy British servicemen appear to display when staring defeat in the face. Morale was not high when the BEF returned. Men allegedly threw rifles from train windows in disgust as they pulled out of Dover. The army was more angry than demoralised. Theatre director Basil Dean recalled finding a pub on the south coast crammed with 'seething soldiery' fresh back from Dunkirk. These were 'dismayed men, savagely wounded in their pride' who sought 'relief in bitter criticism of those set over them'. This was the paradox of Dunkirk. Those that had endured the evacuation could be highly critical of their superiors, while much of the population were almost ecstatic.

J B Priestley's BBC news broadcast of 5 June encapsulated the mood of the country when he claimed, 'Dunkirk is another English epic.' It was so characteristically English, he explained, describing the crucial role seeming innocuous holiday pleasure steamers played rescuing the BEF. 'You do not know whether to laugh or cry,' he said, because they had 'a Dickens touch, a mid–Victorian air about them'. It was this gifted amateurism that so incensed soldiers critical of the conduct of the campaign. Priestley was right, there was indeed something epic about paddle steamers, which 'seemed to belong to the ridiculous holiday world of pharaohs, peers, sand–castles, ham-and-eggs, cheese, auto-matic machines and crowded sweating promenades' that one tradi-tionally associated with British seaside holidays. It was epic, but not professional.

The army's state of mind according to a 1940 British officer John Carpenter was relief on the one hand – 'that was the over-riding thing' – and disappointment 'that it had come to this'. The enormity of the defeat was psychologically crushing. Three weeks would be required simply to sort out the returning disparate trainloads of rescued in-dividuals from the battered BEF into some semblance of formed-unit order. 'We never really thought until the last moment,' John Carpenter confessed, 'that it would be as bad as this – we knew we had been beaten of course.'

One corps commander in France, Lieutenant General Alan Brooke, was enraged how little training had been achieved on the mainland during the BEF's absence. Three weeks after the evacuation he was appointed GOC Southern Command, with heavy responsibilities for coastal defence, and expressed bewilderment in his diary 'as to what has been going on in this country since the war started! It is now 10 months and yet the shortage of trained men and equipment is appalling!' Defences were totally inadequate, yet 'we can only have a few more weeks before the Boche attacks!' Efforts needed redoubling. 'Our briefing was that the Germans may now take advantage of the situation, and that was made very clear to us,' recalled Carpenter. 'Therefore the priority was to get ourselves re-equipped and reorganised as quickly as possible and get ready to deal with it if it came.'

Not only had the army had to come to terms with the reality of defeat. Euphoria after the safe return from the beaches was replaced by a sober realisation within many local communities of what had been lost. The small town of Kidderminster north of Worcester was hit hard. 'It was all very depressing for everyone round here,' recalled one local. 'They all went out with such pride and joy – and half of them didn't come back.' Those that did told horrific tales. Their local regiment, the Gloucesters, had fought on the perimeter, sons had died and many were missing.

In Scotland the loss of the 51st Highland Division began to sink in. Eight thousand 'Jocks' were taken prisoner and over 300 killed. 'There was great trepidation then, because folk started counting on their fingers and wondering who had gone,' recalled John MacInnes, a local government officer on South Uist. 'There was always a loss of maybe one or two in every area, but we were never able to find out until afterwards who had been killed.' MacInnes was careful delivering bereavement messages, because the characteristically Scottish names were very alike. Losing the division was a huge blow, because the 51st had been regarded as one of the premier divisions in the army after the Great War.

Murdo MacCuish was one of those captured and recalled his anguish:

It was degrading for one thing. We were soldiers. We had been surrounded before and fought our way out. Here were thousands in the town [of Saint Valery] – and thousands of French too – and I thought it was the most humiliating thing. I think we should have fought on. I didn't realise how outgunned we were. I didn't cry, but I nearly did I'm telling you. I was twenty and it was heartbreaking . . . marching to captivity.

Anger at the suspected sacrifice of a division, symptomatic of general soldier uneasiness about the conduct of the campaign, endures even today. Tommy Porton, a twenty-year-old Seaforth Highlander, bitterly claimed: 'We were sacrificed by Churchill because he was eager to keep the French fighting. We were placed under poor [French] command and expected to fight alongside men who didn't have the stomach for it.'

Porton recalled charging German positions unsupported with the bayonet 'because French tanks didn't turn up'. There was already a discernible divide between divisions that saw action in France and those left behind, still not properly trained. Porton commented: 'people who weren't there think of it like some black-and-white newsreel, but film will never tell you about the smell of battle or the cries of your friends who are dying.'

Prime Minister Churchill had a ruthless streak. Some Scottish veterans are convinced their division was indeed given up to bolster the French and buy time for Britain to establish a cogent coastal defence. There are parallels with the costly and hopeless defence of Calais to reduce pressure on the Dunkirk perimeter. When Churchill assumed office he bleakly announced: 'I have nothing to offer but blood, toil, tears and sweat.' He personified a dawning realisation on the mainland of Great Britain that disappointments were subsidiary to what now had to be done: 'We shall fight on the beaches, we shall fight on the landing grounds, we shall fight in the fields and in the streets, we shall fight in the hills; we shall never surrender.'

And he meant it. One month after this speech, the day after the Vichy government established itself in southern France, he ordered the sinking of his former ally's fleet at Mers-el-Kebir. Britain was now certainly alone. Hamish Henderson from Blairgowrie was recruited into the newly re-formed 51st Highland Division in Scotland and admitted 'their loss hit everyone really hard. But I honestly never encountered defeatism', because he emphasised, 'it was by no means a tradition of the North-East to acknowledge defeatism.'

Les Pinner conscripted into the 7th Battalion the Wiltshire Regiment was doing basic training in England during Dunkirk. Stories soon emerged about inadequate equipment and in cases, poor leadership, from veterans returning to the depot. 'Even making allowances for a certain amount of "bull" our own experiences during training with "make believe" weapons lent, at least, some substance to what was being said.' Training halted to prepare Molotov cocktails to repel German tanks. 'Devizes was scoured for bottles – any kind,' he recalled, 'filled with petrol and a piece of cloth screwed into the top – all that was required was a match to set the thing alight – and throw at the German tank.' 'Lord Haw-Haw', William Joyce's, broadcasts began with 'Jairmany calling, Jairmany calling, this is news for the English people.' Pinner remembered 'one broadcast making reference to the Wiltshire troops in their barracks at Devizes', conveyed through his characteristic stilted upper-class accent, 'making a plea for the place to be kept tidy until the German troops arrived to take over'.

Across the Channel Wehrmacht officer Eberhard Dennerlein mused: 'after so many successes in such a short time you say "how much does the world cost?" ' On 10 August Major iG Teske, the first general staff officer of the 12th German Infantry Division, earmarked for the second landing wave against England, sent a helpful communication to all the regimental and detachment commanders. 'Due to the lack of useful precedents,' he wrote, 'the following report of 55 BC is submitted', and inserted a copy of Julius Caesar's *Gallic Wars*, describing the Roman seaborne invasion from Boulogne to Britain. Dennerlein remembered 'it was an indescribable atmosphere, euphoric perhaps, because we thought that we were bound to win the war in the near future. The only one in our way was England.'

SCALING CHURCHILL'S MOAT

On a fine day along the Hampshire coast with clear blue skies and a flat calm sea British soldiers started pumps that set off the oil flow. It cascaded down through pipes affixed to the cliff face and out beneath the sea. Viscous black oil soon bubbled up from beneath the surface of the water and expanded into widening circles. Wispy low-lying smoke from flares fired into the black slicks mixed with petrol provided the first signature. Miniature flickers of flame burst into dozens of circular conflagrations that blended into a fearsome slurry of fire that spread further, belching bulbous clouds of thick oily black smoke staining the blue sky. Barely perceptible through the smoke and flames observed from seaward were multiple coils of barbed wire, blocking beach exits.

'This was my father's idea,' said Christopher Hankey, the son of Lord Hankey, the Chancellor of the Duchy of Lancaster in 1940. The employment of 'Greek fire' to repel ancient invaders was not entirely inappropriate to the background reading the German 12th Infantry Division staff had been offered. Hankey recalled his father believed 'why not use this oil to stop them coming up the beaches? We've got vast amounts of it, which is only going to fall into their hands.' A German aircraft over-flew the demonstration and 'we thought, good heavens, they are going to see about this and it won't be a surprise.' Rumours were rife on both sides of the Channel about sightings of burned corpses from failed invasion or raiding attempts. They had heard one going around German troops suggesting that 'if they did manage to get ashore on the British coast they would be burned alive'. Royal Engineer Lance Corporal Alec Johnson recalled 'playing around' with flame warfare:

> One lot would go down to Southampton to practise setting the shingle on fire with petrol tankers on top of the cliffs with pipes going down into the sea and they were turning them on. Then the Navy would fire a flare and the whole sea would erupt, and the idea was to have these waiting and if the Germans came; set fire to them you see.

They were not anticipating Roman galleys. Such a system was dependent upon a calm sea, nevertheless, the conditions required for German seaborne landings. Primitive though the system was, it was, as Hankey explained, 'a discouragement to them, so perhaps we won a psychological advantage'.

Hitler issued Directive Number 16 – a landing operation against Britain – on 16 July 1940, once he realised Churchill would not sue for peace. 'The aim of this operation,' it read, 'is to eliminate the English Motherland as a base from which the war against Germany can be continued, and, if necessary, to occupy the country completely.' There was controversy within the Wehrmacht between the army who wanted a broad front landing, treating the Channel as if it was a substantial river obstacle, and the navy who felt they could only support landings on a narrow front. Goering's Luftwaffe, in the throes of contesting air supremacy over the Channel, paid scant interest to both sides concerns. The initial scheme of a six-division landing between Ramsgate and Lyme Bay to precede forty-one divisions was reduced by practical considerations to a thirteen-division strong landing, preceded by elements of three over eighty miles of coastline between Folkestone and Brighton. Once a bridgehead was established on a line from Canterbury through Etchingham and Uckfield to Brighton, divisions would advance to the first operational objective south of London, between Gravesend on the Thames estuary and Portsmouth. The second operational objective was to be north of London between Maldon and the Severn estuary and then beyond.

British intelligence foresaw the invasion sequence, beginning with a preliminary air and then naval offensive, followed by airborne and then seaborne landings. Hitler's proven unorthodoxy hinted anything was possible, so that seaborne invasion might precede or coincide with other forms of incursion. British obsession with the panzer threat, understandable after the French debacle, suggested Eastern Command would be the initial objective because of open beaches and good tank going in East Anglia. By September British air reconnaissance of invasion disembarkation ports indicated East Anglia and Kent were the two main threatened points.

July was the physical and emotional low point of British preparedness for an invasion following Dunkirk, but the Germans were equally unready. The RAF could only muster 331 Spitfires and Hurricanes. The fifteen nominal divisions available for defence (excluding the reconstituting BEF), lacked striking power and mobility. On the key invasion sector between Sheppey and Rye the 1st London Division had only eleven of its seventy-two 25-pounder guns, four 18-pounders and eight 4.5 inch howitzers left over from the Great War. There were no anti-tank guns, against its establishment of forty-eight, only forty-seven anti-tank rifles, compared to the normal 307 and only twenty-one Bren-gun carriers from ninety, and no Bren-guns at all. Only eighty heavy and 180 light tanks were with the two British armoured divisions, who had lost their entire inventories in France; and each of the fifteen infantry divisions could barely lift a brigade with its own transport. British counter-attacks would have to arrive via rural 'Green Line' buses. General Sir Alan Brooke concluded, 'at present I fail to see how we can make this country safe against attack.' It was up to the Royal Navy and Air Force.

'In England they're filled with curiosity and keep asking "why doesn't he come?"' mocked Hitler at a rapturous party rally on 4 September 1940; 'Be calm, be calm,' he teased the crowd. 'He's coming! He's coming!' The most favourable combination of moon and tide would fall between 19 and 26 September, so the attack date was set for the 21st. Only groups of about 6,700 men – or seven to eight battalions – with supporting panzers, engineers and other elements could be landed at selected points in the first wave. German naval staff assessed they would need a fleet of 1,722 river barges, 471 tugs, 1,161 motor boats and 155 transports to carry them. The plan was to tow the shallow-draught river barges across. German soldier Wilhelm Küchle recalled how difficult it was to manhandle eight- to ten-man rubber dinghies over the sides of fishing boats and then climb inside wearing full combat equipment. 'The boats were little fishing boats which couldn't go to sea above gale-force six.' Training films show how taxed the crews were handling boats in these awkward conditions wearing just recreational swimwear. 'There was nothing we desired more than solid ground under our feet,' Küchle added. Nevertheless, to succeed they would have to breach Churchill's Moat.

John Carpenter, a British officer manning the invasion defences, pointed out 'the biggest problem of course was that nobody knew where an attack might come in'. He outlined the tactics the Germans would encounter from the beaches onward, explaining:

You had two things to do. You had to protect the coast line as far as you possibly could by having observation posts, a thin line of military watching the shore, patrolling the coast. And then you had to retain groups of troops behind the coastline, groups of troops who could react quickly to a sudden landing, where ever it might be.

Observation was also provided by machine-gun armed motor patrol boats. Lieutenant David Howarth, commanding one during the threatened invasion period, explained there was little sleep. 'I stand with one eye on the eastern horizon, expecting I don't quite know what – motor torpedo boats? Tugs with barges full of German soldiers being sea-sick? Or the Scharnhorst?'

Regular units were at the water's edge and Lieutenant Robin Medley, back from France with the Bedfordshire and Hertfordshire Regiment, recalled 'hundreds of holiday-makers banned from the beaches and esplanade sitting on benches watching the army digging trenches just across the road!' He found this unreal. Routine was hard; stand-to in case of attack was from 0230 until 0400 hours, followed by a brief sleep before breakfast at 0700. Digging carried on, interrupted by a sandwich break at lunch, until 1700. One hour's NCO training came after the evening meal and then defensive positions were occupied again from 2130 until 2300. More time could be devoted to training once defensive positions had been built. Lieutenant Pat Mayhew felt the exhaustive wiring on beaches was a waste of time. He was not popular with his commanding officer when he demonstrated that concertina wire barriers could be negotiated by small groups of determined men within twelve to fifteen seconds. 'So I suppose,' he wrote pessimistically home, 'we can say that we gain a second for every month's work, which is rather a depressing thought.' BEF veterans were justifiably suspicious of the value of fixed defences which could be over-flown in any case.

Invasion was pending, but the very psyche of the British, based on the few historical occasions their island had been breached, was resistant to it. Jim Elkin, with the 15th Battalion of the Queen's Royal Regiment defending Dover, was grandly informed by their commanding officer that there had been a sentry posted at Dover Castle for over 800 years. 'Some wag shouted from the ranks,' recalled Elkin, 'that it was about time he was relieved!' Julius Caesar invaded Britain in 55 BC with two legions and mounted troops in ninety-eight requisitioned transports and some warships, but he was not engaged at sea. The Germans were acutely aware of the threat of the Royal Navy. Werner Pfeiffer, a German naval officer staffing Operation Sea Lion, recalled:

> The battle fleet that was on stand-by at Scapa Flow was 20 times superior to our few large ships. As for their superior light fleet, if we had 10 destroyers the English had 80 or 100. And their smaller vessels would also have been deployed immediately to stop any approaching boats from the French coast. The English fleet would have easily appeared in the Channel with no problem – either the same evening or the next morning.

William the Conqueror was aided by the fortuitous invasion of northern England by Harald Hardrada of Norway in 1066. This coincidental deception enabled the Norman invasion to establish a bridgehead in the south at Pevensey Bay using 400 large and 1,000 small boats. Decisive battle followed at Hastings. The Germans planned a similar diversion off the east coast. Herbstreise or 'Autumn Journey' was the name given to a ten-ship decoy involving four large passenger liners that were to set course for Hartlepool from Norway to distract the Royal Navy. Intensive air reconnaissance with air strikes would be conducted against Scotland, the Orkney and Shetland Islands. Freighters were to be assembled and given false funnels and masts to make them appear larger and the empty ships were to be trailed by two hospital ships to give the impression of a substantial troop-carrying convoy.

The Spanish Armada in 1588 encountered such bitter resistance from the English fleet that the Duke of Parma's Spanish invasion army in the Netherlands never reached English soil. Napoleon's invasion fleet, assembled in Boulogne in 1805, also never sailed, blockaded by the Royal Navy until it was destroyed at Trafalgar the same year. Common to all these fleets was the need for shallow draught vessels to land troops. Only commercial river barges were available in 1940, and these would have first to be modified. As with previous historical precedents, Germany sought a decisive battle. Air was the one physical dimension of operations untested thus far by historical precedent. Could the Luftwaffe neutralise the vastly superior British fleet?

Scaling Churchill's Moat required decisive air superiority at least local to the crossing area to protect an invasion. The attack on Kent earmarked for late September was to be conducted by the veteran 17th and 35th German Infantry Divisions from Sixteenth Army, who were to land between Folkestone and Dungeness. To their left would be two divisions from the Ninth Army. Fallschirmjäger (parachute) regiments were to be landed by glider and dropped by parachute to capture the high ground around Lympne airport and Lyminge. Objectives were to secure the Royal Military Canal and attack and secure port installations at Folkestone and Dover. Seven battalions supported by panzer detachments and engineers with advance-guard commando raiders would land between Sandgate and New Romney on this sector. They were to fan out and establish bridgeheads inland toward Ashford and Canterbury. Other units were to land in Sussex with the aim within twenty days of securing a lodgement between Gravesend and Portsmouth.

Ben Angell manned a pillbox on the clifftop at Swingate between Dover and St Margaret's Bay. A new recruit, he recalled shortly after Dunkirk, 'we received some kit which had been salvaged from those who had lost their lives.' They were not confident and neither were they reassured by a young subaltern who visited their pillbox, ceremoniously announcing, 'you are in the front line you know!' 'Some "front line troops" to be sure!' remarked Angell. 'We didn't even have experience in using a rifle!' Sleepless invasion-scare nights followed with Angell pulling an army blanket over his head to blot out the reality of their predicament, thinking, 'I will be taken prisoner by the Germans before waking up.'

Folkestone became an almost derelict town, remembered Frank Brisley, working nearby. Dunkirk veterans were positioned on the outskirts for anti-invasion defence. 'I have to say that they were very trigger happy!' he recalled. They occupied blockhouses and guarded road blocks. 'We found it best to answer quickly when challenged; otherwise you would hear the click of a bullet going into the breech, which showed that they meant business,' he recalled. Troops were nervous but settled increasingly as more time became available to establish defences.

In September British manufacturing output raised the number of 25-pounder artillery pieces to over 400, anti-tank guns were up 176 to 500 and the armoured division's eighty heavies were reinforced by 350 Medium and Cruiser tanks. A plan was developed to contain German bridgeheads with local and mobile forces and overwhelm them with groups of armour and infantry divisions held north, west and south of London. Equipments arrived but training was not complete and neither was the infantry particularly mobile. There were 60,000 Home Guard in Kent and Sussex and many of them would take the initial shock of parachute landings and Brandenburger Special Forces raiding spearheads.

The Home Guard was born of the Secretary of State for War Anthony Eden's announcement during the evening of 14 May for men aged between fifteen and sixty-five 'who wish to do something for the defence of their country'. Conscription had already taken those aged between eighteen and forty-one. 'Dad's Army' as it was later popularly called, were the Local Defence Volunteers (LDV). They came in on a wave of anti-appeasement after Chamberlain resigned. Churchill had called for their formation in 1939. Their tasks were to guard vital installations against sabotage, hunt down enemy parachutists – the Fifth Column, who had been so effective according to rumour in France – and form centres of resistance in the event of an invasion. They were aggressively intent on action, so much so that the government had been reluctant to set up so free-ranging a militia, but people had already begun to arm themselves. Queues formed at police stations within minutes of Eden's statement. Fifteen-year-old Home Guard Private William Fowler recalled 'sensibly they were not taking any notice of people's age' at the police station 'and I was in – simple as that!' The police were unprepared, 'totally disorganised' he remembered, to deal with the mass enthusiasm that accompanied the call-up: 'Forms were literally being turned out on rotary prints in the back and being brought forward to be signed. They didn't expect anything like it. When I got there, there must have been five or six hundred people there.'

Within twenty-four hours 250,000 had signed up and there were one and a half million by the end of June. The military establishment were taken aback, the force was very unmilitary. Volunteers could resign at just fourteen days' notice. When ranks were introduced, leaders were elected, almost like American Civil War militias. Minor rebellions might occur if a leader was imposed. These men were not as obsequious or prepared to unquestionably accept traditional hierarchies as the regular army. Seventeen-year-old Home Guardsman John Graham from the Isle of Wight Battalion explained: 'I think we were rather proud of ourselves. It was time somebody in khaki did rather better than the BEF had done in France, what our Allies had done hitherto. Although we had minimal training and very little equipment and were senile or juvenile, we had good spirit.'

Churchill tapped into their militant mood of patriotism. Once the LDV initials became the butt of jokes – 'Look, Duck and Vanish' – he insisted it be relabelled the Home Guard. It was a volatile *political* force with one and a half million voters in its ranks; they were soldiers second. These were the units that would be pitted against Fallschirm-jäger battalions dropping on the high ground north and west of Folkestone in September. There were 300 Home Guard in Hythe nearby, not all of whom had rifles.

The Home Guard was aggressive in nature and prepared to fight. Its performance, due to its age and loose untrained structure was patchy at best. 'We didn't have rifles, we didn't have ammunition, it was almost like medieval times,' claimed Private Alan Finnimore, 'a scythe was a means of killing someone, anything you could kill with.' He carried a bow and arrow. 'Hun-buster' medieval mace-like clubs studded with 6-inch nails were hardly appropriate to the Blitzkrieg era. Age was also a problem. 'I would say the average age was 60-plus,' announced Private John Shelton. 'We had tremendous morale you know, we were beaten, but we were not going to run away,' he laughed as he added, 'some of us were too old anyway.'

Fallshirmjäger regiment casualties were soon replaced by fresh unbloodied recruits after the fall of France. They were well equipped, resourceful and ruthlessly determined soldiers. During the battles for 'Fortress Holland' and The Hague they successfully held tenuous positions against heavy and determined attacks. They were adept at aggressive fire and manoeuvre and coordinating artillery and air strikes. Company commander Hauptmann (Captain) Hermann Goetzel was despatched in early September alongside the G4 logistics staff of 7th Flieger (airborne) Division to reconnoitre departure airfields in Belgium and northern France in preparation for Operation Sea Lion. Gliders were secretly assembled and all Flieger Division units were instructed to pack away their distinctive baggy parachute smocks. No specialist insignia was to be displayed or worn and no singing of paratrooper songs allowed. Hauptmann Freiherr von der Heydte's battalion was assembled in Goslar, awaiting the call forward from advance parties preparing a departure aerodrome near St Quentin in France.

The 7th Flieger Division had a strength of about 10,000 men, which would have to be flown in multiple lifts. They would be relieved by seaborne landed infantry divisions, numbering 19,000 men each. Initially they would be grossly outnumbered. John Graham with the Isle of Wight Home Guard Battalion emphasised 'it was our territory' and they would have fought. 'We felt the Germans if they came would be at a disadvantage initially, if he parachuted, we did at least know the fields and hedges, and everything else and we'd put up a good show – for about half a day and that would be the end of us. But they never came.'

There was widespread awareness and some trepidation at the prospect of parachute landings. Sylvia Yeatman, a WAAF at Detling aerodrome in the likely line of fire, was shown a row of hockey sticks intended for use by the female aircraftswomen in the event of a German attack. 'I didn't want a hockey stick to hit a German with,' she recalled. She procured a revolver through a friend at the Small Arms School at Hythe. 'The chaps on the base used to look through the window at my revolver on my desk. I don't think they liked that at all. It made them nervous.'

Pilot Officer Jas Storrar remembered hedges were cut down around their air force base to give better visibility in the event of an attack. 'We had boxes of grenades at dispersal in case German paratroopers came down on top of us. We really expected them and it was hard to see that we had enough men or machines to stop them.'

There was considerable apprehension at the pending operation on both sides of the Channel. 'We were all aware that the operation was going to be a bit of an adventure given the means at our disposal,' declared German soldier Wilhelm Küchle, contemplating the likelihood of a seaborne assault. 'Things began to look critical when we embarked on a river barge with full ammunition and combat gear.' Tugs towing Rhine River grain barges with seventy men and four trucks crammed in the hold were unwieldy and made the soldiers seasick. Barges were hastily stripped and fitted with more powerful engines and flak guns awkwardly mounted. Ramps had to be laboriously constructed beam by beam at the water's edge on landing while the barge was secured to the shore by rope. Ponderous barges had also to execute a right turn to land line abreast on the shoreline but only lead boats were equipped with radio, the remainder would have to manage with Verey lights and megaphones at the height of a contested beach landing. Aircraft engines with propellers were mounted at the back of barges to push them ashore over the final two kilometres. 'They made an unbelievable noise,' complained Leutnant Eberhard Dennerlein, 'a crazy idea' he indicated, tapping his head. 'I still have hearing problems that started at that time.' Küchle declared, 'any lance corporal could see that you couldn't land with them.' Any projected assault in their defenceless state he felt 'would have ended in disaster'. German soldiers quietly discussed their survival prospects. Küchle recalled that 'in the long talks amongst us soldiers, the opinion emerged that this was nothing but a suicide mission. We'd come to believe that nobody would return.'

Les Pinner's battalion was erecting scaffolding on the beach in the New Milton area west of Lymington. Solitary patrols were conducted along the clifftop, two hours on and four off, with a rifle and a bandolier of fifty rounds of ammunition. An ammunition reserve with grenades was held at the command post 'just in case'. However, as Pinner confided, 'the fact that none of us had actually thrown a grenade was of some concern!' They were short of everything. There were only three Bren-gun-carriers in the entire battalion, which was 'no exception to the general rule' of the other battalions covering the coast alongside. He recalled how: 'The nightly cliff-top patrols, often under a full moon, with the clouds sometimes obscuring the light could play havoc with the imagination. The shadows created upon the rolling sea could so easily become a German landing craft in every trough, and even waves breaking upon the beach became men wading ashore.'

Exercises were conducted with armoured cars and Home Guard units making practice local counter-attacks, clambering over barbed wire farm fences and hedgerows. Conscript Jack Brunton's battalion was based in Bournemouth and he remembered they were guarding key points with only a rifle and five rounds of ammunition. 'How was I going to stop the German Army?' he asked. 'What could I do the lowest of the low, a civilian soldier who was only there until I could get out again?' Les Pinner's battalion relied on local buses 'to make up the shortfall in case of emergency' to drive to threatened landing spots. 'Oddly enough,' he concluded, 'we were confident in our ability to put on a "good show" if necessary, a confidence which in the light of later information, was perhaps, ill founded!'

The German Navy was even less sanguine than Les Pinner's battalion about their ability to get the troops ashore. Bernd Rebensburg, an E-boat commander, recalled the flotilla chief's reaction on receipt of orders to protect the Sea Lion landings. 'They were brought in by a Leutnant and I remember how Hannes Bütow almost screamed *Madness!* And I think added *Idiocy!*' The E-boat Gruppe crews accepted the perilous nature of the mission. 'Readiness to sacrifice ourselves was expected,' Rebensburg acknowledged. 'So we said the first night, there's eight E-Boats in our group, we're successful and will receive a few medals. But the second night we're reduced by two and perhaps by the third night down to two. And then – who is going to go out at night?'

Werner Pfeiffer, another naval officer staffing Sea Lion, concluded, 'it was the opinion of all the higher naval staffs that the whole thing could not be carried out – we believed it to be "utopia", a still-born child, it could never succeed.' The German soldier was justifiably apprehensive about going to sea in a flat-bottomed river barge. The navy was likewise convinced they stood no chance if the Royal Navy put in an appearance.

Les Pinner exercised regularly with the Home Guard 'and our admiration for them knew no bounds', but they were worse equipped than their own seriously depleted regular battalion. They were poorly armed. 'Their transport consisted of any vehicle which could be persuaded to start.' They had enthusiasm and the will to fight, 'but like the rest of us the ability to survive, if the crunch came, was doubtful'. The coastal area behind his battalion was a no-go area ten miles deep, requiring proof of identity to enter. Signposts had been removed and open fields and flat areas littered with posts, stretched cables and other obstructions to deter glider landings. 'We expected to be invaded,' he recalled, 'the only question in our minds was – when?'

'STOP-LINES' TO LONDON

General Edmund 'Tiny' Ironside, the six foot four inch tall British Commander-in-Chief, decided on a 'coastal crust' general defence plan supported by positions in-depth inland. The concept was static 'stop-lines' up to London and beyond, made up of necklaces of strongpoints designed to soak up the sort of German momentum that had been experienced in France. Stop-lines were to be aggressively maintained with mobile columns directed to threatened points. There were immediate misgivings that too much space was given up too soon, but this was resolved when General Alan Brooke replaced Ironside on 18 July, and relocated operational reserves further forward. Brooke wanted to contain the Germans nearer the coast but by September the construction of stop-lines was well under way. All the earth-moving equipment in the country was employed with 150,000 workmen under civilian contractors. As a consequence many pillboxes were badly sited with apertures and loop holes facing the wrong direction.

'And we played around with what they called a "demi-fugass",' explained Royal Engineer Lance Corporal Alec Johnson. These forty-gallon oil drums were filled with petrol and waste oil and ignited with a large explosive charge that spewed flaming debris across a road. The concept of improvised explosive devices or IEDs was destined to become more familiar in later years as terrorist weapons. They could be disguised as a phantom garage door for a car-parking bay cut into an earth bank. Johnson explained: 'we would find a road which had a nasty bend in it, which meant anything approaching would have to slow down' and then wait for a German tank or vehicle to drive by.

> When it got to the bend we pressed the plunger and the explosive would hurl the 40-gallon oil drum over the hedge and it would explode and set fire to the tank. Now, can you imagine anything more Heath-Robinson than that? A little Sapper waiting – 'Is it there? No – Yes it is!' It was called the 'Phoney War' *and my word*. Well, we carried on like this for quite a while.

Home Guard roadblocks shown here could be interminable. At least a dozen innocent motorists were killed by trigger-happy Home Guards during invasion tensions.

Picture Post magazine tips on how the Home Guard might put a panzer out of action was based upon fanciful advice from its Spanish Civil War veteran correspondents. Such methods were totally inappropriate against the brutal realities of modern Blitzkrieg.

Rumour claimed, 'If they did manage to get ashore on the British coast they would be burned alive'. Rudimentary oil fired anti-invasion flame defences on the Hampshire coast.

Bemused inhabitants in north London receive the first Anderson air-raid shelters. Many did not have gardens to erect them.

Contemporary films of the fugass in action show a tremendous slurry of incendiary flame and material cascading on to a road. Though primitive, newsreels of terrorist devices have shown how effectively such a device can set an armoured vehicle on fire.

London was encircled by a concentric series of stop-lines that began with an outer ring broadly conforming to the present day outline of the M25 orbital motorway. There was a middle-ring encompassing tactically important areas such as the ridge line traversing Shooters Hill, offering good artillery observation possibilities for a bombardment of central London. The final inner-ring or central core was around Whitehall and the Thames. Pillboxes sited on the lines were disguised and painted to appear like a florist shop, the 'Westminster Bookshop' or were concealed beneath haystacks. Anti-tank spigots or launchers were set in concrete and would have been protected by riflemen and Bren-guns. Such deception purchased the ten-second 'stop and think' time that may have been catastrophic for an approaching panzer.

A combination of 'sticky' and smoke bomb attacks were to be employed against tanks, alongside other fanciful techniques illustrated in the contemporary *Picture Post* weekly news magazine. These show soldiers ramming 'a length of tram-line or stout metal bar' into the tracks of passing panzers. The magazine assured its readers: 'it gets drawn in, and either strips off the caterpillar or wrecks the mechanism.' These ambitious tactical measures were suggested by Spanish Civil War International Brigade veterans, including pulling grenade 'necklaces' on to roads with string and draping petrol-soaked blankets over road wheels to snag the tracks and running gear and setting them on fire. 'A tank dangerous at 200 yards,' *Picture Post* contributors advised, 'is almost helpless at six inches!' BEF veterans scoffed.

Tank gunner Karl Fuchs, awaiting the call forward for Operation Sea Lion with the 7th Panzer Division, believed 'the days are numbered for these bums, over there in England'. So far as he was aware 'there is the distinct possibility, actually it seems like a 99% certainty, that we're going to cross the Channel'. They were supremely confident in their capabilities once ashore. 'Our Group is a really terrific fighting unit,' declared Fuchs: 'All of us feel that once we're over there, no one will show any mercy whatever, no matter who's involved. All those bums are the same. If fate sends me over there, I'm going to fight until I keel over!'

Panzers would aim to drive down the main thoroughfares at best speed, so British tactics were designed to get them off the main roads and into side-streets, where they would be more vulnerable. Panzer units employing combined arms, however, generally advanced with accompanying panzer-grenadier infantry or assault engineers to keep opposing infantry away from tanks. Lessons had been learned in Warsaw the previous year. Veteran panzer commanders were adept at providing themselves with close air support and artillery.

Facing such units astride the main London to Dover A20 road was a motley collection of units such as the Swanley Railway Home Guard, securing an important railway junction on the main London to South Coast railway line in Kent. 'This railway Home Guard was a right shambles,' announced fifteen-year-old Leslie Kershaw, one of its youngest members, 'the attendance was very poor due to their duties; if ten turned up they thought they were doing well.' His father was a member 'and all their ages must have been 45 plus with just the odd younger ones'. He painted an evocative picture of readiness akin to a television comedy programme:

> To give some idea of what went on at parade night, all those turning up would be found in the old booking office playing cards. The old Shunter turned Sergeant would turn up and call them on parade, after a while they would shuffle out and form into some decent order. 'Right then, to get your limbs from creaking, we are going to do a smart march to the top of the road and back.' It was roughly 200 yards to the top. On returning the Sergeant would stand them at ease. That was when it started, somebody would break wind, I don't know why, but it would set them all off, and there would be this ragged clap of thunder resounding around the yard as they tried to outdo one another.

Leslie Kershaw was obliged to serve with this particular unit because he was working on the railways, but he judged the 'outside Home Guard' to be better. Ill-equipped regulars and the medieval weaponry wielded by the Home Guard would have resulted in sporadic success at best. Charles Graves recalled when 'a big-shot from Hailsham came down one day' to visit their Home Guard unit 'to ginger us up'. He outlined the general idea of the coming battle, explaining the use of roadblocks and tank-traps. 'We villagers were to "contain" the Germans till the arrival of the real soldiers from the rear,' he said. 'Of course, none of you chaps will probably be alive when they get here and drive the Huns back into the sea.'

'Some of the weapons we used were quite formidable in themselves,' explained Home Guardsman Private Donald Smith. 'What they did to the Germans I'm not sure, but they put the fear of Christ up us I can tell you!' Sticky bombs, explosive devices covered in glutinous grease and designed to adhere to any surface, were especially dangerous. Smith recalled 'it was a bit like a toffee apple' and virtually a suicide mission to employ because 'actually you didn't throw sticky bombs, the only way you could use one was to run up and stick it to the side of the tank'. Private William Fowler agreed. 'You certainly deserved a Victoria Cross for using one of those things.' They were positively dangerous. Once the handle was fixed to the ball filled with explosive the fuse was set. They had a frightening propensity to fall out. Fowler remembered: 'The first person I saw badly wounded was a delightful Guards Lieutenant who stuck it on and got a premature explosion, which was a very common hazard with sticky bombs. It took off his left arm and wrecked his face. He was dead in a reasonably short period of time.'

Although the Home Guard was never to directly clash with the Wehrmacht, it did lose 768 killed and 5,750 men injured.

As obstacles and poles began to be identified on Luftwaffe air reconnaissance photos obscuring anticipated air-landing zones, German plans adjusted to include fast moving 'commando' units, able to capture objectives by coup de main. Fallschirmjäger units dropping further inland might not arrive in time. The German Sixteenth Army plan to capture Dover was adjusted to include the 'Hoffmeister' combat unit of selected soldiers from the 17th and 35th Infantry divisions, supported by the 1st Brandenburg 'special forces' company. Another 130-man group under Oberleutnant Dr Hartmann was equipped with fifty motor-cycles to neutralise strongpoints along the Royal Military Canal. Other units were supplemented by light panzers to get into Dover and prevent the British from sinking block-ships in the harbour. Twenty-five fast motor-boats were earmarked to immediately get inside the harbour installations. Such small actions would have been ruthlessly prosecuted against any opposition. Determination was matched by an idealistic self-sacrificial readiness to accept casualties to secure vital objectives. Major Kewisch of the Abwehr (German Secret Service) visited the 11th Company of the Brandenburg commandos at La Chapelle, prior to their commitment to Sea Lion. Few of them spoke English, he recalled, perhaps fifteen or twenty. It was doubtful they would get through British lines unrecognised. 'Poor boys,' was his comment to a companion on departure.

'It was a shambles,' was Home Guardsman David Conway's assessment of their likely performance against such opposition:

> We'd never even seen a gun in our lives and suddenly we got uniforms; there was short ones, fat ones, skinny ones, old ones, arthritic ones and goodness knows what. But there was a great comradeship, everybody was doing their bit. But what could they expect from civilians all their lives suddenly become soldiers? We'd either be shot or taken prisoners, it was really a 'Dad's Army' only worse.

The essence of the British landward defence was to soak up the impetus of any landed German advance through the series of stop-lines constructed between the defensive crust at the coast and lines of resistance around London. Pillbox construction on bridge embankments and village crossroads were tangible testimony to this effort. But how embedded were the psychological stop-lines, the emotional willpower required to successfully impede an invasion?

The totally unexpected nature of the first twelve months of the Second World War did more than anything else to mould the wartime generation. September 1939 was the point at which this generation left its norms behind. Blitzkrieg followed an unexpected Phoney War period of inactivity that abruptly inverted all norms. Continental Europe was no longer recognisable, conflict was now simply between 'them' – the Germans – and 'us'. Good was pitted against bad. Immediate bonding and acceptance of the situation resulted, rather than any divisive criticism of government policy, despite identified shortfalls. The urgency of the immediate situation was brought home by the close-run evacuation of the BEF from France. Again, there were no recriminations regarding their performance. They were welcomed into the bosom of a nation aware they were needed if it was to survive. If something bad happened, one had to personally take action because the state was unlikely to bale you out. The stunning voluntary expansion of the Home Guard was an indication of a public displaying more aggressive defiance and intent than their politicians, prior to the establishment of Churchill's coalition government. Patriotism was unquestioned. People were determined to do their duty and sacrifice for the greater good. They would fight for this.

The Mayhew family, prolific letter writers with a number of serving sons, commented on the rise of morale that ironically coincided with the nation's declining fortune in 1940. Christopher Mayhew, manning beach defences in Norfolk, identified it as being because 'we're fighting on home ground' and 'because the man in the street didn't like or trust the French from the start'. There was a perverted desire to resist even 'because the odds are now definitely against us' and, interestingly, due to the fact 'the war has entered a novel stage'. The fear of invasion was challenging in a way that what happened in France had not been. 'Tank-traps in Hampshire is somehow quite different from digging them in Flanders.' English people became aware they were living through historically unique and significant times.

'War time events has smashed the silence of the English railway carriage,' announced H E Bates, who regularly commuted to London by suburban train. 'In the whole history of British Railways there has never been, I should think, so much conversation and friendliness per mile as now. The air of silent refrigeration, the arid cross-examination of stares, the snoozing behind the fat peace-time blankets of newspapers – all that has gone.'

Strangers were opening their hearts within an hour of meeting each other. 'People just don't need to be introduced nowadays,' claimed one popular magazine editor. The nation was bonding in adversity.

Nancy Bazin recalled being summoned from Exmouth by the local Devon's Battalion to dig trenches on the beaches. They worked for hours, enduring blisters and 'looking out to sea expecting to see these flotillas of German invading troops come'. The task was 'so obviously hopeless' because the wind, rain and high tide would wash away their efforts. 'But we did it, in this extraordinary way, believing that somehow we were defending.' Leeds nurse Amy Briggs recalled discussions over 'ridiculous' invasion instructions. Resistance and the degree of opposition that resulted was a controversial subject she recorded in her Mass Observation reports: 'What man or woman is going to slam the door in the face of a man with a Tommy gun under his arm? It is only natural for anyone, for the sake of the children behind the door with him, whether it be a man or a woman, to give in.'

Barbara Simon 'overheard my mother telling my father that she'd kill us all rather than allow us to fall in the hands of the Germans'. She found this unsettling. 'I decided that if it came to that I'd run away from home rather than submit to such a fate, and would find my own way of resisting the Germans.' Fear could verge on hysteria. Joan James from Bognor Regis recalled 'we were naturally very afraid of the invasion': 'I know for a fact that in the event of an invasion, if we couldn't get up the road with our suitcases fast enough, two mothers had asked the doctor if he would give them poison to give their daughters rather than see them suffer. Of course the doctor refused.'

Amy Briggs' discussions convinced her 'the situation is very grave'. She assessed prevailing opinion as being not one of 'we are sure to win' but rather that 'we must not lose'.

The reaction to invasion scares is one way of assessing the efficacy of the stop–line defensive concept, which was never fundamentally tested. Bruce Williams, an eleven-year-old schoolboy from Worthing, re-called: 'I remember hearing what I thought was the church bells once' – the agreed signal warning of invasion – 'and nearly wet myself!'

A scare occurred over the village of Bewdley north of Worcester on 30 June when throbbing aircraft noises were accompanied by sightings of ten to twenty parachutes dropping near Ribbesford Wood south of the village. Within an hour police reported parachutists had dropped and this was backed by eyewitness reports. Dickie Doolittle, living west of Bewdley, was stunned. 'I've never seen anything like it, before or since,' he insisted, convinced the invasion had actually started. 'You must realise,' he pointed out, 'that everybody was really keyed up. People were putting up road blocks and there was talk of parachutes and landings in this country.' Watching from his cottage, 'it looked as if we'd got a parachute invasion – scores of parachutes it looked like, hundreds of feet in the air!' Invasion scares were adorned with exaggerations, rumour and occasional panic. German aircraft had indeed been dropping discarded or dummy parachutes, raising tensions as a pre-invasion psychological operations measure.

Invasion alarms revealed the lack of combined arms coordination between the three British services. General Alan Brooke identified the shortfall early on. He asked:

> Who was deciding the claims between the employment of destroyers against hostile landing craft, as opposed to anti-submarine protection on the Western Approaches? Who would decide between conflict-ing calls of the Army for bombers to attack beaches as opposed to Navy wanting them for attacks on hostile fleets?

In the absence of direction, he feared Churchill with his impulsive intuition, which often overrode logic, would interfere. 'Heaven knows where he might have led us!' he declared. Bewdley encapsulated this absence of combined and coordinated direction at the local level. Air reconnaissance could have quickly scotched the confused reaction that ensued.

In Bewdley it was claimed discarded parachutes had been seen and that the Germans were coming up the River Severn in rubber boats. The Home Guard were launched to search for hideouts and the credibility of the worrying reports convinced some locals to depart the village. Church bells rang out the invasion alarm. Phyllis Chennery remembered one such invasion scare further south at Potter's Bar in September. She opened her front door on hearing a crash. 'I could hear people shouting and some hand bells ringing,' she recalled. 'Wardens were on a van going by and they were shouting through megaphones: "Get inside, everybody get inside! – The invasion alarm! The Germans are invading, get inside!"'

She was locked in her bedroom by her husband, a LDV member, who came back with a garden fork and said, 'here you are, this is for you. If any Germans or anybody comes in, you stick this right through their bloody guts, and no arguing!' She smiled at the memory, stating gently, 'I could no more have done that than fly, because I belonged to the third order of the Carmelites and the thought of me sticking a fork in someone – well, I just couldn't have done it.'

Anecdotal descriptions and evidence from invasion alarms provide one of the few yardsticks to assess the type of resistance that might have occurred in the event of actual landings. The 8 September invasion scare coincided with the heaviest bombing raid to date on London. It occurred when an old codeword *Cromwell* meaning the conditions for invasion were right, was widely misinterpreted to mean it had started; a factor of too many and confusing instructions. It resulted in Julia Whitfield, a WVS member at Stoke Abbot, assisting her brother, the local vicar, to ring out the signal on the church bells. Soon all the local churches pealed out their sonorous acknowledgement of the critical news. Her sister asked what she should do, because their WVS task was to set up a first aid centre. Feeling tea might be the appropriate antidote for people in shock; Julia suggested a kettle should be boiled. 'Who for?' her sister drearily responded, 'for the Germans?'

Medieval though the warning system was, it worked, and the Home Guard was called out. At Bewdley at the end of June there were at least four negligent discharges during the crisis caused by careless weapon handling. This alongside crow-scarers banging off in the fields added to the degree of confusion and rumour. Lance Corporal Russell Tailby with the Home Guard recalled the typical experience of being on guard and he 'hadn't been there very long when there was a bang and tinkling of glass'. The adjutant cycled up and advised a rifle had been accidentally fired in the canteen 'and nobody was to put any cartridges in the rifle until the Germans turn up'. Weapons proficiency was poor. 'The first time I got a grenade in my hand I was terrified,' recalled seventeen-year-old choirboy Norris Leedle with the Lincolnshire Home Guard. 'It was scary to think that you have got that thing in your hand and it could go off any time. It was only a few weeks before there was a chap in a dug-out, he dropped it and he'd no time to run out – blew him to pieces.'

The regular army often shared Norris Leedle's assessment of Home Guard potential. 'If the Germans did get across, you'd wonder what'd happen – I don't think we should have done much good.'

In Bewdley the situation verged on farcical as civilian Sunday trippers got in the way of activity as the 'invasion' news spread. Forty-five minutes after the reported landings the nearest regular barracks at Worcester received the message. It took three hours before the first two Bren-gun-carriers, the vanguard of a mobile column appeared. These men were semi-trained and in no shape to comb the local woods and pin down crack German paratroopers. There was no established routine to liaise with or debrief the Home Guard. All that happened was the regular army contingent was held up at a LDV road block. The officer, irritated at the needless delay, was overheard muttering 'LDV – air guns – Pansies!' The Worcestershire Bren-gun-carriers loaded up with several crates of beer in the village before heading south to Ribbesford Wood, looking 'typically bored' according to onlookers. The incident carried on through the night until it was finally established that the 'parachutists' were in fact straw-umbrella shaped haycocks that had been lifted simultaneously into the air by a freak gust of wind. The escapade demonstrated poor observation and reporting and a less than aggressive regular army response, with little appreciation of Home Guard capabilities. Significantly, none of the half-hearted manoeuvring had been impeded by hostile air attacks.

General Alan Brooke, the GOC Southern Command, envisaged an offensive and mobile defence strategy which, due to the training standards and coordination between regular and irregular forces guarding the beaches, left much to be desired. 'I visualised a light defence along the beaches, to hamper and delay landings before they had time to become well established.' Clearly during the critical months of July to September these fundamental capabilities were not at hand, but were gradually beginning to coalesce. BEF divisions were reconstituting and not even reorganised until July and there was little equipment to hand. Of twenty-five British divisions only seventeen were reasonably trained and equipped and just three were in Kent and Sussex.

Stop-lines to break up the momentum of a landed German advance was the only conceivable strategy, accepting the half-trained status of many formations. Home Guard Private Alan Finnimore recalled one of the invasion alarms. 'Allegedly the invasion had started so we manned these strong-points, what for I don't know, because we couldn't have stopped pussy really.' Road blocks were set up and everyone was stopped, not just ARP wardens but the police and even the army. Some army officers were treated like spies. In effect, in the early days it appeared stress had created a Frankenstein-like organisation, in terms of its size and attitude. At least a dozen innocent motorists were killed or wounded by trigger-happy Home Guards, according to numerous newspaper reports. This would of course have hampered the very fluid mobile defensive operations that Alan Brooke envisaged. With the Battle of Britain under way increased Luftwaffe bombing and strafing attacks added to the stress.

Aggression was desirable but high-handedness had its dark side. 'I have lost two officers in the course of ten days,' the CO of the 2nd Anti-Aircraft Division wrote to GHQ Home Forces on 12 June. 'One shot dead in Eastern Command and one shot and dangerously wounded between Nottingham and these headquarters.' William Barnard's father James, a sixty-eight-year-old pensioner, was killed by an over-zealous Home Guard soldier. Despite his loss, he felt he had to admit:

> The stress that the Home Guard must have been under must have been beyond belief. We'd been bombed on a daily basis day and night. To get to work you'd have to pick your way through all the rubble, do a full day's work, come home, put on your uniform and be expected to take on the might of the Wehrmacht, and probably a full time night duty. It was beyond comprehension.

The guilty Home Guard soldier received only twelve months for manslaughter, the judge paying due cognisance to his distinguished Great War service record.

Some of this stress was designed to be applied behind the German soldier, if he had achieved landfall. Secret Home Guard Auxiliary units were set up as stay-behind groups to harass German rear areas as partisans. It was perhaps one of the longest kept secrets of the war. Charles Mason, a poacher, was picked out because he knew his locality so well. He became one of five or six men who operated from OBs or Operational Bases established in underground shelters. These were Nissan huts dug under ground, connected to the surface by tunnels with concealed entrances, containing stored ammunition and sleeping bunks. 'We had priority of the latest equipment,' explained Mason. 'We got plastic explosives before the army got it, the best Tommy gun that came from America, masses of ammunition and detonators – we got it first!'

They were obsessive regarding security. Once Mason learned the local gamekeeper had discovered their location, they resolved to kill him if the Germans landed. 'That sealed his fate,' declared Mason, 'from then on he was doomed.' They would wait for the moment, deciding 'we were going to probably booby-trap him and if that didn't work we were going to shoot him – we had to be rid of him.' Cell members wounded in action would have to be finished off rather than be abandoned to the Germans. That was why the gamekeeper's fate was agreed with such little controversy. Mason explained: 'This is what we agreed on. You leave nobody behind. So how could we tolerate someone like that, when we were prepared to kill our own?'

The existence of the OBs was not released for some considerable time after the war. When asked why the details were never revealed, Mason admitted 'it was rather strange we didn't'. It was simply never discussed, 'I think because we still thought it was a secret.'

In 1974 a group of senior British and German officers, including some who had held positions of responsibility at the time, umpired a war-game at the Royal Military Academy at Sandhurst. The Operation Sea Lion scenario was tested on a tri-service basis, playing the units and tactics of the time. During the exercise the German seaborne landings failed when Royal Navy destroyer superiority dispersed the second wave of barges at sea, despite the initial success of combined Fallschirmjäger and seaborne landings. Most Home Guard veterans acknowledge their resistance would have been patchy and inconsistent. David Conway claimed, 'if they'd started at two o'clock in the afternoon we would have been all finished at three!' Alan Finnimore dismissed the thought of meaningful defence: 'Oh, they'd have just walked through us actually,' but he did concede: 'We thought we would have a go. If they came, we'd give them hell – especially if we'd got some guns or anything to kill with.'

A combination of stop-lines, stay-behind resistance and civilian resolve, at minimum to passively resist, could conceivably have held the ring sufficiently for the Royal Navy, as emerged in the Sandhurst war-game, to have an impact. As Private William Fowler pointed out, 'it was totally suicidal, but you didn't think about that in those days.'

The Sandhurst war-game appraisal of Operation Sea Lion illustrated that the failure of the Luftwaffe to achieve at least local air superiority over the Channel, eventually enabled the Royal Navy to bring its decisive potential to bear. It is clear from contemporary witnesses how shared the invasion emergency experience was. The whole population was, with varying degrees of commitment, fully engaged in this war, which had not been the case prior to May 1940. Having read about it in the newspapers and heard it on the BBC, the nation was now to actually witness the war.

On 10 July the Luftwaffe opened its bid for air superiority, beginning with heavy air attacks on shipping in the English Channel and on coastal towns. This was as the landward defences began to reconstitute. On 8 August the German Air Force opened its main air offensive against south-east England, aiming to bring Fighter Command to battle and destroy it.

For the first time since 1066 Britain was to be invaded, or at least her air space. Moreover, for the first time in her history the majority of the population on the English mainland would see a decisive battle over their own soil. It would set this generation apart for the millennium. The Battle of Britain began to gradually take shape in the skies above them.

5

AIR INVASION: THE BATTLE OF BRITAIN

PRELUDE

'Now you can hear our anti-aircraft going at them now.' BBC reporter Charles Gardener raised his voice above background banging noises. 'There're one, two, three, four, five, six – there are about ten German machines dive-bombing the British convoy which is just out to sea in the Channel.' His live recording of a dog-fight chance encounter seen from the cliffs overlooking Dover encapsulated sights many were to see over the coming months. Dramatic sound bites, commonplace today on satellite TV, gripped radio listeners in an entirely new way as he delivered a vivid oral description of an actuality event: a Stuka dive-bombing attack during the opening stages of the Battle of Britain, recorded on Sunday 14 July 1940.

I can't see anything – no, we thought he had got a German one then. [*Flak banging in the background*] Now the British fighters are coming in an absolute steep dive. You can see their [*the German*] bombs actually leaving the machines and plunging into the water. You can hear machine gun fire but I can't see our Spitfires. They must be somewhere there – oh, here's one coming down now!

There's one coming down in flames! There's somebody hit a German, and he's coming down. There's a long streak and he's coming down completely out of control – a long streak of smoke. Aah! – the man's baled out by parachute – the pilot's baled out by parachute! [*Gardener, now clearly excited, speeds the pace of oral delivery, as if describing a Derby winner.*] He's a Junkers 87 and he's going slap into the sea, and there he goes – SMASH – a terrific column of water! And there was a Junkers 87.

Gardener continued his TV-style recording, which was unprecedented in its day and produced much press comment. 'Hark at the machine guns going!' he reported. 'One, two, three, four, five, six – now there's something coming down on the tail of another.' Excited bystanders can be heard shouting in the background: 'Here they go! They're goin' back home!' Gardener finished his commentary with an excited flourish:

> There's a Spitfire just behind the first two – he'll get them! Ah, yes! Oh, boy! I've never seen anything so good as this! The RAF fighters have really got these boys taped.

One indignant Great War pilot wrote to *The Times* newspaper and complained: 'Where men's lives are concerned, must we be treated to a running commentary on a level with an account of the Grand National or a cup-tie final?' Other readers felt uplifted by the commentary. 'To me it was inspiring, for I almost felt that I was sharing in it, and I rejoiced unfeignedly that so many of the enemy were shot down, and that the rest were put to ignominious flight.' These extracts reveal the degree to which the war had now fully entered the lives of British people. Her population was to *see* the Battle of Britain, a spectator event; the coming Blitz on their towns would be *felt*. Both were to be a shared event and unique to this generation. 'I fancy that [Gardener's] commentary caught something of the spirit of the pilots themselves,' commented one listener. 'If our cause is a just and worthy one, then to rejoice in its success is the obvious thing.'

In the opening days of the Battle of Britain Germany had overwhelming air superiority. Three Luftflotten (Air Fleets), stretching from Norway to France and numbering 3,000 aircraft, could attack the UK mainland from Edinburgh to Exeter. Roughly a third of this force was fighters, versus Fighter Command's 591 single-engine Spitfires and Hurricanes. The key part of this battleground was a rectangular box extending from the English Channel eighty miles beyond London into south-east England, thirty-eight miles between Dungeness and Ramsgate, reaching Northolt beyond the capital and up to five miles high. Major engagements were conducted inside this box and Gardener's live recording was conducted at its south-eastern periphery, on the Channel's edge. Fighter Command's 11 Group covered the majority of the box with seven sectors, ranging from Suffolk to West Sussex, covering London and south-east England. The 11 Group had twenty-one Spitfire and Hurricane squadrons, which could be reinforced by perhaps five from 12 Group and two from 10 Group covering the rest of the country. Air Vice-Marshal Keith Park's 11 Group could call on 300 fighters to engage an anticipated 600 in the box under the command of Feldmarschall Albert Kesselring, commanding Luftflotte 2.

The subsequent attempts at air invasion were to set up the conditions required for a seaborne attack on the British south-east coastline. Initially the Channel was cleared of British shipping with heavy attacks on convoys and coastal towns starting on 10 July and from the 8 August the Luftwaffe sought to destroy the RAF on the ground and in the air. By 6 September Fighter Command was in trouble with its efficiency seriously impaired by extensive damage at five forward airfields and six of seven sector airfields. In two weeks 295 RAF fighters were destroyed and 171 seriously damaged, against only 269 newly produced. Three hundred pilots died, compared to 260 fledgling pilots turned out by flying schools. R H Hawkins, complaining about Gardener's exuberant description of the opening stages of the Channel clashes, presciently asked: 'Does the BBC imagine that the spirit of the nation is to be fortified by gloating over the grimmer details of fighting?'

The Battle of Britain and the subsequent Blitz of bombing raids through into the winter was to have a profound effect upon the psyche of the British wartime generation. It was a formative experience on a par with the shock of events leading to the momentary relief of the Dunkirk evacuation. Fear of invasion was the binding emotion. The Battle of Britain was 'going it alone', when the country remained in its lair and bared its teeth. The welter of emotional experience it produced is best expressed viewing the sequence of a typical air operation conducted against the south-east mainland of England during the summer of 1940.

'STAND-BY' TO 'SCRAMBLE!'

Fighter pilots in England were roused between 0300 to 0400 bleary-eyed after a meagre night's sleep and made to sign a notebook, by torch-light, to record they had received their early morning call. If they were lucky it was accompanied by a hot drink. 'On the ground, our preoccupations were not with the enemy but with food and sleep,' remembered nineteen-year-old Pilot Officer Tom 'Ginger' Neil. Readiness, if called, was half an hour before dawn. 'Christ, we thought, another day.' Having swiftly washed, shaved and dressed, pilots, immersed in their own thoughts or exchanging banter, would gather in the half light of dawn for vehicles to take them to the dispersal hut.

The immediate interest for both sides was the weather state. Pilot Officer David Crook with 609 Squadron recalled the weather being 'brilliantly clear' one morning at Middle Wallop 'and when we got up we shook our heads dismally as we knew there would be a lot of trouble'. Good weather meant intense combat. 'As Mac used to remark, "we should have quite a job to keep the Grim Reaper at bay."' Fitters were already warming up aircraft engines amid the reek of petroleum and making pre-flight inspections as airfields came to life. Flight commanders telephoned operations to confirm when they were ready for action. Any standing patrols required would take off, normally on the look-out for Luftwaffe reconnaissance aircraft, flying patrol lines until it was time to return. Exhaustion slowed the pace of administrative activity markedly from the start of the Battle of Britain.

Pilots dressed informally. Flight Lieutenant Anthony Bartley with 92 Squadron recalled, 'fighter pilots used to go up wearing ties, ridiculous to go fighting in a tie.' Many agreed they shrank if you landed in the Channel or produced irritating neck chafe from the wearer constantly scanning the sky. 'You wore anything,' he said. Silk scarves were not a flamboyant gesture, they protected necks. Pilot Geoffrey Wellum wore open-necked shirts, mufflers and flying boots when cold, but as the summer wore on he flew in shirt-sleeves, 'which was a silly thing to do because you burn'. Flight Lieutenant Allan Wright's flight commander offered immediate and sinister advice on arrival. He pulled out his flying gloves and goggles from a bag and insisted to novices, 'wear these, you'll need them, otherwise you'd be blinded.' 'That was our introduction.' It made one reflect.

As standing patrols returned to land, ground crew looked out to see if the canvas gun ports were missing, a sure indication whether guns had been fired. As pilots adjourned to readiness huts, fitters, riggers and armourers swarmed over the aircraft in their care, refuelling them from lorry bowsers. Squadrons included twelve pilots, divided into two flights of six, which broke down into two, three-man sections. Breakfast for these men was normally a twenty-minute affair, taken by sections based on readiness. It was haphazard in terms of quality, location and duration. 'Breakfast was brought to us at 8 am in insulated boxes, always a fried egg and little squares of rock-hard fried bread,' recalled Pilot Officer Tom 'Ginger' Neil. 'You knew perfectly well what would happen. You'd get the first forkful down and then – Scramble!'

Unlike soldiers and sailors, pilots are not gradually immersed into the world of combat via gradual adjustment to the discomforts of living in an earth trench or rolling decks at sea. They rush from a recreational environment of easy chairs or the civilised confines of a mess to their aircraft. The transformation was as much abrupt as it was bleak. Even the normal domestic routine of a comfortable mess was plagued by insidious ghosts that reminded them of their tenuous mortality. Flight Lieutenant David Crook lost his friend, twenty-year-old Mick Miller, between breakfast and lunch.

> Only a few hours before I had sat next to Mick at this very table and we had chatted together. And now, here we are at the next meal, everything quite normal, but he was dead. That was the one thing that I could never get accustomed to; seeing one's friends gay and full of life as they always were, and then, a few hours later, seeing the batman start packing their kit, their shaving brush still damp from being used that morning.

Pilots often worked a four-day cycle of 'Stand-To', ready to fly within one hour, followed by 'Available', meaning in fifteen minutes. By day three they were at 'Readiness', which meant immediately available for take-off sitting in the aircraft, after which they may be granted 'Stand-

Down' on the fourth day. Most achieved only one day off per week and infrequently at the height of the battle. Cockpit readiness on a hot summer's day with the sun beating down and hot exhaust gases streaming by on either side of an open cockpit was the worst. Waiting passed in uncertainty, tension and fear. 'We'll just have to continue waiting and that's all there is to it,' remembered Geoffrey Wellum with 92 Squadron. 'Relax, try to relax. I suppose that's the answer. Don't know the meaning of the word. Nevertheless, let's make a real effort. Hard work relaxing.'

False alarms were bad for nerves. Pilot Officer Christopher Currant remembered that running was banned in the vicinity of the aircraft, 'because whenever we'd see somebody running, we'd think, "This is us", and we'd all start to run. It was hypnotic.'

Aircraft were spread around facing the centre of the airfield, dispersed against air attack and logically spread to enable pilots to taxi and take off with the minimum of delay. Pilots lounged in and around the dispersal hut, which had sufficient iron bed frames for the squadron, draped themselves across chairs or lay on the grass. 'I couldn't settle down to a book, I just couldn't,' explained Pilot Officer Anthony Bartley. 'If you get into a book and you are suddenly called out, it takes a few seconds or a minute or so to readjust to reality.' He was wary it 'might slow me up'. Geoffrey Wellum thought waiting was purgatory, one eye constantly flickering to the telephone. 'You were like a cat on hot bricks, nervous, *frightened*,' he animatedly explained, 'that's what I'm trying to say, scared stiff.' Allan Wright thought the worst time was sitting on the loo, because 'one's mind tends to wander, there's nothing else to think about, except just sitting there'. Often the telephone would ring with an administrative matter. 'There would be an airman at the end of it,' described Allan Wright, 'and it would either say your lunch would be ready in ten minutes or scramble.' A false ring was sufficient to make a pilot walk out of sight and nervously retch. 'I swear that if ever I own a house I shall never install a telephone, so help me,' vowed Geoffrey Wellum.

Conditions across the Channel for the Luftwaffe pilots were not dissimilar. They too rose at dawn, worn out by operations and an active social night life. They were very confident, the RAF were regarded as lethal sport, not as detested foes. Airfields had been moved nearer the coast after the fall of France. As a consequence, accommodation varied from grand chateau to dispersal tents around small grass-covered local aerodromes. Aircraft were spread around and camouflaged under trees. Meals were taken outdoors and crews passed their waiting times reading and playing cards and board games. Major Josef 'Pips' Priller commanding I/II Gruppe of JG 26 described life on the Channel coast as 'readiness and sorties'. They were often held at virtual readiness until the order to 'go' was received. The first indication of a start for bomber crews lounging beneath aircraft wings might be when their crew chiefs climbed aboard fresh from briefings. Weather dictated the frequency of operations. Routine around the myriad grass-covered airstrips was governed by the insidious loudspeaker. As one pilot recalled: 'They were everywhere, the loudspeakers: in the mess, naturally in the crew room, in the sleeping quarters, on the trees around the airfield, even in the lavatories. No one within the precincts of the aerodrome could escape their din. They didn't say anything welcome but they said it loudly and made the buildings shake.'

Speaker checks, like telephone rings in England, produced nervous anticlimaxes.

Luftwaffe fighter squadrons were not dissimilar to the RAF but they were tactically organised differently. Staffeln, the equivalent of squadrons, also numbered twelve aircraft, but they were tactically organised into looser groups of three, four-aircraft Schwarm with two Rotte, or pairs of aircraft, each. Pilots socialised within these groups, which was a more effective and flexible arrangement than the British squadrons, whose sections flew in tight peacetime-like configurations, easy to see and deal with. Geschwaders of a hundred aircraft or more were subdivided into three Gruppen of three Staffeln each.

The experience of Spain, Norway and France placed the Luftwaffe at the pinnacle of self-confidence in their capabilities. Heinkel III bomber pilot Matthias Henken recalled the plan: 'Our commanders told us that our first job was to eliminate the Channel shipping, then to smash the RAF fighters on the ground; after that we could perhaps land in England to finish the job.'

The Germans launched on the familiar ubiquitous call of metallic speakers rasping out 'Attention! Attention! Action alarm!' Aircraft were led out from beneath trees by walking ground marshallers. After receiving the flickering green light signal Staffeln took off from their rustic grass forward operating strips in clouds of dust. By the middle of summer raids on Britain were so frequent that crews joked they would soon need air policemen to regulate the traffic flow. This was virtually the case as often Geschwaders numbering hundreds of aircraft began to circulate over the Pas de Calais and French coast in order to form up prior to crossing. Traffic monitoring indeed began from the opposing coast at this moment.

Twenty-four-year-old Messerschmitt 110 pilot Gerhard Granz recalled the huge assembly over Calais prior to the 7 September London raid. His formation was almost 1,000 aircraft strong, stepped up in formations one and a half miles high, occupying 800 square miles of sky. They flew over the white cliffs of Dover, emulating H G Wells' futuristic aircraft attack scene from Alexander Korda's film, *Things To Come*.

England possessed a Radio Direction Finding (RDF) or radar system in 1940, the first of its kind operational in the world. Diana Pitt Parsons, a twenty-one-year-old radar plotter, explained: 'you have a transmitter station which sends out a signal which hits the aircraft and the signal comes back to the reception area.' By a process of calibration 'you can judge how far away the aeroplane is and you have, in those days, a pretty rough idea of its height and azimuthal position'. Anne Duncan, a twenty-three-year-old who was plotting from Leighton Buzzard explained its simplicity, claiming: 'it was quite easy in the beginning because anything that was friendly went from England outwards and anything that was not came from France or Holland and Belgium inwards.' This information was passed on to Fighter Command Headquarters at Bentley Priory. 'Yes, they're coming now; there are so many; now we can see them,' recalled Anne Duncan. On average it took four minutes for the radar report to be plotted on the map board. 'Think they're this and think they're that – think there are so many,' she explained.

Once the aircraft crossed the coast they were picked up by the Observer Corps, who provided grid references of what they saw. Group Operations Room decided how many aircraft were needed to respond to the coming attack and would order fighter squadrons to 'stand-by' or 'scramble'. Interception was then the responsibility of sector Airfield Control, who guided their pilots on to targets via coded messages. Wing Commander Max Aitken with 601 Squadron was convinced success was due to this radar coverage. 'Without it we would have been doing standing patrols and with the limited number of aircraft and limited number of pilots you couldn't have done it.' Time and energy was not wasted seeking interceptions, enabling some sleep between sorties and the opportunity of going to battle 'feeling fine, fresh and fit'.

Few British pilots were in that state by September. Heavy casualties resulted in corners cut on training and inexperienced pilots drafted prematurely to operational squadrons. Pilot Officer Bob Doe with 234 Squadron at Middle Wallop recalled 'I was absolutely petrified' the first time he went into action because 'I was probably the worst pilot in the squadron'. His only gunnery training on Spitfires had been ten rounds per gun, which 'I fired into the North Sea, which I couldn't really miss'. Sergeant Pilot 'Bam' Bamberger at Biggin Hill felt, 'I was completely inexperienced and really did not know how to fly a Spitfire – I could fly, but not with particular skill, and as regards gunnery skills, they were non-existent.' Nevertheless, they were committed. 'I really honestly thought I'd be shot down and I didn't think I'd survive the first trip,' recalled Bob Doe. 'I was more scared of calling myself a coward than anyone else calling me one, so I went anyway – and I succeeded, by the Grace of God.'

Most pilots felt like thirty-one-year-old Pilot Officer Ted Shipman with 41 Squadron, awaiting the call to move south to replace one of the exhausted 11 Group squadrons. He recalled: 'I don't think there was too much of the "If only we could be down there in the thick of it" talk. There was one chap who couldn't sit still. Out of the tent, marching up and down. Keen to get stuck in, or scared? Don't know. No one asked him.'

Heroes were not the norm. Pilots 'saying they were always dying to get stuck in, were ones on their own', Shipman commented. They were better avoided. It was better to have a philosophical view. 'We knew we'd go, and then we would do all we could,' Shipman remarked. 'But jumping up and down for the chance? No.'

Fighter controllers had the unenviable responsibility, alongside the advantage of watching huge formations of enemy gathering on the

French coast, of deciding when and whether to launch. Flight Lieutenant Peter Brothers pointed out 'the problem for the Fighter Controllers was – do you think a raid was genuine or a spoof?' Allan Wright with 92 Squadron explained: 'London is only 50 miles from the coast and another 30 miles is 90 miles to France. They would gather up their aircraft over France and when they got their formations, they would turn in.' Detecting this moment was critical to maximise fuel, ammunition and, in particular, height to intercept. 'The controller had to be absolutely certain this was the real thing,' Brothers commented, 'that meant he had to delay.' Invariably 'that meant we were always late and struggling for height', complained Brothers, and Wright concurred. 'So you could never meet them on that advantageous basis just outside London.'

'Waiting for the orders to take off was called "scramble" and that was worse than actually being up in the air in combat,' revealed Sergeant Pilot 'Bam' Bamberger. 'We'd wait for the dreaded telephone to go and it would say: '92 Squadron scramble! Angels 20 [20,000 feet] enemy 100+, approach over Southampton.' Adjusting their flapping gear as they ran, pilots leaped from chairs and piled out of dispersal huts and sprinted to their aircraft, some in tunics others in shirt-sleeves. As Geoffrey Wellum describes: 'As one we all make a dive for the door. Cries and curses I have heard so often before: "Start up, Start up", "Out of the bloody way", "Move, for Christ's sake." I race for my Spitfire. Blimey, out of breath already.'

'You ran to your aircraft,' recalled 'Bam' Bamberger, 'the parachute was already there,' resting on the wing, 'you have to get strapped into the parachutes, turn on your Oxygen.' Ground crew riggers would already have removed the starter plug and pulled the trolley clear. 'The fitter looked at you and as soon as he saw you climb on the wing, he leaped out of the cockpit and put you in it.' Everything conceivable that could be done to connect, strap or cut practical corners was done to assist the pilot. 'And you were off the ground in three minutes hammering into the blue yonder against this Teutonic monster,' declared Wellum, even now so long after the event with an excited inflection to his voice. 'Yes – bastards.' 'You hadn't time to feel scared,' claimed Bamberger, 'in fact it was almost a relief to get into the air.'

Once fighters scrambled and were away, the war was again immediately apparent to civilian bystanders. Twelve-year-old schoolboy Andy Robertson with his trio of pals was like thousands of others along the south coast alerted to the noise of war, and looked skyward in expectation, watching the defence network unfold. 'We used to cycle up to the top here at Goodwood and see this magnificent vista across to the English Channel,' he recalled.

> We could hear sirens going off in either Chichester or Portsmouth and we could see barrage balloons coming up mainly in Portsmouth. After a period of time you would see – but at the time didn't realise what it was – Germans coming in over the coast. Down [below him] here, there was West Hampnett aerodrome, Tangmere a little further along, fighters taking off up in the air. When I think back now, it was literally like watching an air show put on for us.

The civilian populations of Sussex, Hampshire and above all Kent had found themselves practically involved or bystanders during the Dunkirk evacuation. Those living within a triangle formed by the Thames estuary, the coast between North Foreland and Beachy Head and a line drawn from Eastbourne to London occupied ringside seats for the spectacle of the Battle of Britain. July and the beginning of August had witnessed daily small-scale raids over the south, but once the RAF airfields of Fighter Command were subjected to the main Luftwaffe offensive after 12 August, the sights and sounds of aerial combat were a regular backdrop to the lives of civilians on the ground.

'In some cases we came to aircraft where there were still the bodies of the pilot,' recalled ten-year-old Peter Dyson at Wareham, 'and occasionally a body with a parachute attached to it lying around.' He was amazed with curious child morbidity that, when three bodies were taken out of one German aircraft that crashed nearby, they were buried on the spot, 'almost to within an hour or two of their death'. German airmen are interred at his local church, Lady St Mary's, their graves marked by a simple iron cross with a simple inscription, *Ein Deutscher Soldat.*

'I watched a huge mass of German aircraft coming along the skyline there,' indicated former schoolboy Leon Taylor, watching an attack on the radar towers at Ventnor on the Isle of Wight. Their progress was marked by flak bursts as a group of twenty JU 88 twin-engined bombers broke off from the main formation and droned across the radar pylons on the hills above Ventnor, which they proceeded to dive-bomb. The pylons disappeared beneath bomb bursts and smoke. 'To my amazement, when the smoke cleared the pylons still seemed to be standing, and the planes disappeared over the horizon to seaward.' Schoolteacher Rene Howe, observing the 'mass of planes' from a balcony, thought it 'looked as though the whole of Ventnor had been hit'.

Common to most eyewitness accounts was the size of the bomber formations observed flying and the sinister intent they manifested. 'There was oh – four or five hundred altogether – but they were in batches of roughly thirties and forties.' Massive Geschwader formations over-flew fourteen-year-old Eric Baker's cricket match at Hurst Green near Hastings en route to London on 15 September. 'You look up and you saw great big swathes of black planes going steadily overhead, with the fighter escort up much higher.' Fourteen-year-old Leslie Kershaw remembered, 'this was the first we knew of the war.' He lived at Swanley on the A20 road into London. 'We used to see squadrons of planes coming over, not just half a dozen, but blooming groups of 50.' Puffs of anti-aircraft smoke marked their progress. 'The River Thames was in their favour,' he declared, 'a highway to London, the water lit up by moonlight, a [navigation] sign post to London.' There would be a pause, a momentary clearing of the sky, 'and then the next wave would come, I'm not exaggerating when I say a formation, blooming long group of 50 of them, at least four abreast, and they would cover quite an area in the sky.'

Heinkel III bomber pilot Matthias Henken recalled 'my first view of England; it all looked very green and tidy.' So much so, he felt, he would like to return to holiday along the south coast and perhaps visit London. 'The sun was shining and it was very warm in the plane and the war seemed far away.' He was in a formation of fifty aircraft, with Dornier bombers flying nearby. 'I did not see our fighters but knew they were there somewhere.' Twenty-year-old Leutnant Heinz Mollenbrock, flying the September attacks on London, recalled 'the sun was glinting on the aluminium skins of the fighter aircraft' and it was a beautiful summer's day. Anti-aircraft guns were punching flak into the sky around the formation of Heinkel bombers. Below the River Thames clearly indicated the route. 'You see the water clearly,' Mollenbrock observed, 'not as a blue river, but a shining silver lining of water.' Alan Lee Williams, a fourteen-year-old fire messenger, heard their sinister 'humming tone' approach from the ground. 'Over 700 planes appeared coming up the Thames,' he recalled, 'it was a sight to be seen – unbelievable!'

Gerhard Granz, a Messerschmitt 110 pilot, remembered 'as we got closer to London we became very tense and excited because we were expecting attack from Spitfires and Hurricanes. By September some German aircrew were beginning to experience *Kanalkrankheit* or 'Channel sickness'. Many had already ditched in the Channel, short of fuel or badly shot-up on homecoming. 'Utter exhaustion from the English operations had set in,' wrote fighter pilot Helmuth Ostermann of III/JG 54. 'For the first time one heard pilots talk of the prospect of a posting to a quieter sector.'

Pilot Matthias Henken, basking in the sunlit heat from his Perspex-fronted Heinkel bomber, recalled: 'we crossed the Channel at about 15,000 feet and flew on over the Kent coast and then I heard someone shout "Fighters!" – and the Hurricanes were among us.'

INTERCEPTION AND DOG-FIGHT

'Angels 25, many snappers, "snappers" being the code-word for Me 109s,' explained Geoffrey Wellum. 'Enemy now heading for East End, Sheppey, vector so and so. You should see them in two minutes and there they were.' They were looking for dots in the sky. The very size of the formations they sought aided detection. 'It was like a lot of gnats on a summer evening,' described Geoffrey Wellum.

The imperative and frustration with delayed scrambles was to gain height. It took ten minutes to fly the channel but twenty minutes to gain attacking height. 'If you were scrambled you'd be fighting as soon as you got to the appropriate height,' commented Flight Lieutenant Allan Wright, '10 minutes or 15 perhaps.' Once sighted, conflict was about speed, agility and firepower. 'Take a bombing formation coming in at 230 knots and you're closing at 300, that's a closing speed of 530 knots,' explained Wellum, 'and that doesn't take long.' Flight Lieutenant Peter Brothers persistently emphasised during interviews that 'if you've got the height, you've got the advantage – speed'. The size of an aircraft in a rear-view mirror at 600 yards normal firing distance is an indistinct dot, totally invisible if coming out of the sun. Surveys have revealed that 80 per cent of aircraft were shot down by 20 per cent of the aces and these are essentially 'shoot in the back' ambushes. This height advantage was rarely in the hands of belatedly scrambled fighter interceptions. Brothers explained, 'we very often found we had to attack head on, because we had just about struggled up to the same height when we met the bomber formation.'

RAF Hurricanes and Spitfires were a complementary self-supporting pair. The Hurricane was a strong and stable gun platform, well suited for dealing with bombers. Spitfires were 30 mph faster at 350 mph, equally manoeuvrable and could fly higher than the Hurricane. It was more suited to contesting other fighters, being able to out-turn its primary adversary the Me 109. On the German side, the twin-engined Zerstorer Me 110, with its heavy cannon and machine-gun (MG) forward armament mix, was unsuited to contesting air superiority with fighters. Its Me 109 companion was a far different proposition, able to out-climb the Hurricane, faster than the Spitfire, and had a more devastating cannon and MG mix. 'The two cannons and the inverted carburettor and the instability of the aircraft in the hands of an experienced pilot made the Me 109 a deadly weapon – really deadly,' revealed Flight Lieutenant J G Sanders. 'The thing was, there weren't only one; there were 30, 40, 60 and a hundred – a whole gaggle of them. So one of them is going to get you!'

The best of the German bombers was the Ju 88 whose top speed was close to 290 mph, which made it difficult for a Hurricane to catch. The bomb load of about 2,000 lb matched that of the Heinkel III and Dornier 17 and 215. They were efficient machines and with armour-plating could absorb fearsome punishment and still fly. In tight formation utilising coordinated return fire, they were difficult to shoot down.

German fighter pilot Norbert Limmiker believed 'Hurricanes slower and more clumsy' but 'they were capable of taking more punishment than the Spitfire'. 'Tommies were brave flyers,' he assessed, 'but if you could catch them in a dive or by surprise then there was a real advantage.' RAF ground control quickly gained the grudging admiration of German pilots. 'Whenever we appeared over their coast,' Limmiker admitted, 'they always seemed to be there waiting to pounce.' They always sought to use the advantage of height in stepped up formations to dive down from the sun or in strong light.

Like ground eyewitnesses, veteran Fighter Command accounts are permeated with descriptions of the staggering and dismaying numbers of enemy aircraft they encountered. 'What bothered me,' admitted Peter Brothers, 'was the number of them. Massive hordes, which made you think – ah – there are 12 of us and at least 200 of you chaps steaming towards us, where do you start?' Squadron Leader Ronald Adam, the operations room ground controller at Hornchurch, remembers the radio snatch of a New Zealander pilot on sighting the enemy. 'Christ Almighty, Tally-Ho, [the accepted code for attack]. Whole bloody hordes of them.' 'You've got to shoot down four enemy planes before you are shot down yourself,' Sergeant Pilot Philip Wareing was told by his squadron commander, 'because that's what the odds are. Otherwise you're wasting your time.' There were tenuous compensations as Allan Wright explained: 'I didn't mind the big odds, if most of them were German you didn't have to bother much whether what you saw in front of you was going to be German and not one of your own.' It saved vital seconds considering 'is it one of ours or one of theirs?'

Roland Beamont, flying a Hurricane with 87 Squadron, described the final moments of an interception, a fleeting experience allowing little time for consideration:

Almost immediately the clear sky ahead started to turn into a mass of little black dots. It could only really be described as a bee-hive – we used to call them the 'bee-hive'. This mass of black dots appeared developing ahead. Our CO continued to lead us straight towards it. I just had time to think, 'I wonder what sort of tactic he's going to employ, is he going to turn up sun and try and dive out of the sun at them or go round to the right and come in behind . . . what's he going to do?' While I thought that, it was quite apparent he wasn't going to do anything. He bored straight on into the middle of this lot until we seemed to be going into the biggest formation of aeroplanes you ever saw. Then his voice came on the radio and he said: 'Target ahead, come on chaps, let's surround them.' Just nine of us.

A British fighter's standard armament was eight .303 Browning machine-guns each carrying 300 rounds, firing at 1,200 per minute. 'You had about 12 seconds and in two attacks I finished off those 12 seconds of ammunition,' explained Geoffrey Wellum. The combination of cannon and MG fire from German fighters was twice as effective in destructive power as the British. RAF pilots aligned their guns to converge at 250 instead of the regulation 600 yards to increase damage, which of course required a far closer interception. 'It was not straight forward shooting like at a bird or something, it was deflection shooting,' explained Flight Lieutenant Anthony Bartley, 'coming in from the side, coming in from underneath, from all different angles.' The deflection angle was the 'aim off' to ensure the cone of fire converged on to the moving target at the correct range, so that the opposing pilot was obliged to fly through it. 'It was too quick,' claimed Geoffrey Wellum. 'Half of them were snap shots,' he indicated with a quick head jerk as if a plane was flashing by. 'It was a straight forward maths thing.' 'I got behind a Heinkel' and 'gave him a real good dose,' explained Flight Lieutenant Ted Shipman with 41 Squadron:

> People write about the rattle of the guns: with eight firing together it's never a rattle, more a great sustained roar. His wing caught fire and down he went spiralling. The thing I remember is that this rear gunner kept potting at me right to the moment it went in. So I didn't jump for joy at this either. I was never elated at a success. Some did, some in my squadron took extraordinary pleasure from a kill. Never me.

Down below, railway worker Robert Barham pointed out, 'one could really distinguish the comparatively slow "tump, tump, tump" of the German fighter's cannon from the throaty roar of eight Browning machine guns carried by our Hurricanes and Spitfires.' They could produce spectacular results. 'I was looking upwards, towards the south, almost overhead, when suddenly a huge orange flash dimmed the brilliant sunshine,' recalled Dudley 'Doug' Gardiner, near Warmwell in Dorset. 'It was followed by a pall of dense black smoke, out of which spewed a mass of debris. Parts of aeroplane started to flutter gently to the ground, leisurely twisting and turning whilst large black objects sped swiftly past them.' The pilot did not make it, a parachute emerged from the debris, but not in mushroom form. 'In its place was a useless fluttering thing, a little thicker than a line, to which was attached a sandbag-like object beneath it.' Gardiner watched its progress with macabre fascination. 'I followed it down and within seconds it disappeared behind the rooftops.' Hubert Bowden with 55 (Wessex) Field Regiment RA saw twenty-one-year-old Pilot Officer Brooks bale out of his crippled Hurricane and float down. 'As he glided to earth a German fighter shot him to bits.' They were horrified and 'powerless to act'. The great heights and spectral beauty of the environment within which this battle was conducted belied its implicit bitterness. There were men inside these toy-like aeroplanes dodging and weaving against a majestic backdrop of royal blue summer skies, and they were trying to kill each other.

'Kill the pilot or set the aircraft on fire,' advised Flight Lieutenant J G Sanders, 'that's why I insisted on having one in four linked incendiaries and try and kill the pilot and the aircraft would come down.' An ambush execution was always the preferred option, dog-fighting was less predictable. 'Very often if you're in the right aeroplane at the right time you can sneak up and get in close, 50 to 100 yards, and you hardly need a fight for that,' declared Allan Wright. He narrowed his eyes and described how 'there he is just sitting there and you just pull up and you get a bead on him like this', demonstrating with his hands and 'brrrr – you've got him'.

Apart from being emotionally frightening dog-fighting was an intensely physical affair. Cocooned in his cockpit, a pilot was subjected to colossal stresses and strains imposed on his body from gravitational pull, high altitude, centrifugal force and other pressures. 'A huge dive and the change in air pressure just bust my eardrum,' recalled Anthony Bartley. In a sharp turn Pilot Officer Dennis David explained: 'You were pushed way down into your seat. Your eyeballs were pushed down in your face. It was like swinging a bucket around. The bucket goes around but the water [the pilot] stays in the bucket.'

German bomber aircrew could be subjected to this centrifugal force trying to extricate themselves from a downward spiralling crippled and often burning air frame. Hatches were barely man-size and could be obscured by rushing flame, wreckage or deformed metal. Crew had literally to climb up or down the fuselage side trying to get out as the aircraft corkscrewed or violently gyrated.

Three feet in front of British fighter pilots was a twelve-cylinder Rolls-Royce Merlin engine screaming at full power, while eight Browning machine-guns roared and shook the frame of the aircraft on firing. In his earphones was the mush and crackle of static, alternating with urgent warning shouts from other pilots and the occasional despairing shriek of one going down. Cockpit smells were an offensive mixture of high-octane fuel, hot metal, burning rubber, cordite and often vomit forced out through dizzying spirals and tight turns. Anything beyond 4G or four times the gravitational pull of the earth could produce disturbing side effects. '4G I can reasonably cope with over a long period,' stated Allan Wright but 'anything over 6G and the blood drains from the head into the stomach and legs and therefore your brain can't cope properly.'

A steep dive to left or right can produce as much as 6G or 7G and colour starts to blend into monochrome and may result in blackout. 'There are situations,' explained Wright, 'when you can't control this, and the next thing is that everything goes black.' Not for long, but a temporary lack of clarity that blunts fighting effectiveness. 'When you come to, the memory is all gone. Cockpit? What is it a cockpit of? You don't know anything. It comes out fairly quickly, but for those first few seconds your mind has gone – all you've got is eyeballs!'

Pilots learned to counteract the force by squeezing muscles in the lower half of the body to keep blood to the head, clenching like mad, to pull up as much G as possible to retain consciousness. Jet pilots would later be aided in this by specially made pressure suits. 'You could hold it, you knew what was happening, but if you kept on pulling G, you would eventually become unconscious,' explained Geoffrey Wellum. 'We got adept at just keeping it on the groin.' All this was untaught at flying schools and could only be picked up by experience or in conversation with veterans, who may not wish to dwell on their individual terrors. In order to survive the pilot had to discipline his mind for cool concise thinking, to anticipate his opponent's next move, retain sharp eyesight and accurately calculate deflection. At the end of a mission pilots were bathed in sweat.

The toll on the pilot's nerves was apparent on the ground. 'There was an indescribable tension about the whole thing,' recalled Jean Mills, a plotter at Duxford, on the edge of 12 Group. 'We could hear the crackling voices of the pilots come back and although we had headsets on and the work was quite intensive and required a lot of concentration we used to manage to ease one earphone off so we could hear what was going on.' It was a combined effort, ground and air, the pilots 'were very much our pigeon' and 'we were all rooting for our boys to come back'. Distressingly they were able to hear those that did not. Corporal Claire Legg remembered the girls monitoring the pilot's radio channel at Tangmere. 'What they heard often distressed the girls very badly' after battle was joined. 'They knew the pilots and they heard them screaming and going down. It was horrid.' Sergeant Tom Naylor manned the plotting table at Hornchurch sector and recalled the system breaking down due to the density of traffic at the height of the 15 September bombing raid on London. Distracted pilots simply switched off their radios, which 'was a good thing because the language that usually came over the loudspeaker from the pilots could be awful'. It also recorded the pathos. Naylor remembered one Canadian pilot 'who obviously had been hit': 'He came on and said, "Three-Two." That was his call-sign. "Give my love to mother." He never came back.'

The Luftwaffe grew increasingly nervous as casualties rose. Aileen Clayton was a WAAF officer belonging to Y (Radio Interception) branch monitoring German Air Force traffic at Kingsdown in Kent, on the direct flying route to London. 'It became obvious to us that there was a growing tension among German fighter pilots. They would lose their tempers, get irritable with each other, and at times sound downright panicky; and our knowledge of German swearwords increased considerably.'

By September, fatigue and a discernible lowering of morale were becoming evident in the Luftwaffe. 'There is no fun or enjoyment in that kind of incessant war time flying,' declared Heinkel bomber pilot

Matthias Henken. 'It just becomes a dirty, noisy, dangerous job that wears out your nerves' and it was having a cumulative impact. 'I have seen worn-out young men who aged before your eyes.'

Dog-fighting was sheer physical effort, countering G forces, seeking more power, short deflection bursts at snap targets while seeking to retain a sense of the overall situation amid fleeting images. 'I was so het up and frightened and gulping I thought I was going to be sick with sort of excitement, I suppose,' recalled Geoffrey Wellum. 'We always flew with a very high throttle opened, and before we went into action, every time I pressed the emergency booster over-ride.' Each ounce of additional power could be life-saving. 'So I had 6 lbs a booster, I think it was, up to 12 lbs from six – and you used it – to hell with it.' Height was crucial. Allan Wright explained that covering 2,000 feet at a dive was three seconds compared to three minutes to pull up the same distance. 'He's worrying about you and you don't have to worry about him.' Hesitation had no place in aerial combat. 'You must go,' Wright emphasised, having acquired a potential victim, 'you can't just turn away and find another target.'

Tactics within this close fighting arena were untaught. Before the war it had not been envisaged that large scale fighter on fighter conflict would occur. 'The bomber would always get through' had been the pre-1939 maxim. England and Germany were too far apart for fighters to confront each other, but this was transformed by the fall of France. 'Beware of the Hun in the sun' was the first rule of the new air fighting Wellum advised, alongside quick reactions and aggression:

If you try and look at the sun, you look at them through your fingers or put your thumb over it and squint around the edge. You just get a fleeting glimpse of something. You don't ask questions then, you break into it. You never query it. If you see something that you don't like coming out of the sun at you, pull into it straight away. Always turn into it – go for him!

Wellum flew to a simple maxim. 'Never, but never fly straight and level for more than 20 seconds. If you do, you'll die.'

It became apparent that the only way to break up a bomber formation with inferior numbers before it reached its target was to

Tension marks this pilot's face as he awaits the signal to take off.
They could be airborne within minutes.

One fireman felt he was 'stalked' by the fires. 'If you see a
bulge, drop everything! Out!', before the collapse. A
building falls in London during the Blitz.

'I didn't really know what had happened', admitted one young child who lost her little brother. A bombed London East End child and his foster-mother.

tackle it head on. Individual bombers would seek the nearest cloud cover, drop down to sea or ground level, dodging and weaving at high speed or apply dive brakes with a jink turn and hope the attacking fighter would overshoot. The best policy, and one applied in a disciplined way by the Luftwaffe, was to maintain tight formation and fight it out. The only recourse then was to shoot down the lead bombers, which also tended to disperse the formation. The Heinkel III was poorly armed with just three 7.9mm MG 15s, or 'marmalade throwers' as their crews nicknamed them. These were situated singly in the nose, dorsal and side positions. The Heinkel's nose was also fully glazed, which produced reflection problems in sunny weather and water rivulet obscuration in bad. More significantly, nearly all the crew were enclosed together just behind the Perspex dome. Flight Lieutenant Brian Kingcome with 92 Squadron recalled how vulnerable they must have felt. 'As you came at him' in a head-on attack 'you'd see him nervously getting ready for you, bouncing around long before you were within firing range.' They felt completely exposed, intently observing the approaching menace with tracer arcing past the cockpit. 'They had to be very, very tough and very, very brave to keep going steadily onward.' 'You got to judge when to break,' explained Flight Lieutenant Gerry Edge:

But once you knew how, a head-on attack was a piece of cake. When you opened fire, you'd kill or badly wound the pilot and the second pilot. Then you'd rake the line of them as you broke away. On one attack, the first Heinkel III hit crashed into the next Heinkel. There was a lot of crashing among bombers we attacked head on.

OVER TARGET

Fifty years after the Battle of Britain former German Zerstorer Me 110 pilot Gerhard Granz flew a commemorative raid route in a light aircraft. 'Here,' as they flew over the Isle of Sheppey, 'just when we could see the Thames ahead, the interception by the RAF would often start.' The bomber streams were minutes from their targets in London. 'Flying in a group was not so easy,' described Leutnant Heinz Mollenbrock, following the river line from the Thames estuary. 'I was in the final Kette; the final three [of the Schwarm, or formation mass] was the most dangerous position to be in.'

Derek South's house at Chislehurst in north-west Kent overlooked the lower river valley of the Thames, providing a ring-side seat to observe the massive German fly-in. Two separate formations of sixty aircraft each droned by with no sign of British fighters. 'The track of the planes was constant and inexorable,' he recalled, noticing the sun glinting fiercely on Perspex front turrets as they headed for the docks. 'We didn't take cover. It was as though there was a feeling of total vulnerability and acceptance of enemy domination. Even a sense of admiration.'

Gerhard Granz in the covering force of fighters recalled flying over Sheerness. 'Our battle began somewhere here, over the north side of the river, to the east of London.' He had the advantage of height and observed a Hurricane coming up from below and attaching itself to the rear of a Heinkel III. 'I broke formation and went after it, got in a burst and I think I downed it, but didn't have time to check because suddenly there were Hurricanes all around me and I was taking hits.'

Bombing runs began, aided by the navigational indication provided by the twists and turns of the River Thames. Thick clouds of smoke shot up, punctuated by the flash of bursting bombs among the docks and built up areas both sides of the river. 'You have to look to your comrade flying in front and to the left side, flying close together,' explained Leutnant Heinz Mollenbrock. 'Only by this group could they assemble a strength of 27 machine guns against the attacker.' On 7 September the RAF had been aloft guarding their airfields; nobody had thought the Germans would go for London. Nine miles of waterfront and docklands on both banks of the river below Tower Bridge were set ablaze.

Sixteen-year-old George Mooney living in Stepney remembered 'a beautiful Saturday afternoon' on that day, 'the sky was a beautiful turquoise blue'. They were suddenly alerted by the sirens 'and you saw the vapour trails in the sky . . . There was hundreds and hundreds of vapour trails. It was as if someone was painting white patterns in the sky. Then all of a sudden the bombs started dropping.'

He ran home to check on the safety of his mother. For much of the population this was the culmination of the unreal scenarios they had only viewed in cinemas, worry about which the inactivity of the Phoney War had allayed. Bernard Kops, a fourteen-year-old living in the heart of the Jewish community in Stepney Green, recalled, 'we lived very close to the docks, so we were obviously for it if we had thought about it.' But this was the point; no one considered themselves a *target*, so the initial raids were a real shock. 'We lived in this tight world,' Kops explained and it was populated by people they knew. 'There was Aunt Katie, Aunt Sarah and Aunt Rose and Aunt Millie.' They were a poor community. 'Every day was like an uphill struggle,' Kops remembered. He had to scavenge the streets daily for old shoes to be burned as coal. 'It wasn't could we get through to Saturday, could we get through today!' Suddenly the war intruded on all this. 'My God, it's all over!' they thought during the first few days, 'everyone is going to die!'

Alan Lee Williams, a fourteen-year-old watching along the Thames, had a totally different perspective viewing the spectacle. 'We saw the Spitfires and Hurricanes diving in – weaving in and out, we thought if this is war, we love it – it was like a cricket match!' Paul Wenzel, a young boy in shorts, remembered 'it was the sound of the machine gun fire that was striking to me. It was nothing like you hear on the films; it was just like running a stick along metal railings.' Adults like twenty-three-year-old Rose Cadby, living in Aldgate, held the more prevailing view that 'anybody with any sense would be scared of something coming out of the sky'. It was the stuff of science fiction brutally come alive. 'If anyone's coming toward you to hit you,' she rationalised, 'you could have a go, but a bomb coming from the sky – where could you run?'

Class became an issue in the targeting of the Blitz on London before shared suffering produced a degree of social levelling. Seventeen-year-old Josephine Russell lived in the fashionable part of Knightsbridge and admitted, 'I wasn't aware of being a "Londoner".' That was to occur later as Home Front propaganda got under way. 'We knew they were having a terrible time in the East End and one heard stories of what was going on.' There was reluctance to intrude by offering assistance. 'One would have been regarded as a sightseer and getting in the way of something that was very difficult for them, and they had to get on with.' Bernard Kops remarked on the perception that the West End was untouched while the East End was pulverised. 'A few bombs dropped in the [Hyde] Park,' he remembered, 'but you'd go through the West End and there wasn't any damage – there's no war on!' It was encapsulated by Josephine Russell's domestic servant's exchange with her mother. 'Oh Madam dear, they've hit the Westminster Bridge,' she announced. Her mother, aghast, responded, 'How awful, I'd no idea' – but Josephine clarified what was meant. The Germans had destroyed the Westminster Bridge pub.

There were insufficient shelters in the densely populated East End. 'Service shelters were useless,' Bernard Kops announced. 'Maybe you'd go in there if you were a teenager to cuddle a girlfriend – or to have a piss – but they were dirty, cold and damp. We didn't feel safe,' he admitted. Inactivity during the Phoney War and a reluctance to trash gardens led to too many Anderson shelters stockpiled unused in depots. George Mooney, searching for his mother at the height of the early September raid in Stepney, felt equally unsafe. He found his house had imploded on receiving a direct hit and had disappeared into the cellars 'flat on the ground'. He found only his mortally wounded nine-year-old female cousin, who plaintively asked, 'Am I going to die?' 'No, love,' he replied, but she did later in hospital. Seven members of his immediate family were killed – 'bang–gone', and by nightfall he had given up hope of ever finding his mother. 'I wasn't a cuddly fellow, but at nine o'clock when my Mum came round the corner, you couldn't have given me a better present. It was " 'eres me Mum – *Cor it's Mum!*" I was as happy as a pig!'

The East End bore the brunt of the early air-raids. Paul Wenzel, a young lad, recalled one near miss:

It was this vivid blue flash, never heard a thing. Never heard a bomb coming, just a vivid blue flash and this great pressure and even the hurricane lamp blew out, followed by – it seemed to go on for ages – the noise of blast and masonry falling. Then we heard people shouting 'Are you alright?' It was obviously the firemen pulling at the masonry. 'We'll wait for the lull and we'll get you out.'

In time Wenzel became used to the sights and smells of bombing raids. 'There was arms and legs and things hanging around' in the aftermath of an explosion in the flats opposite. 'My Mum grabbed my arm and said, "you don't have to look."' Jessie Stansfield remembered a hit on the United Dairies less than a hundred yards away. 'They were still using horses and the horses caught on fire and were running about just going berserk. I'll never forget the screaming, they were literally burning, there had been a direct hit on the stables.'

It was not all grimness for Jessie Stansfield because she met her future husband at the height of an air-raid. 'He pushed me to the ground and all I was worried about was me stockings.' When they married a few months later the wedding ceremony was speeded up as it was interrupted by yet another air-raid.

Tragedy was commonplace. Sylvia Piper was in an Anderson shelter in Tilbury during the September London bombing raid. Her father had just returned from leave and was in uniform when the house received a direct hit, blasting through the shelter. One of her brothers was killed, another hit in the shoulder and her father so badly injured he never recovered. Her mother received head wounds and Sylvia a hole in the chest, 'hot shrapnel – so it burns as well as damages'. The pathos of the scene is a memory that endured to this day. 'The sun was absolutely glorious' on that day and the shelter peppered with holes allowed the rays of the sun to gleam through and illuminate aspects of the carnage within. 'And being eight years old, I didn't really know what had happened.' She never forgot what her surviving brother told her, tearfully recalling: 'I saw it was Eric, and I knew it was him because he'd got a hole in his shoe. What was so awful about it was it was my turn to sit on that seat.'

'He has never got over it,' she admitted.

Battle inside the bombing target area was taken up by the Fire Service. Coping with the fiery consequences of intense bombing was tangible confirmation to the civilian population that war had arrived and they were all in it. 'It was a terrible shock to feel so suddenly that the enemy was close,' admitted London fireman Richard Holsgrove. The hum of enemy aircraft overhead gave substance to the string of contemporary magazine articles about failed invasion attempts in 1588 and 1805 that had encouraged a degree of complacency. It was a stark realisation for Holsgrove 'to know that someone was trying to destroy us, and trying to destroy the city'.

Fire-fighting was physically and mentally akin to actual combat, not a world removed from the desperate dog-fights in the skies above. Conflict was more against a remorseless rather than quick-reacting foe. 'You see those buildings at the end there?' George Wheeler, a former fireman, pointed while reminiscing about a scene. 'You look up and all of a sudden while you're watching you hear *Wheee – crash!*' Then another series of whistles followed by violent concussions. 'Then suddenly you feel the heat behind you, you look round and the buildings on the other side have caught fire. So then you've got a very dangerous situation. By the time they've dropped the first one, you could have another 50 or 60 fires going. The bombs would explode and spread it.'

It was like combating a live opponent. 'The centre of the fire would change,' explained fireman Richard Rosoman. 'There it would be flaring up like an enormous candle, and then it would blow away and disappear.' It was as if the conflagration was feinting. 'It fluctuates all the time like this, so one is more and more bewildered.' Rosoman was also struck by the sheer violence of the blazes they attempted to control. 'It's so shocking, so powerful,' he described. Like in combat, the unwary succumbed. After the war Rosoman became an artist famous for his portrayal of 'The Falling Wall', which captured in oil one of his comrades being buried by falling burning masonry tackling a fire in a narrow East End alleyway. 'It haunted me, it still does a bit,' he admitted. The picture was a way of exorcising ghosts. The wall fell with a 'sound such as I had never heard in my life, it absolutely filled everything and then all movement stopped.' One of his friends was quickly pulled clear; the other had to be abandoned beneath twelve to fifteen feet of red-hot brick rubble. 'We all knew it was pretty hopeless trying to rescue him'.

George Wheeler recalled the intimidating nature of fighting this almost tangible fiery opponent. 'You're looking up and you can see all those showers of sparks and they're all coming towards you.' Fire-storm raids later in December could lead to firemen being suddenly overwhelmed by a rushing conflagration, akin to a tropical storm, as cold air inversion rushed in to replace rising hot air, occasionally achieving hurricane strength. This was like combating some form of mythical monster. 'You then start to feel the heat getting greater and greater,' recalled George Wheeler, 'you can feel your face beginning to tingle.' They were in effect being stalked. 'You're watching, particularly the buildings on either side, if you see a bulge, drop everything! *Out!*'

The sights, sounds and emotions of the Blitz on London were followed by the 'Baedeker Raids' on provincial towns such as Canterbury and Coventry, Bath, Norwich, York, Hull, Poole, Exeter and Grimsby. These continued upon other cities also, right up to the 'Doodlebug' V1 and V2 Flying Bomb attacks that were to come in 1944. The shared experience produced an indelible imprint upon the psyche of the wartime generation that endured it all. The feeling of community it fostered was not necessarily a totally uniform feeling, but it has since remained historically unique to that generation. 'Of course the King and Queen didn't leave London you know and they were bombed and very popular,' claimed Jessie Stansfield. 'They were one of us and that's all there is to it.' Losing one's house was no longer a novelty, she explained. 'You couldn't just go in and say "I'd lost my house last night" because they would just say "so did I!"' Shared though the experience was, there were different interpretations. These are more commonly expressed today, in an age moulded by alternative values and influences.

Rose Cadby from the East End had a jaundiced view of royal visits to bomb sites in the East End. The royal family was, in effect, suggesting 'I can look you all in the eye because now my home has been bombed.' This was true, there was damage, but the Queen's main quarters were untouched. 'But it was only her railings,' Cadby observed, 'wasn't it lucky, eh?' She and others less advantaged in the East End might be cynical. 'Come on! Poor people coming out of the shelters, their houses reduced to rubble and poor Queen Elizabeth had her railings done in – oh my God,' she commented ironically. Rose Cadby encapsulated the East End penchant for strong opinions and a wicked sense of irony. 'It's funny they missed the palace, wasn't it?' she asked disingenuously.

Cynicism came from dreadful scenes witnessed after the 'all clear' siren sounded. 'It was difficult to take it in,' fifteen-year-old Jessica

Jacob observed, recalling the destruction, 'it was so extensive'. 'The smell and every now and then you heard one of the damaged buildings collapsing a little more. If you could find something that was familiar, it was something you could hang on to.'

Fireman George Wheeler described how in the aftermath 'you would run your hands over the rubble, any signs of life of any sort, you look for it.' Finding children was especially important and upsetting for firemen who immediately redoubled efforts when it was suspected the young were beneath the rubble. 'If the young child's still alive – it's so precious,' confessed Wheeler. One rescuer recalled grasping the hand of a fifteen-year-old girl, completely buried in an Anderson shelter, trying to console and quieten her panic. Her mouth was full of soil, which he managed to clean out. As she laid back catching her breath 'sort of breathing heavily, some stupid devil walked over the top of the shelter, soil came down and went back in the girl's throat and as she squeezed my hand like that she just faded out.' This grim memory never left him. 'Now I had the feel of that girl clenching my hand for weeks and weeks and weeks. I could never forget it and I don't forget it now.'

Indomitable spirit does not cloud grief. Winnie Feldon lost her parents and sister in one London raid. 'Oh I still miss her a lot now, I could do with her here now I'm on me own, but got no one left,' she remarked over sixty years after the event. 'Still I'm not bitter about it – ah no. I do get upset,' she admitted, breaking into tears. 'You mustn't be upset,' and she cried again. Her eight-year-old brother survived the experience, but he 'never spoke about it'. Fireman George Wheeler felt however, 'the more we were hit, the more we had this spirit.' The population of Britain was fully immersed in the crucible of war. 'I think they actually thought they could bomb us into submission,' Wheeler declared, 'but it did the opposite.' Any half-prepared Sea Lion invasion attempt would likely have met stiff resistance. 'The more that was done to us, the more we responded by "OK, we can take it, get on with it, we are not going to submit."'

Churchill had offered the nation nothing more than 'blood, toil, tears and sweat'. That is all they got.

THE KILL AND RETURN TO BASE

The Luftwaffe switch from attacking RAF airfields to bombing London meant a longer flight to get back, with only ten minutes German fighter endurance over the city. Gerhard Granz, flying a commemorative flight fifty years after the event, recalled he was shot down over Great Burstead near Billericay. He abandoned his cockpit at 500 feet, not the 1,500 feet he flew that day. 'But I do remember that cemetery,' he pointed out, 'it was very close to me in every respect – in 1940 I thought it was waiting for me.'

Despite return fire from the bomber he was stalking, Pilot Officer 'Boy' Geoffrey Wellum focused intently on his dodging and weaving opponent. 'My target, concentrate, the target. Looking at him through the sight, getting larger much too quickly, concentrate, hold him steady, that's it, hold it . . . be still my heart, be still. Sight on, still on, steady . . . fire. Now!'

Guns made a noise like 'tearing calico', he remembered.

'As soon as you fired people would see the tracer or become aware of you,' declared Flight Lieutenant Allan Wright. With only fifteen seconds of ammunition it was a question of lining up on a dodging and weaving target, employing three to five second in speculative and hopefully accurate deflection shots. Anthony Bartley liked De Wild incendiary ammunition because 'you could see flashing as it hit'. Deflection, as discovered by Flight Lieutenant Colin Gray with 54 Squadron, was a hit and miss affair that became effective with experience. He accidentally shot his target aircraft down because after limited success in a tight turn he had to give twice the deflection he thought he needed. 'To my astonishment my first burst caught him amidships and the pilot immediately baled out.' From then on he 'always allowed twice the deflection I thought necessary and maybe a bit more for good luck'. Allan Wright's policy was to pour in incendiary bursts until he saw a result. 'You don't know if there is any damage until you see smoke, or a chap hops out, or it flips or whatever.' Tell-tale signatures gave some indication. 'You get an oil pipe and it catches fire so you get black smoke, or you get a coolant and that makes white smoke.'

The pervasive smell strapped into the claustrophobic confines of a fighter cockpit was of high-octane petrol. 'You pretty well had 87 gallons of petrol in your lap, it was just behind the instrument panel,' explained Allan Wright. This was due to the elliptical shape of the Spitfire's wings. Hurricane wings did have fuel tanks, which were protected, but not where the wing came into the fuselage beneath the pilot. The Spitfire had its main tank behind the Merlin engine, the Hurricane its twenty-eight gallon reserve there. The pilot therefore sat behind a bath of volatile fuel, sloshing around during the exigencies of flight. 'So if it went up, *it* went up,' declared Allan Wright, 'the business was to get out in time.' That meant within six seconds at best, because as Hurricane Sergeant Pilot Jack Perkin explained:

People who stayed in a burning cockpit for 10 seconds were overcome by the flames and heat. Nine seconds and you ended up in Queen Victoria Hospital in East Grinstead in Dr Archie McIndoe's burns surgery for the rest of the war. If you got out in eight seconds, you never flew again, but you went back about 12 times for plastic surgery.

Perkin got out between four to five seconds with his hair on fire.

'I got a *clink* in my starboard tank,' remembered Squadron Leader Tom Gleave, 'an incendiary, and it burst into flames.' Within two or three seconds an aircraft became virtually unflyable. 'It burnt so quickly, it was unbelievable,' recalled Gleave. Getting the cockpit hood open, a routine action, became terrifyingly complex in the mind-numbing context of a catastrophic fire. Gleave forgot all he needed to do was pull a toggle instead of clawing at the cockpit hood. 'As the hood came back, there was a God Almighty explosion,' which propelled him clear amid a huge sheet of flame.

In a screaming high revolution dive burning fuel was sucked into the cockpit generating an invisible blue flame of blow torch intensity that melted the instrument panel and seared all exposed skin. Every object grabbed or twisted to release straps and levers to get out was barbecued by a torrent of rushing fire. Anything exposed, face, neck, hands, bared legs above flying boots and the groin, all was cooked and melted. Any protrusions such as nose, lips, ears and eyelids were seared off. 'A petrol flame is more intense, hotter and fiercer than almost any other fire I know of,' remarked Sergeant Jack Perkin and with the fuel tank configuration 'you had that straight in your face. You can only think, *I must get out of this.*'

Gleave fell clear of his aircraft tumbling head over heels until his parachute opened. His face, hands and legs were swelling even as he descended. 'Most of my clothes had gone. I was pretty badly burnt – about 30% burns. I lost all the skin off my right foot. I still get holes occasionally, things sometimes come out, bits of bone. I lost all the skin off my hand and most of my face. My eyelids and nose went.'

Tom Gleave was married and understandably anxious at what his wife's reaction to his pitiful condition might be. He lay in his hospital bed with hands, forearms and legs encased in dried tannic acid, while his face had swollen to 'the size of the proverbial melon'. Peering through the slits in his mask he heard footsteps approaching the bed. His wife stood gazing at him. 'She flushed a little,' he recalled and asked, 'what on earth have you been doing with yourself, darling?' He found it hard to answer. 'Had a row with a German,' he eventually managed to respond.

Squadron Leader Bill Simpson was burned and disfigured on the first day of the Battle for France. Nursing sister Mary Godson recalled his wife did not want to see him, 'he was not a pretty sight' and not long married, 'he had been a nice-looking lad'. His fingers had come away from his left hand when his dressings had been inexpertly changed while in France and only stumps remained on his right. Simpson later expressed his misgivings in writing, reflecting: 'will he ever find a girl who can love him physically and mentally to the extent he desires and needs, irrespective of his ugliness?' His wife thought not, but Bill Simpson was subsequently to marry one of his nurses and she was to bear him two children and support him in a successful business career.

Once the Luftwaffe bomber stream was turned away or headed for home the RAF focused attention on any labouring or crippled aircraft. Pilot Officer 'Boggle' Bodie selected one such damaged Dornier bomber: 'He appeared to be having difficulty with one engine. I fixed that by stopping it altogether for him. He looked a bit lop-sided then, so I stopped the other one too, and he started a long, steep glide down.'

Conditions inside these shot-riddled aircraft were nightmarish. 'Two of my crew to my mind nearly dead in the plane badly wounded,' recalled Leutnant Heinz Mollenbrock, nursing his crippled Heinkel III. Four or five attacks were endured flying on one engine until Mollenbrock, badly wounded, baled out with his observer. He ironically ended up in Woolwich hospital with RAF pilot Henry Higginson, whose Hurricane had riddled their machine in a frontal attack. 'I saw a couple of chaps baling out of a Heinkel,' recalled Geoffrey Wellum, 'and one poor sod got caught up on the tail and there he was wind-milling about on the back of his aeroplane, he went straight into the deck. You know – it has an effect on a chap of 18.'

Radio operator Horst Zander's Dornier 17 belonging to the KG 3 'Blitz' Geschwader was hit on the way back from London. 'A blinding flash and black smoke poured through the cabin, directly followed by an icy gale.' The flight deck occupied by the majority of the crew was reduced to a shambles: 'The cabin was full of blood. Our pilot was hit. On the intercom I heard him say feebly [to the observer] Heinz Lambe, "you have to fly us home".' This particular aircraft, 'bucking like a horse' managed to touch down at Antwerp.

German soldiers awaiting the invasion call near coastal airstrips, must have reasoned from the frequency of crippled and smoking returning bombers that there was time yet before the call forward to embark on landing barges.

'Boggle' Bodie flew down to confirm his damaged Dornier actually went into the ground. Coming alongside he assessed the pilot of the 'pretty well riddled' aeroplane was either dead or badly wounded. 'He didn't even turn his head to look at me, or watch out for a place to land, but stared straight ahead.' Then he spotted a pair of legs emerge from beneath the aircraft as the gunner tried to bale out, but he only got as far as his waist. He wriggled, squirmed and thrashed about all to no avail. Bodie recognised: 'Good God he's stuck! Poor devil, he couldn't get in or out, and his legs, all I could see of them, flailed about wildly as he tried to release himself.'

There was nothing Bodie could do about it, he felt guilty and almost physically sick. He observed with macabre fascination as first one flying boot and then the other was kicked off. Bodie felt himself willing 'he'd better hurry, or it'd be too late'. With the dead pilot slumped over the controls the Dornier descended to 1,000 feet. 'He had no socks on,' Bodie recalled, 'his feet were quite bare, it was very pathetic.' He would be cut in half on landing 'like cheese on a grater'. Appreciating he should not be allowed to die like that, Bodie focused his sights squarely where his body would be and delivered a short burst. The legs were stilled. As the aircraft exploded, 'I saw pieces sail past me as I flew low overhead. I didn't feel particularly jubilant.'

RAF pilots returned to base once their ammunition was exhausted while the Luftwaffe cripples attempted to nurse their shot-up machines across the Channel. Fuel was the perennial problem for German fighter pilots. Oberleutnant Ulrich Steinhilper recalled a September mission with 1/JG 52 when the bomber stream missed London and carried on using two-thirds of its fuel before giving up and turning for home. Steinhilper's fighters stayed with the bombers as long as they dared, fighting off harassing fighters until fuel ran too low. 'We literally wave-hopped hoping our fuel gauges were wrong, and that we would have just enough to get to France.'

The mission became a disaster, rough water prevented belly landings so the only option was to gauge fuel consumption as accurately as possible and then pop up at the last moment to gain height to bale out. 'Our track across those wild waters became dotted with parachutes, pilots floating in their life-jackets, and greasy oil slicks on the cold water showing where another Me 109 had ended its last dive.' Steinhilper's Schwarm of four made it back to Boulogne to refuel. 'All along the coast near Boulogne we had seen 109s down in the fields and on the grass, some still standing on their noses.' A secret memorandum later revealed nineteen pilots had drowned on his mission and only two were picked up by the Seenotflugkommando (air-sea rescue) sea-planes.

The Channel was truly 'Churchill's Moat' because every German pilot on crossing it, who became a casualty over England, either lost his life or became a prisoner. British pilots operating over their home bases received a second or third chance. German pilots ditching in the Channel fared better than their RAF counterparts, however. German fighters carried dinghies and bright green chemical stain to aid rescue by an air-sea rescue service of thirty Heinkel He 59 twin-engined sea-planes. British air–sea rescue methods were not properly organised until well into the battle.

Coming down in the Channel was perilous for both sides. Once clear of the aircraft, RAF pilots pulled the rip-cord of their parachute and kicked off their flying boots or shoes and inflated the Mae West life-jacket, if it was not punctured on the way down. Neck fastenings needed to be loosened and they had to clear the parachute shrouds on entry into the water. If not, they might be dragged by a half-inflated parachute and drown. Pilot Officer Peter Stevenson, flying a Spitfire with 74 Squadron, drifted eleven miles out to sea for twenty minutes after being shot down over Deal. Snagged by his left foot he was dragged with his head underwater for three minutes at 10 mph until almost unconscious before he was released. British pilots were often reliant upon local boats or motor torpedo boats (MTBs) to be picked up. Rescue was, however, an imprecise art. Pilot Officer Jas Storrar watched his friend Guy Branch shot down in the sea over Poole harbour. He circled him until he saw the lifeboat was to within fifty to a hundred yards away and returned to base. With some relief he was able to telephone his wife and report what he saw, but it all went wrong. 'I simply couldn't understand how somebody in the water wearing a green Mae West, couldn't be spotted. But he wasn't. For a long time, his wife lived in hope that he'd been picked up by the other side. But he hadn't been. He died that day. He shouldn't have gone then. His number wasn't really up yet.'

Sorties lasted between forty-five to fifty minutes on average. RAF pilots flew about three or four or more during the height of the battle. Exhausting day followed exhausting day, beginning at 0330 hours. There could be a pause for breakfast at about 0800 and there was a traditional slack time between 1300 to 1600. Stand-by alternated between action until 2130 or the onset of darkness. Pilots often preferred not to talk much on landing, content to simply sit and unwind, to begin mentally generating further reserves of courage. Allan Wright accepted 'that God will do with me what He wills'. When he prayed, 'I daren't ask to come right through. I just ask for "give me tomorrow" and when tomorrow came, and that night I was still there, I'd ask for the next day.' Complete unadulterated relief came with the final day's landing. Geoffrey Wellum described how:

Dusk is mauve and purple, its not red and you're coming in and had it at the end of the day, its all quiet. Smoke coming up from the chimneys in cottages, and you feel a sort of unknown presence, a feeling of tremendous peace. So much so you feel there is something there, of course there isn't. You've only got a small cockpit and when you look around, there's nobody there – or is there? I dunno, but fighter pilots know what I'm talking about. Then you get a sense of beautiful loneliness and think, I've got to get down because my mates are on the ground.

'It was so lovely to see the ground crew,' he recalled. 'How did you get on, sir?' 'Well, I sprayed bullets all over Kent'. 'What again, sir?' They were elated if something had been shot down.

'It didn't pay to get too friendly because you learned very quickly that the changeover was rather rapid,' recalled ground crew George Wood. 'Somebody is there today, you talk to them, and they're not there the next day, they're dead, gone missing – they're gone and you get a new face comes in.' Affection between pilots and ground crew varied. Survival beyond the norm cemented relationships, however reluctant. Ground crew became adept at forecasting this, based on their close observations of how well the pilot handled his aircraft, the performance on take-off and landing. 'He's either a pudding or he's a good pilot,' remarked Wood. But trainees were short-coursed to replenish losses and these were immediately apparent. 'You know in your own mind,' Wood observed 'that some of them should never have been there.'

Death was reluctantly discussed on RAF bases. 'I don't think it would have done any good to brood on that in the unit or the certain circumstances we found ourselves in,' explained Sergeant Pilot 'Bam' Bamburger. They kept it to themselves. 'Chaps baling out and their parachutes not opening, chaps on fire, seeing your mates burning and things like that,' reflected Geoffrey Wellum, 'yes – it's not easy.' 'I was having a bath the next night and I realised Pat was not going to be coming back, I was never going to see him at all,' recalled Allan Wright. 'It got to me, and I wept, I must say, the only time I ever cried. But after that – well – the best German is a dead one.' Across the Channel the Luftwaffe were more Wagnerian, sentimentally setting an empty place at the dinner table in memoriam. Not so the RAF, someone had simply 'gone for a Burton', commented Bamburger. 'That was it – they'd had it.'

Both sides lived their perceived short lives to the full. 'In the evening we were in the pub as a unit, as a squadron, or what was left of us,' recalled Geoffrey Wellum. 'Who's missing?' might be asked. 'Pilot Officer X,' 'Who is Pilot Officer X?' Wellum arched his eyebrows to reinforce the point. 'Oh, he arrived last night.' Wendy Webster, a WAAF working at RAF Lindholme, remembered the emotionally charged atmosphere. 'Air crew had priority over everything, including sex,' she remarked. 'There was this feeling that they lived for the moment, so if a WAAF went with one of the air crew then it was definitely a body and soul job – he wanted the lot because he was a pilot and might not be here tomorrow.' Many were out four nights a week, as Flight Lieutenant Peter Brothers explained. 'Quite a number of the chaps used to nip off in the evenings to Kit-Kat or night clubs, spend the night roistering and come back and fall asleep in a deck-chair waiting to be scrambled.' Brothers got his life organised, aspirin 'that would knock me out completely and sleep like a dog', then Benzedrine from the doctor in the morning 'and now I was back on the ball again'. An infusion of pure oxygen, inhaled prior to take off was the final head-clearing remedy.

Well before the end of the Battle of Britain Winston Churchill praised the RAF, claiming 'Never in the field of human conflict was so much owed by so many to so few.' One anonymous pilot wag responded immediately, 'I thought he was talking about our mess bill!' It did, however, strike a chord throughout the country. Flight Lieutenant Alan Deere with 54 Squadron recalled what a 'hellish day' it had been, talking with his friend George Gribble. 'I heard what Churchill said about the many and the few' and said 'by Christ he can say that again – there aren't many of us left.' Gribble did not survive. There was most certainly a universal feeling of gratitude. 'We were heroes to the people and were greeted and treated as such – they bought us drinks,' announced Anthony Bartley. Nursing sister Mary Godson treating Dr Archibald McIndoe's 'Guinea-Pig' burns patients recalled their total resolve to return to action. Richard Hillary, who wrote a famous wartime book about his fighter pilot experience, she remembered 'was bitter about his disfigurement' but he went back and was killed. 'They were all so brave and ready to go back, their aim was not to get well again, but to be able to go back.' She recognised it much later as patriotism, which was not remarkable then. 'They were fighting to save England, everyone dreaded that Germany would take over.' Nobody could foresee what might happen. 'We did think they might,' she recalled. 'It had happened to Poland and France, yes, I was warned Britain might fall and we were the next step. Why should we escape when others had not?'

Major Graf von Kielmansegg with the 1st Panzer Division based near Orleans was summoned from a local cinema on 28 August to report to his Chief of Staff. Shot-up returning aircraft bespoke obvious Luftwaffe difficulties in achieving air superiority, but he was convinced this summons meant 'we were finally going to be told that Sea Lion had been given the green light'. 'Are we on our way?' he asked. He was told to sit down. 'Yes, we're on our way,' the Chief of Staff replied, 'but not to England – to East Prussia.' Sea Lion, von Kielmansegg appreciated, 'was a dead duck'.

Frederick Winterbotham, working in British Intelligence, had access to Ultra the top-secret decoding of German high level signals radio traffic. Having detected signs of preparations for a possible German invasion of Russia, it was calculated that the invasion of England must occur by mid- September at the latest or not at all. An innocuous signal was intercepted directing that air loading bays in Holland were to be dismantled. Winterbotham had to brief at a subsequent conference General Hastings Ismay, linking the Service Chiefs of Staff, Air Chief Sir Cyril Newall and his superior, Sir Stewart Menzies, the head of the Secret Intelligence Services. 'I pointed out that if these loading bays were dismantled it meant they would not have proper air support and that in fact Hitler had given up the idea of invasion.' Newall, on being asked to comment by Churchill, agreed: 'that is entirely our view, with the dismantling of this, the invasion is off.' Winterbotham recalled the impact on the Service Chiefs who sat back surprised in their chairs, 'they didn't know what this was about.' Churchill apparently 'smiled and pulled out a big cigar and lit it'.

On 14 September Hitler postponed the pre-decision date for a Sea Lion launch until 17 September. It was then decided the order issue would be delayed 'until further notice', interpreted throughout the

Wehrmacht as being 'for good'. On 19 September the order was issued to cease assembling. 'Churchill's Moat' would not be breached, Hitler had turned his attention eastwards.

The people of Britain had no idea the Battle of Britain was over. Indeed the term was not yet being used. The Blitz was to continue for four long years. One correspondent recalled a Stepney man reading a newspaper headline 'East End Faces Hitler With Courage And Humour', and adding, 'it's about all we have got to face him with.'

6

COMMANDO RAID

THE COMMANDOS

In the half light of dawn on Boxing Day 1941 the German look-out south of Vaagso by the fjord shore spotted seven blacked-out ships gliding silently past. It was unfortunate to be on duty the morning after the festivities celebrated in town. Christmas was a sentimental time for the German soldier away from home.

A detachment of fifty soldiers from Regiment 341 of the 181 Infantry Division had arrived to share the holiday leave. Half were veterans of the campaign fought in northern Norway the previous year. After two and a half years of Axis victories in Europe, America and Japan had entered the World War and two weeks before the German advance had stalled in front of Moscow. Vaagso port formed part of the island chain that embraced the northern Norwegian coastline, hundreds of miles from the nearest point of conflict. The English had 'shot their bolt' and German soldiers celebrated Christmas secure in the knowledge they were serving on the periphery of the war.

The look-out telephoned Hauptmann (Captain) Butziger who commanded the battery of four 75mm guns on Maaloy Island, directly opposite Vaagso town, but there was no reply. He was shaving and his orderly continued to industriously buff his boots. He next tried the harbour commander's office and reported seven blacked-out ships were in the fjord but was told not to worry because a merchant convoy was expected. When the frustrated look-out persisted these did not look like merchant ships he was accused of being drunk. It was Christmas and a quiet sector. Persevering, the look-out despatched a signal to the naval signal station on Maaloy Island, a hundred metres off the town. 'Unidentified warships entering fjord,' he transmitted. The signaller, uncertain how to handle this curious information, rowed across to the town and personally delivered it to the Naval Headquarters in south Vaagso. Had he alerted the army battery, he was asked, on the island from which he had come? 'No, sir,' he responded, 'it's an army battery and this is a naval signal.'

On board the sinister blacked-out ships were over 500 British Commandos. As Alec Johnson, a demolition team member from 3 Commando, recalled: 'It was Christmas. It's a good time to raid, you see, because soldiers are invariably sleeping in after the night before, or, you know – having a drink or something.'

Forward looking strategists soon recognised that to hit back at the Germans and regain Europe would mean seaborne attacks against enemy-held territory. Lieutenant Colonel Dudley Clarke, the Military Assistant to the Chief of the Imperial General Staff (CIGS) Sir John Dill, conceived of and proposed the idea of guerrilla warfare to initiate this. Churchill enthusiastically embraced the idea of 'storm troops' able to harass the enemy coast and Section MO9 was set up at the War Office. CIGS decided the new force would be called 'Commandos' after the Boer bands that had so successfully harassed the British during the Boer War at the turn of the century. Clarke was influenced by his Middle East experience of the Arab Rebellion in Palestine in 1936 when regular Imperial troops were bogged down fighting irregular insurgents. On 14 June 1940 a 'Commander of Raiding Operations on coasts in enemy occupation' was appointed. Appreciation that all three services would be involved to prosecute such operations resulted in the formation of a Directorate of Combined Operations, directly responsible to a Committee of the Chiefs of Staff and Minister for Defence.

Three weeks after Dunkirk the first amateurish raid was conducted between Boulogne and Berch during which Clarke, the innovator, was wounded. As the four air-sea rescue launches transporting the raiders straggled back into Folkestone harbour they were initially denied entry and then the bedraggled-looking occupants were arrested on suspicion of being deserters.

Lessons were assimilated and the new raiding force set up and organised. Commanding officers were specially selected and these in turn chose their own junior officers who were permitted to tour British Army units to select the best men. Recruits were not told what they were volunteering for; they had to be fit, able to swim, not prone to seasickness and be ready to cross country by day or night and live off the land and engage in 'scouting' activities. Service would be dangerous and personnel not up to standard were to be returned to their units. Churchill was insisting to the War Office by August that 'we must develop the Storm Troop or Commando idea' and 'we must have at least 10,000 of these small "bands of brothers" who will be capable of lightning action'.

'I wanted cheerful officers, not groaners,' declared Lieutenant Colonel John Durnford-Slater, who was tasked with setting up 3 Commando. 'A good physique was important, but size was not. I looked for intelligence and keenness.' Frustration at inactivity and a desire to get back at the enemy in any practical way provided the motive to join. Tom Sherman with 2 Commando recalled 'the standards were so high we'd cream off the best in the regiments'. This understandably caused rancour and inter-unit jealousy. 'There were COs who refused to allow people to volunteer,' Sherman added. Durnford-Slater interpreted the stuffiness of high commands as 'part of the 1940 mentality' that had already contributed to military failure. 'The War Office regarded us as Winston Churchill's private army and wanted to abolish us,' he commented. Commando Lieutenant Michael Burn felt the antagonism: 'the regular army were doing their best to get us disbanded, they hated us, some of them,' he declared, 'we were a nuisance.'

Commandos attracted unconventional characters who wished to reverse the perception of failure in the army, and saw they would be the men to do it. 'Everywhere almost, we were in retreat,' remembered Michael Burns, who served with 2 Commando, 'and people were really becoming negative and Churchill wanted something which would be successful for aggression.' Newly joined Peter Young was adamant: 'we were overrating the Germans.' Having fought in France he appreciated: 'If you took them by surprise, they would run away; if you opened fire on them, they would take cover; if you shot them they bled. In a word they were human.'

Captain John Smale had joined the army in 1936 and survived Dunkirk as a company commander and received an influx of young boys aged eighteen to replace heavy losses. 'After working with wonderful and efficient soldiers, all reservists with about five or six years regular service in India, and a full and true sense of service, I found it frustrating to find myself with these young boys learning elementary training on Bren-guns.' He felt he should do more and joined 3 Commando. Commandos were soon actively training amid the invasion scare climate of August 1940 and caused some consternation to holiday-makers. 'Our arrival from the sea usually caused grave panic among the mothers and children enjoying themselves in the sun on the beach,' admitted John Durnford-Slater, even though 'we invariably sent an officer on ahead to warn them.'

Two raids were conducted in 1940 and ten in 1941 as the Commando organisation expanded. Raids started as pin-pricks and increased in severity and scale. Each Commando was initially configured with ten troops each of three officers and forty-seven other ranks. Very soon lurid press accounts of butcher-and-bolt deeds produced an image at variance to facts. Commando John Gibson from Edinburgh recalled how: 'The media took over and spread stories of derring-do. But that was never the reality of the Commandos – the skulduggery, devil-may-care, gangster-warfare kind of thing. That was never the style.'

Training was fearsome but designed to inculcate controlled aggression. Commando instructor James Dunning explained: 'the key element was getting them to convince themselves they could do anything. You can only do that in the military sense if you train people to overcome their inner fears and give them supreme confidence.' Bill 'Tiger' Watson with 2 Commando, for example, regarded his toggle rope – used as a climbing aid – six-foot long with an eye at one end and wooden grip at the other as infinitely more useful than the stiletto Commando knife. 'Though taught the grisly techniques of its use in combat, as far as we were concerned, it lay in its concealed pocket as an emblem only.'

Raiding is part of the fabric of British history, from the Angles, the Saxons, the Jutes, and the Vikings with their longships, on down the centuries through the fire-ship raids conducted against the Spanish Armada and Napoleonic fleets to the costly raid against Zeebrugge in 1918. In the Second World War the Commandos inherited this tradition and were seen as equally fearsome. Commando Harry Sullivan recalled:

Unarmed combat sounds horrible now, but I and most of my friends felt that we and our families were going to get killed. Our way of life was going to be totally destroyed. So when people taught me how to disable a man with a knife, I didn't rear back in horror. You know: how to cut his tendons, how to cut his throat, how to stop thinking you didn't kill a sitting target – and how to welcome a sitting target. If the fellow was sitting with his back to you, you were in luck.

There was a war on, he who hesitated with the knife, cosh or whatever weapon came to hand was lost. Commandos were taught to kill and disable with properly targeted and delivered blows. Durnford-Slater revealed the extent to which perception was applied to identify men capable of fighting this way.

I always avoided anyone who talked too much, and soon learned a lesson in this when a fine athletic-looking fellow who had taken part in many sports proved useless and boastful and had to be discharged. We never enlisted anybody who looked like the tough-guy criminal type, as I considered that this sort of man would be a coward in the battle.

Awareness continued during and after battle. He addressed his Commandos after their first hard-fought raid and then added: 'a very few of you didn't like the Vaagso operation and must leave the unit forthwith.'

'I thought I was a fit young boy till I got there,' declared Alec Johnson when he turned up for his Commando selection course. 'You didn't walk or march, you did it at the double, you double-marched.' Conducted at Achnacarry, a remote location in northern Scotland, the course lasted twelve weeks initially before being cut to five. It covered offensive demolitions, all aspects of close combat and opposed assault landings using boats and climbing equipment and was often conducted under live fire duress. Forty Commandos died on the course. Tactical endurance schemes covered everything from small-unit battle drills and ambushes to living off the land. Johnson described the pace:

You had to do 30 mile route marches in about 10 hours with a 50lb pack on your back. When you came in you had to start fighting each other with your fists, and the chap next to you would have to have a go at you and you him. I always hoped I would get my friend who was about my size rather than a six foot five inch giant. Sometimes our feet – you couldn't get your socks off – the blood had congealed.

Training encompassed abseiling and climbing to achieve those surprise beach landings in difficult locations, which were unlikely to be covered by enemy fire. 'When I see them abseiling now,' Johnson remarked, 'I have to smile'. They've got these harnesses on. You can't fail, you can just hang. You can't fall, rather, we just had the rope wrapped around us and if you were silly enough to let go it was three weeks in hospital.'

Or worse, as Niall Thomson, a Commando instructor recalled, when seven men drowned after their rope snapped on the death slide. 'They were blown off' by live explosives into a river and 'they weren't able to make it'. Living off the land meant, as Johnson explained, 'we learned to eat insects, worms and things like this – they didn't do any harm.' It was these shared excesses during training that established an esprit de corps, eventually rewarded at the end of the course with the award of the distinctive green Commando beret, but not in the early days. 'Cos at the time,' Johnson explained, 'we said no, it would have just meant trouble. People would say, "Right, Commandos – let's pick on them!"'

Speed marching promoted determination and developed endurance. One unit achieved sixty-three miles in nineteen hours and another marched up Mount Snowdon and down again in seventeen and a half hours. As Commando instructor James Dunning pointed out: 'Determination is the most important thing, even on speed marches, where our great aim was to get the chaps over 15 miles in full kit in just under three hours. Finish up with the assault course and firing and then leisurely up to the top of Ben-Nevis, mentally equipping them to do anything.'

Raids conducted before the end of 1941 were mainly small-scale and met little resistance. This meant non-stop harsh training for the majority of Commandos with little prospect of actual combat. 'We had been looking for action, you know,' recalled twenty-one-year-old George Parsons, who had recently completed his demolition course. There had 'been a lot of time training and people were getting a bit irritable, you know, they wanted some action'. Brigadier J Charles Haydon, commanding the new Special Service Brigade, recognised the growing irritation with postponements and 'being harried from pillar to post, onto ships and off them, into billets and out of them, and so on'. There was disquiet. 'In short, a sense of frustration,' he admitted. 'It seemed that we were *never* going to see a German,' complained Lieutenant Peter Young, and 'the fire-eaters – who were legion – vowed they would go back to their units.'

There was more to raiding than swashbuckling adventurous landings, lethal though they were at the small-scale tactical level. Raiding in 1941 was constrained by the realisation that larger and more important targets would be heavily defended and were therefore best avoided. Improved Commando assault techniques and the advent of specialised landing craft encouraged the selection of more ambitious objectives that would also require naval and air force support to achieve an opposed landing. Such combined operations required seamless cooperation between land, sea and air forces, complex procedures. The arrival of over 500 Commandos slipping unobserved into the Vaagso Fjord at dawn on Boxing Day 1941 was the first indication of a previously unappreciated capability to both sides. It was to be even more forcefully applied against the port of Saint-Nazaire in March 1942.

Both targets, Vaagso and Saint-Nazaire, were economically important and had strategic significance. The northern Norway strike was designed to inflict damage on fish oil stocks which were vital for the manufacture of glycerine explosives and as vitamin supplements for German U-boat crews. It would also promote the wasteful garrisoning of German troops, better employed elsewhere. Saint-Nazaire possessed the only dry dock on the French Atlantic seaboard able to house and maintain the German pocket battleship *Tirpitz* which, after the damage her sister ship *Bismarck* had inflicted, was of strategic significance in the hard fought convoy battles of the Atlantic. Likewise Hitler's Europe could be shown to be vulnerable, with implications for the French. An examination of the various sequential stages of a Commando raid, utilising these two examples, gives some indication of the Commando experience during this bleak period of the war, when Britain was obliged to rely upon her own devices to strike back at the continent.

RAID PLANNING TO FINAL APPROACH

Security and the detailed combined arms coordination planning needed to conduct such operations meant their commanders were granted scant time to rehearse and prepare. Barely three weeks were permitted for Vaagso with little allowance for the likelihood that poor December weather might well impede practical raid rehearsals. Complex navy and air force requirements had to be worked out. RAF bombers needed two hours to transit the 350-mile approach to provide fire support and cover over an objective that took the Royal Navy as many *days* to reach and to arrive at precisely the same time. Enemy airfields had to be neutralised so that the navy could shoot the Commandos on to their objectives. Bad weather delayed the Royal Navy who would be approaching the objective even as the aircraft in support took off from England.

The Saint-Nazaire commanders had one month to finalise the plan. A converted US lend-lease destroyer, the *Campbeltown*, loaded with four and a half tons of explosives, was to ram the dry dock caisson gates at Saint-Nazaire and disembark Commandos alongside others transported by motor launches (MLs). They were to carry out demolitions in the port area to fully incapacitate the dry dock. Only eighteen days were allocated to convert the ship from a four-funnel lend-lease US destroyer to a two-funnel silhouette resembling the German *Möwe* small-destroyer class. Armour plating was erected against the bridge and alongside the decks to protect the Commandos during an anticipated suicide run-in. Some of the delay was caused by Royal Navy and RAF reluctance to participate in a scheme predicted to have little chance of success. The newly appointed Director of Combined Operations, Vice-Admiral Lord Louis Mountbatten insisted with characteristic under-statement that 'the fact it is regarded as impossible makes it possible', rationalising 'the Germans would never think we would attempt it'. After the debacle of the exercise dummy run conducted at Devonport naval yard labelled a 'fiasco' some planners might have concurred. Almost everything possible went wrong and the defenders triumphed.

Tactical handling of small boats or assault craft during a raid was vital. The Vaagso raiders were equipped with the new Higgins armoured landing craft, that could carry half a troop or thirty men apiece. These disembarked from a retractable drawbridge ramp in the bows. They could only drive at 6 knots, during which time they had to approach a hostile shore unseen, land troops under fire, then stand-off and await the re-embarkation phase once the Commandos had finished their mission; a vulnerable moment, pausing under control in hostile waters. Both raids relied on darkness for the approach. The Vaagso raid, launched at dawn, synchronised with smoke screen and bombing support from RAF Hampden aircraft.

The Saint-Nazaire scheme was to utilise the 18-knots speed of the MLs to run the gauntlet of fire from both sides of the Loire estuary alongside the destroyer to get inside the harbour defences through bluff and shock surprise. Commandos embarked fifteen apiece where there was only space for twelve men on wooden launches festooned with additional fuel tanks. Speed was their only protection. Frank Arkle, the First Lieutenant on ML 177, recalled painting their launch in great zig-zag pastel colours to cloak it against the anticipated mass of searchlights. However, during the Devonport dummy run they found their boats 'shone like diamonds' in the glare of the port searchlights and 'we spent the next two days repainting them all over in the famous battleship grey'.

Commandos were task-organised into small groups for a raid. Assault or attack groups of twelve opened the way for demolition teams of four, six or twelve, depending on the mission. Demolition personnel carried pre-prepared explosive charges the size of infantry small packs with plunge igniters to initiate detonation. Small groups of four to six men formed protection parties that acted as bodyguards to the demolition teams at work. This organisation was in stark contrast to infantry platoons of thirty that formed conventional rifle companies of 120 or more men in infantry battalions. Task-organised meant that specific teams were given the requisite men and demolition materials to do the job. This organisational structure reflected the individual initiative raiders were expected to display in going about their tasks. 'People were left to make up their own minds,' explained Lieutenant Michael Burns. This was not the hierarchical and closely supervised *modus operandi* that characterised the traditionally organised regular army. 'In a war anybody, everybody could be killed and what decides the action may be the action of a private soldier who is left to command a trench.' Burn emphasised, 'we were all individuals', reflecting 'the feeling we were given was that every one of us might be as important as a brigadier.'

Such independence was inculcated from the start. Commandos were not housed in barracks, they received 6s 8d (36p) per day as an allowance for 'digs' in a nearby town. Neither were they closely supervised. 'You weren't shouted at,' declared Tom Sherman with 2 Commando, 'there wasn't any of this shouting and bullying and anything that you got in the regular army.' Reliance was placed on initiative. The lodging system reduced the administrative 'tail' of a Commando to the minimum, enabling it to focus on training. It further aided security when a unit relocated prior to an operation. 'Instead of saying parade tomorrow on the main square in Weymouth,' explained Commando instructor James Dunning, 'it might be parade tomorrow at 10 o'clock in the market place at Dorchester – and find your own bloody way there!' Self-sufficiency made the Commando a tenacious and unpredictable opponent. They could continue the momentum of a raid attack despite officer and NCO casualties.

Security demands in effect reduced eve of operation concerns because soldiers were excessively busy completing last minute administrative tasks – or so wound up at inactivity that when action beckoned it was welcomed. The numerous small groups contributing to a team task had to coordinate with each other and rehearse their individual roles among each other to perfection. Small arms, primarily Thompson sub-machine-guns, the .303 Lee Enfield 4 Mark 1 rifle and other weapons, such as throwing knives, cheese wire for silent strangulation, black-jacks, coshes and bronze knuckle-dusters, alongside 3-inch mortars, explosives and ammunition, had to be stockpiled, cleaned, checked and double-checked. The thought of action raised tense expectancy rather than fear and the primary frustration was that of postponement or cancellation.

The Boxing Day Vaagso raiders were delayed for twenty-four hours in the Shetland Islands through bad weather. Lieutenant Peter Young described how: 'The usual rumours were rife – the whole show had been cancelled, the raid had been postponed because the Pope wouldn't think it cricket if we fought on Christmas Day and so forth.

As usual there were fire-eaters who proclaimed that if the raid did not come off they would go back to their units.'

A raid is a calculated and cold-blooded act of aggression. There are few civilian-life comparisons. The nearest is the tension associated with the start of a boxing or rugby match, when one anticipates some pain, or a free-fall parachute descent, but there nobody dies. 'Tense I suppose would be the thing,' admitted Commando Bill 'Tiger' Watson, 'and anticipation – yes.' Commandos glancing at their fellows as they boarded boats for the final approach *knew* that somebody was going to be seriously mutilated or die. Peter Young was impressed by his 2nd Troop Sergeant Culling who was compellingly fatalistic. 'I am afraid of damn all,' was what he said, 'quietly and without any trace of boasting. He was as good as his word.' The Saint-Nazaire raid was predictably going to result in heavy casualties and produced mixed feelings. 'You were doing all this heavy training and nothing's happening, so very frustrating,' recalled Eric de la Torre with 3 Commando. 'So when we were finally briefed, we thought, well, this is going to be *something*.' Bill 'Tiger' Watson with 2 Commando 'thought we would get away with it' and chuckled as he reminisced 'that I would be wounded romantically and a beautiful nurse would look after me in hospital – I was very young.' Others, such as Corran Purdon with 12 Commando, had been training indefinitely on demolitions, 'so when we found we were going to blow up the dock installations at Saint-Nazaire, there was I suppose a feeling of elation.'

The biggest fear was to show it. 'The thought that crosses your mind,' claimed Eric de la Torre, 'is I hope that I am going to do my part without being overcome by fear.' Corran Purdon with 12 Commando remembered that as he chatted among his demolition team about 'what we are going to do', at the back of his mind was the thought, 'my God, I hope that I'm not going to show fear in front of my men if I'm frightened.' Shame was a potent stabilising emotion. Letters were left behind addressed to the next of kin labelled 'To be posted in the event of failure to return'. Michael Burns recalled Sergeant Bill Gibson. 'I remember seeing his face and I knew he was going to be killed.' Surviving veterans often and without prompting remark upon the moral differences of this age compared to their own. A unique characteristic of the wartime generation was its closeness to and recognition that death was an unavoidable consequence of war. Bill Gibson's final letter to his father encapsulates their preparedness to serve selflessly. 'My dearest Dad' his letter began:

> By the time you get this I shall be one of the many who have sacrificed their unimportant lives for what little ideals we may have . . . I can only hope that by laying down my life the generations to come might in some way remember us and benefit by what we have done . . . at a time like this, I turn to you Dad and God. I hope that there will be peace for everyone soon.
>
> My love to everyone. I'll remember you. Your loving son Bill.

Bill Gibson failed to return. Eric de la Torre felt, 'somehow I always thought it was unlucky to write last letters to your parents.' 'No – my attitude was *I'm coming back!*'

Men going into action tend to focus on their surroundings with the intensity of cinema-goers looking through three-dimensional viewing spectacles for the first time. Nature's detail becomes finely etched with a totality that is understandable only to those who have experienced the near proximity of death. 'It was a terrific sight, you know, when dawn came,' remembered Alec Johnson on the Vaagso raid, 'because we were silently coming up this fjord'. 'A spectacular passage,' described Lieutenant Colonel John Durnford-Slater, 'between great snow covered hills.' Major Robert Henriques, witnessing the scene from the bridge of the cruiser HMS *Kenya* gliding across the motionless waters of the Vaagso fjord, thought, 'it was a very eerie sensation entering the fjord in absolute silence and very slowly.' Every domestic detail could be picked out in the growing light of a majestic dawn, whose stillness was about to be shattered by the violence of war.

> I wondered what was going to happen for it seemed that the ship had lost her proper element, that she was no longer a free ship at sea. Occasionally I saw a little hut with a light burning in it and I wondered whether that light would be suddenly switched off, which would mean that the enemy had spotted us or whether it would continue to burn as some Norwegian fisherman got out of bed, stretched himself and went off to his nets.

Landing craft were lowered into the water at forty-minutes before H-Hour. The first light of dawn began to reflect on the hilltops, as blacks in the fjord below became formless but visible greys. Movement is detectable in such light and groups of landing craft motoring towards their objectives at 6 knots peeled off in sub-groups as they neared their landing sites. Henriques observing from the bridge recalled they 'could just be seen through glasses, black beetles crawling in the shadow of the mountains up the black waters of the fjord'. Total surprise was achieved at Vaagso. Aircraft were heard overhead and tracer arced up to meet the sound in the distance. With an ear-splitting succession of cracks the cruiser's guns opened up, followed by the subsidiary crackling of star shells spluttering over Vaagso and Maaloy Island. It was H-Hour.

H-HOUR

Few plans in war survive the crossing of the start line prior to an attack. Remarkably, the RAF Hampden bombers arrived on time at the end of their 350-mile journey and skimmed the fjord surface at 200 mph at low level to drop smoke bombs to cloak the Commando run-in. One aircraft disabled by anti-aircraft fire dropped a phosphorous bomb inside one of the lead landing craft and plunged into the fjord. 'Bursting, the phosphorous inflicted terrible burns amongst the men' in such a confined space recalled Lieutenant John Durnford-Slater. 'People were jumping out into the sea on fire and their clothing on fire,' recalled Alec Johnson with Group 2, 'and it wasn't a very good beginning for it.' Half a troop was taken out by an own goal even before landing. The craft burst into flames and 'grenades, explosives, and small arms ammunition were detonated in a mad mixture of battle noises,' observed Durnford-Slater. Men were shocked at the immersion in freezing water but fortunately the craft was near the shore. Phosphorous burned the skin for so long as it was exposed to air and caused horrific injuries. The landing craft was pushed out of the way, burning and spluttering, into the deep water of the fjord.

Commando raids depended upon surprise and at Vaagso it was complete. The German four-75mm gun battery on Maaloy Island was devastated by the naval bombardment, while the RAF smokescreen cloaked the amphibious approach. In one of the lead boats approaching Vaagso town was Eric de la Torre who was Durnford-Slater's radio-operator. 'Stand-by,' he heard, 'and we touched down, and we all rushed off.' Jumping over rocks, 'the first thing I saw was a friend rolling about in the snow with his battledress smouldering', one of the survivors from the stricken landing craft. There were a few bursts of machine-gun fire and they broke into the town's edge. John Woollett with 6 Commando recalled the successful shock impact of this synchronised arrival:

> The attack came in and then just as we were coming round in sight, in came the Air Force and blotted us out. And again, the timing of the whole operation was such, I mean – the Germans never heard about it and they didn't realise. They realised that there was an attack from the air and went into their bunkers. By the time they came out we were there.

'It was one of those things that worked perfectly,' he emphasised. The Germans, situated so far north, had no inkling at all of likely landings. Unrehearsed, their officers were not in control. 'We were straight on up over the thing,' claimed Woollett, as the demolition teams clambered over the battery positions. 'The Germans were just coming out of their defences just as we were arriving' and quickly succumbed in their dazed state to the ruthless assault.

Surprise can be a two-edged weapon in an unpredictable engagement. Once the Commandos had landed on the island, Woollett observed, 'it wasn't the same on the main shore, the main part of it', Vaagso town across the hundred-metre channel. German soldiers in the process of forming damage control groups to deal with the consequences of the air-raid that had barely passed overhead suddenly realised there were British soldiers ashore. They were not in their defence positions on the shoreline but in the town under their officers. 'They were spread out in the town,' recalled Woollett, 'and quite a nasty battle took place down the streets.' Commando raids were short, sharp and fast-moving high-intensity engagements by design, they did not anticipate set-piece engagements.

The Saint-Nazaire raid relied upon darkness to penetrate the Loire estuary and traverse treacherous sandbanks to achieve surprise. H-Hour was a rolling event, dependent upon when the enemy opened fire or when the dry dock gate was rammed. Massive U-boat pens were under construction nearby. Admiral Karl Dönitz, the Commander in Chief of Germany's submarine forces, had asked his flotilla chief at this strategic French Atlantic port what he would do if the British mounted a raid. He was assured emergency plans had been prepared, but no one seriously anticipated such a raid at Saint-Nazaire. 'I shouldn't be too sure of that,' Dönitz tersely replied. There were over eighty artillery and anti-aircraft guns securing the Loire estuary and 5,000 troops in the town. The Germans could be forgiven a degree of complacency as the flotilla of seventeen small craft and the destroyer *Campbeltown* stole along the estuary in a mile long column two gunboats abreast.

An RAF deception bombing raid, synchronised with the assault bombing singly to avoid French civilian casualties, alerted the Germans. Kapitän zur See (Captain) Mecke, the German Naval Flak Brigade commander, noticed this unusual behaviour and signalled Wehrmacht defence units at midnight that 'the conduct of the enemy aircraft is inexplicable and indicates suspicion of parachute landings'. Only the previous month a British parachute raid at Bruneval along the Channel coast had resulted in the capture of sensitive radar equipment. Official reputations were conceivably at stake. Reports then reached Mecke at 0120 hours that a force of small vessels proceeding up the estuary had been challenged. Korvettenkapitän (Commander) Dieckmann ordered his estuary batteries to stand by to engage naval targets and the anti-aircraft batteries began to lower their guns to the shore-defence role. Mecke issued a warning order 'Beware landing' and searchlights were switched on. Totally illuminated in mid-channel, the column driving purposefully onward had two miles to run.

Bluff and deception was part of the Commando raid *modus operandi* to achieve surprise and close upon its objective. Steel plating was erected along the starboard side of *Campbeltown* and behind this lay Commando assault and demolition groups. 'The run-in was desperately exciting,' recalled Lieutenant John Roderick with 3 Commando, commanding an assault group, 'the suspense over the haggling about who or what we were, the opening fire from the banks, the silence and then the final opening up of all the guns.' Two shore stations challenged the ships. 'Proceeding up harbour in accordance with orders,' was the response. Some shots were fired by the nervous gunners, which was immediately followed by the appropriate return signal for ships being fired at by friendly forces.

During this nervous stand-off the troops crowded inside the vulnerable wooden MLs felt appreciably naked. Michael Burns condemned the MLs as 'death traps' in retrospect and the decision to employ them as 'disgraceful'. But he philosophically accepted the prevailing view 'at the time we didn't think much, we just thought "Oh well, it's all they've got – we've got to do it and that's it."' Naval crew suspected what was coming. Frank Arkle, the First Lieutenant on ML 177, remembered his friend Mark Rodier confiding to him on the bridge as they stole along the estuary, 'making provision for letting his mother and father have his belongings back when we got back from Saint-Nazaire'. Arkle tried to brush it aside. 'What is all this about?' he argued, but his friend 'had absolute conviction that he was not going to get out alive'. Signal wrangling gained them a further mile before, as Arkle described, 'all hell broke loose'.

Once the ruse was exposed, speed and the violence of the assault was the only option. *Campbeltown* raised its white ensign battle flag and the race for the last mile, the final six minutes was on. The flotilla laid down such a weight of fire itself, supported by eight 20mm guns and the 12-pounder on the bows of *Campbeltown* that some German guns faltered, and searchlights were hit. Roderick 'was filled with admiration for the gun crews who suffered severe casualties, I think'. It was a two-way exchange of fire, with many of the shore batteries likely convinced this was a seaborne fight, seeking to inflict damage rather than land. Frank Arkle saw: 'There were tracer bullets going in every direction, a very colourful sight because the British tracers were all orange in colour and the Germans were all a blue-green. Very pretty! The shells weren't quite so pretty when they started to fly around the place!'

Harbours have numerous inlets and entrances. Under a bewildering intensity of fire and searchlight glare *Campbeltown*'s captain had to pick out the entrance to the Avant Port, avoid this, pass the East Jetty and Old Dock and look for his final checkpoint, which was a lighthouse at the end of the Old Mole. Once located, he had to pull out to skirt the

Dawn, Commandos about to land at Vaagso, Norway, Boxing Day, 1941.

Commandos flushed out resistance by setting fire to strong points during the
Vaagso raid.

HMS *Campbeltown* successfully rammed the Saint-Nazaire dry-dock gate; here examined by curious German soldiers shortly before she exploded.

A mortally wounded Commando surrounded by his captors at the Saint-Nazaire dockside.

obstruction and select the correct ramming course slightly right of another inlet. Corran Purdon with one of the demolition groups on board remembered, 'there was an awful lot of stuff hitting *Campbeltown* and absolutely hitting the poor MLs, but *Campbeltown* was the big target.' The port line of MLs began to peel off heading for the Old Mole, which had two fortified gun emplacements upon it, flaying them with fire.

Commando Bob Wright recalled, 'the air was filled with things that whistled, hummed and shrieked.' Commander Beattie captaining the destroyer suddenly realised an error, having chosen the wrong lighthouse, and corrected. She surged through the water at more than 20 knots, with little chance of rapidly responding to slow steering. 'I remember a red-hot shell passing through the wardroom and going on out,' recalled Corran Purdon, 'it didn't explode.' Down below in the engine room the stokers were shovelling coal into her furnaces up until the very last moment, despite the cacophony of bangs, concussions and objects shrieking by, to maintain a ramming head of steam.

Campeltown's decks were lashed with fire. Grimly enduring this storm behind the armoured deck-plates, Lieutenant John Roderick saw his assault group taking casualties around him. He reached out 'to find whether Corporal Finch was still in position following a particularly dirty explosion'. Corporal Donaldson with one of the bamboo scaling ladders was already badly wounded and was to die when the fighting began. 'He was quite one of the nicest members of the troop,' Roderick remembered. 'A quiet soft spoken Scotsman with a charming smile and a most proficient soldier.' Roderick's men had large pans of ammunition fitted to their Bren-guns for the run-in when 'we fired at as many targets as we could make out'. Eric de la Torre was on one of the MLs running the fire gauntlet. 'You can't imagine all your senses being so alert, every sense – hearing, looking and your heart pumping.' Tracer sped over the launches and connected with huge oily explosions, the noise was indescribable as oil fires broke out around stricken MLs off the mole. 'It was the most exciting thing in my life,' de la Torre admitted.

Campbeltown ploughed through the anti-torpedo nets draped before the dry dock at 20 knots with sparks raining off from shell strikes, and smashed into the caisson entrance at 0134 hours. A plume of water ballast jetted into the air from the gates and the destroyer reared up as if biting the gate, as a forty-foot lower jaw appeared at the bottom of her bows which were torn out as if by a can-opener. Roderick was intrigued that 'the crash of the bows came with surprisingly little jolting'. She began to settle at the stern as water cocks were opened to flood her in place.

After the shock assault of H-Hour the fight-through and demolitions phase could begin.

RAID FIGHT-THROUGH AND DEMOLITIONS

The greatest problem raiding at night is to retain control. The Commando tactical organisation's sub-division into small and mutually supporting teams aided this. Assault groups overcame opposition and secured the target areas within which demolition teams worked with protectors. The Saint-Nazaire raiders did not blacken their faces and wore webbing blancoed white to aid recognition. But, as so often happened, plans did not survive the shock of H-Hour.

As Lieutenant John Roderick moved forward with his assault group to the bows of the *Campbeltown*, perched atop the dock gate, 'it was a bit of a shambles with many wounded chaps lying about the deck'. Corran Purdon with a demolition group recalled, 'we went up on deck and forward to the 12-pounder where there were a lot of dead bodies, I remember Johnny Proctor lying there with his leg blown off, cheering us on.' 'Flames met me in opening the Forward Companion way door,' described Roderick, 'and I had to shut it quickly.' Their bamboo ladders were damaged by gunshot so they had to innovate, using lengths of cable to clamber down on to the dock gate. This was not the composed and controlled way they would ideally wish to initiate the assault. Commando Bob Wright recalled:

When I came up on deck there was a brilliant flash and ear-shattering explosion and I felt a blow on my knee that felt like a sledgehammer and it knocked me to one side and I fell to the deck. I was lying there and somebody grasped my pack and pulled me on my feet and said, 'Are you all right, lad?' It was Major Copeland and he said, 'Bundle over the port side, don't hang around here, it's decidedly unhealthy.'

'Motor Launch 192 was the first ship to be hit,' claimed George Davidson with the 20th ML Flotilla. He need not have been on the raid, having accepted a transfer for parachute training, but decided at the last moment because 'they had an interesting party coming up'. The launch had been surging past the Old Mole: 'When we were completely stopped, I mean the machinery stopped, the boat was still moving. The engine room was on fire and instead of passing the Old Mole we ran into it.'

There was a German flak emplacement on the mole and stick grenades came raining down. Frank Arkle on ML 177 saw the port line of MLs turn in towards their landing points alongside the Old Mole and dockside. 'They started to get into some serious fire,' he recalled, 'and fire broke out on board on several of them unfortunately.' It was a stand-off at the dockside. German fire lacerated the approaching launches and stick grenades were tossed inside to finish them off. External fuel tanks burst apart in cascades of burning petrol, adding to the flashes, smoke and confusion along the landing points. Many of the ML-borne Commando groups were repelled. Demolition team member Eric de la Torre clung grimly to a life-raft, listening to a sailor sing out the hymn 'Oh God our help in ages past' as men burned and died in the water around him. Controlling the boats in the crucial stand-off phase prior to re-embarking the Commandos was not an option.

Some MLs did manage to get their Commandos ashore in the vicinity of the *Campbeltown*. Frank Arkle on ML 177 experienced 'a very funny feeling as they went ashore silently in their rubber boots and disappeared into the shadows on the dockside to do their duty'. His gun crews engaged positions on the Old Mole and they 'fired a lot of shots into these [U-boat] pens but we couldn't see what the results were because it was completely dark inside.' Any formed group that did penetrate the dockside area could be lethal. Lieutenant Stuart Chant, with four wounded Commandos, had only ninety seconds to negotiate the myriad of metal steps inside the dry dock pumping house before it blew. One of the naval ratings aboard ML 7 was deeply impressed with the results once they got their Commandos ashore. Their progress into the town of Saint-Nazaire was identifiable from the chain of fires and explosions that went off one by one. 'Once they got cracking,' he observed, 'they *did* get cracking.'

After they were ashore and into the confusing network of warehouses and quays the odds against the Commandos reduced in the sharply contested one-on-one skirmishes at which they excelled. Organised within tightly knit and self-contained groups with predetermined tasks, they could operate with more focused coordination than the Germans, uncertain whether a landing had occurred or not. The Germans lost control of the night and not until daylight could they organise and coordinate heavily-armed groups of sailors operating as infantry into counter-sweeps. Supported by lorry-borne anti-aircraft guns used in the ground role, they suppressed the small groups of Commandos that tried to break out through the town.

As in any urban fighting at night around dock installations John Roderick recalled 'there was and had been a hell of a lot of firing going on and it was difficult to pinpoint where it was coming from'. German reports of success around the mole were contradicted by the bedlam breaking out in the dock area behind them. 'There was a number of Nissan huts into which we threw grenades with the most terrific bangs,' recalled Roderick, 'and in another concrete building we killed a further batch of the enemy.' Street fighting 'was particularly exciting and fraught with surprises', he pointed out. 'I think without any exaggeration we killed at least our own numbers and possibly more.' But attrition reduced the small groups even further. 'We had quite a large area to cover,' he explained, 'and with our reduced numbers it was a full time job keeping our eyes open to all around us.' Each sharp engagement cost more men. 'It was as much as we could do to maintain our position on the ground and maintain the defensive perimeter that was one of our main objects.' Eventually, lacking ammunition, the Commandos pulled back to the mole in order to re-embark.

The estuary alongside the dockside was festooned with blazing wreckage. Returning demolition teams recognised there would be no pick-up. 'Chaps were drowning, there were pools of burning fuel on the water,' recalled Eric de la Torre in the water, 'you had to kick your feet like mad to try and steer the raft away from the flames – it was an absolute inferno.' All Corran Purdon with 12 Commando could see 'was a sea of black, you could see sinking boats and hear shouts coming from the river.' They were told to break-out through the town. 'That was a bit of a tall order,' Commando Bob Wright recalled. They would have to fight their way out of the docks area, across the bridges and through town and Spain was 350 miles away.

The Saint-Nazaire experience was in stark contrast to the Vaagso raid, designed to achieve a night approach with a dawn H-Hour, to enable the fight-through and demolitions phase to take place in broad daylight. The violent initial naval bombardment, synchronised with RAF low-level bombing runs, quickly overcame the four-gun 75mm battery on Maaloy Island, which was anticipated to be the toughest nut to crack. The real difficulties occurred when the Group 2 assault and demolition groups broke into the town. Intelligence had not been able to predict the German High Command despatching an extra unit to Vaagso to enjoy their Christmas leave. 'So there were twice as many to fight,' remembered Alec Johnson. 'Not only that but they were star troops, so they knew how to fight and we had quite a battle.' This was bad news, the aim was to secure the area for raiding demolitions, not engage in a lengthy set-piece battle. Barely two hours was available to achieve their objectives before the Commandos would have to be taken off and clear the fjord before enemy air attacks came in.

Once again the small-group organisation proved easier to control. Lieutenant Colonel Durnford-Slater commanding the raiders ashore employed his 'floating' reserve and pulled out more reinforcements from the successfully captured battery on the island. The German conventionally organised defence with platoons and companies was more difficult to coordinate because the surprise assault had caught them dispersed in the town and not manning shore positions. Half the defenders were there on holiday and not subject to any pre-arranged rehearsed defence scheme. A savage and costly street fight broke out during which most of the Commando assault group commanders were killed. So many officers and NCOs fell that the momentum of the attack slowed. Durnford-Slater's radio operator remembered the colonel being told 'Captain Giles is dead, sir' and 'that was a big shock': 'You know Captain Giles, he played rugger for Hertfordshire and he boxed heavy-weight for the Commandos, and, you know, to lose him so soon after you've landed, you thought "My goodness me, we are in trouble here."'

Street fighting quickly consumed men in chance encounters at corners with sudden bursts of automatic fire. Isolated skirmishes broke out around buildings, backyards and narrow alleys. The Commandos were assisted by the basic town layout, which was a high street bordered by houses and warehouses with the fjord to the right and rocky high ground to the left. They had simply to drive south to north. Because of the scarcity of time, risks were taken and this cost officers and NCOs in the attempt to maintain impetus. The Germans, threatened on their flanks, fell back to isolated improvised strongpoints, such as the Ulvesund Hotel in the southern part of the town. Here they made a determined stand. 'The good ones – Germans – got on the hill behind the villages and sniped,' recalled Alec Johnson, 'and if you showed yourself you were a goner.' Because the buildings were wooden it soon became apparent they could be penetrated by heavy machine-gun fire, and they burned. 'Now they're good soldiers, the Germans,' Johnson admitted, 'but some wouldn't give in.' Buckets of petrol were brought forward and splashed inside. 'We set fire to the buildings and they were just burned to death.'

Second Lieutenant Denis O'Flaherty was struck in the eye by a sniper and the bullet came out of his throat. Peter Young, continuing the desperate house to house fighting, saw him pass by supported by two Commandos. It was not encouraging, 'O'Flaherty looked as if he had a plate of strawberry jam flung in his face,' he remembered. Snipers and opportunity grenade-throwers received little mercy. Durnford-Slater recalled avoiding a grenade then seeing the thrower gunned down despite shrieking 'Nein! Nein!' when cornered on surrender. 'Can a man throw a death-dealing grenade one second and surrender the next?' Durnford-Slater later reflected. 'I can hardly think he can expect much mercy.' The Ulvesund Hotel, the main centre of resistance, was soon blazing. 'On my way back, when the flames had died down, I counted 12 German corpses inside,' Durnford-Slater commented.

As soon as areas were secured the demolition parties got to work. John Woollett with 6 Commando began destroying the four-gun 75mm battery on Maaloy Island. 'I had a whole lot of explosives in sand bags you see, and you tied it with a rope round the gun. We had practised this, and then you fired it and it shrank the barrels and made the gun useless, but didn't scatter gun fragments and kill lots of people there.'

Next, they turned their attention to fuel storage tanks. 'We blew the tanks and that was quite a messy job.' Alec Johnson surveyed the incendiary process with some relish. The herring factory was blown up, providing vitamins 'A or B or something' for sailors on U-boat crews. 'Well our job was to blow them up,' and an orgy of destruction followed: 'any accommodation, anything German, which we did – a tank [a panzer], the little lighthouse, the accommodation.' If it was not blown it was burned. Then, as Johnson remembered, 'we got the signal to return at about half past three or a quarter to four.' Lance Corporal Eric de la Torre, remembered a 'recall rocket' was fired from the cruiser HMS *Kenya*. 'They had a message that the German bombers were on the way and the Navy didn't want to be caught in a fjord, and so the whole thing was called off.' The Vaagso Boxing Day raid of 1941 was the blueprint for a successful combined arms raid; it was never equalled.

AFTERMATH

The most difficult phase for any raid is to successfully extract after the action, invariably under fire. At about 1500 the Vaagso force withdrew, intermittently harassed by Heinkel 111 bombing raids, which were broken up by heavy anti-aircraft fire and intervention from top cover flying Beaufighters. It was a daylight withdrawal and the force was back at Scapa Flow, the start-point, by the following day.

The Saint-Nazaire extraction conducted at night was as painful an experience as the run-in. Eighteen vessels engaged in the raid, of which eight were left stranded or blazing around the dockyard area. Ten attempted to re-embark surviving troops and break out but only five of these got back to England. Frank Arkle on ML 177 took off at 18 knots, having recovered many of *Campbeltown*'s crew, to re-run the gauntlet of eighty-eight guns in the Loire estuary. 'The first shell hit us in the engine room and it apparently shifted one of our engines right on top of the other and they were both out of action.' As they drifted helplessly another shell slammed home 'and I can see to this day the funnel folding apart, what appeared to be quite slowly and the shell bursting in the middle of it'. His friend Mark Rodier took the full brunt of the blast fulfilling his earlier premonition of death. Arkle 'felt my right eye on my cheek and I was convinced that my eye had been blown out of my head and was hanging down on my cheek, and I felt there was only one thing to do about this so I plucked it out and threw it overboard.' Fortunately it was to be flesh and not eye. They abandoned ship and clung to wreckage in the water until 'we were beginning to get seriously affected by the cold' before being picked up at dawn by an armed German trawler.

Capture was a high risk experience for Commandos unable to re-embark. There was no extraction for those marooned in the dock area trying to evade the German combat groups re-establishing control and mopping up. Lieutenant John Roderick's surviving group members were captured at 1030. 'Our captors were not particularly pleased and pushed us against a wall and searched us. We thought we'd had it!' Eric de la Torre was washed ashore, flung into a lorry and driven into town to be incarcerated in a big room with other prisoners. This was a perilous moment for Commando captives totally reliant upon the self-control of their unpredictable captors.

George Davidson, taken after ML 192 sank alongside the mole, had only the overalls and plimsolls he stood up in. He warily regarded his trigger-happy guards, who were luckily officered by a 'steady type'. 'Fortunately I had lost my service revolver in the swim as I am quite sure that if I had been armed when they caught me, it would have been the end for me.' He was asked during interrogation by a high-ranking officer if he had any weapons, whereupon the Commando with him took out a hand-grenade and laid it on the desk 'which caused a bit of a panic'. After such a shocking and confused night action it would take very little for stressed out armed sailors to resist opening fire. 'The Germans brought in a sailor they had fished out and said you try and revive him,' recalled Eric de la Torre, in the big room where the captives were held. 'We tried to get the water out of his lungs.' Tension was palpable, 'by this time' he pointed out, the delayed action fuses deep within the destroyer rammed into the dry dock gates had still not exploded. 'The *Campbeltown*, you know, it hasn't gone up!'

Lieutenant Commander Beattie who had steered *Campbeltown* into the dock gate was being interrogated in a hut nearby. The harbour area was not cleared of Commandos until dawn and the surrounding area much later. As a consequence hundreds of curious Germans and souvenir hunters were belatedly converging to pick over the ship. 'They were patting us on the back, the Germans were amazing!' declared Eric de la Torre. 'They couldn't believe it, that any one would venture up into a submarine base, heavily defended.' Everyone came to witness this achievement, adding to the real possibility the bomb would soon be discovered. 'I was interrogated by a German who spoke very good English,' Beattie recalled: 'He discovered that I had been in *Campbeltown* and he was remarking "it was no good ramming a stout caisson like that with a flimsy ship". At that moment there was a bang.' A tidal wave of water gushed into the dock, battering the merchant ships within while the four and a half ton explosive charge virtually vaporised the crowds climbing over her decks.

'Jerry doesn't like these blokes,' declared a 1942 British *Movietone News* clip entitled *Commandos Raid Again,* 'he doesn't know when they're coming, or where.' The camera panned across blackened grinning faces of well-equipped Commando troops with Tommy guns, woollen head warmers and festooned with toggle ropes, ammunition bandoliers and demolition carriers. This was absolutely true, the Germans did not like them. At Vaagso 120 enemy were claimed killed and ninety-eight prisoners brought back, the largest concentration taken in Europe since Dunkirk. All the German military offices in the town, as well as cars, lorries, a 16-ton panzer, five 75mm guns, petrol tanks, ammunition stores, barracks, telephone exchanges, beach mines, searchlights, lighthouses, radio installations and four factories were demolished. Generalmajor Kurt Woytasch the 181st Division Commander had enormous difficulties reconstructing events for his report when he arrived to survey the desolate scene. It was as if the Four Horsemen of the Apocalypse had ridden in and out. Corpses were strewn about snow-filled streets and charred remains of soldiers were identifiable inside skeletal burned out houses and warehouses. Not a soul remained on the fortress garrison of Maaloy Island opposite the town, all were killed or taken away. In the fjord British destroyers had sunk nine merchant ships and an armed trawler that yielded the radio call signal of every German vessel in Norway and France, along with challenges, responses and emergency signals.

Three months later the Atlantic seaport of Saint-Nazaire received its punishing visitation. The implications of a raid on such a strategic installation could not be ignored. Delayed action torpedoes fired around the U-boat pens exploded sixty hours later and triggered off a French riot. Nervous German soldiers engaged in the distressing work of recovering the remains of comrades scattered hundreds of yards around the dock area after the *Campbeltown* explosion lost control and fired into the demonstration. The crowd believed the raid was the precursor to the rumoured Second Allied Front and scattered, while German troops engaged them and German Organisation 'Todt' workers, whose uniforms vaguely resembled Commando raiders.

Five months later the major port of Dieppe was hit by an even larger scale raid that included twenty-nine Churchill tanks. It was a total debacle, a frontal attack relying on surprise but with insufficient fire support. The raiders lost 1,027 men killed, including 900 Canadians and 2,340 prisoners. Lessons were not necessarily learned for the subsequent invasion of Europe. In fact Lieutenant Colonel Charles Carrington the Army Liaison Officer with RAF HQ wrote: 'nothing to be learned from Dieppe, except how not to do it, a little late in the war to learn that lesson.' But the Germans were perturbed. The newly formed 1st SS Panzer Division was called out of its barracks at Evreux and directed toward the Channel coast before being recalled. Hitler issued his 'Commando Order' in October 1942. 'From now on, all enemies on so-called commando missions in Europe or Africa . . . even if they are in uniform, whether armed or unarmed in battle, or in flight, are to be slaughtered to the last man.' Nicolaus von Below, Hitler's Adjutant, recalled, 'he was becoming very uneasy at the increasing reports of saboteur commandos behind the German lines in both Russia and France.'

In England the raids were proof the island could hit back and was a shot in the arm for morale at a low point in the war's fortunes. 'A thrilling raid on a Norwegian island came off according to plan, with 90 or so Germans captured and a few quislings [Norwegian collaborators] too – 150 killed,' wrote Mrs Clara Milburn in her diary. 'And all completed in a quarter of an hour, less than the time allowed.' The British public relished the reports of spectacular damage and casualties inflicted behind enemy lines. John Durnford-Slater remembered how 'the press shouted the story' of the Lofoten Island raid in March 1941: 'The people talked of it in tones of pride. Even German radio grudgingly had to praise the secrecy with which the raid had been mounted and the complete success of its execution.'

In March Clara Milburn noted 'a daring raid on Saint-Nazaire', another spectacular achievement, but unfortunately 'some of our men could not be re-embarked, which was a pity'.

Colourful though the raids were they came at a price. Commando soldiers accepted this and the odds, and rationalised their own survival chances. 'It sounded dangerous to be in the Commandos,' acknowledged Commando Ronnie Williamson, 'but actually you were probably a lot safer because you had people around you who could react instantly – at a moment's notice – to anything that happened.' Vaagso was highly successful but the fighting in the town had been intense. Two officers and fifteen men were killed and five officers and forty-eight other ranks wounded, seventy casualties in two hours. The RAF lost thirty-one aircrew killed. Saint-Nazaire was especially costly. The Royal Navy lost 55 per cent of its component and eight of every ten Commandos did not return, 144 of the 630-strong force were killed.

Commandos lived among their small domestic communities, not in barracks. Intimate relationships developed, romantic as well as domestic. Lieutenant Peter Young referred to their landladies as 'a fine body of women with tremendous esprit de corps!' His Commandos planted their feet in some very friendly hearths. 'Some of the soldiers developed the system to such a fine art that they would get the people in their billets to clean their equipment, or would send them round to Troop Headquarters to read orders!'

Dr David Paton, a medical officer with 2 Commando, was on one of the few motor launches that got back from Saint-Nazaire. When the remnants of the unit mustered for a parade and march through Ayr after the operation 'the women stood in layers in the streets and wept. Terrible to see.' Four hundred men departed Ayr for the raid, only sixteen were available for the parade.

The raiders came from the sea and the population of England were very much aware since their ejection from Europe that they were an island race. Indeed, Commando casualties were invariably buried at sea during the return voyage. Eric de la Torre, returning from Vaagso, recalled, 'that was something I will always remember.' Captain Johnny Giles, rugby player and heavy-weight boxer was one of them: 'It was very moving and the chaps were standing around with their bandages on, their dressings on, which hadn't been attended to yet, their faces blackened for the raid . . . it was a moving ceremony.'

Phoney War never applied at sea. Within four hours of the declaration of war on 3 September 1939 the passenger liner *Athenia* was sunk. There were no lulls and it continued as such until the last day of the war. The war at sea much influenced the psyche of a generation aware of their dependence upon the goods that came across it to prosecute the war. It too exacted an awful price.

7

NORTH ATLANTIC CONVOY

On 25 September 1941 the Liverpool-based liner *Avoceta* was torpedoed with great loss of life. She carried mainly women and children. Two days later, nineteen-year-old Roy Bagot, the second officer aboard the MV *Coxwold* with the same convoy, saw the sinking of HMS *Springbank*, one of their naval escorts. 'Two torpedoes hit her as she went in' to search for a U-boat he recalled, 'both on her port side, one aft and one for'ard, and great columns of water and smoke rose up to meet the rain as she rolled away with her wounds'. Ignoring a heavy sea whipped up by gale-force winds, Bagot's captain risked lying off to windward of the stricken ship to mount a rescue attempt. 'There were sailors in boats, sailors on rafts, sailors just swimming, and sadly there were those we watched just drifting away.' They snatched as many as they could in the teeth of a 'screaming wind'. Delaying meant there was no hope of catching the convoy so *Coxwold* returned to the Mersey, berthing close by the Liver Building where the ferries disgorged passengers. Anxious friends and relatives waited behind the canvas screens that sheltered the quay as survivors began to walk down the gangplank. 'And do you know,' Bagot remembered:

As we came down to greet them, these waiting people, as if they had known what had just taken place, started – very slowly, shyly at first, not all of them knowing the words but each one of them understanding the message – these people started to sing:

> *Eternal father strong to save,*
> *Whose arm hath bound the restless wave . . .*

Oh hear us when we cry to Thee
For those in peril on the sea.

Roy F 'Dick' Dykes, serving with the Royal Navy Volunteer Reserve (RNVR), summed up the attitude of Battle of the Atlantic veterans, reflecting 'every one of you has shared the same experiences, the same feelings'. Bagot found himself reflected in the glow of this intangible emotion, felt in all English coastal towns, which created part of the legacy of this wartime generation. It can be viewed through the medium of a typical North Atlantic convoy sailing. 'You have the same feelings,' Dykes stressed, 'when you bring survivors on board who can't stand up or are completely unconscious because of their time in the water.' Grim though this experience was, 'it was a family affair'.

Both sides were equipped or preparing themselves for a fleet encounter at the outset of war. Günther Prien's U-47 crept inside the Royal Navy anchorage at Scapa Flow in the Orkneys in October 1939 and changed all that by sinking the battleship *Royal Oak*. The 'Bull of Scapa', as he was nicknamed by the adoring public in the Third Reich, altered strategic opinion and the direction of Germany's resources into the coming Battle of the Atlantic. No longer was the submarine viewed as the instrument to sweep coastal waters, picking off what survived surface raiders. The submarine was to dominate the largely unseen Battle of the Atlantic. Britain was proud and dependent upon her surface fleet, which captured most of the publicity during the Phoney War. Service was as tedious as it was dangerous. 'Dearest Mum,' wrote seventeen-year-old William Crawford serving on the battleship HMS *Hood*; like many young servicemen, he was homesick.

I am writing again today just because it makes me feel nearer to home, I know it's wrong to say but I sure am fed up. I feel kind of sick, I can'nae eat and my heart's in my mouth. We struck bad weather today. Talk about waves as big as houses, they're crashing over our bows. Even as I write this we're heaving and I can hear the waves smashing on the focsle. The last leave was the happiest I've ever spent, sitting around the fire talking with a good dinner beneath my belt . . . I wonder if it would do any good Mum if you wrote to the Admiralty and asked them if there was no chance of me getting a shore job at Rosyth. You know, tell them you have got two sons away and that. Be sure to tell them my age. If only I could get off this ship it would not be so bad. Well, cheerio Mum, my very best love to you all. Bill.

Crawford likely volunteered in order to get the service of his choice. Elsie Crawford received a telegram on 28 May 1941 from the Portsmouth Naval Barracks stating baldly: 'Regret to report that your son William McFarlane Crawford, boy, second-class is missing.' Four days before the *Hood* had spectacularly exploded during an engagement with the German pocket battleship *Bismarck*. Only three of the 1,419 crew survived; William Crawford was not among them. Irishman John Manning was similarly motivated to join the Merchant Navy. 'With the war on and reading the papers and seeing all the action that was going on I wanted to be amongst it.' He appealed to his father, 'Hey Dad, get us away to sea,' and he did. 'He put my age down as 16, I was only 15.' But he was in.

The loss of the passenger liner *Athenia* within hours of war being declared was an object lesson to all that the Atlantic had psychologically widened and England's island status was dramatically confirmed, as also the need for convoy protection to keep it afloat. Archie Smith, on regular Atlantic crossings with the liner *Cameronia*, passed the *Athenia* on their outward trip to the United States. 'We were terrified of being torpedoed,' he remembered, 'and when we got to New York there was quite a feeling of revolt that we weren't going to be escorted home again.'

Violence came earlier to merchant seamen before all others in this war and losses proportionate to numbers serving with the other armed services was greater. Twenty-eight thousand were killed and several thousand more died from wounds from sinkings and shipwrecks from 4,800 ships, representing 21.2 million tons of the Merchant Marine. Geoffrey Dormer, a junior officer on the armed trawler HM *Cape Argona*, recorded the loss of over three dozen ships personally boarded or known to him by December 1940. 'I mention the subsequent fates of various ships,' he wrote in his diary the following January, 'to emphasise the extremely hazardous nature of the Merchant Navy's task.'

Their vital role was soon appreciated, more so after the fall of France, because every gallon of fuel burned by aircraft, tank and ship, as well as metals, war equipment and food, was shipped to Britain by sea. Britain produced enough food to feed only half its population at the outbreak of war with only a few months' reserves. By 1941 it was understood Britain could live and fight on about 26 million tons of imports, less than half the pre-war total. Yet merchant seamen never personally felt appreciated for this effort and the losses incurred. 'We know what we did,' claimed Jim Paterson a Merchant Navy seaman from Durham, 'I'm not sure whether other people knew. But then they must, because otherwise they would have starved.'

The impact of rationing and the human and material cost of transporting the goods across a tenuous Atlantic life-line etched its mark on this wartime generation. 'Making-do' was a unique characteristic of 1939–45 wartime society and they fully appreciated why. Cardboard wedding cakes soon appeared by necessity and at the end of 1940 most family store cupboards had been emptied. Onions disappeared once the Channel Islands and France were under German occupation, as did lemons as the war expanded, for the duration. Hens were slaughtered with reductions of foodstuff imports and eggs became scarce. The banana became an object of wonder to young children who were born and raised in a world where you did not see one. Ironically it improved the nation's health, alongside the more equitable economic distribution of scarce resources enabled by wartime full employment.

Lack of appreciation for merchant seamen's efforts was partly conditioned by their own cynicism shaped by pre-war conditions at sea. This coloured their attitude to the unwelcome war suddenly foisted upon them. Crewman John Carroll remembered the rigours of unemployment in coastal towns and ports in the 1930s, adding, 'prior to the war, the only job you could get was around the dock or on ships.' By 1939 the Merchant Marine had reduced some 18 per cent since the eve of the last World War in 1914. The UK was dependent upon many Danish, Norwegian and Dutch flagged ships and her tanker fleet halved from 50 per cent to 25 per cent of the world's fleet. As a consequence, anything that could float was commandeered for the war effort. Government and ship-owners, finding they could get more than the scrap asking price from dubious tramp steamers, were more than happy to oblige. Crewman Ray Kease felt little obligation to either the government or such unscrupulous shipping lines. 'The war coming into it was really nothing to do with us,' he claimed. 'It was a damn nuisance because we didn't want anything like that, it was a civilian force.'

There were substantial differences between the psychological make-up and attitudes of the Royal Navy compared to the Merchant Marine. Independently-minded merchant seamen regarded their uniformed colleagues as 'the pansy RN with its perishing gas and gaiters'. Pay differed substantially; a Royal Navy seaman earned four shillings a day (20p), whereas a merchant seaman was paid £12 12s 6d (or £12.65p), rising to £24 in 1943. But a merchant seaman's pay stopped the day his ship went down. 'Naval ratings used to look down on us,' recalled Archie Smith from Glasgow. 'I remember one time a naval rating said, "Medals – what do you guys get them for?"' These differences had an intangible effect upon the seamless cooperation needed when ships' masters had to be harassed into a semblance of convoy order by their Royal Navy protectors on convoy operations. 'Professional seamen, certificated officers who had served their time,' remarked John Harding-Dennis, a merchant seaman radio operator, 'took less kindly to being talked down to by some, likely reserve, wavy-navy ex-shop assistant dressed up in a little brief authority.'

Readiness to defend was not the same to hard–bitten men tempered by grim pre–war conditions, who received scant sympathy from successive governments and shipping companies. 'We'd come through a long period of depression and the ships were old,' declared merchant seaman Vernon Miner. Wages fell after the First World War and conditions did not improve. 'The men that were sailing were basically seamen,' he recalled, 'and this was their career from which they'd started out, and having come through this period of depression where they were so long unemployed that they never dared leave their ship.' War was employment. As the new threat emerged, it was easier to identify with what *was*, rather than *might be* in any imagined future. Merchant seaman did not form part of the Royal Navy's disciplined hierarchy. One naval convoy commodore described the merchant masters under his convoy jurisdiction as 'ordinary, unpretentious people'. He was impressed, regarding them as self-contained, confident and calm individuals who 'uphold discipline by sheer character and personality – for their powers of punishment under Board of Trade Regulations are almost non-existent.'

The Merchant Marine crewing the convoys employed 120,000 sailors, captained by 4,500 masters. These were backed up by 13,000 deck officers and 20,000 engineers with 36,000 deck ratings making up the bulk of the service, and 30,000 engine room ratings and 17,000 stewards. They endured harsh conditions. John Foster was dismayed when 'I saw this huge rusty hulk of a ship and I thought: I've got to sail in that!' Boarding with ten others, he dismally looked over his future crew quarters, which were 'absolutely filthy, old mattresses and blankets and everything – never been washed'. Cook Ray Keese was equally dismayed by the galley he inherited. 'When it came to rice and all dried foods like flour and lentils and so on, they seemed to be invaded by little insects or beetles – everything had to be sieved on that ship.' Facilities on the *Empress of Australia*, John Carroll described, provided few comforts to cushion the rigours of an Atlantic convoy crossing: 'Sometimes you slept in what they called the "Glory Hold" and you had to get your grub in there with 26 people. You slept in there with your gear until the end of the voyage . . . and we got our eats standin' up, sometimes you had nowhere to sit down. With the majority of companies, you got treated like dirt.'

Small wonder crews had little respect for rank; they were a con-glomeration of officers, donkey-men, greasers, deck-hands, stokers, trimmers or stewards drawn from all races and creeds across the British Empire. A third were Lascars – indentured coloured seamen – three-quarters of whom were Indians. Crews came from Bombay, Chit-tagong, and the Punjab, Arab seamen from the Gulf ports and Malays and Chinese from Hong-Kong. Saif Othman from Aden sarcastically recalled Winston Churchill's appeal to sign up: 'Come in my children, we need you, this is your country,' he was assured. 'As soon as we win this war we will grant you anything you desire.' Tension with this caustic ethnic mix was endemic. 'Sometimes you would overhear them and they would be using derogatory words like "nigger" and "sambo" and all the names that they called black people,' complained Caribbean crewman John Foster. Being a boxer he recalled, 'when I used to hear that, I would offer to take them out on deck.' 'It was hard work,' declared Saif Othman, 'I've never worked so hard.' There were of course language difficulties and few of these men understood the politics or the nature of the war they were involved in. 'I didn't know anything about the war,' Othman remarked and was totally shocked when his chief mate threatened to throw him overboard for lighting a cigarette during the blackout. He was very young. 'It was all very strange,' he confessed, 'I didn't know what to say – I couldn't understand.' Many merchant seamen at sea when the war broke out typically heard about it through word of mouth.

Churchill was fearful about the possible outcome of the Battle of the Atlantic. 'The only thing that ever really frightened me during the war,' he later admitted, 'was the U-boat peril.' Admiral of the Fleet Sir Dudley Pound was even more succinct as First Sea Lord in 1942, pointing out 'if we lose the war at sea we lose the war'. Convoy vulnerability increased after the fall of France, making the Atlantic readily accessible to U-boats. *Rudeltaktik* or 'wolf-pack' submarine tactics were introduced in 1941, and the Battle of the Atlantic was jump-started with Victor Oehrn's sinking of ten ships totalling 41,000 gross registered tons (GRT) on a single U-boat patrol. Between June 1940 and March 1941 Otto Kretschmer's U-99 sank thirty-nine merchant ships of over 200,000 GRT over eight patrols. German success peaked in November 1942 with the disposal of 750,000 GRT, just short of winning Grand Admiral Karl Dönitz's 'tonnage war' when sinking ships outweighed launchings.

Merchant seamen were pitched into this maelstrom with little appreciation of the nature of the conflict to come. 'I wanted something a little more dangerous or exciting,' admitted American gunner's mess boy George Goldman, who was an accountant when the war broke out. 'I didn't know what I was getting into, but it looked hot.' The irony was that this supremely strategic contest was not fought out in a series of major identifiable campaigns like the other major land and air theatres of Second World War; it was conducted anonymously and out of sight of land. These ordinary men were led on both sides by only 'junior' commanders. 'The extraordinary thing was that the Battle of the Atlantic was the most important naval action in the whole war,' declared Convoy Escort Commander Joe Baker-Cresswell, 'and yet it was fought by no one more senior than a commander' (or lieutenant-colonel battalion commander equivalent). U-boat signaller Herbert

Ohrsen recalled the tension aboard his submarine under depth-charge attack. Escape 'depended naturally upon how clever the commanders are,' he explained, 'the destroyer commander and the U-boat captain.' It was not a conflict where naval units were deployed en masse in one area. 'So it then developed into a little private war,' commented Ohrsen, but no less fierce or deadly.

CONVOY UNDER SAIL

Atlantic convoys were briefed at conferences, frequently at Liverpool, attended by every ship's master and the commodore, the senior Merchant Navy convoy leader. They attended in uniform or whatever attire that took their fancy. Royal Navy escort commanders might not attend as they were at bases in Londonderry or on the Clyde. They could be colourful events. Sub-Lieutenant Geoffrey Dormer recalled one convoy commander Admiral Goldsmith regaling assembled masters by warning: 'if you let your ships make smoke', the tell-tale signature that attracted marauding U-boats, 'you are nothing but a fucking murderer!'

An average convoy might be between fifty to a hundred ships, a vulnerable target spread across a large area of sea. Cargo vessels, varying from 3,000 ton vessels to 7,000 ton tankers armed with a solitary gun, formed up in perhaps twelve columns of four to five ships each, sailing at 8 to 10 knots. This configuration minimised ship exposure to flank attack, showing mainly a smaller bow or stern target. The front of such a convoy was five to six miles wide and two and a half miles deep. The resulting assembly of ships 'was a sight to behold' declared Ordinary Telegraphist (signaller) Derric Breen watching an ocean-going convoy from his escort destroyer HMS *Egret*. 'It was an awe-inspiring sight, impressive and martial, but displaying its own vulnerability as the mass of ships showing a seven to eight mile front steamed along at 4 to 5 knots, extending backward for three to five miles.' The fours sides of the convoy represented a combined front of fifteen to twenty linear miles, which had to be screened from U-boat attack by a group of about six escorts, often four corvettes and two destroyers. Their task was to prevent U-boats slipping inside the convoy, keep them under the surface and, if possible, sink them. It was the equivalent of patrolling the outskirts of a small city.

Managing this flock of ships was the job of the convoy escort commander. Station-keeping was chaotic, because engineers and masters struggled to keep in their allotted columns by finely adjusting propeller revolutions to maintain a constant speed. This was totally contrary to the peacetime norm of comfortably and more safely sailing alone. Crewman Billy MacLean recalled sailing in one convoy with 122 ships at 7 knots, 'the speed of the slowest – zigzagging all the time to mislead the submarines'. Escort commander Evelyn Chevasse RN, commanding the destroyer *Broadway*, generally departed base 'with butterflies fluttering wildly in my stomach' at the prospect of assembling ten or a dozen columns 'for which there was no room in the narrow waters of the north channel off Liverpool'. 'Now the odd thing was,' confessed convoy escort commander Commodore Joe Baker-Cresswell, 'that before the Second World War, we had never really practised convoys.' They had to relearn painfully compiled 1914–18 instruction about unrestricted German submarine warfare. 'You would have thought that we might have learned our lesson' because 'we were completely unprepared for the sort of war we had to fight.' So it was with some trepidation that escort commanders set off in the early days with 'no real rules to follow'.

Royal Navy escorts shepherding their charges at speed on the fringes of the convoy were less exposed than slow-moving merchant vessels feeling acutely vulnerable inside. Sixteen-year-old John Harding-Dennis recalled 'constant tension, fed by harrowing memories' when sailing the Atlantic danger zones, lying fully clothed on his bunk with life-jacket, sea-boots and a survival bag within reach. 'Then, the slightest bang – a steel door clanging shut, a dropped spanner in the engine room – would make you jump up in a panic of sweat.' His subconscious was dominated by the image of a 'torpedo track heading for you straight amidships'. The Royal Navy was not impervious to these fears. Sub-Lieutenant Geoffrey Dormer on the armed trawler *Cape Argona* recalled one early captain 'insistent that the very first thing to do on joining a ship was to learn the way from one's berth to the upper deck with one's eyes shut, for fear of being trapped below'. Motivating him throughout was the litany of sinkings he recorded in his diary. Saif Othman from Aden recalled only three of a hundred compatriots signing on with him surviving the war: 'When you sign on a ship and it sails – goodbye. You are no longer human. You are finished – dead. When it sails you are like one of the dead. You're not alive until Allah, glorious and exalted is he, delivers you safely ashore. You say thank God I am safe, the world is a good place.'

'The first ship I ever saw going down was a ship carrying iron ore,' recalled merchant seaman Reg Clarke. 'The two halves went down in opposite ways and she was completely gone in about 30 seconds.' John Foster was especially scared of being caught within the narrow confines of the engine room below decks. 'It was the most vulnerable place to be whenever you were attacked by torpedoes. Mostly they targeted the midships where the engines were situated. Then, if you were down there, that was you finished. There was no such thing as anyone being saved, if any one was, it was a miracle.'

'When we finally got the ships into their proper places,' remembered convoy escort commander Evelyn Chavasse, 'and all my butterflies had flown, we settled down to our long slog across the Atlantic.' This might take ten or more days depending on the weather and convoy speeds. Air escort coverage did not cover the full distance, creating the mid-Atlantic air gap, a freezing expanse of 300 miles referred to as 'the gap' and, with losses, as the 'Devil's Gorge' or the 'Black Hole'. German U-boat wolf-packs straddled the gap.

Life for Royal Navy escorts was primarily drudgery and routine. Conditions within their cold and cramped boxes was harsh. A typical destroyer according to correspondent Douglas Macdonald Hastings was 190 men living and eating in an area 'about the size of a couple of double-decker buses, and as about as uninviting as the inside of a boiler'. Eight or ten officers ate and lived in an iron box above the ammunition magazine, and slept on top of chests of drawers in cabins the size of a typical taxi. The 1936-designed Tribal-class destroyers, built for 220 men, had a complement of 262 by 1939 and expanded to 300 later in the war. Smaller corvette crews of forty-seven at the outbreak of war were expanded to eighty-five by 1943.

Royal Navy ships were conditioned to sailing and operating in lines, merchant ships were not. 'I did not like these big hunks of iron riding up on me all the time,' admitted US crewman George Goldman. 'There was nothing we could do about it,' he laughed:

> No two ships seemed to travel at the same speed, no matter how they tried to adjust the revolutions of the propellers. You'd turn around and here comes a ship slowly moving up on you, and a ship damn near rammed into us one time. Where the hell it came from I don't know, but the first thing you know she was right up on top of us . . . Everybody started hollering and waving, but she didn't hit us. But when you see two big monsters like these coming together it's frightening because of the power, you can just imagine the steel buckling.

Reg Clarke recalled the biggest fear aside from enemy action was collision and 'on that account they always kept well clear of each other, [in peacetime] when they were independent'. Leslie Harrison, a young second mate, remembered one occasion starting watch and 'inheriting an excess of revolutions', which recorded in his sparse log narrative meant they 'charged up abreast of leaders; then completed disorderly four hours by being overhauled by ship astern at precise moment two ships of starboard column got to grips and fell over on me, with result that for 10 pregnant minutes we were all six running in line abreast, with a couple of feet or so between us.'

The only recourse was 'hold your hat on and steer a most precise course'. Collisions did occur, such as when the twin-screw tanker *Athelviking* became 'unmanageable' and sank the cargo vessel *Rossington Court* in March 1940. Merchant seaman Derrick Cutcliffe experienced a terrifying encounter scraping by a passing ship at a combined speed of 30 knots. 'The noise and feel of 30,000 tons of ships crashing into each other at that speed was unbelievable,' he remembered. 'Men were screaming in pain and fear' and simply writing about it fifty-nine years after the event 'still makes me feel sick to the pit of my stomach, so vivid is that awful dreadful memory'.

Much of the 'slog' involved in crossing the Atlantic was the combination of exhausting watch routines combined with the vicissitudes of the weather. Navy escort crews were often divided into three watches of eight hours length. As officers had to be on the bridge at all times and there were fewer, they were split into six four-hour watches, which meant two stints every twenty-four hours. This exhausting routine exacted a toll. Telegraphist Derric Breen changed to a two-watch shift pattern when U-boat attacks intensified. 'We grew more and more weary, the struggle to keep awake becoming increasingly unbearable,' he recalled. 'The W/T office was a small haven of warmth and freedom from the water which seemed to be everywhere in the ship.' Chain-smoking kept them awake.

Edward Butler, serving on a navy escort, remembered living on corn-beef and hard-tack because 'the seas came in and put the galley fires out and you just couldn't cook anything hot'. They were steadily ground down by fatigue and constant water immersion. Nightmarish winter storms caused ships to gyrate seemingly through three dimensions at once, inducing nausea among even the hardiest. All sense of orientation and even the ability to reason coherently could be lost amid constant retching, bringing forth little but bile. Keeping clean was also a challenge. 'There was no hygiene there,' Butler admitted, 'you really started smelling after a week if you didn't watch it.' Deep concussive booms continuously sounded out as waves battered hulls amid shrieking winds lashing open bridges with stinging spray. Derric Breen recalled that even his 1,250-ton destroyer was subjected to a 'fight for survival'.

Out of this welter of breaking waves we would stagger to a crest; from this peak we would often see the whole of the convoy. There were, however, times when we staggered to the crest, only to find that the entire brood we were protecting had themselves disappeared into a trough. Again and again; *Egret* buried her bow into an unheralded monster and she staggered to a standstill in a chaos of breaking furniture and straining gear. We were in waters which had been known to rip the turret from the deck of a battleship.

Such storms might last for days. Ships might broach like whales with fan-tailed exposed propellers momentarily spinning spray as vessels seemingly arched backs before plunging into the next trough. Inches of filthy bilge water sloshed across decks inside, slopping against bulkheads and raising the effusive stench of oil, vomit and flooded toilets. Breen remembered all the cups and plates were gone within days and had to be replaced with Nestles milk tins to drink tea. 'What, however, was the real agony,' he confessed, 'was the never ending, muscle crippling effort to hang on to something, to find a corner in which to wedge, so that for the odd minute the strain might come off legs and arms.' 'The lucky ones had hammocks,' recalled Edward Butler, 'and the unfortunate ones had to lie on the lockers.' They had then to endure the discomfort that accompanied watch changes. 'You would get chaps coming down from the middle watch, four o'clock, wet through, and just clambering on the locker and the poor chap who was already trying to get some sleep would get soaked.'

Life was no different on merchant ships. George Bathie recalled waves ominously taller than the bridge of the ship. 'Now the ship is out of the water maybe 30 feet – we can stand on the deck of the bridge and look up at the water.' 'When they're coming, they make a hell of a noise!' exclaimed merchant seaman Sidney Kerslake describing crashing waves: 'They rush at yer like big white phantoms. The wind is howling like mad, and whistling through the rigging. It's a terrible noise really.'

Bill Short claimed, 'it was phenomenal. The ship was getting thrown all over the place. I was on a ship of 5,000 or 6,000 tons,' he rationalised, 'and it was getting treated like a small rowing boat.' John Carroll, working in the galley, remembered, 'the crockery is falling against the bulkheads, the chairs are getting washed up against the bulkheads, the galley – the pans – everything. It's impossible to cook.' The systematic demolition of the ship's lifeboats was even more disconcerting: 'The next minute I heard an almighty smash, I really thought we'd been torpedoed or something, the bang was tremendous. One of the lifeboats had got carried away from its davits and that was it, finished with.' They lost them all and the life-rafts. 'We were not so much worried about U-boats,' John Carroll admitted, 'it was the weather.'

Conditions for U-boat crewmen were little better than those for the surface fleets they were seeking. The mainstay of the Atlantic U-boat fleet was the Type VIIC submarine, which had only eight bunks for thirteen petty officers and twelve bunks for the remaining twenty-five men. Even larger Type IXCs had eight bunks for twelve petty officers and twenty-four for thirty-four men. Beds were shared because everybody stood one watch in three and engineers one in two every twenty-four hours. Routine was a succession of watches and maintenance. There were just two electric hot-plates to serve entire crews of forty-four or fifty-six men. Torpedoes, equipment and provisions had priority of space over crew, who often had to sit on the floor or boxes and balance plates on knees to eat. Carbon monoxide levels were high with the total absence of air-conditioning or heating systems on operational boats. One of only two latrines on board was always used as an additional store room. Kapitän Leutnant (Lieutenant Commander) Klaus Anderson on U-481 recalled the ability of crew to attune themselves to accept these harsh conditions as normal. 'I always had great problems with foul air,' he remembered. 'Even with the ventilation fans running efficiently there were parts of the boat where the putrid air hardly stirred.' So crowded and cramped were U-boats that crew living forward might rarely if ever visit friends aft, perhaps for the entire voyage. 'The poor blokes in the bow torpedo compartment, or even worse, in the oily atmosphere of the engine room, must have suffered enormously,' Anderson commented. Discipline in these trying and frustrating conditions was rarely an issue; leaders coped.

U-boat wolf-packs were strung out like a fishing net astride antici-pated convoy routes. It was an observation line. Any part of the line snagged by a convoy resulted in the rest of the pack being pulled in by radio. The preference was for the darker winter and autumn nights with troublesome seas and sufficient wash to cloak the raising of a periscope.

U-BOAT STRIKE TO ABANDON SHIP

A six-ship convoy escort would typically have two destroyers five to nine miles in front, ideally overlapping radar and visual coverage. They would rotate in an elliptical pattern, 'sweeping' the sea ahead with Asdic. Two more corvettes would be three to four miles out screening each flank and two more as 'tail-end Charlies' protecting the rear. Radar range was fifteen miles and Asdic echo-sounding swept 2,500 yards ahead. 'High price' ships such as tankers and troop ships would be in the centre of the convoy. Ammunition ships were dispersed and tank and aircraft-carrying boats would be bounded by more expendable cargo

Torpedo strike. 'Ship-flash' or the first detonation of a torpedo was often the only warning merchant crews received they were under attack.

Exhausted and coated in oil, this freezing survivor hangs
on limply to the rescuer's guard rail.

Marooned in the Atlantic in an open boat. Small boat-handling skills in the
merchant marine were poor. 'They were screaming for help', recalled one
survivor, 'but it was only possible to shout back encouragement'.

vessels carrying raw materials. Archie Smith, a troop ship steward, recalled 'it was fascinating to see how a convoy was composed' to protect the vital cargoes. As he gazed about, 'you could see a black flag going up and you knew there was a submarine alert – and you'd hear depth charges. But being right in the centre of the convoy you felt "quite" safe.' U-boats used their 17-knot surface speed to get ahead of the convoy and engage on the surface possibly at night or from periscope depth by day.

Aboard naval escorts crew would endeavour to rest and catch up with meals during the day and sip a last hot drink at dusk before the ship was closed up for action stations at dusk. Nights were long and tensions high. 'We had the feeling it was a necessary job,' recalled Edward Butler on close escort. 'I'm not so sure that we realised it was all that important.' Maintaining motivation was not easy, 'to us,' he declared, 'it was a very boring job' . . . We were on look-out for anything that might come up; and it was bitterly cold on an open bridge in all weathers. It was little more really than trying to keep dry, rather than realising we were doing an important job.'

'I was leading the convoy, up in the front,' remembered convoy escort commander Joe Baker-Cresswell. 'I suddenly started to get this feeling, this instinct, that something wasn't quite right.' 'Ship-flash' from a torpedo strike was the first indication something was amiss. Atlantic veterans often testified to a feeling of mute helplessness when they saw sister ships erupt in flames.

First contact for U-boats was if the four-man bridge watch sighted a ship on the horizon. Having identified it as friend or foe, merchant or warship, the identification book of ship silhouettes was consulted to estimate the draught and determine how deep the torpedo should run. Speed and direction of travel was all important because manoeuvring into firing position could last days. A straight shot was the ideal, like an aircraft deflection shot, whereby the ship sailed into the torpedo target lane. Angled shots were worked out on a calculator with variables such as range, speed and course updated and entered, like panning a gun on a moving target.

Under the surface the U-boat commander wore red-tinted glasses prior to action, to retain night vision in the event of a surface engagement. As ranges closed to 4,000 or 5,000 metres only momentary confirmatory peeks were made with the periscope a few centi-metres above the water to avoid splash. Taking frequent looks, the submarine stealthily approached at slow speed. Steady nerves were required to get close to a convoy. Horst Elfe the twenty-three-year-old second watch officer aboard U-99, recalled the cold-blooded precision of his captain Otto Kretschmer. 'Silent Otto as he was called was always very matter-of-fact, very unemotional, but he was not without a heart.' Kretschmer had proven judgement, and luck.

At 1,000 metres a 'fan' of torpedoes might be fired, each com-pressed air launch released as the commander ordered '*Los!*' This was the signal for the torpedo-room watch officer to begin timing the stop-watch run to target. Throughout the attack, the hydrophone man listened out for propeller signatures indicating an approaching destroyer. Groups of ships would be attacked, firing all torpedoes to capitalise on the confusion generated from the first shocking ship-flash and explosion. The jarring concussion of a strike and the collapse of creaking bulkheads inside stricken ships as they sank were audible to the entire crew. Werner Kronenberg, a U-boat engineer, remem-bered, 'those squeaks, the bursting of the bulkhead, this noise when she goes down, a noise which gets into your bones. That is not a pleasant sound,' he reflected.

'I was sitting on the poop with my watch-mate and there was a tremendous explosion, really tremendous,' recalled merchant seaman Ed March. 'It tore the deck open, tore the tanker's cat-walk apart, great big hole in the side of the ship and it breached the engine room.' 'Contrary to what one might think, there wasn't an almighty big explosion and great big fount of sparks and things,' claimed tanker crewman Reg Clarke. 'There was a thump like we had bumped into something. The effect wasn't immediate. It seemed to be a short while afterwards before the forward hatch seemed to erupt, and it was full of palm oil, not aviation spirit or fuel, which we'd been told was almost non-inflammable. But it turned out not to be the case.'

Surface attacks were equally surprising. George Goldman, the gunner's mess boy, recalled often being distracted by sailors using the steam line to wash their clothes in the laundry room next to his bunk. The hissing and clattering was disturbing and he stepped inside to quieten the racket. But there was no one there. As he turned back another shell tore through the forward end of the alleyway leading to the engine room. Running alongside the tanker at 16 knots was a surfaced U-boat, steering parallel to them on the starboard side. 'It raked the deck with machine gun bullets and started to pump shells into us.' On board was 50,000 barrels of high-octane fuel and 20,000 barrels of diesel.

Three-quarters of most ships, including over 200 assessed within a survey of 269 vessels, sank within fifteen minutes of being torpedoed. Reg Clarke saw the demise of an elderly iron ore ship, which disappeared in thirty seconds: 'Well, the torpedo hit this ship, right slap-bang in the middle and she just broke in half, because of the weight and the fact the water went straight into the engine room, straight into those two holds and completely filled the air space that were in those holds in a very short space of time.' In such circumstances ships went down with the engines still revolving propellers and scalding the engine room crew.

A further survey found that 26 per cent of deaths occurred between the moment the ship was attacked and prior to boarding lifeboats or rafts. Death rates doubled when it was dark and again if the sea was rough. Confusion was thereby highest at the time of sinking and attempts to escape. Reg Clarke recalled how volatile his alleged 'non-inflammable' cargo of palm oil could be:

> It simply erupted into a huge fountain that shot up into the air and down, so it was raining fire. The skin on my fore-arms was hanging down in strips and there were puddles of this oil on the deck and I was wearing gym shoes. The ship was listing and going down a bit and I had great difficulty in finding my feet. I kept falling down into these puddles of blazing oil.

Confusion killed men at this stage. Long after the event Reg Clarke involuntarily brushes himself down and slaps his body while telling the story, as if still on fire, an indication of the mindless terror he endured. Numbed minds were incapable of clear thinking. Reg Clarke thought only of getting off the ship and found one lifeboat on deck already quite full. 'I felt quite guilty if no one had said get off, abandon ship or anything like that – but obviously it *was* being abandoned.' But no order came.

Ships' masters were aware even before the war that merchant seamen were not good at handling small boats and whalers, the very skills needed on abandoning ship. Esprit de corps in the traditional Royal Navy sense did not apply to a Merchant Marine who saw scant point in inculcating intangibles such as allegiance and unity of purpose to workmen employed in a semi-militarised industry. No formal survival training was given and poor safety awareness standards added to the death toll that ensued in the confusion that reigned between attack and abandoning ship. Disciplined Royal Navy crews had crew rehearsed what to do. There is evidence to suggest that proper training in lowering and handling small boats was neglected, while actual practice was to be conducted in disorganised and nightmarish conditions. 'At about the time we got the boats out and before we could lower away we got another torpedo on the starboard side,' recalled tanker crewman Ed March, illustrating the point: 'The ship didn't last a minute, seconds after that, she just rolled over and sank. We just let the one and three go, let the falls go and jumped into the boats. We didn't have time to get the oars out, the ship rolled over on top of us. It took us and the boats down.'

Journal of Commerce correspondence early in the war cited a Board of Trade Advisory Committee recommendation that proposed creating boat training centres at the main ports as early as 1913. Any ship's crew unable to abandon ship in five to ten minutes without smashing, fouling, overturning or swamping boats, the correspondent claimed, indicated 'in nine cases out of ten' they are 'due to the incompetence of the men handling them'. 'Hey John, I'm going over,' was all that John Manning heard from his sixteen-year-old shipmate. 'As he went over, the boat that was next to us along the ship's side, the falls snapped and went on top of my mate – killed him actually, and probably a few more that was with him *in* the boat.' Incompetence cost lives.

' "What's happening? What's happening?" someone kept demanding in a high-pitched wailing cry, full of agonized bewilderment,' remembered Michael Page, describing the chaotic sinking of his ship:

One minute we had been on watch on deck or in the engine room, or sleeping snugly in our bunks; the next we were engaged in a frenzied scramble through the dense shrieking blackness which assailed us with squalls of freezing spray, and slipped and fell on the wet iron decks which canted faster and faster into the hungry sea with every passing second, hurting ourselves cruelly on things which we could not see during our wild rush towards the boat.

The highest percentage of deaths among crews was the 42 per cent from the engine room and over 25 per cent of deck ratings. These were the men down below. There was nothing orderly about scrambling off ships and little direction if they sank within the average fifteen minutes. No part of their training and temperament prepared peacetime ships' masters to cope with bombs and torpedoes and lead men as untried as themselves in the face of enemy action. George Goldman realised he could not get off the flaming side of his crippled tanker and nobody could see through the smoke. 'So we waited for orders and orders never came.' Crew deaths as a percentage of the ship's complement varied from 16 per cent to 28 per cent during the war; one in four died.

Much of the rest of the convoy could do little during or after enemy action except sail on. Derric Breen on the escort destroyer *Egret* 'sailed into a nightmare without end'. Night attacks stretched nerves taut. Merchant radio officer John Harding-Dennis recalled the cumulative impact 'when you'd been at action stations almost round the clock for three days and nights, with no sleep and precious little food, the tendency was to jump at every sound as you strained through the darkness with indifferent night-glasses'. The slightest hint of a tell-tale phosphorous track or glow on the surface inspired immediate shouts from somewhere of 'torpedo starboard beam'. The sea reeked with the stench of discarded petroleum and engine oil. Distant booms and rumblings heralded contacts and distress rockets would shoot up while 'snowflakes' – escort star shells – would illuminate the convoy outline in an effort to spot surfaced U-boats. 'That's right, you stupid bastards – give them a good target to aim at,' was John Harding-Dennis's frustrated view. 'Snowflakes could only have been dreamed up by some bright bugger sitting smug behind a drawing-board,' he claimed.

Telegraphist Derric Breen recalled a surreal cameo of death and destruction: 'A world in which ships about us went up in flames; in which ships carrying explosives simply disappeared. Worse than all these, struggling to provide some kind of screen for those ships ploughing stubbornly on, we could not stop for our dead and our dying, the living in the boats and in the water were beyond our aid.'

The role of Royal Navy escorts was to attack U-boats, not save lives. Breen's crew accepted the concept of having to abandon survivors to an uncertain fate because: 'Britain's survival depended upon our pushing each convoy through,' he explained, 'no matter the cost.'

Well-trained escort groups conducted immediate counter-measures rehearsed during pre-convoy 'beat-up' training sessions. Escorts nearest the suspected attacker fired snowflake illuminating rockets during sweeps to force the U-boat beneath the surface, where it became blind and vulnerable to Asdic detection, and less able to use its considerable surface speed to escape. Asdic operators swept a cone of water 2,500 yards ahead with a beam of sound pulses whose 'pinging' echo response would expose a target. This pinging noise was disconcertingly audible to U-boat crews beneath the surface, as also the splash of dustbin-size underwater bombs or depth-charges that sought them out. These were lethal if blown within twenty feet of a submerged hull. U-boat crewman Hans Börner recalled the momentary relief of avoiding a depth-charge pattern, but 'one knew that the next would come'. There would be a splash: 'we could hear that! But where was it? In front? Aft? Larboard?'

The chances of a successful kill were enhanced if the hunt was coordinated between two escorts, with one listening and maintaining Asdic contact while directing the other for attack runs. 'Hedgehog' mortars, firing twenty-four bombs, were developed in concert with superior radar to shoot ahead of improved 147B Asdic, enabling contact to be maintained throughout the whole attack. Hedgehog projectiles armed on entering the water and exploded on contact. 'We saw two distinct flashes as we passed over the position,' described Captain Raymond Hart on HMS *Vidette* during such an attack run.

Conditions beneath the surface in the attack area were bleak, as described by Oberleutnant Hans-Norbert Schunk, recalling the impact of a depth-charge attack. 'Suddenly, a lot happens; glass breaks, valves burst, one had to go into deeper waters.' Cracking and creaking noises heard throughout the boat disconcerted crews as she descended below 200–240 metres. 'One after the other turns white. Not a squeak can be heard.' There was nothing that could be done except wait and endure, while gasping in carbon-dioxide enriched with pure oxygen needed to induce over-pressure.

Raymond Hart's attack run was successful: 'Our bows virtually lifted from the water as a result of the U-boat breaking apart and the escaping air. And there was great exhilaration on the bridge, because this was our first kill. We had no feelings at the time I'm afraid of destroying 70-odd people. One had control of one's emotions by then after three years of war.'

The Battle of the Atlantic was an anonymous war conducted at small-unit level. Raymond Hart did not overly reflect. 'It was *us* or *them* and on that occasion it was *them*.'

SURVIVING

Entering the water was merely the first part of the sunken seaman's struggle for survival. Those fortunate enough to be picked up by 'tail-end Charlie' escorts or rescue ships prepared to take a risk and pause were virtually incapacitated by the extreme elements. Choking on sea water and with oil-filled lungs, they hung limply from recovery nets, shaken off when they were hammered against the ship's hull by the violent motion of storm-flecked waves. Benzene was used to clean the oil off the victims. Merchant seaman Jimmy Thomas found these recovery attempts a traumatic experience, there was always the danger of being torpedoed yourself. 'One had never been *so* frightened,' he admitted. 'When you went down on the mess decks, which were warm, the men cried with the pain of being thawed out.' He was particularly disturbed by 'the fact that – you saw men float away – and just die'.

Sidney Kerslake hung rescue nets over the side of his ship amazed that anyone could emerge alive from the water. 'I don't know how they lived to swim from a ship to our ship, it was that cold – freezing.' They lay limp on deck like netted fish once hauled aboard. 'They couldn't help themselves at all.' Kerslake and his companions pulled them up, tried to administer rum, 'rubbing their arms for them, trying to get their blood flowing again'. He recalled 'one lad, about 18 or 19, trying like hell to get to us'. But the tide whipped him away down the side of the ship. He ran along the deck to cast a line: 'He was so tired or frozen he couldn't grab the rope and I kept shouting to him, shouting to him to "Pick it up! Pick it up!" Then all of a sudden he just vanished beneath the surface of the sea.'

He paused and closed his eyes during the interview as if to erase the memory. 'I could see him go down for four or five feet or more out of sight.'

Two-thirds of surviving crews were generally picked up within a day, according to studies, and almost half of these within two hours; while less than one-fifth endured small boat or raft voyages lasting more than a week. Only three in every hundred remained stranded at sea between three and seven weeks. Survival depended on the climate. Nine of forty men, according to one study, picked up after one hour in water at 1.1°C died afterwards on the rescue ship. Sea temperature also influenced lifeboat mortality, with over half perishing if the range dropped to between 10 to 19.9°C.

In April 1943 the P&O cargo liner *Shillong* was sunk during a snowstorm on a North Atlantic convoy. Later that day Peter Gretton commanding HMS *Tay* passed by: 'Close to the rafts of the *Shillong*, surrounded by the bobbing red lights on the lifebelts of many men in the water. It was a ghastly and unforgettable experience; they were screaming for help, but it was only possible to shout back encouragement. In the middle of a battle there could be no question of stopping to pick up survivors.'

One boat got away from the liner while twenty to thirty survivors had to jump into the sea to board a raft. Overcrowding and rough seas caused it to swamp three times, losing men each time until only nine were perched precariously on top. Five more died during the night and the four left were rescued by the sole remaining lifeboat with thirty-eight already on board. Eight days later seven were left alive inside when found by a destroyer, all afflicted by frostbite. The teenage cadet in charge who had inspired them to keep going lost both legs and nearly all his fingers were amputated. Survival was a question of circumstance, luck and the innate will to live, all factors that might bedevil calculated scientific study assertions.

The most traumatic experience was the immediate plucking of survivors from the waves. 'Worst of all was the sight of a tanker going up,' recalled John Harding-Dennis, 'burning like the pit, wreathed in a pall of black, greasy smoke.' Getting away from the flames was all the more difficult in reduced visibility. 'The whole of the water,' recalled John Manning animatedly spreading his arms, 'was alight while we were trying to get away.' 'And all we could hear was screams all round the water that we was in. And the poor buggers was thick with oil and some of them was burning while they was in the water, trying to swim in the water that was lit.'

Heat from the flames engulfing the Anglo-American Esso tanker *Cadillac* was so intense that the men in Second Mate R A Smith's lifeboat panicked. Blinded and enclosed by suffocating walls of flame, they leaped into the water with the oars. 'They were nearly mad with the heat and pain,' he recalled, 'and some of them were calling out and others were praying; they did not know what they were doing.' Smith prostrated himself at the bottom of the boat in about a foot of water until someone said, 'we are getting out of it.' Only five men were left.

'Even the strongest man alive would get frightened to hear the sounds of screams,' admitted John Manning, haunted to this day:

Big men screaming, bawling 'Help me! Help me!' they were shouting. And we were grabbing all we could. Eventually we grabbed as many as we could on board and rowed as much as we could. While we was rowing they're *still* screaming for help and we was saying 'we can't help you no more! We can't get anymore in it [the boat], because we were all lying different ways [to maximise space].'

Seaman were traumatised by sights and sounds that endure to this day. George Goldman's enduring memory is of survivors frantically blowing away at the life-preserver whistles, but the water was too choppy to see them. 'You could hear those whistles blowing, blowing, and I can still hear them today,' he admitted. Reg Clarke epitomises the tough merchant seaman image, he was one of fifty-five men squashed into a thirty-five-man lifeboat. His ship had carried sixty to a hundred passengers, most of them nurses homeward bound. Their lifeboat capsized on entering the water and pitched the women into the dark sea. 'The sort of thing that you could hear, was the sort of thing you don't want to hear for the rest of your life,' he confided. 'I don't anyway.'

Once clearing the stricken ship, survivors were often accosted by the very U-boat that had sunk them. Norwegian merchant seaman officer Birger Lunde frantically shouted at his lifeboat crew to row and avoid being run down by the submarine speeding past. Walter Gibb, the chief officer of the torpedoed MV *Richmond Castle*, remembered: 'at the time of our sinking [4 August 1942] rumours were rife that U-boats were surfacing and opening fire on lifeboats.' The approaching surfaced U-boat, with guns manned, was regarded with some trepidation. 'In fact they treated us with courtesy and compassion, passing down field dressings, tinned butter, bread etc, giving us the course and distance to the nearest land.' A sample of Admiralty debriefings of merchant survivors between October 1939 and March 1944 yields fifty-six encounters with U-boat crews and no attacks. Most encounters saw German apologies for the sinking – 'it is war' – with navigational advice and provisions passed across. Walter Gibb recalled their departure call, 'Cheerio, goodbye and good luck.'

Survivors may have lived but luck often deserted them. The first impression recalled by Peter Franklin, also from the torpedoed *Richmond Castle*, was 'how small a lifeboat looked on that vast sea'. Next came the feeling of solitary loneliness as the mother vessel slipped beneath the surface. 'Look, the ship's going,' was the shout Franklin remembered. 'There was a sudden hush and in dead silence we watched what had been our home, to some of us for a long time, completely disappear beneath the sea.' The moment exuded finality, she was gone in eight minutes. With the departure of the U-boat they were completely alone. It was very difficult to settle during the first night because they were 'thinking of the night before', Franklin recalled, 'when we had been sleeping peacefully in our bunks dreaming of the good time we were going to have on leave this time.'

Isolation was even more pronounced when lifeboats drifted apart, driven by buffeting waves in the night. 'You've no idea how much confidence can be given,' Franklin admitted, when they were all strung together, 'and how much can be lost' once separated. The ocean became that much bigger. The water ration was two tablespoonfuls per day for each person with one biscuit, two chocolate squares and two malted milk tablets. Constantly soaked by spray or rain, engine room survivors were generally only dressed in singlet and trousers. Many had no shoes. 'We just watched ourselves shivering and couldn't do anything about it,' Franklin remembered.

Richmond Castle was torpedoed in the middle of the summer and, despite this, survivors suffered considerably; the winter experience was worse and grim in the extreme. Birger Lunde's interview gave the impression of a man wishing to entirely disassociate himself from the nightmare scenario he described. He related events dispassionately, as if from afar. 'We sat there holding on,' he remembered, with wind and high sea making it impossible to keep pace baling out water. 'We moved to the back of the lifeboat and sat there with water up to our chests.' Bill Short on an Arctic Convoy recalled he was 'like an icicle' when he clambered sodden wet into his boat and rapidly froze from head to foot. 'People might think you're childish but when you're subjected to such cold you just lose your strength,' he admitted. 'I just cried like a baby I was so cold.'

Merchant seamen marooned in open boats had mostly not received survival training. It was not a disciplined Royal Navy hierarchy where all contingencies were briefed and trained for. Moreover, there was no accumulation of survival lore passed on orally because crews were populated by individuals contractually thrown together by chance, who tended to go their separate ways during port or home leave. The very nature of their tough profession and the general attitude of servicemen belonging to this generation was to make light of misfortune and get on with life. 'I sat there watching the men,' reflected Birger Lunde, 'they died one after the other.' As each one succumbed the mind became a little more immune to the sorrow. It was a question of individual willpower which these drew on to live. 'I thought about everyone at home,' recalled Lunde:

I was worried that I would lose my mind too. One man began to undress and asked me to give him an injection. I was the officer who used to give the men injections for illness. He undressed and just fell into the sea. The men shivered and shook. We were holding them as they died. Even the captain died. It was so sad, one after the other, seventeen men, one every hour.

Bill Short's saturated clothing was coated with ice. 'I was just like an ice man,' he described. 'Our lips were all frost-bitten, our eyes and our eyebrows were all white and we were just pale, frozen stiff.' Exposure to continuous wind and spray resulted in catastrophic drops of body temperature. Derrick Cutcliffe, a *Richmond Castle* survivor, recalled the onset of hypothermia 'or "exposure" as we called it in those days, is an insidious and deadly enemy, killing you slowly and surely'. Symptoms are akin to drunkenness prior to collapse. 'Exhaustion eventually sets in,' he observed, 'and the mental processes fall apart.' 'It is important to keep your spirits up,' Birger Lunde commented, 'not to give up one little bit,' he stressed further, 'not to let go even an inch.' Those who lost this spirit, he pointed out, gave up and died. He began to hallucinate, remembering with a pained expression how 'I saw everything so clearly – warships ready to pick us up'. But they were not there. When he came to he determined: 'I knew I must not fall asleep again because it would be the end. So it went on, day after day.' He freely acknowledged it was luck that eventually saved him. An American crewman on the *Monroe* from Baltimore said to his captain, 'there are two men standing on the water waving.'

Bill Short was picked up by the Russians with seventeen of his boatload of thirty-seven still alive. He was taken to hospital where 'they covered me from head to foot in goose grease and bandaged me' in order to raise his barely registering body temperature. 'They put a tube into my stomach and poured tepid water into it to try and get rid of the ice that had formed in my stomach.' His frostbitten legs were amputated without anaesthetic. 'When I came to I discovered they'd just chopped my legs off, the bones and everything else were still sticking out and the gangrene and poison was pouring out.' Bill Short endured hell for five months. 'The first letter I got when I got back was an income tax demand for what my wages had been for the previous half year,' but his wages had been stopped the day his ship went down.

On the ninth day at sea Peter Franklin and the survivors of the *Richmond Castle* in his boat were rescued: 'I won't attempt to describe our feelings. I couldn't. Life just began afresh – I felt that I had been given another chance in the world, and that God was good.'

This was not always the outcome. Merchant seaman Jimmy Thomas recalled his first home leave. 'They didn't even ask me where I'd been,' he remembered:

Eh – and p'raps they thought they were doing me a kindness you see, but in fact I was screaming to talk about it, and didn't really have anybody to talk about it to. The conversation over the table was still about somebody having a baby, and I couldn't have cared less; and the local amateur dramatic society and what they were doing, and the fact that the beer had run out of the pub, and women, horrifyingly were being allowed in the snug bar.

Many parts of the Merchant Marine felt unappreciated. Ray Kease believed they received insufficient publicity. Because they were dressed as civilians 'they took you for an army dodger', he commented. 'I used to have fellas spitting at me,' recalled John Carroll and he would be 'called all kinds of names' walking out with friends. Ed March was dropped at the dockside by a destroyer having survived a tanker sinking in which nine to eleven of his mates had died and they had a severely injured crew mate with them. 'He had a rivet in his right eye, in fact he had no right eye, he had a rivet there, and he was crying and screaming and in terrible shape.' They suspected he might die. Standing alongside them was a nine-man Royal Navy guard crew that was rescued with them. A red-cross vehicle turned up and took the 'unharmed' navy guard away, 'but they were not going to do anything for us'. Ed March indignantly remonstrated: 'We were civilians – the devil with us. And here we are with somebody we think is dying and the rest of us not in good shape and most of us have practically no clothes and we were nothing!'

Peter Franklin, rescued by Royal Navy corvettes, was simply grateful to get a second chance of life. They had been tenderly helped across the decks 'by sailors who absolutely radiated kindness – they gave us their food, they gave us their bunks, and the five days we spent with them still gives me a warm feeling inside whenever I think of them.' Ray Kease in contrast was bitter at the lack of appreciation for what they had endured. Only their mothers thought of them, certainly not the ship-owners: 'You had no sentimental letters from the owners of ships. You had a letter stating your son is lost at sea, nothing has been heard of him, we presume the ship must be sunk. Goodbye, Ta-Ta, his money stops from this day forward.'

Ships were living organisms. When they went down they took a part of the community with them. As most seamen came from Liverpool, London, Glasgow and the Tyne, in that order, the loss of a ship with many local people aboard was quickly circulated because it had emotionally shocking as well as sociological impacts. Over half of the crew of the *Ceramic*, lost with her entire 288-man crew in December 1942, came from Merseyside. Postal districts were effected both sides of the River Mersey, affecting many from households adjoining Wallasey, Birkenhead and dockland areas. The impact was akin to that of a disastrous Blitz air-raid. Likewise a Merseysider might survive a nightmarish Atlantic convoy crossing only to discover his family had perished in an air-raid on return.

Veterans of the Battle of the Atlantic were awarded a medal for an anonymous conflict fought – in land terms – at platoon and company level; a searing experience. Unlike the more famous, but arguably less strategic but no less fierce Battle of Britain, hardly anybody saw it. 'Now perhaps I realise what people mean,' declared Peter Franklin, 'when they talk of the Brotherhood of the Sea.' It was a universal experience that meant many things to many men and forms part of the unique heritage of the Second World War, understandable primarily only to those people who experienced it.

The Battle of the Atlantic revealed the vulnerability of tenuous contacts with the Dominions and Empire. Italian air power closed the Suez route to the east for three years. Government neglect of the need to defend Britain's imperial assets militarily quickly became apparent. Everything east of Suez had virtually to be fought for, but to get to Suez required a 13,000-mile voyage around the South African Cape of Good Hope, a stark contrast to the pre-war 3,000-mile trip. Contact with the Far East was even more difficult. Bombay voyages increased from 6,000 to 11,000 miles. Not only was import capacity reduced by 25 per cent, but re-routings and the delays involved assembling convoys and protecting them, increased average round voyage times from ninety to 122 days. Fighting for the Empire was another aspect of the unique experience of the British 1939–45 generation, its necessity as unquestioned as the pre-war popularity of Empire Day. Resources and resourcefulness of the motherland were to be stretched to the very limit.

8

DESERT AND JUNGLE

DESERT TANK MEN

School children perhaps felt geography was more relevant when one-fifth of the globe and 25 per cent of its population formed part of the British Empire, a factor celebrated every 24 May on Empire Day. By the middle of 1942 much of it had been lost. Rommel's panzers were knocking at the gates of Cairo and the Japanese Army had reached the Irrawaddy valleys in Burma, bordering India. Schoolboy geography was to be revised during long journeys British and Commonwealth soldiers undertook to reach these threatened areas. War became a form of military tourism. Ironically the wartime generation was physically exposed to Empire on the eve of leaving it, granting them a unique appreciation of what they were to leave behind.

'I felt spell-bound,' announced Tank Sergeant Bert Rendell with the 1st Royal Tank Regiment (1 RTR) at his first exposure to the Western Desert, 'we were back to biblical times.' He gazed wistfully at camel trains plodding by with date-filled containers on their backs. The desert was uniquely foreign, exotic, mysterious and a surprise to many. 'Our fondly imagined pictures of the desert culled from Hollywood's presentations of endless sand-dunes' was not what they encountered, recalled Captain David Ling with 44th RTR. Such mirage-like illusions 'were to be rudely shattered'. Ling gazed at a reality that was far less accommodating:

The Garden of Allah was a stony dusty and endless track, sparsely covered with dry scrub and heavily populated by ants of infinite variety, the largest spiders . . . the unpleasant scorpion, much more pleasant chameleons and lizards, occasional snakes, centipedes, great lumbering black beetles and the one great pest that surmounted the unpleasantness of all the others four-fold, the filthy persistent Egyptian fly in their millions.

The desert was a land of physical and colourful contrasts. Despite its desolation David Ling observed, 'it seems absurd to say,' but, 'I know of nowhere which produces such lovely and varied wild flowers as the Libyan desert.' It was either loved or loathed. 'The vastness of the whole thing just gets you,' admitted Major A F Flatow with 45th RTR on the eve of the battle of El Alamein. 'At times I used to feel horribly swallowed up in it and it all became rather eerie.' It made him crave human contact, 'to get back into the bustle of the [tank] leaguer'.

It was a long way from home. Sergeant Alan Wollaston with the 3rd RTR left Glasgow in September 1940 and sailed via the Cape to arrive at Suez just before Christmas. An average voyage took two months. Jake Wardrop with 5th RTR, like much of the British soldiery following their father's out to familiar imperial battlegrounds, exploited every opportunity military tourism had to offer. 'The weather was lovely and the tan was improving daily,' he confided to his diary crossing the equator and nearing the Middle East. 'I sat on deck and read a lot and I also dipped in the little pool which we had made – what a life!'

The desert campaigns were fought across a surface akin to the moon along a sixty-kilometre-wide strip of land along the coastline of Cyrenaica, Libya and Egypt up to the mountainous terrain of North Africa. To the north was the sea, while an impassable sand and salt-lake interior stretched out to the south. Large parts of the operational area were level plain, a sand-top model where armoured operations were developed in virtual laboratory conditions. The pendulum nature of the campaign spawned the 'Benghazi handicap' nickname conferred by those who fought to and fro across it. Desert emptiness reduced an army's ability to sustain prolonged advances across long distances, with few natural features, unlike Europe, upon which to hinge a defence. Beginning with General O'Connor's British victory that expelled the Italians from Egypt, losing 130,000 prisoners in the winter of 1940–41, the German Afrika Korps under General Erwin Rommel arrived. Rommel counter-attacked and the campaign pendulum swung six

times with offensives and counter-offensives between the start line at El
Agheila and Benghazi, east to the Egyptian border and beyond during
1941–2. The final handicap was run after British victory at El Alamein
when the Afrika Korps retreated to North Africa, where it finally
surrendered in 1943.

This was primarily a battle between the tank and artillery and anti-
tank gun. Air power and material superiority steadily tipped the balance
in the Allies' favour until the pendulum stopped swinging after 1942.
Sergeant Bert Rendell with 1st RTR 'completed the ups and downs',
as he described it, 'of the army in the desert'. There were many
disappointments. 'Sometimes spirits were high only to be dashed again
by the brilliance of Rommel,' he admitted. At the beginning, British
and Allied tanks with crews of four or less were inferior to German
Mark III and IV Panzer tanks, crewed by five. Feldwebel Hermann
Eckhardt with Panzer Regiment 8 in the Afrika Korps thought: 'the
British two-pounder tank gun was shit – thank God!' Corporal Peter
Watson with 2nd RTR claimed 'we were outgunned by the German
tanks by about a mile. That meant for the first mile of an attack they
could hit us but we could not hit them, which meant we literally had to
do a cavalry charge in our tanks. We used to kink to left or right to try
to avoid the shots.'

Technical parity was temporarily achieved for the British with the
advent of the Sherman tank with its 75mm gun, which went into mass
production and was seen as a likely war winner. It was completely
outclassed by the emergence of the monster German Tiger I with a
fearsome 88mm gun that appeared in the final stages of the war in
North Africa. The technical pendulum swung every bit as much as the
operational.

Following the disaster of France the British Army came of age in the
desert crucible. The learning process was brutal. Sergeant Bert Rendell
complained about 'men who should have been in a canteen serving
cups of tea' and they were given to him as crew 'after ten minutes on
this and ten minutes on that, 2,000 miles out from England and straight
into the attack'. This was the low point of 1942. 'It was frightening,'
Rendell emphasised. 'I'd like to get it to the BBC, to tell people so they
understood that a lot of boys who had parents that idolised them never
had a chance from the moment they left England to go to the war.'

Casualties and the raising of mass conscription armies produced sociological change through a form of social levelling, and nowhere was this more apparent than in the stultifying claustrophobic confines of the tank turret. There were no secrets here and all inhibitions had to be shared by necessity. Grammar school officers replaced previously predominant public school, and seasoned senior non-commissioned officers (NCOs) began to be commissioned from the ranks. A professionally orientated army emerged from the traditional and Territorial-based citizenry that first arrived in the desert. Victory at El Alamein in late 1942 was the tangible turning-point.

Over everything shone the sun, its 'brilliant heat beating on a land, severe and complete' observed tank signaller Peter Roach with 1st RTR. During the hottest months of June, July and August mid-day temperatures could reach 140°F, falling to 5° at night. Rain seldom fell and only in winter. *Ghiblis* or dust storms created bizarre physical conditions every four weeks or so, reducing visibility to three metres and bringing operations to a standstill. Peter Roach justifiably concluded, 'a man was unnecessary here and seemed to feel it.' Despite the human physical difficulties, the tank was appropriate to the flat rolling desert vista. 'If wars have to be fought,' wrote twenty-two-year-old 'Jimbo' D'Arcy Clark with the Queen's Own Yorkshire Dragoons, 'they should be reserved for . . . desert and other places like it, where there is no living thing to be ruined by destruction.' The war between tanks was conducted across this pitiless terrain. 'In fact desert seems a fitting place for wars,' concluded D'Arcy Clark.

An average day for the members of a four-man British tank crew would begin at first light between 0400 to 0500 hours, depending on the time of year. Tank maintenance, repairs and refuelling would have taken place up to 0100, a few hours before. A testy sleep, interrupted by clanging tank repairs and routine 'stag' or guard, would have lasted barely three to four hours. 'The grey dawn, icy, unfriendly, was streaked to the east with the vivid slashes of colour only desert awakening knows,' described Captain David Ling with 44th RTR in the Gambiut area in the Western Desert in November 1941. During operations there would be an approach march at night normally preceding a dawn advance. Fighting would develop by day, with likely a crisis occurring by the second night, resulting in either a further night's advance or, worse, a retreat. Leaders could go two nights with no sleep and often three or four nights with little or none. After five nights in action at El Alamein Major A Flatow with 45th RTR remembered, 'we could walk, and talk and move our tanks but our minds were sluggish – they refused to work or think things out', a condition exacerbated even further by the emotional rigours of combat. Somehow they had to retain alertness in order to rapidly plan and conduct moves, which meant at best a meal shortly after dusk and maybe another at dawn. At dawn there was time only for a quick brew, biscuits and jam, before, still groggy from cumulative exhaustion, tanks were driven from the harbour area – a box-like tank park for security – out to patrol or battle positions. These had to be reached before first light.

The majority of days following stand-to were spent waiting for rather than being in action. Heat afflicted them all. 'It was incredible, incredible,' recalled Trooper Paul Rollins with 40th RTR: 'I mean the sweat comes through your shirt, it dries. You have a drink of tea and that comes out again. You wear the same shirt and it gets dust on it with the sweat. It sticks on your face, the dust's on your face, you're covered in dust, and there's nothing to wash with.'

Water was short. 'The four pints per tank meant that we had to take turns as to who washed first,' remembered Lieutenant Jock McGinlay, a troop commander with 7th RTR. 'Being first or second wasn't too bad, but quite often I passed up my turn when I was to be last.' 'One pint per man, per day – perhaps!' declared Rollins: 'It's nothing, is it? And its chlorinated – Oh God, I hate it – Foul! And when you make a brew, all the scum was floating on the top and around your cup there's three million flies!'

Flies, food and the dead went together and were reflected as such in popular desert vocabulary. The Afrika Korps staple was Italian tinned tough beef labelled *AM* or *Administrazione Militare*. This was promptly christened *Alter Mann* or 'Old Man' by the Germans and *Arabo Morte* or 'Dead Arab' by the Italians. The British subsisted on bully beef, prepared in hundreds of variations. Flies got into everything. 'They fed on the dead,' complained Private Penn with the Eighth Army at El Alamein, 'then came round trying to feed on our water and food.' Rollins declared: 'they sent people mad . . . they're in your eyes, wherever there's moisture.' With bodies around, 'well, you wouldn't know if it was a piece of body because it was all black with flies, and when you get near them they all fly off and you can see it's a bit of head or an arm, or something lying there.' Minds became inured to death. 'Of course the flies "wanted water just like we did", announced Penn, "they would dive-bomb our tea" and would float on top. "The only way to get rid of them was not to tip it out, it was to sieve the tea with your teeth and just blow it off." '

Getting into a tank means clambering up the steep sides to gain entry via the turret. 'A turret four feet in diameter, and chock-full of the clap-trap of war – two pounder breech, wireless set, ammunition etc is not conducive to easily entering,' recalled Captain David Ling, worming his way into a Matilda Mark II turret. This action might recur countless times during any given day. 'Swathed as we were in greatcoats and leather jerkins, the operation was one requiring time and skill with much final shrugging and twisting to bed down in comfort,' not the pathway desired for speedy exits under duress. The desert was cold at night in the summer and in winter, but temperatures rose steadily after sunrise.

Once inside the turret, visibility was immediately restricted to an 18 × 6 inch letterbox vision-slit view of what was going on outside. Not being able to see clearly raised tension and obliged crews to be totally reliant upon each other, because the machine in which they fought was a weapon system. The commander's function was to lead the crew and possibly other sub-units, he also gave instructions to the gunner, who fired the main gun. The driver had to best position the tank in battle to survive and enable the gunner to successfully engage targets from cover on direction from the commander. Fourth and later fifth crew members were radio operators, responsible for the commander's communication with other tanks, doubling as a tank gun-loader or operating the hull-mounted machine-gun. Survival was a factor of the crew's ability to work seamlessly together. They could see more of each other inside the tank than looking out. 'These boys down in the tank they can't see,' recalled Sergeant Bert Rendell commanding a Cruiser tank. 'They know nothing but can hear the rumble of tracks.' The driver looks out but does not control a weapon, yet the others are reliant upon his judgement to identify good going over ground and demonstrate agility and skill in action. Drivers felt acutely vulnerable. Rendell once recalled his driver with his protective slit visor down, barely able to see, mumbling to himself, 'I am going to die, I am going to die.' He snapped him out of this self-imposed stupor by giving him 'a couple of heavy blows on the head and he came to'.

Not being able to see accentuated the claustrophobic nature of the crew predicament. Air inside reeked of petroleum, waste oil, exhaust fumes, and cordite when the guns were fired. No personal secrets could be withheld by men operating under such confined conditions, which meant they often knew each other too well. Enduring relationships were forged but it only took one man to break the symmetry required to successfully fight the machine and survive. 'Hoggard was a rather mediocre elderly little man and I would rather not have had him in my crew,' confessed Major Flatow, referring to his radio operator: 'He was the only one who showed he was windy and who readily admitted it. But that is nothing against him. The main thing against him was that he made a noise when he ate!'

Most crew were prepared to die for each other if necessary and did so. Lieutenant Eric Allsup with 8th RTR, now in his eighties, admits, 'I know the names of my tank crew to this day – I forget a lot else.'

Tank designers focused on the gun, armoured protection and mobility, paying little attention to the requirements of the human component. Design effort was expended on the 2 per cent of time engaged in combat rather than the 98 per cent spent getting there. British tanks were inferior to their German, American and Russian counterparts. Panzer crews managed the man/machine interface more competently, realising quickly the need to group individuals inside the tank so that the turret command trio and hull duo could look at each other and derive moral support as well as exchange tactical and technical information. This was important within the noisy confines of a metal box in battle. Loud noises within sanitised the awful sounds of battle without, adding to the unreality of their situation. Radio mush on head-sets, interrupted by tense reports or the screams and curses of other crews fighting elsewhere, added to the surreal nature of the experience.

Once the tank crew occupied its battle position shortly before dawn, the rest of the day's events would evolve. This often involved an 'advance to contact' which meant a move forward to find and engage the enemy. Tank actions normally began in the early morning or late afternoon because the heat haze that rose between those periods was sufficient to obscure accurate fire. Desert limitations applied to both sides. 'The African land and climate made its mark on this conflict,' observed Panzerjäger (anti-tank gunner) Günther Halm with the Afrika Korps: 'When the heat became unbearable in one tank battle, both sides got out of their tanks – the English as well as the Germans. When it became cooler in the evening they climbed back inside and started fighting again.'

An advance was particularly tiring because of the buffeting ride the crew had to endure traversing rough ground. Tank commanders were particularly fatigued having to stand virtually the entire day with their head just beyond the turret ring, scanning the undulating horizon for enemy. Not finding him raised stress levels that would often abruptly climax in the form of an unexpected meeting engagement. Captain David Ling confessed to this acute fear on his first advance. 'This fright was as nothing compared to the fright I was to know in later battles – fright backed by knowledge of the previous fright,' he admitted. There was no tell-tale gun flash, 'only silence and stillness'. Crews feared the vulnerability that came with over-caution by commanders. Ling was urged on by his corporal loader – 'Don't go slowly, sir, Keep moving, sir.' When he requested his driver to slow down to better enable him to focus his binoculars on suspicious ambush sites he was urged, 'Christ's sake – keep moving, sir!'

Locating well camouflaged and feared 88mm Flak guns was about luck. If one survived the initial engagements there remained the possibility of developing the future canny instinct to pick out potential ambush positions. Ling's baptism began when: 'The whoosh of a shell close to my head surprised me and I redoubled my efforts to find a target. There should have been a trace of the gun after firing. Dust should have been kicked up and – whoosh, whoosh. Where the hell was the damned thing?' His Matilda was struck at the enemy's fourth attempt.

The noise of battle in such chance encounters added to the total shock and confusion of the moment. 'If you're in a tank and an armour-piercing anti-tank shot just misses you, it sounds like this . . .

MEEOOW!' claimed Corporal Peter Watson with the 2nd RTR. 'If it hits, you hear just a thud, you don't feel much, but if it penetrates you feel just a little shake and depending where it lands, you either survive or you don't.' In peculiar desert climactic conditions a direct hit could sometimes be detected with the onrushing shock wave cleaving the air apart. One Grant tank commander saw such a round, 'a strange phenomenon which only occurs when one is looking right along the line of sight of a shot'. German 88mm Flak guns fired a projectile ten times the weight of the standard British 2-pounder, the shell crashing in at a velocity of between 800 to 1,000 metres per second.

Armour-piercing solid shot bores through metal drilled by kinetic energy jetting molten metal into the fighting compartment, which invariably sets off an ammunition explosion. An artillery direct hit explodes on the exterior and the shockwave can break off a jagged metal 'scab' which then ricochets around inside the vehicle, lacerating occupants and likewise detonating ammunition. Survivors testify to a blinding 'instantaneous flash' inside the tank interior on impact. 'On entry,' Captain Ling explained, 'it burned all exposed hair and seared the surface of the eyes.' This shock occurred on impact even if the projectile failed to penetrate. He surmised, 'it was thought that the impact under certain conditions sparked the fuel fumes and the aluminium interior painting in the turret.' Near misses were terrifying, both within and outside the hull. Major Flatow at El Alamein recalled seeing a large 88mm shell 'literally bouncing along the ground at a terrific speed and singing as it went'. The cumulative impact of these noises 'was all rather hair-raising', he recalled. 'Big black shells kept bursting among us and also shells with a peculiar double-crack.'

Death within the claustrophobic confines of a tank turret was nasty and brutish. David Ling momentarily blacked out after the strike and came to to find his gunner, Trooper Bucket, sprawled across him, 'his head split in twain'. He was entangled with the body, trapping the crew below beneath a corpse whose 'hot blood poured over and through me, a black glistening stream from the back of his crushed skull'. Buckled machinery and corpses often pinned crews, who had only seconds to get out of blazing tanks. Ling and his crew heaved the body aside to get out. 'I remember,' Ling recalled, 'I stretched my arm to push him forward and away, and that two of my fingers went through the hole in his skull, into the warm softness within.'

The all-pervasive fear was that of fire. Only about five to eight seconds were available to bale out, an achievement accomplished even by crewmen missing limbs. Oxygen was rapidly consumed in the flames, so that shouting and screaming was the equivalent of a drowning man blowing out his remaining air. 'Donaldson died well' was Ling's testament for a brother officer:

> His tank was hit and raging with flames, he told his crew to evacuate as the ammunition exploded and bit into their legs and bodies. Out went the radio operator and Donaldson, demanding to go last, passed with all his strength his gunner over him and heaved him up, badly wounded. They fell to safety to see their commander lift himself and fall back into the spluttering steel, his last strength spent.

John Donaldson had run out of air.

'The flames shoot up, 30 to 40 feet high, and if you're not out in a few seconds you are dead,' recalled Corporal Peter Watson. He and his crew managed to evade the German infantry sent out to apprehend them after baling out and made it back to their own lines. 'I felt a queer feeling on my face, so I put my hand up and water was pouring down. I had blisters as big as saucers, and I'd lost my pride and joy – my moustache. That went for a Burton, my eyebrows went, my ears were burnt, the whole of my face.'

A medical sergeant trying to comfort and assist offered, 'I'll cut that off for you, Corporal'. 'Cut what off?' Watson responded. 'Good God man, look at your arms and wrists.' And Watson glanced down and began to comprehend the future misery he would undergo. 'Hanging down about a foot,' he observed, 'was skin on both arms, like an umbrella.' Years of painful surgery followed. 'You think you're going to look like an ape for the rest of your life, don't you, Corporal?' he was provocatively asked by his skin specialist from Harley Street. Watson was inclined to agree, he was in a terrible state with 'lips about an inch thick and all crusted, my beard had grown and sand has stuck on the burns, there was puss and I had gone black'. His doctor, 'a smashing bloke' Watson recalled, promised he would 'tidy' him up. Years later he humorously confirmed during interview, 'and he was right – look how handsome I am!'

At about 2100 opposing tanks tended to break off action and began to pull back for the night to seek their respective harbour areas. Under cover of darkness attempts were made to recover the human and mechanical flotsam from the scarred desert expanse. Often the move back required a two- to three-hour night drive, with straining eyes and tired minds attempting to focus on navigation across a featureless terrain, while exposed to the choking dust clouds of vehicles moving ahead. On arrival, tanks needed to be refuelled, rearmed and minor repairs and maintenance carried out. Sleep rarely came before 0100, and then only three hours or so, interrupted by guards with briefings for leaders before the dawn stand-to. Food cooked twelve hours previously at B Echelon would arrive, usually quite unpalatable and often after the men had retired to sleep. Rest was preferred to food. 'Under such conditions,' concluded an official report, 'the fighting efficiency of crews falls off very seriously after a week's continuous fighting.'

The desert campaign and victory at El Alamein in November 1942 was a peculiarly British and Commonwealth triumph. Church bells rang in England for the first time since the invasions scares after Dunkirk. Victory was achieved by resourceful and pragmatic soldiers 'making do'. The very vocabulary of the desert campaign reflected the suspected muddling through that had occurred. 'Fart-arsing around' or 'swanning about the Blue' (i.e. the desert), without knowing where one was, encapsulated to many the questionable generalship and organisation that characterised early stumbles during the 'Benghazi handicap'.

There was realisation Allied tanks were inferior to the panzers until the arrival of American-designed and manufactured variants, which were put into mass production at the point when they had achieved tentative technical parity with the panzers. They were to lose it again by the end of 1943. Major success was achieved before the American landings in North Africa, which occurred soon after El Alamein. It held a unique place in the wartime generation's psyche as a turning point. 'Now this is not the beginning of the end,' announced Prime Minister Churchill. 'It is not the beginning of the end. But it is perhaps, the end

The tank crew view of the desert war, seen through the driver's opened vision block of a Grant tank.

Tank bail-out. 'If it hits you hear just a thud . . . you either survive or you don't', explained one crewman. Baling out of a crippled cruiser tank, this crewman scrambles to get away.

Primary senses – sight, sound, touch and smell became all-important in the jungle. There are eight soldiers moving through the foliage in this picture taken from the tree canopy.

of the beginning.' There was still a long way to go. The invasions of Sicily and Italy followed in 1943.

Success, however, had still eluded the British and Commonwealth in the Far Eastern reaches of the Empire.

JUNGLE INFANTRY

At night in mid-March 1944 floating bridges were launched across the Chindwin River. When they came to rest on the western bank, swarms of Japanese soldiers crossed. Bullocks carrying collapsible carts, soldiers pulling metal hand carts and others toting ammunition boxes on their shoulders streamed across. At dawn the bridges were swung back and hidden beneath the protective overhead jungle canopy and dismantled, to await the next night.

Three Japanese divisions were on the march, the 31st to the north, the 15th in the centre and the 33rd in the south, heading westward on foot along Burmese jungle trails toward the Tiddim, Imphal and Kohima road to Dimapur bordering India. 'We had to cross the rugged Arakan mountain range for about 200 kilometres from east to west,' recalled Captain Shosaku Kameyama with the Japanese 58th Infantry Regiment forming part of the 31st Division advance on Kohima. Each man carried two weeks' worth of rations, ammunition, shovels and clothes; a total weight of forty to fifty kilograms. 'This was so heavy,' Kameyama remembered, 'that once we sat down to rest we could not stand up by ourselves; we had to be pulled up by someone.' They trickled along jungle tracks across the high mountain ranges assisted by only oxen and mules.

Both sides had been ready to go on the offensive that spring in the difficult terrain of the Indian-Burmese border country. The Japanese U-Go and Ha-Go offensives had stolen the march, crossing these wild hills with no roads and initially undetected, as they had done when ejecting the British from Malaya and much of Burma in 1941–2. Once more they gambled on making deep penetrations and living off captured Allied stocks. Up to now the Japanese had dominated jungle operations.

Whereas the forerunners of the Eighth Army were familiar with and had fought in the desert, there was no such reservoir of imperial traditional skills to be handed over for jungle fighting. 'My father served in the First World War in the desert,' recalled Private Reed with the Eighth Army, 'and I had a fair idea what to expect.' The terrain was as familiar as the traditional German enemy. He was a known entity, Christian, and exposed to the same European ideological and social influences as the British. The Afrika Korps proved a skilled, resourceful and bitter foe, likely better led, but the British soldier had total confidence he would be beaten. Not so the Japanese soldier. He was different, austere, totally committed to his Emperor and the warrior *Bushido* ethic that required him if necessary to die for a righteous cause. Japanese soldiers in Burma were young, averaging between twenty and twenty-two years, and were from tough healthy peasant stock, used to hard work. Harsh brutal recruit training coupled with the pitiless veteran experience of the war in China had produced an implacably aggressive foe, completely at ease in the jungle. 'The Japanese were animals but great soldiers,' declared Captain Neville Hogan with the Burma Rifles. 'Their battle drills were fantastic. You couldn't help but admire them.' The British, however, at the outset had naturally assumed they would be better than ten foreigners in any imperial contest. They were proven completely wrong.

The seven-week Malayan campaign, ending with the fall of Singapore in February 1942 to a numerically inferior Japanese force, with its surrender of 90,000 British and Commonwealth troops, was a humiliating disaster and was ultimately to loosen the fabric of the Empire. An incredulous Major General Henry Bennett recorded in his diary at the beginning of 1942 that 'this retreat seems fantastic. Fancy 500 miles in 50 days – chased by a Jap army on stolen bikes without artillery.' His soldiers were equally nonplussed. Ian McKenzie, who was captured with the Gordon Highlanders in Singapore recalled: 'And I got a shock when I'd a right look at the Japs. Is that what the hell beat us? Raggedy shirts and rubber boots. What the hell are we letting them beat us for?'

Over 10,000 casualties came from the fighting retreat by British and Indian troops 1,000 miles across Burma, of which 3,670 were killed or wounded and 6,366 missing. General Alexander wrote despondently to General Wavell commenting upon the declining effectiveness of Allied troops retreating across the River Irrawaddy. 'They DO NOT KNOW their jobs as well as the Jap, and there's an end to it.'

Jungle fighting was the problem, both tactically and psychologically. Japanese tactics were based upon mobility and speed. Opposition was bypassed by infiltrating through the jungle and encircling road-bound British, Commonwealth and Indian units who sought to block the few jungle thoroughfares. David Marshall, with the Malayan Straits Settlement Volunteer Corps, assessed inexperienced British soldiers as jungle shy, claiming they were 'stiff with fear and had really lost the battle psychologically before it began'. Captain Teruo Okada, a Japanese intelligence officer, felt 'the jungle is not such a terrible place'. And 'it did not have the fear that it seems to have had for some Allied soldiers'. Camouflage and night fighting was extensively taught in the Japanese Army and normal training sufficed for both the deserts of China and jungles of Malaya and Burma. 'You see we can live on rice, salt and sesame seeds and salted fish, this can keep a soldier going a long time, also we can find things in the jungle to eat,' Okada explained. Fear of the jungle inculcated a British road block mentality, amateurs versus professional Japanese infiltration and encirclement tactics. Marshall commented, 'going into that jungle he was afraid of all the unseen terrors and only too glad to get away.' Another British commander in Malaya concluded: 'It was the eeriness, they dreaded the insects and snakes, they hated not being able to see the dangers. They imagined that death lurked behind every tree, they could not move, forward or backward except with great difficulty and they felt glued to the spot, with threats all around them.'

As in the case of the Western Desert, reinforcements despatched from rural and urban communities in England to reverse the disaster travelled a long way to fight. They were to witness the exotic sights of the Empire in the Far East previously only viewed from school text books or celebrated on Empire Day. Raymond Cooper, a Border Regiment company commander, enjoyed a virtual 'peace-time cruise' aboard the liner *Orcades*. They languished in first-class cabins, lounges, swimming pool, concert hall and strolled across the large promenade deck. Down below the soldiers had 'tiers of hammocks slung along the mess decks as thick as cells in a hive' and 'queues formed half-way round the ship for meals, canteens, even for baths'. Michael Lowry, a twenty-three-year-old lieutenant in the Queen's Royal Regiment, recalled the 'optical illusion' of ships floating on the desert traversing the

Suez Canal. They experienced the ferocious heat of the Red Sea and the wonders of flying fish; 'before breakfast on the boat deck it was 110 in the shade,' which rose to 120 degrees. It was military tourism at its best.

All this represented a new experience. 'I don't think the troops were ever prepared to like India, about which they were one and all lamentably ignorant,' declared Raymond Cooper on arrival. He blamed 'the narrowness of general education in Britain, which apart from its other faults did not seem to have imbued anyone with the desire to learn more than was immediately connected with the earning of his living'. This was combined with 'the good old feeling of it's not like that in my back garden so it can't be right out here'. Immersion in this new environment would change attitudes. Michael Lowry was amazed to see heaps of bodies lying about the streets of Bombay until he appreciated that 'Indians would doss down when and where they felt inclined and cover up their heads to keep off the flies'. 'It was a very long way from home, and had taken a lot of hot weary travelling to get to,' declared Private George MacDonald Fraser with the Border Regiment. 'It was a far corner of the world,' he recalled and when opening mail one 'saw the well-remembered writing, you had the feeling that it came from another planet'. The Fourteenth Army that formed in Burma to reverse Japanese success was a British–Indian Army, of which the British formed only 30 per cent. As MacDonald Fraser expressed it, 'the final echo of Kipling's world, the very last soldiers in the old imperial tradition'. It was to prove a unique experience.

'Jungle warfare was still very much in its experimental stages and "Bungle Warfare" still seemed to most people a better description of our efforts,' declared Raymond Cooper prior to the battle around Kohima. The geography of the Indo-Burma frontier made movement extremely difficult east-west across the grain of the country. 'We began to enter a part of the earth dominated by the landscape and not by its inhabitants,' described Cooper. This massive theatre of war had virtually no communications through the jungle-covered mountains up to 3,000 to 4,000 feet high. Large-scale military operations, only able to utilise the few roads and all-weather tracks were exceptionally difficult. There was a massive engineering commitment to bridge rivers and streams transformed into raging torrents by the Monsoon rains. Fighting was conducted at the end of lengthy and precarious lines of communication. 'Perhaps the best way is to compare the jungle to a very beautiful woman,' described Lieutenant Colonel O G W White: 'The pin-up dream girl in full Technicolor, cool, alluring, beautiful and attractive in the heat to look at but once approached and negotiated with, full of the greatest possibilities of danger and death to the unwary. This simile is particularly apt because, like the figure of a pin-up girl, the jungle is never flat.'

'The physical hammering one takes is difficult to understand,' claimed Signals Officer Lieutenant Horner with the 2nd Royal Norfolks. 'The heat, humidity, altitude and the slope of almost every foot of ground combine to knock hell out of the stoutest constitution.' Every pause appeared to signify yet another false crest, with a path still snaking upwards: 'You gasp for air which doesn't seem to come, you drag your legs upwards till they seem reduced to the strength of matchsticks, you wipe the sweat out of your eyes. Then you feel your heart pounding so violently you think it must burst its cage; it sounds like a drum, even above the swearing and cursing going on around you.'

Yet the strength required was constantly sapped by disease and privation. 'I had Malaria 17 times,' declared Private Joe Hammersley with the Fourteenth Army. 'I was in hospital exactly 21 days and then came out and went into action. I'd been in action again for about five weeks and I was taken out with dysentery.' After four more weeks in hospital he was back in action again. The climate in Burma is one of the unhealthiest in the world; hot, humid tropical jungle covered the mountains and lowland areas on the central Burma plain, which reached temperatures of over 100°F before the Monsoon rains. These occurred between November and February in the north-east, and mid-May to mid-October in the south-west and enveloped Assam and Burma with exceptionally heavy rainfall of up to 200 and 500 inches in parts. Fifteen inches of precipitation was recorded on one day in Arakan alone. Living conditions in this sodden environment were difficult in the extreme, permanently wet troops found their equipments became mildewed and rotten. 'If you haven't seen the Monsoon burst, it's difficult to imagine,' described George MacDonald Fraser:

There are the first huge drops, growing heavier and heavier, and then God opens the sluices and the jets of a million high-pressure hoses are being directed straight down, and the deluge comes with a great roar, crashing against the leaves and rebounding from the earth for perhaps a minute – after that the earth is under a skin of water which looks as though its being churned up by buckshot. Before you know it you are sodden and streaming.

Leeches proliferated in such conditions. 'New British blood was apparently nectar to them,' declared Michael Lowry with the Queen's Royal Regiment. They crawled through bootlace holes and 'got so bloated by this apparent bottomless pit of blood that they would never have seen daylight again had it not been for the pain the men felt as the swollen leeches tried to share a boot which only just fitted a swollen foot'. The more adventurous 'took more juicy blood from around the crutch' and soldiers despaired, as Lowry confirmed, 'they were the devil to extract as their strong suckers at the mouth and the rear appeared to be glued to the human skin.' Salt or cigarette burning 'usually did the trick' but 'you can't always light a cigarette and salt isn't always to hand'.

Throughout the war malaria, amoebic dysentery, cholera, scrub typhus, dengue fever, smallpox and other assorted tropical diseases endemic in South-East Asia caused far higher casualties to both sides than enemy action. Malaria accounted for 50 per cent of all recorded sickness between 1942–4. 'Half the section was feverish to some degree and scoured by dysentery in its various forms,' complained George MacDonald Fraser with the Borderers. One of his Cumbrian friends complained, 'Ah'm crappin' ivvery clour bar blue.' Excessive rainfall 'puckered the skin in a revoltingly puffy fashion', he recalled, 'and brought forth a great plague of jungle sores on wrists and ankles'. One officer recalled a soldier, not prone to grumbling, declaring with some exasperation, 'this ain't fighting bloody Japs; it's fighting bloody nature!'

During the relative pause following ejection from Malaya and much of Burma at the end of 1942 to late 1943, the British and Commonwealth troops came to terms with jungle life. Patrolling and minor tactics took on crucial importance. It was found roads were better secured by employing fighting patrols from defended localities. Immediate action battle drills were developed to screen, identify the enemy and replicate Japanese tactics of moving through the jungle to fix, then encircle, enemy penetrations. Company commander Raymond Cooper explained, 'I was an enormous believer in battle drills of various kinds, something which would give us instantaneously the best reaction to ambush, to sudden attack on a hidden bunker, or to the quick shaking out of a patrol into a defensive position.'

The antidote to Japanese infiltration tactics was the advent of the 'defensive box' which, with the achievement of Allied air superiority, could be re-supplied by air. There was no longer regard for a conventional front line, surrounded troops simply held on within the box and were re-supplied by air until the Japanese with over-extended lines of communication were forced to concede in static battles of attrition. Soldiers were better jungle-trained and as Raymond Cooper explained, the apparent previous invincibility of the Japanese jungle soldier could be contained. 'So many of our supplies were already being dropped by air,' he recalled, 'that the idea of being surrounded caused no despair.'

The Japanese Ha-Go and U-Go offensives against Imphal and Kohima began in March 1944. They gambled on capturing British supplies by launching a surprise infiltration attack with three divisions across the grain of the deep valleys and steep jungle-covered mountains west of the Chindwin River towards India, accepting tenuous all-weather tracks as lines of communication. Japanese battalion commander Lieutenant Colonel Ichii Sugita recalled his pessimism 'because they told us the operation would be a success but I told them we had no air superiority'. He was well aware of the immense physical difficulties: 'At that time the soldiers and officers I met spoke of adverse conditions, especially due to short supply on the spot and they believed that they are unable to succeed.'

An infantryman often had to have his equipment packed ready to move in darkness prior to the dawn stand-to. Invariably he was soaking wet from rain or sweat and would have to feel around in the darkness to sort out his weapon and kit. Patrolling was a feature of life, whatever the position. A clearance patrol would stealthily circle the perimeter at dawn to confirm security. Patrols were employed to seize the initiative, disorganise enemy encircling operations, gather information and dominate the surrounding jungle. A fighting patrol might be employed to capture prisoners, assault an objective or lay an ambush. 'Tiger' patrols with three to five men formed the smallest sub-unit, whereas a fighting patrol could be up to platoon or even over a hundred-men company strength.

Getting ready for a patrol was an activity suffused with expectancy and latent tension. 'It was all very business-like and unhurried,' recalled Private George MacDonald Fraser describing one such event. 'Quiet voices, magazines being charged and safety catches going on, feet shuffling, the light of the storm lantern reflected on faces.'

Navigation was difficult and virtually impossible at night in secondary close-bush jungle, which required hacking through. Direction was calculated by compass with time and distance measured by a 'pacer', who monitored progress based on average distances that could be achieved in primary jungle – high trees with little bush – and secondary, more closely packed jungle. Recognisable headgear was worn to aid night recognition. A platoon-size patrol would be headed by two scouts at visible distance to the next element, the lead section of ten men, followed by the headquarters with mules, two more sections and a tail-end Charlie pair to the rear. 'An emergency rendezvous (RV) was arranged every few hours in case we had to scatter,' recalled company commander Raymond Cooper with the Border Regiment.

Stealthy movement was difficult. 'Just try it with a hundred men!' enjoined Cooper. 'Speed was hard to regulate with obstacles to climb over or through, and gaps would occur.' A man, realising he had lost contact with the fellow in front, would say to himself, 'Oh well, I'm bound to catch him up in a minute.' Within half an hour such a large fighting patrol might find itself in two halves a mile apart. Taps on the shoulder were passed along when visibility was lost, to halt the column. Trust, experience and cool heads were needed to make the company-size 'snake' single-file column work. All this had to be conducted quietly and stealthily. 'After not raising one's voice for a fortnight,' Cooper recalled after a long range penetration patrol, 'it is difficult to get out of the habit, and I have several times returned from a long patrol and surprised everyone by continuing to talk in a whisper.'

Traversing the difficult Burmese terrain was both physically and mentally draining. Dehydration leading to the onset of heat exhaustion was a common hazard. Minds began to wander as symptoms became more apparent. 'As the hours passed,' recalled Cooper, 'the hills ahead seemed to get steeper in my thoughts, and the jungles thicker and more Jap infested.' A winding path at night could be particularly frustrating. 'Every time it wound our leading man walked straight into a bush, and we were very scratched and bad tempered by the time we suddenly came out on a broad path.' Tension while moving was all-pervasive. 'I remember every step,' claimed George MacDonald Fraser, 'as I walked on eggshells.'

There was always the immediate hazard of unexpected and sudden contact with the enemy. MacDonald Fraser claimed his senses were heightened to the point he could detect the odour of 'Jap'. 'I can no more describe the smell than I could describe a colour, but it was heavy and pungent and compounded of stale cooked rice and sweat and human waste and . . . Jap.' Primary senses – sight, sound, touch and smell – became all-important. Visibility in secondary jungle was inferior to the more open spaces beneath the luxuriant canopy of primary jungle. Little could be seen so dependence was upon sound signatures. 'We froze to verify every noise,' recalled Raymond Cooper on patrol. 'Ears can carry further than eyes in that country, and we could afford no risks when even the crackle of a leaf or the cry of a bird might prove to be a slant-eyed patrol.' George MacDonald Fraser learned to 'take your time' and 'don't lose contact' with the other patrol members. 'When in doubt, sink down and listen, and try to remember that darkness is a friend, because with experience came the knowledge that Jap was certainly no better in the dark than we were.'

The whole point of the patrol was generally to make contact with the enemy. Quite often they would see nothing, only hear other patrols clashing in the distance. 'Somebody's having a duffy,' was the comment during MacDonald Fraser's patrol on hearing distant firing. When the enemy did take tangible shape it was often emotionally unexpected and set the senses racing. After discerning Japanese voices nearby Raymond Cooper struggled to control his feelings:

In the next few interminable minutes I remember cursing myself for just having removed my bayonet for fear it was shining in the sun, feeling convinced my rifle would misfire, fearing Robinson would give the show away by re-appearing before the Nips reached us, wondering the height from the ground of a Japanese stomach and what they were talking about, and envying Spearitt for already eating his sardines.

Events took place hiding and lying at leaf top level which obscured vision, therefore one was totally dependent upon sound until the enemy actually appeared. 'It was not easy to find a place where we could shoot without being seen,' observed Cooper. At this point decision and action had to be immediate. Once committed, there could be no subsequent reflection in hindsight. 'The decision by an ambush commander as to when to open fire, particularly at night, is pregnant with problems which have to be solved almost instantaneously,' remembered Michael Lowry with the Queen's Royal Regiment. 'At close quarters covering a track in thick country at night, and in the misty gloom, a soldier cannot really see his rifle or gun sights, and so to make sure of success, the enemy is invariably taken out at very close quarters.'

'Contact', or the fight, was invariably nasty, brutish and short. 'The difference of one or two seconds could be too soon or too late,' explained Lowry, 'it is ultimately life or death.' The incident Lowry described was a close-quarter fight with Japanese sword, automatic weapon and rifle and bayonet. Private Wally New with the Fourteenth Army vividly recalled if the Japanese were ambushed 'they were at you in 20 to 30 seconds'. It was primarily the clashes between opposing patrols seeking jungle supremacy that characterised the fighting in Burma beyond a small number of large set-piece conventional conflicts. 'The same old thing happened again, patrols went out and many of our chaps got bayoneted and the Japs suffered casualties as well,' explained New. 'But it wasn't a major big battle like it was in Europe, more close fighting on these patrols.'

During the U–Go Japanese infiltration offensive beginning in March 1944, that culminated in heavy defensive battles around Imphal and Kohima, British and Commonwealth infantry primarily manned hastily established defensive positions to block unexpected multiple Japanese advances. It was here that the myth of Japanese jungle invincibility was laid to rest. Initially the speed and timing of the sudden Japanese advance after 9 March, as on the Malay peninsula, caught the British off-guard, but the Imphal road was not cut until 29 March. The fiercest fighting was at Kohima and the siege at Imphal held because air superiority enabled substantial reinforcements to be airlifted, while jungle defensive boxes were supplied by air. It proved the decisive battle in Burma.

Material superiority was not decisive during the early Malay and Burma campaigns. What transpired beneath the jungle canopy was a world apart from the focused way material superiority was applied in the battles for north-west Europe. Beneath the trees it was man against man and British and Commonwealth infantry blunted the Japanese offensive against India.

'I found the British infantry has the staying power,' concluded Major Mike Calvert, a British jungle-warfare expert. 'He may not be the best attacking troop in the world, he's not terribly good at pursuit and he doesn't like hitting a man when he's down.' 'Kohima being a small place we did not expect the resistance they put up,' remembered Japanese intelligence officer Captain Teruo Okada. 'We just hoped to cut them off but the resistance was such we could never completely isolate them.' The core of resistance in the confined and quite often isolated series of battles fought in the jungle came from the physical and mental resilience identified by Calvert 'which would win in the end and which was kindled by the jokes of the British troops which kept one going again and again'.

At the heart of this community of resistance was the basic ten-man infantry section, stemming from its wider tribal family, the regiment. 'Even the most cynical reluctant conscript was conscious of belonging to something special,' recalled George MacDonald Fraser, surrounded by Cumbrian friends in the Border Regiment. 'If he came from the regimental area, the tie was all the stronger' The section, MacDonald Fraser explained, 'was his military family . . . Those seven or eight other men were his constant companions, waking, sleeping, standing guard, eating, digging, patrolling, marching and fighting, and he got to know them better perhaps than anyone in his whole life except his wife, parents and children. He counted on them, and they on him.'

Within the section each man had his own 'mucker' or mate, a functional as well as emotional attachment because most tasks required two men to do them. This involved digging trenches, carrying stretchers, one might cook while the other watched out. In action they provided each other with covering fire every time they moved and would rescue the other if one was wounded. It was not dissimilar to the emotional bond between any two spear-men in the ancient Macedonian phalanx of Alexander's day. Everything was subsumed to maintain an unbroken wall of spears, meaning only two of the phalanx of spear-men were impacted should one be wounded. As MacDonald Fraser reminisced, they complained and laughed together and took pleasure in reviling each other: 'I remember those section brew-ups as some of the friendliest gatherings of my life.'

Manning a defensive line at night in the jungle in anticipation of an expected Japanese infiltration attack, was the time of greatest tension for the infantry soldier. 'A stag was a two-hour watch of two men, armed with rifle and bandoliers, normally standing in one pit,' explained MacDonald Fraser. 'It was eerie, but placid enough; you got used to the night-sounds and to the odd tricks that your eyesight can play you, causing bushes to stir when they're perfectly still, or detecting movement from the corner of your eye which isn't there when you look at it directly.' Company commander Raymond Cooper recalled nights when he was able to reflect on the beauty of his surroundings, but such esoterics were rarely shared at section level: 'The soldier staring out into the vast silence hour after hour and wondering if he heard the crackle of footsteps or the click of a detonator – wondering in many cases what a Japanese looked like anyway – found little to admire even in those innumerable masses of tropical stars or the pale brilliance of the Burma moon.'

Michael Lowry thought the conditions 'all very eerie'. Not being able to see, they were dependent upon sounds. 'The monkeys at night appeared to be playing at being noisy soldiers as they simulated the movement of humans,' he recalled. Natural sounds accentuated the Kipling-like scenery. 'During those nights there was also a continual pitter-patter of dew falling from leaf to leaf, and a mist which formed at about midnight and did not completely lift until 9.00 am.'

At the heart of tension lay fear and hatred of the Japanese. 'I hated the Japanese then and I do now,' declared Private Leonard Brown with the Queen's Own Royal West Kent Regiment. 'As soldiers I think they were very good but to torture prisoners – that's not soldiering, that's butchery.' Private Joe Hammersley recalled prisoners subjected to nail pulling and castration and the rape of English nurses. 'They'd torture you until you gave them the position of your own troops,' he remembered, 'we could hear the prisoners screaming.' Despite the abomination of the Holocaust that emerged in Europe, the bitterness directed against the Germans was not comparable to the deep emotions raised by the Japanese fighting the Fourteenth Army. 'Many people in this war have had worse times and harder fighting,' commented Major Norman Durant with 77th Brigade, 'but anyone who has fought the Italians, French, Germans and Japs will say with no hesitation that the Japs are the ones to be avoided.' His view was totally uncompromising:

> Somehow one can imagine that under different circumstances one could have a drink and a cigarette with a German and a quite amiable talk and a cup of tea with a prisoner, but having once met the Japs one can only imagine kicking their heads in. They look like animals and behave like animals and they can be killed as unemotionally as swatting flies. And they need to be killed, not wounded for so long as they can breathe they're dangerous.

Attacking a jungle defensive position was fraught with difficulties for both sides. Michael Lowry described the obvious onset of a Japanese attack, given away by 'the beating and hacking of trees and scuffling of feet' demonstrating it was 'decidedly coming ever closer to us'. 'Sometimes the Japs would be about five or six yards in front of us and it would be hand grenades and rifles,' described Private Joe Hammersley. 'They could speak English as well as we could – and they'd call out 'Over here, Taffy', or 'Over here Bill'. You'd get up and bang, the Japs had you.' Lowry described how the ominous approaching noise rose to a crescendo until 'in the half-light we could see them about eight yards away'. In such close-foliage conditions fighting was close-quarter, almost medieval. Lowry lost three men cut down by a Japanese sergeant major wielding a sword – two killed and one wounded. Grenades were bowled to nullify this particular approach: 'We ducked into our slit trenches and the Japs knew nothing of us until the grenades burst literally between their legs. Amid shrieks and moans and some chatter, the enemy fell back down the hill in the direction from which they had come, but the close blasts of the grenades and the smoke they gave off temporarily blinded us.' Bodies were later recovered with pieces of grenade stuck in the woodwork of their rifles.

Fighting around Kohima developed from a jungle contest to a First World War pockmarked landscape of shattered tree-stumps and water-filled craters. Allied material superiority in conditions of a stripped-off jungle canopy could be more effectively applied as artillery churned up the landscape and air superiority enabled – weather permitting – close support and the air transport of whole divisions as reinforcements. The Japanese siege was broken. 'We were in Kohima for three weeks,' recalled Major Boshell, a company commander with the 1st Battalion the Royal Berkshire Regiment, overlooking the tennis courts at the heart of the battle for the settlement. 'We were attacked every single night,' he claimed, 'they came in waves, it was like a pigeon shoot.' It became a battle of attrition. 'Most nights they overran part of the battalion position, so we had to mount counter-attacks.' His company was reduced from a hundred to sixty men. By 8 July the Japanese decided to withdraw, its Fifteenth Army effectively destroyed in a series of protracted battles that cost 30,000 men for the loss of 16,700 Allied casualties. The destruction of Japanese power in north-east India effectively paved the way for the Allied invasion and conquest of Burma from the north in 1945.

These events were not immediately in the public eye back home. They were a distant side-show in the public mind, beside the great events about to occur in France and north-west Europe. It was not even realised how decisive the battles around Kohima had been.

Up to this point there had also been no decisive battle on the European mainland in the west. One year before Home Guardsman Frank Edwards recalled, 'this evening I saw a very thrilling and awe-inspiring sight.' It was dusk and he was alerted to the roaring sound of approaching aircraft engines. Beginning with three flying low, more and more followed:

Until the sky over our end of the road seemed to be full of these mighty bombers. Some had their lights on; some had just the tail-light; and some just a white light on top of the plane. All these planes, although well apart, were going in the same direction and no doubt would join up in formation when further out. Evidently starting at this hour they were going on a long journey and I should say we were seeing the start.

Sicily was invaded in July 1943, followed two weeks later by the fall of Mussolini. When in September the Allies invaded Italy the new government agreed an Armistice and declared war on Germany. But the principal offensive directed from the UK mainland at Germany remained the bombing offensive, now in concert with the Eighth US Air Force. Although it received generous media coverage, compared to events in Burma, little was known about it, apart from those actually serving on bomber air stations. Only when they took off was their reassuring and appreciably growing mass apparent to the general public. As Frank Edwards recalled: 'we watched them going over until after blackout time when we had to light up, but the roar of these planes lasted for over an hour.'

They came and went most nights, depending upon the hours of darkness, almost like inter-city commuters. With the continued absence of a Second Front on mainland Europe, they plied their deadly night-time trade over Germany with a frequency approaching bizarre routine.

9

RAF BOMBER RAID

'YOU'RE ON TONIGHT' – TAKE OFF

They landed in twos and threes one after the other at irregular intervals during the final dark hours preceding dawn. Viewed from above, the conglomeration of runway lights switched on to guide them appeared in places to enclose each other or overlap. Over 1,000 airfields criss-crossed the UK, covering some 360,000 acres of land, densely packed around Lincolnshire, Nottinghamshire, Norfolk and Yorkshire. Most bombers were down and crews asleep before the last late-comers touched down with relieved tyre squeals. Apart from cripples coming in the whole process could be likened to commuters routinely arriving at home bases after a night shift. Leading Aircraftswoman Joyce Bayes was with a squad of WAAFs marching to the camp area at RAF Mildenhall, home to two Lancaster bomber squadrons. As they strode along they became aware of the noise of an approaching aircraft, flying so low that it was obscured by the woodland bordering their route. Two of four engines were screaming at full power and belching oil and smoke when it suddenly flew past. Marching lost its rhythm as they meandered to a distracted stand-still, gazing at the stricken bomber with some apprehension.

They saw: 'Its fuselage and wings were badly scarred, with large pieces of metal flapping and banging against the framework in the slipstream. Part of the tail and the rear gun turret was non-existent and the starboard under-carriage leg hung grotesquely at an angle, like a broken limb.'

The ugly image 'somehow intensified each second', juxtaposed as it was against a crisp clear September morning in 1944, 'sharply defined against the blue, cloudless sky'. Joyce Bayes never forgot the moment. The squad 'willed the aircraft with simple but profound prayer to continue flying for the last few miles and to land safely with its crew having come this far to reach its home base'. They were snapped back to the present by the authoritative voice of their NCO who said, 'Pray for them. Just pray.' Discipline restored, the march continued as they anxiously scanned the horizon ahead 'waiting for the dull ominous thud in the distance that precedes the explosion of a crashing aircraft, with the tell-tale pall of black smoke rising skywards – but it did not come'. There was just silence. Canadian mid-upper gunner Jim Moffat with 427 Squadron at Topcliffe remembered his badly battered Lancaster survived a German night-fighter mauling, barely making the return runway. The wreckage was promptly parked in a hangar and the door locked. 'They didn't want anybody to see it. It would be too demoralising,' he commented.

A typical RAF station like that at Hemswell in Lincolnshire, a No 1 Group RAF Command airfield, might have two squadrons. This housed 150 and 170 Lancaster Squadrons with twenty aircraft each, which meant 2,500 personnel accommodated on base, of which one-tenth were aircrew. Crews would still be asleep when the day ground crew took over from the night shift. Lancasters were alive with engine mechanics, riggers, electricians, instrument fitters and radio mechanics swarming over the four-engine aircraft. Working around the clock, damaged engine changes that took a week in peacetime were replaced in five hours. Maintenance took place at dispersal points on concrete pans around the airfield. Ground crew were possessive about their charges, but there was little mechanical wear and tear to remedy because the average operational life of a Lancaster bomber was only about forty hours' flying time.

A routine day began with evaluation of the previous night's raid while awaiting the signal for 'the target for tonight'. Once this objective was selected about six hours remained for technical and logistic preparation alongside detailed operational planning. Photographic and meteorological checks were flown over the routes to and from the target, while aircraft crew compositions were compiled and chalked up on notice boards. Operational directives enabled fuel and bomb loads to be made up so that by about lunch-time the shape of the impending operation was beginning to emerge and final flying tests completed. Daily routine for aircrew began when they were awoken by a shake on the shoulder with the unwelcome news, 'You're on tonight.'

'In the morning you would go down to look at the operation list,' recalled Flight Sergeant Louis Butler with 467 Squadron, 'you find you're on for ops and you would say to your mate "we're on for tonight."' For the remainder of the day there was apprehension. 'Where to, tonight? Berlin again? The Ruhr? One of the hot-spots? Where?' 'You get a feeling in your stomach like butterflies and that feeling then stays with you all the time,' he recalled. Eighteen-year-old Canadian Doug Harvey with 408 'Goose' Squadron based at Leeming began to calculate likely objectives based on what the ground crew were telling him about the fuel and bomb load. 'The shorter the target, the less gas, the more bombs,' he recalled. 'If you saw the refuellers putting the whole load on, 2,154 gallons, you knew it was a long stooge.' Flight Sergeant Jack Currie declared, 'I knew it when they put 1,850 gallons in the tanks. I thought it'd be Berlin,' a flight time of six and a half hours. Loading bombs was labour intensive for twenty or forty aircraft, requiring tractors with trailers fanning out to the concrete pans loaded with 10,000 lb mixes of high explosive, 4,000 lb 'Cookies' and incendiaries. Electrical or mechanical faults could have disastrous consequences during this sensitive process. A 4,000 lb 'Cookie' exploded during loading at RAF Scampton on 14 March 1943, killing several men and destroying six Lancasters and badly wrecking five others.

Bomber crews operationally commuted to Germany following a typical day on, day off timetable, four out of six days or four operations in seven days. There might be a rash of operations for a month and then a long pause. Frequency of missions was dependent on the weather, moonlight and night-time hours. 'People easily forget,' explained Air Chief Marshal Arthur Harris, commanding Bomber Command, 'that for over a third of the year we could hardly get in Germany at all because there wasn't any darkness that would take you any further than the north German coast.' Short summer nights meant distant targets were too far. The resulting armchair-to-action character of operations imposed considerable strain because each trip was an emotional cold shower. 'It is difficult to describe but for five or six hours you entered a different world in which you were completely cut off from your normal life,' explained Sergeant Bill Rae, a Wellington bomber rear gunner with 142 Squadron. 'On landing back at base you suddenly switched back to real life – the next op.'

The 'Brylcreem Boys' label, applied by the envious army, encapsulated the comparative good life that aircrew enjoyed between operations. 'There was a bed for you to sleep in with sheets,' remarked Squadron Leader A F Wallace with 620 Squadron; 'there was food on plates; there were glasses to drink from.' This made him feel guilty:

> I remember contrasting these things with our friends and colleagues serving in the desert; in the jungles of the Far East; or perhaps at sea almost anywhere in the world. When we went into the Mess dining room, there was a glass of milk for the aircrew. I always felt slightly embarrassed because there was none for the ground crews on whom we were all dependent.

Accommodation varied from spartan Nissan huts on featureless airfields to well appointed quarters. 'Good food in the Sergeants Mess,' wrote Sergeant Robert Raymond, 'and I am lodged in married quarters, have my own bath and fireplace if we care to use it.'

Even so, 'the condemned men ate a hearty breakfast' recalled aircrew Ron Read, echoing his pilot 'Morty' Mortenson's macabre sense of humour voiced at the traditional bacon and eggs treat reserved solely for flying aircrew. 'We all ignored him and chewed on,' he remembered. Mortenson's prophesy was shortly fulfilled and he was killed when their Halifax was shot down by German night fighters. 'It was no wonder that aircrew were the favourites of the young girls, lonely wives and widows of surrounding districts,' Read remarked, 'but it was rather like fattening turkeys for Christmas.' Operational pressures and tension ate into these apparent comforts like corrosive acid. 'It was like going to hell and coming back to paradise,' remarked twenty-one-year-old Canadian RCAF Joseph Favreau from Quebec. 'Piccadilly Circus, warm pubs, good times. Then the next morning back to hell.' Death and comfort provided strange bed-fellows, admitting: 'This for me was the worst part, the to and fro. Many times coming back from a raid, all by myself in the back of the aeroplane, I cried, I cried like a baby, I had to. That was the only way to get out of it.'

Cumulative strain was handled alone within the routine of airbases or civilian accommodation. Only aircrew could identify with their inner turmoil. Some drank too much or sat seemingly preoccupied with an 'operational stare', the distracted expression that blocked out both the good and bad times. Riotous behaviour was another release. One Yorkshire man recalled, 'on nights when the weather was too bad for flying, the bomber men would come riding on their bicycles into our village of Sutton-on-the-Forest.' They would hit the pubs, talk to the people and the Canadian airmen handed out chewing gum to the children. 'They used to take away my father's Alsatian dog and get it drunk,' he recalled with some amusement and 'once they did the same thing to our goat.'

Recognition of these peculiar strains led Air Chief Marshal Harris to grant a leave allowance of six days in every six weeks for bomber crews. Aircrew going on leave during the height of the bombing offensive during 1943–4 witnessed a wartime society in transition. Although there was increasing confidence the war would be won, this was tempered with war weariness. Edie Rutherford, an immigrant housewife from South Africa in her late thirties, recalled the war appeared to have bogged down at Cassino in Italy. 'News this morning is of the big defence Jerry is putting up there,' she wrote pessimistically in her diary. 'He seems invincible – shall we ever break the Nazi heart?' she asked. Emotionally confronted by the twenty-six-year-old young wife of an RAF bomber crewman living in their shared flats exposed her to the reality of the air war. He was declared missing. 'It is difficult to know what to say to a wife in such trouble,' she confided in her diary after seeing the 'regret to inform' telegram. 'I did my best, poor lass. Felt myself as if my inside had fallen out.'

Britain was being flooded with American soldiers and airmen forming part of the so-called 'Sweet Invasion' of two million US servicemen preparing for the Second Front, while the 8th US Air Force spearheaded the daylight bombing offensive. Severe losses had driven the RAF to bomb primarily by night. 'There are so many

Americans around just now that I am sure at times you wonder whether you are in England or the States,' declared Home Guardsman Frank Edwards. 'There seem to be three or four American soldiers to every British Tommy,' he observed. By now there was appreciation that Britain, far from going it alone, was on the verge of passing the lead power baton for the war in the European west to the United States. This glimpse of the approaching obvious had yet to be fully digested by British society, at present reeling sociologically from the American onslaught. They were welcomed, but there was some distrust and resentment in some circles about Yanks 'overpaid, over-sexed and over here'. The American jibe in response was that Tommy was 'under-paid, under-fed, under-sexed and under Eisenhower', a reference to the inevitable strategic direction Allied leadership would follow. The absence of many British servicemen serving overseas ruptured marriage to the extent it was believed values such as loyalty and fidelity were under threat. Dawn Gould, a seventeen-year-old willowy blonde, was swept off her feet by a GI she agreed to marry. She remembered:

> I think it was the manners. They were so polite, they call everybody 'Mam' and they say 'excuse me Mam, pardon me Mam', the things we weren't used to. The English boys had very very rough cloth [for uniforms], and sometimes it was impregnated with anti-gas material and it smelt awfully sulphury. With the Americans they had this very good quality cloth and you could feel the difference. They had the advantage of the after-shave, lotions, lovely white teeth, beautiful uniforms and of course our boys did get a bit jealous and you could understand why.

Not surprisingly both sexes in wartime Britain lived for the moment. 'There would be a tendency to "ease" moral standards,' recalled RAF ground crew Malcom Sisson with a knowing smile. Life could become complicated, as Edie Rutherford explained when she heard about a married woman who had been unfaithful with another married RAF officer: 'Suddenly one day she heard the lover was killed and her husband returning home . . . she is now in a fever wondering if incriminating letters she sent her lover are with his kit which will be returned to his wife, and if so, will she turn up when her husband is there.'

The absence of so many men away on service required most young women to either serve or work. Many felt their active participation in the war effort gave them a new voice. Barbara Davies worked assembling Lancasters at the Armstrong Whitworths aircraft factory at Baginton. Its very size offered tangible proof of the part she felt she played: 'The place was vast. The work sheds seemed to stretch for miles. Huge aircraft were parked on the hangar apron front ready to be flown away. I found it all unbelievable.'

Her living conditions were deplorable and women workers were not welcomed by well paid men who then had to opt for poorly paid military service. 'There was not one familiar face,' she recalled, 'this was real loneliness and I would have crawled all the way back to Calderdale if I had been given the chance.' The quality of life was bleak. 'One girl I got to know, Jane, was living in a hovel' in which 'drinks were served in jam jars and food offered straight from the tin.' Other unwelcome developments included 'our host' running the accommodation who 'turned out to be sneakily lecherous'. Complaints at work regarding conditions were met with the stony response, 'There's a war on!' Eventually she moved into purpose-built housing for migrant workers, but her pay was half what the men received. 'Equal pay and opportunities was unheard of,' she commented. As a consequence she recalled, 'the seeds of dissent were probably sown at this time.' Union membership was mandatory, but it brought few benefits to women workers.

There were no unions in the armed forces and the experience was not dissimilar. 'I had a captain working under me when I was a major's rank,' recalled Muriel Gibson, an anti-aircraft battery officer, 'and he was earning more than I was.' When required to take over her section when she went on leave he confided, 'I ought to get your pay, you know, while you're away.' Muriel completely agreed. 'Fine, you take my pay and I'll take yours!' Society was in transition, it had yet to change, as Agnes McLean from Glasgow reflected: 'I found in the main that adversity really brought people together. The class divisions sort of disappeared for a wee while. But politics didn't.'

Conflict insidiously changed the role of women both morally and economically for this wartime generation. 'Our experiences had changed us for ever,' wrote Barbara Davies, 'our aspirations were higher. We wanted something better than the mills and sewing shops.' Little was achieved in their lifetime, but their future daughters were to benefit from attitudes instilled by unrewarded wartime austerity.

'Dear God, 40 planes lost last night,' announced Edie Rutherford in her diary, 'we watched 100 bombers pass over us last night at dusk, such a noise they make.' Edie Rutherford had sensitively deduced the implication of their passage and the likely cost. 'It made me quite ill for the evening, just thinking of the poor lads, the risk they take and what they would be doing to fellow humans, for we *are* all fellows of each other. What utter folly war is,' she reflected.

Crowds of aircrew turned up at the wooden briefing huts at about 1600 or 1700, arriving by lorry and coach or carelessly pitching bicycles among the provided racks outside. With short confirmatory test flights over, the chattering groups in blue serge battledress, enveloped in neck scarves and wreathed in tobacco smoke, filtered into the briefing room. All eyes sought the large wall map that would confirm the 'buzz' they had already picked up from ground crew loading fuel and bombs. Front gunner Fred Sutherland with 617 Squadron likened the atmosphere to an exam room. 'You can go in there and feel the tension in the air – everyone – just keyed up.' They sat stiff-backed with tension and waited for the 'Griff'. When the base and squadron commanders entered they were called to attention and the briefing began. Without further ado the wall map displaying the 'target for tonight' was unveiled and the red-ribbon trail across it pointed directly to the objective. Certain targets raised the emotional temperature. As Flight Sergeant Louis Butler pointed out:

As soon as the Wing Commander said that the target was Essen, the atmosphere changed and you could have cut it with a knife in the room. Everyone knew the reputation of Essen. You could see the gaunt look on their faces, the white faces. You knew that when you went to Essen the defences would throw everything bar the kitchen stove at you.

'I am not ashamed to admit,' declared Sergeant Neville Hockaday, a New Zealand pilot with 75 Squadron, 'that after briefing for my first trip to Essen . . . I had to wash my underpants. That evening I knew the real meaning of fear.' Berlin aroused similar emotions. 'Berlin. Christ,' declared Flight Sergeant Doug Harvey with 408 Squadron, 'you could see the hearts sinking down through the boots, the faces getting a little wan.' Berlin was the 'Big City'; the Ruhr was 'Happy Valley'. There followed a succession of briefs: from the met man, the flying control officer coordinating the taxi from pans and take-off; the intelligence officer describing German defences; squadron and station commanders offered their veteran advice and the navigation leader, after his piece, ended the briefing with a synchronisation of watches. Base commanders summed up with a final word that could include a message from the Bomber Command C-in-C, Air Chief Marshal Harris. 'He sent the most amazing signals,' recalled Group Captain Hamish Mahaddie from the Pathfinder Force. One he never forgot was: 'Tonight you go to the Big City, you have the opportunity to light a fire in the belly of the enemy and burn his black heart out.' Mahaddie commented: 'Well after the crews stopped cheering a thing like that they didn't want aircraft. Just fill their pockets with bombs and point them towards Berlin and they'd take off on their own.'

'We used to call that Met guy Cloudy Joe,' explained Canadian Doug Harvey, because there was never any good news and the information he offered was always incomplete:

He didn't know what the hell was happening on the continent. From the weather stations he knew a bit about the fronts coming in, but predicting the weather in England is a crap shoot. And he would tell you all kinds of nonsense like the base would be open, and when you got back, of course it was foggy. And the target would be clear tonight; no trouble finding it. And of course it was ten-tenths cloud. It was so ridiculous; it relieved the pressure a bit for me.

Trooping out amid nervous chatter and some horse-play, crews went for a quick meal before drawing flying kit. Many were too nervous to eat. From this point onwards seven-man crews drew inexorably closer, deriving comfort from the men who would share their fate or fortune, rather than to exchange any technical information. Flying gear was worn piecemeal depending on personal preference and the aircraft crew position. The Lancaster heating system blew warm on wireless operators and roasted the bomb-aimer, whereas the navigator and rear-gunners would freeze. The latter wore the entire gear from leather Irvin jacket and fur-lined flying boots down to silk under socks, anticipating six hour flights in cramped and static positions at Arctic temperatures. Pilot parachutes doubled as a seat, whereas the others clipped theirs on to forward harnesses, stowing them elsewhere until needed. Mascots and lucky charms were legion, because high casualties bred superstition. There were pronounced aversions to women anywhere near the flight pan. Stone throwing was not unknown to keep unsuspecting WAAFs at bay. Any innocent WAAF who happened to have more than one boyfriend failing to return from operations was labelled a 'Chop Girl' and shunned. Debates occurred whether or not to take locker-keys because doors were forced if they did not get back, as evidenced by the large number of bent locker doors. Flight Sergeant Jack Currie was fatalistic about his. 'Bollocks,' he declared, 'I'm coming back. I'll keep the key myself.'

Driving out to dispersed aircraft pans could be a cheerless occasion, despite the attempts at forced banter. Just the noise of aircraft engines turning, producing high-octane fuel and exhaust smells, was sufficient to trigger emotionally induced physical reactions. Jasper Miles expressed his earthy fears in verse:

> There are many different grades of fear,
> From simple fright to scared severe,
> And each can cause the bowels to itch,
> This, vulgar airmen call 'Ring – Twitch'.

Canadian pilot Ken Brown recalled the moment 133 airmen boarded their buses to take them off for the suicidal Dambusters Raid on 16 May 1943: 'Normally when you were on a bus, there was a little bit of chatter, someone has a story, someone is talking about his fear or something else. That didn't happen – there was silence. We were all frightened, there were so many misgivings.'

Aircrew often recall that the last twenty minutes or half hour waiting about on pans before take-off was the worst time of all. A van might suddenly emerge from the darkness and announce a delay, which made it even worse, or offer salvation in the form of a 'scrubbed op', which could be one in two. Thoughts inevitably dwelt on the 'chop rate', the remorseless logic that dictated whether they would return or not. Survival chances deteriorated year on year. Over 800 bomber aircrew perished during the Battle of Britain, they doubled the following year and had quadrupled by 1943–4. Average life expectancy on operations was fourteen missions when thirty were required to complete a tour before the respite of a possible training or staff job presented itself.

The first three trips were five times more dangerous than the average, while the following thirty had a 5 per cent wastage rate. The maths did not add up for long life but everyone assumed for sanity's sake they were the exception to the rule. Morale was high for the first five trips, descending to pronounced tension by the eleventh or twelfth. A downward spiral followed, characterised by fatalism and callousness at the deaths of friends and others. The minimum effect was a changed demeanour. By the end of the war 55,000 aircrew had perished on operations. Doug Harvey's 408 Squadron lost twenty crews or 100 per cent of the squadron-established number of aircraft. Statistics proved and disproved a number of assertions, one of which was the logical premise that experience purchased time.

Mathematician Freeman Dyson, working at the Operational Research Section of Bomber Command, calculated by 1943 that: 'The total effect of all the skill and dedication of the experienced crews was statistically undetectable. Experienced and inexperienced were mown down as impartially as the boys who walked into German machine gun nests at the Battle of the Somme in 1916.'

Aircrew were blissfully unaware of this at the time. Sergeant Eric Masters felt: 'One was just as likely to "buy it" on the first trip as on the thirtieth,' an assessment he confirmed when he was shot down on his thirtieth mission over Cologne.

Apprehensions were not openly discussed. 'People often say to me "Were you frightened?"' confided bomb-aimer George 'Johnny' Johnson with 617 Squadron. 'My answer to that is anyone who says he wasn't frightened, is either completely emotionless or a bloody liar.' 'Every time we beetle down the runway I wonder if we are going to make it back,' admitted Pilot Officer Ralph Wood a Halifax navigator from 76 Squadron. 'I've seen too many guys go for a Burton this past year.' The expression was derived from a Burton Ales advertisement, which always showed someone missing from a group of people – they had gone for a Burton Ale. Wood explained it was barrack-room language for 'gone for a shit', which he felt more meaningful in the context of the bowel-clenching fear he always experienced 'necessitating a quick trip to the can'.

The ultimate sanction that kept aircrew flying was less death than a fear of being labelled LMF or Lacking Moral Fibre. Flying Officer Barney D'Ath-Weston, a New Zealand air gunner with 105 Squadron, recalled meeting a colleague after the war who had declared he could not continue flying. 'He was stripped of rank etc and finished the war cleaning toilets.' 'It must have been hell on earth for some of these once brave aircrew whose nerves were stretched to breaking point,' recalled wireless operator Flight Lieutenant John Price with 150 Squadron. 'Thereafter they peeled potatoes in the kitchen or were forced to perform menial tasks.' Ron Read, a Halifax pilot with 78 Squadron, felt 'many more cases of LMF might have surfaced if we hadn't been of the generation we were'. The consequences of refusing to fly were more horrific than continuing. Read explained it in terms of 'self disciplines, born to respect authority and obey orders. Above all,' he emphasised, 'we regarded any show of fear as an appalling breach of code.' Men suffered in silence and generally kept their fears to themselves. Being branded LMF resulted in a formal stripping of rank on parade and public humiliation. Canadian Doug Harvey witnessed one such ceremony after which the disgraced young man went behind a hangar and hanged himself.

Confirmation of 'Go' for the target for tonight resulted in last minute nervous pees on aircraft tail-wheels for luck, and a hurried final drag on a cigarette before clambering aboard. Closing the hatch was like closing a chapter, bleak finality to flagging spirits that the raid was on; aircraft smells triggered memories of what was to come.

As many as forty Lancaster heavy bombers at dual base squadrons had to taxi their machines from dispersed aircraft pans to the main runway, a complex operation conducted in total radio silence. Marshallers on foot and light signals indicated the way. Steering a heavy bomber was not easy, pilots had to keep them on narrow fifty-foot perimeter tracks employing brakes, rudders and carefully judged bursts of power. If they misjudged, the undercarriage might sink in the grass at either side and initiate a catastrophic explosion or at least impede the entire base launch. Jack Currie, standing on the side-line, recalled 'the air was becoming filled with heavy noise' rising and falling as each bomber passed his vantage point. 'I put my fingers to my ears and wondered how much noise the night could hold.'

Whatever the weather, there were always groups of spectators to wave them off. 'You cannot watch them go unmoved, nor see them return either,' reflected correspondent J L Hodson viewing a mass take-off in October 1944. The caravan at the side of the runway controlled the departure flow, shining red to pause and then green through an Aldis lamp. On 'Go' the pilot opened all four engines to full power and released the brakes. As the heavy bomber trundled off, the next aircraft in line would swing on to the main runway.

'You start building the speed, slowly slowly, like a great lumbering truck,' explained pilot Flight Lieutenant Doug Harvey. The flight engineer called out the air speeds as the pilot concentrated on keeping the aircraft straight on the runway. 'With the stick forward as far as you can get it, you try to get that tail up,' explained Harvey, 'you watch the end of the runway and the trees just off it, everything alert.' At 95 mph, 100 mph, 105, 110, the end of the 2,000 foot runway is getting closer and closer and 1,394 hp from each of the four engines can lift 65,000 lbs, so with 2,154 gallons of fuel, seven crew-members and a mixed bomb load of 10,000 lb of high explosive, any engine failure at this point could be fatal as the undercarriage slowly lifts. 'You just work it up slowly, watching the trees. Sometimes so heavily loaded,' remarked Harvey, 'you're just skimming them. It's dark, but you know damn well how close you are.' Controls were not power assisted so it required all the pilot's strength to heave flat control surfaces into the slip-stream. At 120 mph then 125 mph the engineer snaps up the wheels 'and then

Bomber stream. 'Our end of the road seemed to be full of these mighty bombers', declared one civilian observer watching the raids depart.

An RAF bomber crew de-briefing on return. Bleary eyed, 'their facial muscles slackening', described one aircrew as reluctant crews moved from table to table answering interminable technical questions.

'Tail-end Charlies' had the highest loss rate within the crew. They were the first target for German night fighters.

finally you got flying speed and you start to climb' recalled Harvey. 'And the sweat's dripping down. Get up, you bastard. Yeah. Yeah.' The safety speed is 130 knots and at 300 feet the flaps are up as, far below, other aircraft are rising into the twilight sky. With so many aircraft taking off from the densely packed East Anglia airfields traffic control was crucial. 'Everybody was nervous,' declared nineteen-year-old rear-gunner Jim Moffat with 427 Squadron. 'The most dangerous part of the whole trip, we figured, was take-off. Once take-off was over your battle was half-won.'

FLIGHT AND TARGET APPROACH

As the bombers popped up they became visible to the German *Himmelbett* belt of radar stations in occupied Europe. From this point onwards German radar operators tracked the aircraft. Freya was the codename given to the early warning metal graticule-shaped construction that was as large as a house. Mythical Freya was the Nordic watchkeeper who could see a hundred miles in every direction by day or night and these were the first to direct their pitiless beam at the approaching bomber streams. Shorter range Würzburg electric bowls as big as windmills provided a more precise fix after the direction of approach was alerted by Freya. Würzburg operators radioed the circling night-fighters that rotated inside stand-by boxes situated inland from the Dutch coast. These homed in on the bombers supplementing the Würzburg pointer with Lichtenstein, an on-board radar with a narrower and more precise beam. They sought to join the bomber streams, nicely lined up for their attention.

For every 1,000 feet the bombers climbed the air temperature dropped $2.5°$ and after 8,000 feet oxygen masks were needed. Aircraft interiors darkened as they nudged their way through thick cloud seeking the opaque blue twilight beyond. It took the bomber stream about half an hour to reach the Dutch coast. From there the Ruhr was a further fifty minutes for Lancasters cruising at 225 mph. This gave German defences nearly fifty minutes killing time on average each way, or more for targets beyond to Berlin. The intention was to thin out as many of the night-time commuters as possible with a combination of radar-directed searchlights and flak and night-fighters. By mid-1943 the Nachtjagd Night-Fighter Arm employed 565 twin-engine fighters and about a hundred single-engine Messerschmitt 109s and Focke-Wulf 190s. Flak was achieving a 23 per cent kill rate against 76 per cent from night-fighters. Chance now dictated the maths of the bomber crew chop rate.

The bomber stream was an unwieldy slab of aircraft, which on many nights did not even see each other. They conducted a lonely war, unlike the 8th US Air Force's massive daylight formations, relying upon the collective firepower of mass employed .5 machine-guns. The RAF flew by night, lightly defended and with minimum armour, utilising the cover of darkness to maximise the bomb load. They could rarely identify men who simply disappeared in a blinding flash of light. The meteoric parabola of a stricken fiery bomber was an impersonal phenomenon. Bomber streams were stacked at various heights because the older Stirling aircraft could not get above 11,000 feet or at best 18,000, not beyond the range of 88mm flak. Lancasters flew at 20,000 feet. Individual navigation to targets meant that aircraft might fly as much as fifteen miles either side of the red-ribbon route shown on briefing maps. As the lead bombers neared the Dutch coast over the North Sea the rearmost aircraft were still taking off.

Bomber crews generally kept their own company. Pilots and navigators did associate occasionally with their opposite numbers from other aircraft, but less the gunners and the rest. There was a bond whose genesis came from the initial crewing-up process, which happened once basic training was completed when the RAF in its customary do-it-yourself way allowed crews to pick their own. Fred Allen, a Halifax rear-gunner based at Lisset, recalled: 'There were probably 300 in the room, and you didn't know who's who. You just started walking about and if you liked the look of someone: "Have you got a gunner?"' He assessed one pilot passing by who he thought 'can handle anything' and 'we hit it off and that was that'.

These same characters were now packed within a constricted aluminium tunnel of runners and equipment no wider than a motor car and about ninety feet long. Moving about inside to reach the escape hatches and climb over the main spar – quite an obstacle – was tricky on the ground; but when wearing a parachute in the dark and with an aircraft spinning on fire and awash with fuel and hydraulic fluid, was impossible. Five of the seven-man crew were at the front in the cockpit space. The pilot was usually in his early twenties and had the only armour protection remaining about his head, because the rest had been long stripped out to increase bomb loads. There was no co-pilot. He could be assisted by the flight engineer who sat next to him, whose job was to provide a running commentary on fuel and the state of the four engines. As flying was intensely physical and not power-assisted, even after an uneventful flight the pilot would be left with aching shoulders and spine from constantly heaving on the control column, inducing advanced fatigue by the time he got back. The pilot was the captain, even if a flight sergeant flew officer crew members. He was joined in the front cockpit by the wireless operator, bomb-aimer and navigator.

The mid-upper gunner could not wear his parachute and had to stow it elsewhere, knowing he would have to retrieve it in the dark impeded by radio and oxygen lines should there be an emergency. He only had a stiff hammock slung beneath the turret to sit on during bottom-numbing seven-hour trips. The rear-gunner had to clamber along the fuselage, over and into the claustrophobic gun cradle at the back of the aircraft and then close the turret door. His was the coldest and loneliest post of all, enduring temperatures of 50° below zero. All he could see on looking behind was the barely discernible feet of the mid-upper gunner. 'Tail-end Charlies' had the dubious distinction of having the highest loss rate in the crew, being the first target for an approaching German night-fighter, despite removing Perspex hoods to improve visibility. To exit in extremis meant he had to turn the turret inwards, open the door, clamber out, find his parachute – hopefully not damaged – in the dark, and crawl to an escape hatch. It was especially noisy at the back of the aircraft. Engine noise required one to shout without the aid of intercom even at the front, while the rear was worse; added to which the tail wing bumped and groaned in the buffeting slipstream and aluminium constantly chinked under pressure.

'Enemy coast ahead!', announced by navigators, signalled the next hurdle as climbing aircraft had likely clawed their way to 15,000 or

16,000 feet; Lancasters were aiming for 22,000 feet. Flight Sergeant pilot Doug Harvey steeled himself for the first flak on viewing the approaching searchlights. 'They're standing up on the coast as you're coming across the North Sea to Holland, Belgium, France. There's a wall of these damned things. Right on the coast,' he recalled. They now entered the fifty-minute gauntlet leading to 'Happy Valley' in the Ruhr. Bluish-white 'master-beams' were directed by radar at the approaching stream and manually controlled slave beams clustered around any highlighted bombers like a moth in the intense light. 'One of the beams would pick us up and the dark interior of the plane would burst into brightness like a star,' described twenty-one-year-old Canadian Joseph Favreau: 'It was more devastating than being shot at. You had the feeling that everyone was watching *you*. Every gunner, every fighter had picked *you* out.'

All that could be done was to dive steeply and weave, so that Favreau explained 'my nose was bleeding, my eyes were bleeding from the pressure'. Planes might be 'coned' by searchlights for as long as ten minutes. Everyone felt for the unfortunates so highlighted. 'You were heartbroken to see a guy beside you coned,' admitted pilot Doug Harvey, but selfish self-preservation overrode all else: 'Your mind said, "Hold that bastard, hold it, till I get past . . . Jesus don't shoot him down yet, I'm not past yet, I've got to sneak by here, in this dark space between these two great big cones." '

'Other bombers in the stream avoided their luckless colleagues like the plague!' admitted Flight Sergeant pilot Philip Gray with 186 Squadron. Radar-directed flak came up in battery clusters of four explosions, all at precisely the same height. Gray experienced such flak by day and night. On approaching a daylight target 'we could see the latest shells exploding all across the action and, equally intimidating, all the spluttering smoke puffs of their predecessors hanging there in their hundreds like delegates of doom and disaster.' By night it 'was greatly subdued' because 'mercifully, those hundreds of hideous pock puffs of spent flak could no longer be seen'. Radio broadcaster Edward B Murrow, flying with Lancaster D for Dog over Berlin in December 1943, described night flak as 'a cigarette lighter in a dark room: one that won't light – sparks but no flame – the sparks crackling just below the level of the cloud tops'. Twenty-four-year-old Squadron Leader Denis Peto-Shepherd recalled one close burst during a daylight run over Rouen:

> It was the most incredible experience for at the moment of the burst, so close in my line of sight, I was positive that this was it and that neither of us in the cockpit was likely to survive. At that moment, time all but stood still and I saw the burst in the most amazing slow motion. At first sudden, tiny and immobile, suspended seemingly over the nose of the aircraft and only as big as my fist; it then grew, oh so slowly it seemed until it was a black-brown seething evil and flame-gashed puff as large as a football. And then suddenly, as I watched it, the slow motion effect ceased and all hell was let loose as the seething puff exploded with terrific violence and a sickening hollow thump. We were flying directly into the splinter cloud and coincidental with the thump the aircraft lurched and shuddered in the blast as the splinters thudded and ploughed into it.

The stream flew on in absolute darkness seeking 'blackness again, complete blackness', recalled pilot Doug Harvey. Losses were instant, catastrophic and anonymous. Pilot Ken Brown with 617 Squadron remembered, 'the anxiety is worse when you have a fellow on your starboard side, and he explodes, a huge ball of fire, orange, which lit up the whole valley.' Crews were required to log these disasters en route so as to identify the victims when they got back. It could be a distracting as well as melancholy process. Flight Sergeant Jack Currie, a Lancaster pilot, described distant night combats between bombers and predatory German night-fighters, attracted to interceptions by searchlight activity. 'To watch the battles to the end was tempting,' he recalled 'but the secret of survival was to keep a roving eye.' There was no end of distractions. 'Flame spurted from a slowly falling Halifax' on their port beam he recalled, 'and like a scavenger, a Junkers 88 prowled and pecked about the dying bomber'.

Air gunner and radio operator Norman Thom from 100 Squadron remembered his nervous flight engineer repeatedly announcing examples of downed aircraft with a fearful sounding voice. 'Ooh look, there's one that's bought it. Oh Christ! There goes another one.' He was near the end of his tether and oblivious of the impact it was having on the rest of the crew. 'We could have done without his mournful patter,' Thom admitted. Pilot Phillip Gray fixed his gaze ahead and concentrated. 'There were things taking place outside my own front windscreen I wished I didn't have to watch,' he confessed.

With thirty minutes to go before the target the bomb-aimer left the front gun turret in order to set the aircraft's speed and position on the bomb sight, as the crew looked out for signs of target indication flares. Other aircraft might be dimly observed flying in their formation. The danger of collision at this stage, during the straight bombing run, was as pronounced as it was on take-off. Bouncing and bucking from the backwash of preceding aircraft would become apparent. Bursting quartets of thickening flak began to flash around in the night sky. Target indication markers normally appeared in sequence, firstly red marker 'finders' illuminated with high explosive 'supporters' and then the 'illuminators', sticks of flares at the aiming point, where lastly the 'primary markers' might be seen. These were yellow flares with perhaps green back-up target indicators.

'Bomb doors open,' ordered by the aircraft captain, heralded the most testing and vulnerable part of the mission, because the bomber had now to fly straight and level for twenty to thirty seconds. Flight Sergeant Louis Butler with 467 Squadron thought this was 'the absolute worse part of the trip' because 'it seemed a hell of a long time when they are throwing all that muck up at you'. A lifetime of seconds filtered by as the bomb-aimer directed 'left − left, right, steady' − with the inevitable joke offered by Louis Butler: 'back a bit − but of course you couldn't do that'. When the bomb-aimer announced 'bombs away' the aircraft lurched and abruptly rose by 200 to 300 feet as 10,000 lb of high explosive and incendiaries dropped away.

Variable height differences between the ageing Halifaxes and Stir-lings below and Lancasters above, amid the difficulty of seeing each other, meant some bombs fell among the aircraft below. There is no conclusive evidence of how many who failed to return were hit in this way. 'Photoflash' images of target impact, used after missions to assess accuracy, often showed other bombers beneath. Pilot Frank Phripp recalled one Lancaster releasing its bombs on top of his friend Andy, flying a bomber alongside his own. The previous run-in had been a 'piece of cake' so no flak or fighters could be blamed. Bombs suddenly crashed right through the accompanying aircraft and carried on down. 'Suddenly a flash of flame and smoke where Andy's aircraft had been,' he remembered, and 'no parachutes'.

Despite the impersonal gap of 10,000 to 20,000 feet between aircraft and target, there were few illusions about the nature of the impacts below. Flight Sergeant Robert Raymond piloting a Lancaster over Essen in January 1943 saw 'destruction on a colossal scale and terrifying in its concentration and intensity'. Long strings of red tracer hosed up from the ground like 'liquid corkscrews' as he watched:

> Brilliant flares that hang interminably between heaven and earth and never seem to move, the photo flashes exploding near the ground with a piercing blue-white light, then the long strips of incendiaries being laid out in geometrical patterns among the buildings, and the great mushroom explosions of the 4,000 pounders.

Flight Lieutenant A Forsdike recalled the aptly named *Gomorrah* fire-storm raid on Hamburg in July and August 1943, when the city 'set in the darkness' resembled 'a turbulent dome of red fire, lighted and ignited like the glowing heart of a vast brazier'. It made an indelible Dante-like impression on him: 'Above the city was a misty red haze. I looked down fascinated but aghast, satisfied yet horrified. I had never seen a fire like that and was never to see its like again.'

'I had no qualms. It didn't worry me,' declared Squadron Leader Doubleday with 467 Squadron. 'I was briefed on targets in which I knew that civilians must become engrossed.' His view was that 'we didn't set the code for the pattern of the war or the behaviour' that was established by the Germans at Warsaw, Rotterdam, London and Coventry. As far as he was concerned 'the whole future of civilization, I believed, was at stake'. He had no dispute about what Bomber Command was doing. 'The lesser of two evils to me was to get the thing over, hit as hard as you could and get the people, who were in the concentration camps and in the countries that were overran, get them free as soon as you possibly could.' Aircrew rationalised that, despite the regrettable cost, they were determined to see the mission through.

Flight Lieutenant John Price taking part in the 1,000 maximum effort raid on Cologne, saw the rash of red crosses denoting Cologne's hospitals in the city centre on his map. 'I would have nightmares after the war thinking about all the women and babies we killed that night,' but he accepted 'that we in England were determined to save our land whatever the cost'. He calculated 'killing the enemy, of whatever gender, was the only answer.' Housewife Edie Rutherford, listening to even more reports of Berlin bombings, remarked, 'I hope Hitler remembers how he in the past ordered certain places to be rubbed off the map.' Nevertheless, she was 'sorry for the Germans' but appreciated she would not feel the same 'if they had done to me . . . what they've done to many'. Her husband was uncompromising and had 'no pity for them whatever – says they wrecked his career and health 25 years ago which is true,' admitted Edie. She was less bitter on reflection, although 'it has affected me'. Group Captain Hamish Mahaddie was as pitiless as her husband. 'If you couldn't get the German worker in his factory it was just as easy to knock him off in his bed,' he reckoned, 'and if his old Granny on the seat by the door got the chop that's bad luck, it didn't bother me in the least.' He had observed fires at Rotterdam in 1940 burning for a week, flying over the Humber.

Having dropped their bombs 'we would get the hell out of there' recalled Flight Sergeant Louis Butler. This obliged the bomber stream to turn back into the very prevailing head winds that had ironically propelled them more quickly into enemy territory. It would take twice as long to get back; which meant twice as dangerous.

FROM TARGET TO HOME BASE

'Like trying to catch a fly in a darkened room' was the German night-fighter verdict on the difficulty of achieving a night-time bomber intercept. At the end of March 1944, Leutnant Martin Drewes, piloting a Messerschmitt 110 twin-engine fighter fitted with a Lichtenstein SN 2 radar array, operated by Feldwebel (Sergeant) Pelz and aided by observer Gefreiter (Corporal) Hendke, realised he was in the middle of the bomber stream they were seeking. Vectored in by ground-mounted Freya and Würzburg radars, they had a choice of three target blips visible on the screen. Closing to within 1,000 yards of one, Hendke warned his pilot Drewes 'he must be right ahead of us and a bit higher'. Four little flickering exhaust flames became identifiable and then a brief silhouette view of a moonlit bomber.

The maximum peril for bomber crews was shortly after 'bombs away', when with relaxed euphoria they emerged alive on the other side of the flak belt. Some crew became drowsy enough at this point to doze. Certain characteristic smells arose within returning aircraft, which were noticeable to aircrew, explained Warrant Officer Eddie Wheeler with 97 Squadron. Particularly pungent odours were apparent over target: wet cloth smells from chemicals mixed with charred wood and the odour of burning alongside that of acrid brick dust. Now on return Wheeler described the distinctive 'combination emanating from the heating system, creating body odours, the smell from the dope covering various patches of the fuselage from previous damage, the strong pungent cordite smells when one had experienced a heavy flak barrage or after the plane's guns had been fired'. There was also 'a constant smell of fear about the aircraft during flight, emphasised by the odd trips to the Elsan [chemical] toilet' at the back of the aircraft. Rubber oxygen masks could cause problems with sweat and condensation. Gunners kept their turrets turning little circles in the sky, tired now from constantly conducting vertical and horizontal sweeps. They could not see below.

Leutnant Drewes slowly crept up beneath his unsuspecting prey. The Lancaster continued flying straight and level. Adjusting his speed to that of the bomber they slowly climbed to within fifty yards, three pairs of German eyes riveted to the black mass thundering along above them. Drewes placed his eye to the reflector-sight on the cockpit roof, aiming for the port inboard engine. It made little sense to fire into the body of the aircraft, which might still be carrying a full 10,000 lb bomb load. His sight was aligned to two 20mm cannons mounted behind the cockpit which fired upwards at a 72-degree angle. *Schräge Musik* it was called, or 'slanting' music, an expression that colloquially suggested jazz or 'crazy' music. It was played at this hidden slanting angle so that the target was engaged from its blind spot below, while the attacker flew parallel beneath its victim. When he pressed the firing button hits flashed on his opponent's wing, bathing both aircraft in green light as he fired 520 19.5 gram 20mm shells per minute. Ammunition could be exhausted in one seven-second burst. Drewes remembered the Lancaster's death struggle lasting five minutes, flying horizontally like a blazing meteor, until it fell steeply earthward. Other flaming torches indicated the route of the bomber stream.

'We were hit just like as if it was a three-ton truck. BANG!' recalled Sergeant JS 'Johnny' Johnston, a Lancaster flight engineer with 103 Squadron. 'We held together for a minute then she screamed right across the port wing, hit the propellers and we went out of control. Both engines burst into flames.' Fighter interceptions lasted barely two to three seconds:

> I got thrown to the floor and banged my head. I got up, or tried to get up. I could see Alan [the pilot] trying to get her straight. Then she dipped her nose and I went straight into the nose with all the junk that was on the floor and landed on top of the bomb-aimer. All of a sudden, the nose broke off. I just saw it start to crack. The bomb-aimer and I fell out. I was surrounded by bits of plane cowlings, pieces of metal – floating all around me.

Four of the crew were killed. Jim Pesteridge's 102 Squadron Halifax was similarly shot down from below west of Mannheim on 10 August 1943. With no warning, 'suddenly there is a thudding on the port side, I look left and up through the wing there is, what looks like, a short stream of electric lamps rising between the two engines.' They were hit by incendiary bullets from below. 'Neither of our upper or rear gunners can see the enemy.'

The only recourse during a night-fighter attack was for the bomber pilot to 'corkscrew' the aircraft. This was often initiated by one of the gunners – 'Corkscrew port!' No questions were asked and the captain would immediately heave on the controls and dive to port, then climb to port, roll and climb to starboard and dive to starboard, roll, dive to port and climb to port, all the time chanting a litany of proposed directions to the rest of the crew. 'Between us, the gunners and I evaded four attacks,' on one occasion recalled Flight Sergeant Jack Currie with 626 Squadron. Despite the eleven degrees of frost clinging to them at their height, 'I was sweating like a horse and my muscles were aching.'

After the carnage wrought on the ground, often engulfing their own families, night-fighter attacks were pursued with murderous determination. Major Wilhelm Herget was one of the *experten*, the few really effective pilots, with fifty-eight night kills to his credit. 'I was flying through the propeller wash,' he recalled in December 1943, having penetrated the middle of a night bomber stream near Frankfurt, 'and my plane was shaking and so I dived on the first plane in front, the next to the right, the next to the left.' Firing no more than four to eight cannon on each pass at the fuel tanks between the two engines on each wing, he had five successes on the outward stream, carrying bombs, and intercepted another three on the way back. Herget was old to be a night-fighter pilot and physically and emotionally drained by the mission. 'At that time I was thirty-three years of age and I was not able to climb out by myself, to get out of the plane. They had to lift me out.'

Baled out aircrew received scant sympathy, the so-called 'terror flyers' might be beaten by irate civilians. Norman Thom's Lancaster Z for Zebra with 100 Squadron was shot down by a twin-engine Junkers 88 returning form Friedrichshafen in April 1944. They went into a spin and he was trapped by 'a rush of air' that 'ripped through the fuselage with the speed of an express train'. Pinned and unable to move he had resigned himself to die until an internal explosion blew him clear of the aircraft and his parachute opened. His pilot 'Dinger' Bell was not killed outright in the crash in occupied France, and Thom recalled: 'Eye-witnesses told him they had seen Bell moving. He had fallen on his knees which had gone some way into the ground. He wept and called for his mother before dying of his injuries. The Germans ignored Bell and did not call a doctor to help him.' The airmen were murdering their families back home. They considered they had got their just deserts.

Aircrew were officially told they had good survival prospects if they were shot down. Survival was, however, proportional to the distance they had to scramble, crawl or find their way to the nearest escape hatch. About 50 per cent of American aircrew successfully baled out of their various types of stricken aircraft. There was a better than 25 per cent chance of getting out of the older RAF Halifaxes and Stirlings, vulnerable at the lower heights, but only 15 per cent, or one in seven escaped Lancasters, flying at higher altitudes. The explanation, according to Freeman Dyson, a wartime member of the Operational Research Section at HQ RAF Bomber Command, was: 'the Lancaster hatch was in various ways more awkward and harder to squeeze through. The awkwardness probably cost the lives of several thousand bomber boys.' There was the additional horror of not being able to locate the stowed parachute in the dark and confusing confines of a plunging aircraft fuselage or, worse still, finding it damaged. Flying Officer 'Blue' Rackley recalled his bomb-aimer Des Morgan tried to save the life of the rear-gunner Taffy Davis whose parachute was damaged when they were badly shot-up returning from the Ruhr in June 1944. They baled out of their crippled Lancaster over England tied together. The jolt of the opening parachute tore Davis from Morgan's grasp; he fell free and was killed.

The final hazard before reaching the safety of the British coast was the prospect of ditching in the North Sea, the fate of crippled aircraft or those detouring because of navigational errors and running out of fuel. German flak ships haphazardly prowled the enemy coast at night beneath likely bomber stream return routes hoping to catch over-relaxed crews unawares. Noel Belford and his Lancaster crew in T for Tommy with 12 Squadron in Lincolnshire came in over the North Sea following a gyro compass error even as the rest of the crews had landed in England in early January 1944. With twenty to thirty minutes fuel left they opted to ditch with the benefit of full power. Belford made several dummy passes, his navigator Arthur Lee recalling he 'decided to land across the troughs using the wave crests to slow the aircraft down'. Only the engineer and pilot stayed forward, the rest climbed over the main spar 'and squatted down with our hands clasped behind our heads ready for the impact'. Landing in the sea at speed was like landing on uneven concrete rubble. Arthur Lee described: 'We hit the water with an almighty crash, the sea poured in through the open hatches, and we thought we were going down, but the inrush was caused by the waves breaking over us.'

Other witnesses liken the experience to flying into a stone wall. They hit so hard the crew were thrown around the fuselage. Aircraft generally sank within a minute, so escape hatches had to be opened and escape ladders positioned before impact. Sergeant Parachute Jump Instructor L Brown experienced a ditching in a Halifax in August 1944. 'Bracing for impact' meant sitting as forward as possible with backs to the bent knees of the man directly behind. 'The aircraft struck the sea with a terrific shock and there was an immediate inrush of water into the cockpit and fuselage.' Confusion was caused by equipment and men washed back into the radio operator's compartment. Equipment often snagged escape hatches. These men were saved because conditions were generally calm. Ditching in rough seas was the equivalent of landing in a wood or group of buildings, aircraft could cartwheel or snap wings off while slewing around, accelerating the sinking process once the back of the aircraft fuselage was broken. There were rarely survivors in such conditions.

Fog on returning airbases could result in a further two-hour delay before the survivors of the squadron 'stacked' over airfields could be talked down. Radio silence did not apply on return. Desperately weary pilots would seek the tell-tale signs of runway lights, red dots merging into white dots for the main runway length. Correspondent J L Hodson witnessed one atmospheric bomber stream return in October 1944:

> Dawn has broken, thin and grey over this bleak countryside, over these Nissen huts, so cold that your sleep has been small, when the first faint roaring comes again and yonder black speck grows into a great Lancaster.
>
> Since you last saw her she has been beset by shells, night fighters have flung their rockets at her in parabola curves, she has been silhouetted over a sheet of cloud that, lit by flares from below, shone like frosted glass; she has narrowly escaped collision, even narrowly escaped a Cookie 4,000lb bomb that fell from above, 20 feet ahead of her nose. Yet, incredibly, she is here – here almost to the minute.

A green tag was placed on the main operations board signifying the return of each aircraft. Mascots were superstitiously touched once wheel squeal signified a safe return. 'Well you've never had a bowel movement as great,' announced pilot Ken Brown with 617 Squadron returning from the successful Dambuster raid of 16 May 1943. 'We made it!' So exuberant were they that nobody noticed the obviously distressed state of some of the ground crews. 'Rather disturbing to think we were rather elated that we had made it back and here was a bunch of people crying.' They did not realise until Flight Sergeant 'Chiefie' Powell approached them, 'tears were just pouring down his face'. 'What's wrong?' they asked. 'Have you any idea where any of the other boys are?' he responded. Of the nineteen crews that had left Scampton several hours before, only eleven aircraft returned. Fifty-three aircrew had perished on one raid. Four of the six targets were hit and two dams destroyed.

Tea was served at the debrief well laced with rum. Crews moved from table to table as they were questioned by numerous intelligence officers. What was the target indication like? Did you see any aircraft go down? Specialist questions came from the technicians: aircraft problems? Radios, instruments, guns, fuel systems and so on. Throughout it all, 'the crew slumped uncomfortably in the slatted folding chairs,' recalled Flight Sergeant Jack Currie. 'Their facial muscles slackening, showing grimy shadows where the oxygen masks had rubbed against the skin.' Debriefings were unpopular but essential, crews were desperately tired, many still feeling the effects of chill kept their neck-scarves on, gazing back with bleary swollen eyes, many chain-smoking cigarettes. Presently the room emptied, apart from scattered papers, cigarette ends and dirty cups and plates. Quite often the squadron commander and WAAF intelligence officer would be sitting there alone, still awaiting late arrivals who might or might not come. As correspondent J L Hodson described it: 'the little anxiety becomes a great anxiety and still no news.'

'He always phoned me when he came back,' declared WAAF Jan Birch married to airman Brian Reid. 'I waited and waited and the whole place emptied and I sat down and looking at my watch, I thought I'd wait a few more moments.' She lost her first fiancé on the second day she was engaged. 'There was no call' from Brian she wistfully recalled, he did not return. For the living 'the sweetest smell of all was when one entered the mess after debriefing, to that marvellous aroma of fried bacon and coffee,' recalled Warrant Officer Eddie Wheeler with 97 Squadron, 'or was it the realization that one was a survivor?'

Touch-down for late-comers could often be catastrophic. Twenty-two-year old Canadian Ken Brown recalled the arrival of a crippled Lancaster, the navigator dead and the pilot badly wounded. He just managed to land when the aircraft flipped on its back:

> The plane came apart. The turret rolled right across the airfield like a ball. The rest of the plane broke up. The rear-gunner was still in the turret, the guns embedded in his body. His legs were up around his ears. A mess, but he was still alive. When he spoke even though it was sort of garbled, I realised he was a Canadian. And he said, 'If you move anything I'll die.'

This was an inevitability. Brown asked him where he came from and he responded, 'Ontario, its good to be with a Canadian when I go.'

Of the 125,000 aircrew that served in Bomber Command, over half – 73,741 – were wounded or killed. The Commonwealth made its contribution, one in five alone was Canadian. In all, 55,000 'Brylcreem Boys', the majority highly educated and technically proficient selected aircrew, the technological cream of the crop, perished. Most of them were in their late teens and early twenties. One glance at the operations board the morning after a raid sufficed to determine who had not returned. Crews bonded ever more closely in a self-preservation instinct. It was the *other* crews that never made it. As Flight Sergeant John Waldridge, a bomb-aimer with 49 Squadron remembered: 'One night you'd be out drinking with them and the next they weren't there. Their beds would be empty and someone would come the next day and collect their kit.'

Meanwhile the end of the day had been reached. The deadly commute over enemy territory would perhaps continue the following day or, depending on weather, several times that week. There might be a pause and then it would continue, giving the lethal law of averages governing their survival time to catch up.

The fire-storm raids on Hamburg in August 1943 and Dresden in early 1945 realised the apocalyptic vision set out in Alexander Korda's film *Things to Come*, that had so disturbed British cinema audiences in 1936. The bomber would always get through was the nagging fear, although Germany's population in 1939 were less concerned. It was logically assumed that air power alone would be sufficient to win future wars. Despite the worst that had been directed against Warsaw, Rotterdam, London, Coventry, and now the Ruhr and Berlin, this did not occur.

The decisive conflict against Germany in the west was eagerly anticipated by both sides in 1944, it would be on land, and would decide the outcome of the war. As in 1940 it would be in France.

10

THE D-DAY EXPERIENCE

THE EVE OF 'THE DAY'

By the spring of 1944 the cocky defiance of 1940 in Britain was replaced by a war-weary desire to finish the job. The night-life gaiety of the West End of London packed with Allied troops from every nation to enjoy this was a veneer, flimsily cloaking the unknown outcome of the likely decisive year of the war. Would the invasion to launch the Second Front really cost 50 per cent casualties? Had the Germans developed secret weapons? How many dancing couples enjoying themselves in London would be parted by violent death this year? 'We knew D-Day was coming but nobody knew when,' confided twenty-six-year-old Wren officer Moyra Macleod, working with Naval Planning Staff, to her diary: 'The sea was absolutely chocker-block. Torbay was jammed with craft, you could almost walk from one to the other. It was the most exciting thing.'

Excitement was tinged with war-weary fatalism. It had been a long wait. Housewife Clara Milburn had questioned the calls for a Second Front in her diary two summers before. 'One has no doubt that as soon as we can do it, we shall,' but there was risk, because she added, 'only no more Dunkirks for us.' 'Invasion' no longer meant the Germans may come, 'now it is spoken of as a settled plan with the date fixed', a secret, 'but it is the invasion of the Continent this time.' This became increasingly apparent up and down the country; Clara Milburn living near Coventry found local roads blocked off and soldiers guarding restricted entrances. 'We found the Straight Mile closed,' she recorded. 'I was told it was packed with tanks all getting ready for the invasion.' Driving on she saw 'many double roads have one side closed, and one sees scores of vehicles massed on either side of the road.' There was a flurry of Luftwaffe bombing raids in the spring of 1944 designed to impede these preparations. War-weariness was exacerbated by the lack of a known date. 'Haven't you noticed that nearly everybody looks ten years older?' declared a forty-five-year-old Chelsea man to a Mass Observation reporter. 'That dreadful bombing at the World's End has offended a lot of people.'

'Thank God. At last,' declared Lieutenant H J Sweeney in D Company the 2nd Oxfordshire and Buckinghamshire Regiment (Ox and Bucks) glider infantry, shortly due to land in one of the first gliders in Normandy. 'We had been waiting for this day for years and years. Finally here we were about to take part.' Twenty-year-old Parachute signaller Harry Reid claimed, 'I don't think any of us could see beyond D-Day.' There could be no thought of future prospects until it was over. 'We were being conditioned to do everything in relationship to that.' It was the event that shaped all training and preparations for the immediate future. Parts of the British Army had been engaged in the Western Desert, North Africa and Italian campaigns and others in the Far East, but the vast majority of it had tediously trained in England awaiting this day. D-Day was high risk symbolically as well as psychologically. As with the catastrophic fall of France four years earlier, most British people would recall what they were doing at the moment D-Day was announced. Despite progress on other fronts there was recognition that the war could only start to come to an end when Allied soldiers stepped ashore in France. Germany too recognised the potential emotional ambiance of this moment, relishing the opportunity to bloody the Allied nose and throw them back into the sea. They could negotiate an acceptable peace from the resulting stalemate.

The invincibility of the so-called 'Atlantic Wall' had a tangible resonance fed by German propaganda newsreels about massive guns set in reinforced concrete emplacements surrounded by imposing bunkers and wire. In the spring of 1944 the German Army *Wehrmacht* magazine proclaimed the existence of 'The Armoured Coast'. War correspondent Oberleutnant Walter Köhler reported 'no less than 9.3 million cubic metres of concrete had been built into the 2,100 kilometre coast along the Channel and Atlantic and more than 6,000 guns direct their barrels against the enemy.' In reality there were too few heavy guns, only 15 per cent of shelters at the anticipated landing points were bombproof and only four of 50 million mines had been laid, but the perception was it was a formidable obstacle. Information from landed frogmen, low-flying air reconnaissance and the French Resistance indicated that in places it was. There were 'Belgian Gates' to snag landing craft at low tide, ramps and stakes mixed with star-shaped metal 'hedgehogs' studded with mines, designed to rip out the bottom of landing craft. Beaches beyond were registered by machine-guns, mortars, anti-tank guns and artillery. Sea walls were festooned with barbed wire bunkers and fortified houses. Anti-tank ditches and minefields were in abundance at beach exits, covered by infantry and hidden gun emplacements.

'Worst of all,' declared Sergeant Ian Grant, a cameraman due to land with 45 Commando, the French Maquis had identified underwater pipes leading out from concrete bunkers that could set the sea on fire 1,000 yards from the shore. 'They would then act like a chain of flame-throwers, thus setting up a virtual wall of flame, through which our line of landing craft would have to navigate.' Flail Tank crewman Joe Minogue due to land on Gold Beach recalled being jauntily told by his Division Commander Major General Percy Hobart, 'we're expecting 70% casualties you know, but if any of you chaps get there I'll see you the day after D-Day.' There was realisation from Prime Minister Churchill down to the lowliest private soldier that this enterprise could not afford to fail. Royal Marine Ken Oakly, who had barely survived the amphibious landings in Sicily the year before, recalled a pep talk given by a senior officer the night before the invasion: 'Many of you will not survive the first assault wave, some of you might survive the second, but not to worry, we shall just pass over you until we have captured the beach. That's the thing that *must* be done. You must capture the beach.'

The date of the impending invasion was unknown. 'My fiancée said "we'll get married on such-and-such day," ' recalled Alastair Pearson, the Commanding Officer of 8 PARA soon to jump over Normandy. 'And it dawned on me that *a* I wouldn't be there, and *b* it was perilously close to D-Day.' Commando Peter Wild remembered 'we'd have to tell lies' to their girlfriends; 'we'd arranged to take Wrens out that night, never to turn up!'

The risk of this enterprise not succeeding was considerable. Thirty-seven Allied divisions were available in Britain to face fifty-eight German combat divisions in France. Deception played a huge role, diverting German attention to a mythical First Army Group commanded by the American General George Patton which was anticipated to land in the Pas-de-Calais area and another poised to assault Norway. The German Fifteenth Army, with twenty divisions, including two panzer, covering the 550 kilometre Somme-Calais area, would be held waiting as the main Allied blow descended on the Seventh Army in Normandy, holding more than twice the distance, some 1,600 kilometres with six fewer divisions and only one panzer. The Allied D-Day plan intended to checkmate the German defence by moving ten to fifteen Allied divisions against five spread out German divisions during the first five days of the assault.

'Just before D-Day there were soldiers everywhere,' recalled Chief Wren Katherine Andrews. 'We didn't know when the invasion would be of course, so it just seemed as if one minute they were there, and the next they had just vanished.' Soldiers were confined to transit camps. Ursula Norton, a young child in Southsea near Portsmouth, recalled soldiers sitting on the beaches waiting to embark. She was with her three-year-old cousin Malcolm and 'one man with a beard hugged us both and burst out crying'. 'I remember him telling me he had a little girl just like me he had left behind.' They were asked to post letters as 'I think they had been ordered not to write home at that late date.' Wren Moyra Macleod remembered the poignancy of men 'giving me envelopes' saying 'would you please post this, this is for my family you know, this is money for the stamps.' She was visibly affected by the moment, 'it began to be very moving.' Dawn Gould had to wave goodbye to her American fiancé through the wire of a transit camp. 'I didn't get right close to him, because it was not allowed.' They were engaged for three weeks. He did not come back.

'Confinement within a wall of barbed wire was all about lectures; constructional and destructional,' recalled Sergeant Ian Grant with 45 Commando. Memories were of 'boredom; eating, sleeping; sprawling in a tented city' with 'warm, spring sunshine giving promise of the summer ahead'. The incongruous part was that everyday life continued around them as if nothing had happened. Buses turned around the terminus as usual carrying people back to Southampton's homes, shops, cinemas and pubs. 'Was it real?' he asked himself, 'us and them?' Some men were afloat as early as 1 June, an unwelcome move because, Grant discovered, 'after the scent of clean sea air, the atmosphere below was foul', a cocktail of 'nauseous fumes' from diesel mixed with fresh paint applied to the interiors. Parachute and glider troops at transit camps inland alongside airfields were equally uncomfortable. Nineteen-year-old airborne glider soldier Denis Edwards was 'cooped up for several days': 'It was hot inside our small tents and I suspect that like me, few of the others slept very soundly. On my mind was the thought that the task that had been allocated to us seemed so great and our force so small.' He recorded the atmosphere in his diary: 'nerves were taut and the air seemed charged with tension.'

Weather conditions in May were remarkably good while waiting, with a glorious heatwave, but as the day approached freak gales battered the country and south-westerly winds tore up the English Channel. A long line of depressions began to develop in the Atlantic, threatening disastrous consequences for the shipping due to launch on 5 June. Nothing like it had been seen in June for forty years. The navy needed winds no stronger than 12 mph, good visibility and no prolonged high winds in the Western Approaches for the days immediately preceding the operation. Sid Capon, due to jump with 9 PARA against the Merville Battery covering the Orne estuary, recalled: 'It is a bloody awful day, wind and rain that was to get worse as the day went on. The solid ground had now turned to mud and it is now evening and we awaited to get on the lorries that were to take us to the waiting aircraft.'

The operation was scrubbed. 'Gentlemen, back to your tents', they were told. 'It's been delayed for 24 hours.' It could not have been worse. Bed rolls meticulously packed into parachute containers had to be re-opened. Sid Capon's battalion was earmarked for a virtual suicide mission, to storm a vital German battery. Heavy losses were anticipated. 'We go back to our tents and sleep and awake in the morning and my thoughts were if there had not been the 24 hour delay our task would have been completed at Merville.'

'I suppose it gave a lot of fellows another 24 hours of living,' reflected airborne signaller Harry Reid. All Sid Capon could think of was 'now we must go all through the procedure again'. Some of the fleet had sailed and had to be recalled.

On 5 June a high pressure ridge was assessed to be shadowing the cold front sweeping over the Channel so the decision was 'Go'. 'Next morning there was no hesitation and we sped away in trucks,' recalled Sergeant Ian Grant heading for the dockside, 'racing through South-ampton's streets, with passers-by knowing full well what was about to happen – blowing kisses, weeping and cries of good luck.'

Nursing Sister Brenda McBryde remembered a services dance at the coastal town of Littlehampton, a still evening, enjoyed by those cooling off on the flat roof as the sea quietly lapped below on a deserted beach. A scarcely perceptible vibration 'began to overcome the muffled fox-trot beat they could hear outside'. The noise grew louder and louder until: ' "Look!" somebody cried out in amazement and we watched a cloud of tiny specks in the sky behind us, fanning out and multiplying as formation after formation of planes rose from the land thundered overhead on their way out to sea.'

The noise was deafening and soon brought out the dancers below who gazed up at swarms of Lancasters, Stirlings and Halifaxes, some towing gliders, moving purposefully across the sky towards France. A great sigh of 'Ah–ah–h–h' went up from all those watching 'as we realised we were witnessing the opening of the Second Front', Brenda McBryde recalled. 'It was a moment of elation and awe.' Alastair Pearson, flying overhead with his parachute battalion, knew the wedding was off, but his fiancée Joan, did not: 'It didn't honestly dawn on her until the morning of D-Day when an old boy she knew asked her if she'd heard the aeroplanes go over last night. She said she hadn't and he said, "Well you'd better turn on the news, because there'll be no wedding on Tuesday!" '

Troops buffeted at sea were steadily coming to terms during last-minute briefings with the intricacies of scaling the mythical 'Atlantic Wall' at the very moment their airborne compatriots were flying over it. Flying across in the face of a much weakened Luftwaffe was likely achievable, holding on until the seaborne troops arrived was another matter.

FROM THE SKY

'At the airfield we sorted ourselves into sections and platoons and were provided with a hot cup of tea and sat on the edge of the runway smoking and cracking jokes,' remembered Private Denis Edwards, part of the glider coup de main that was to land on the Orne River and Canal bridges. 'Whilst we all affected an air of total unconcern I am sure the others, like me, had stomachs that were churning.' Airborne signaller Harry Reid had never appreciated until confined to the transit camps why there were so many wireless operators until 'I learnt that they expected 50% casualties on the landing, and that's sobering.' There was trepidation: 'It would be true to say that we knew we were in for a very, very difficult time, and I think you could get quite emotional about that because you had to work out whether in your heart, in your mind, whether what you were going to do, what was expected of you, was worth putting your life on the line.' But he reflected, 'there was no way back was there?'

Soldiers had less to ponder than officers and commanders and busied themselves smearing hands, necks and faces with camouflage grease. 'As one wag pointed out,' remarked Edwards: 'Cor blimey – we don't need no bleedin' weapons – just the sight of us will scare 'em to death!' Airborne Sapper Tom Barrett assembled with 9 PARA for the drop on the Merville Battery. 'By this time we were definitely shaking and the 'planes for locating the dropping zones were already away.'

Officers churned the plan over through their minds. The British 6th Airborne Division was to protect the left flank of the Allied invasion and secure the area east of the River Orne to enable Montgomery's 21st Army Group to break out at a later date. Six American parachute regiments from the 82nd and 101st Airborne Divisions were to fly in and protect the opposite western flank of the invasion. They loaded 13,000 men upon 822 transport aircraft taking off from nine airfields. The British loaded another 7,000 men in six battalions from airfields south of Oxford, which were carried in 266 transport aircraft and 344 gliders with air landing infantry and heavy equipments. It was a challenging plan. Brigadier James Hill commanding the 3rd Parachute Brigade had to capture the bridges across the Orne River and Canal, silence a vital enemy battery covering Sword beach, destroy five bridges across the River Dives, and secure the prominent ridge line between the River Orne and Dives. Tasks covering some twenty-five square miles had to be secured by his division during the hours of darkness from past midnight to the seaborne H-Hour at 0700 hours on D-Day morning. It was the practical difficulties of achieving these as yet unseen objectives on the other side of the Atlantic Wall that taxed the intellects of these commanders as they made ready.

'Remember,' Hill later explained, 'the country was strange to us – infested by Germans and it was a dark night as well – *no mean task*.' They were short of aircraft. Hill remembered Major General Richard Gale, the commander of the 6th Airborne Division 'was so upset about no aeroplanes that he managed to persuade Bomber Command to let him have aeroplanes from bombing Berlin and that sort of thing'. Of course 'you cannot train parachute aircraft in a month', Hill commented and this was soon apparent to the emplaning soldiers. Corporal C D Weightman with 12 PARA, on meeting the aircrew and shaking hands with the skipper, was told 'either in innocence or to pull our legs, "I haven't dropped paras before."' Eyes rolled skyward; 'that was a great start,' he recalled.

'Fully dressed and kitted up we looked like a string of pack mules,' observed glider soldier Denis Edwards. Packing a personal container for a parachute assault involves an interminable debate over what to take, the dilemma of load priorities: ammunition versus rations and the rest. The finished bundle must be parachutable and has to be suspended on a harness within the claustrophobic and bucking confines of an aircraft in flight at night. Major A R Clarke with 13 PARA packed a sten gun, spare magazines with 9mm ammunition, two pounds of plastic explosive (HE), two 36 hand grenades, two full belts of Vickers .303 ammunition, wire cutters, radio batteries, small pack and webbing harness, forty-eight hours' worth of rations, water and cooking and washing kit. Further heavy items were spread about his pockets: a loaded .45 automatic pistol, medical kit, another 2 lb of HE, knife, survival kit, toggle rope and all the other personal things a soldier feels he needs to take into battle. With his parachute, he carried an all-up weight of 110 to 120 lb, which meant he could barely stand unaided.

The simplicities of life became all-important at the airfield before take-off. Should one accept the final tea and biscuits? Air sickness may result while a final nervous pee could involve the unbuckling of pre-checked parachute equipment and maybe a complete rejig of personal equipment stowage; a decision not to be taken lightly. As soon as one man felt the need to urinate, everybody else would want to go. Sergeant R A Pead with the 9 PARA mortar platoon recalled 'sitting about waiting to get into our equipment and move, playing cards to pass the time. You have a queer feeling in the stomach – a kind of sinking feeling, and the frequent trips to the latrines.' He did well at cards and sent the winnings home to his wife because 'it was no use where I was going'. Little sleep was achieved over the previous forty-eight hours with laborious packing and pre-paration interrupted by the postponement. Small pleasures raised morale. George O'Connor with 13 PARA noticed a small note attached to his parachute from the female packer, which read 'Good luck' and was signed 'Elsie'. He never forgot it. 'It's many years since, but thank you, Elsie, the 'chute worked OK.'

Soldiers going to battle become aware of their mortality and felt the need to communicate with their God. This was a generation of churchgoers. Some were hard-bitten veterans but the vast majority, as James Hill explained, were twenty-one years old, 'not a great age you may think' and 'they had never seen a shot fired in anger before, with the exception of myself and three officers'. Major Clarke attended the 13 PARA airfield service feeling it 'to be the most natural in the world'. They knelt, scratching and bruising knees from the weight of their equipments on the perimeter gravel in the act of contrition: 'So all six hundred of our battalion, led by Padre Boy Foy, acknowledged our need and our dependence, our fear and yet our trust, our inadequacies and yet our resolve.'

More than half of them were destined to become casualties. 'Whether you are an atheist or have no ideas of God or anything else, you pray,' pointed out James Hill. He insisted his command attend church parades once a month. Many of his men later conceded this provided comfort. Hill explained:

You have to pray to something. Now those chaps had all been to church, into the garrison church, and when they were flying in their aeroplanes they may have felt we don't know anything about God.

He doesn't mean anything else but we have been into his House and that gave him a lift and that came back to me on several occasions.

The order came to emplane, and as Sergeant Pead with 9 PARA passed between 'lines of men who were not going with us at that time' he saw many had tears in their eyes. 'They knew what the chances were,' he realised. 'I had a job to clamber into the plane,' remembered George O'Connor, 'a member of the ground staff gave me a shove and I was aboard.' At 2200 hours Denis Edwards heard the 'emplane' order and 'gave the earth by the runway a hard stamp in the hope that a little bit of English soil would accompany me on my journey'. The jokes and air of good humour were a fragile veneer cloaking real tension. 'It's too late now mate – yer shouldn't 'av joined!' Edwards became even more scared as he buckled into glider seat 12A, because unlucky 13 was not a recognised number. The sounds and smells of engines spluttering into life were sufficient to trigger psychological and physical reactions. Adrenalin comes first with the fitting of the parachute harness, a definite action that signifies the operation is definitely on. The second adrenalin rush comes with the start-up of engines; individuals had now to come to terms with what was about to happen.

Movement and direction inside taxiing aircraft can be discerned through bumps, sudden spurts and halts, accompanied by the bird-like chattering of rudders and control cables. Adrenalin surged again as the heavily laden aircraft accelerated down runways, one after the other, an interminable rise and fall of engine note. 'At 2256 hours the steady hum of the bomber engines suddenly increased to a deafening roar,' recalled Denis Edwards as his glider set off with a violent jerk and 'twang' as the slack on the tow cable was taken up by the tug plane. 'My muscles tightened,' he remembered, 'a cold shiver ran up and down my spine, I went hot and cold and sang all the louder to stop my teeth from chattering.' Inside the parachute aircraft the bumping and lumbering developed into a lurch, another change of engine note and steady vibration as they rose into the air. They were airborne; there was no turning back. 'I thought it was going to shake to pieces before it left the ground,' remembered George O'Conner taking off with 13 PARA. There was a 'clunk' as the wheels of his Dakota transport aircraft clamped into their pockets. 'I could hear sighs of relief and everyone

Local roads blocked off with masses of vehicles in the south of England were tangible evidence the Invasion was pending.

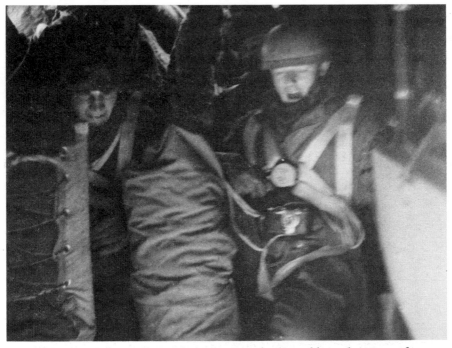

Action Stations in the night sky above Normandy. 'I could see the crests of waves. The wind and engine noise was shattering', recalled one paratrooper about to jump over Normandy. Waiting at the jumping hole of an Albermarle.

Crammed together, cold, sea-sick and lashed by spray, assault craft head for the beach on D–Day.

Seeking a reassuring glance the soldiers scramble down the ramps into the obstacle-strewn surf, under fire from the houses to their front.

began to talk at once.' By the time the aircraft formed up in streams and were vectored towards the coast the troops began to settle down for an average two-hour flight.

Oberst Oelze, commanding a Luftwaffe radar unit on the occupied island of Guernsey, telephoned the German 84th Corps HQ at Saint-Lô in Normandy shortly after midnight with news of a disturbing intercept. His Freya and Würzburg radar screens had spotted formations of four-engine bombers, followed almost immediately by other unidentified aircraft at regular intervals. They might be gliders. Seventh Army in Normandy was in its fourth year of an uneventful and largely peacetime occupation. The weather had been indescribable. It was a routine evening with units of the 21st Panzer Division on exercise near the proposed landing areas with practice ammunition. A phlegmatic duty staff officer at Corps HQ teased the radar operators on Guernsey reminding them they should watch their alcohol consumption and 'be on the look out for small ghosts only'. Leutnant Raimond Steiner meanwhile, manning a coastal bunker at Franceville beach with Artillery Regiment 1716, was intimidated by a vast fly-past of enemy aircraft, recalling 'the vibration in the air caused the sand in the dunes to crumble'.

Lights were dimmed inside the aircraft. Sergeant Pead with 9 PARA recalled how quiet things had become. 'I should imagine each of us had our own thoughts and fears.' George O'Connor flying with 13 PARA conducted a familiar debate with himself while pretending to sleep. 'What was I doing here?' he pondered. 'I was about to parachute into a foreign country and kill or be killed, what for?' His thoughts echoed those of his fellows from similarly deprived social backgrounds. His generation was convinced the post-war world must offer a new deal for ordinary people. 'The country had done nothing for me, except kept me poor and hungry.' He resolved: 'If I live through this I might get a better future, for helping the country out, I might even get a home for my wife and myself. I wasn't worried about a home "fit for heroes to live in" as promised by the government, even a room of our own would do for a start.'

Inside the gliders was noisy. Denis Edwards remembered 'a continual high-pitched scream of wind and slip-stream forcing its way through the cracks and crevices in the thin fabric of the fuselage'. The door left open in flight to enable an easy exit on touch-down intensified the noise. Air pockets and a buffeting slipstream made it difficult to prepare for action within the dimmed interiors of parachute transports. Major E S Lough with HQ 5th Parachute Brigade recalled: 'we had only a faint light in the aircraft and considerable difficulty was encountered in getting the right kit bags to the right chaps and in finding the quick-release pins, some of which had come undone.' It took them nearly forty minutes to sort themselves out before being ready to hook up.

Flying transport aircraft in a 'Vic' or 'V' formation of threes for parachute dropping is not easy in darkness. 'Formation flying is not part of a transport pilot's expertise,' claimed Flight Lieutenant Bristow of 575 Squadron, 'and here we were on a particularly dark night.' Having lost sight of the aircraft ahead, he closed up, only to quickly discover 'there were four of them', so he throttled back, preferring to take his chances alone. Peering through his cockpit window trying to pick out the enemy coastline ahead, he recalled: 'Shortly before we made landfall something exploded on the land right ahead. A vast sheet of yellow flame lit up the sky for a second or two, and in that I saw a line of aeroplanes all going in the same way, all at the same height, and I was part of this mad game of follow-my-leader.'

'*Prepare for action!*' was the call-point over the sea nearing the coast when it became a struggle to fit equipments to parachute harnesses in dimmed aircraft interiors, buffeted by the slipstreams of those converging for the drop zones ahead. Exertion and the realisation that *this was it* produced sweat, the stench of nervous flatulence mixed with the sour smell of vomit, as aircraft started to bob and weave. As the Stirlings neared the coast, the jump-floor hatches were opened in readiness for despatching. Dakota aircraft generally flew with open doors. Lieutenant Richard Todd with 7 PARA recalled, 'all 20 of us, cumbersome, heavily laden figures, jostled and swayed while all the aircraft yawed in search of the exact line of flight.' *Action stations!* and *Stand to the door!* meant 'we hooked up our static lines and shuffled to our jumping positions'. Todd was jumping number one, which meant he straddled the broad end of the jump hole: 'For what seemed an age we flew like this. Looking down, I could see the crests of waves. The wind and engine noise was shattering.'

Dispatchers busied themselves among the paratroopers, colliding with them as aircraft jinked up and down and side to side, as they completed equipment checks. Nervously looking through open doors, men could make out the ships and invasion craft on the moonlit water below. 'The most magnificent sight,' recalled Private T. Buckley with 12 PARA, gazing through his Stirling hole, 'thousands of ships, battleships, destroyers, corvettes, tank-landing craft and others.' He found it awe-inspiring, 'a wonderful sight which I will never forget.' Then came the indistinct line of surf below indicating one and a half minutes to go. Red lights came on above the exit doors reflecting a pronounced red glow visible even at the back of the stick, deep inside the aircraft interior. Excited paratroopers repeated the dispatcher's warning cry *Red on!* They were thundering into the final approach to the drop zones.

Aircraft slowed down and began to lose height. Major Clarke, a company commander with 13 PARA, heard the dispatcher sing out *Carbourg!* And then 'we were into the flak. It came up at us rather like fireworks.' 'Suddenly our aircraft is all swaying and the ack-ack from the enemy guns send us into turmoil,' recalled Sid Capon with 9 PARA. Moments of sudden weightlessness were replaced by crushing weight on bent knees as gravitational pull compensated over air pockets. Men were thrown left and right against fuselage walls as aircraft weaved and yawed to avoid flak bursts. Some luckless paratroopers attempting to maintain balance fell out of doors into the sea; a lonely death but drowning was accelerated by the weight of equipment. 'Something hit us,' Clarke recalled, 'the sound was rather like that of a dustbin being emptied.' Sergeant Pead with 9 PARA 'could see the tracers creeping up towards the plane and flashing by, the flak was knocking on the fuselage.' The pilot took evasive action 'which threw us about a bit'. Aeroplanes throttled back to jump speed and began to vibrate inside as they slowed almost to stalling speed to facilitate a safe exit. Turbulence increased as slipstreams merged. Paratroopers fought for balance so they could achieve the vital clean exit. All eyes were on the red light, willing it to change to green.

An unbalanced exit is a paratrooper's nightmare. Failure to achieve this precondition can result in snagging the aircraft door, twisting parachute lines, tearing equipment and weapons free or, worse still, impeding the full deployment of the parachute canopy. 'I was about to stand up, when I was nearly thrown out of the door by another blast of gunfire,' recalled George O'Connor. 'Not yet lad,' restrained his dispatcher. 'I regained my breath and noticed the rest of the lads were rolling about on the floor, they were so tightly packed together they were getting tangled up.' This was potentially catastrophic in the confines of a bucking aircraft; not knowing whether they were still hooked up. If not, the parachute would not deploy and they had no reserve. His stick was definitely not ready to jump. His aircraft suddenly banked and turned, the red light came on, followed almost immediately by the green. The dispatcher shouted *Go!* and started to push the number one and two out of the plane, 'as he pushed me out, I heard him shouting *Good luck, lads!*' His chute opened with a snap amid tracer rounds flashing and cracking past.

Major Bill Collingwood's aircraft was hit by flak crossing the coast; he was Brigadier James Hill's brigade-major. 'He was blown out of the door and left dangling and spinning underneath,' Hill recalled. 'He had a 60lb kit-bag attached to his right leg.' As the aircraft limped back over the English coast the crew managed to haul him back on board. On arrival at Odiham, the emergency airfield, he commandeered a jeep, and despite his damaged right leg, flew back in a glider the next day. 'What an example of sheer guts and mental toughness!' Hill exclaimed.

'When the light went on to jump I think we were all on our hands and knees,' remembered Sergeant Pead with 9 PARA, 'and the weight of our equipment made it awkward for us to get to our feet.' Nevertheless, he got to the door 'and fell out, that was the only way'. Glancing about, 'it seemed like the 5th of November, tracer bullets flashing by and fires burning below.' Sid Capon had a similarly untidy exit:

> The amber glows of the flak outside can be seen. 'What the effing hell's happened?' We are all sent sprawling and again within the turmoil the shout of *Red Light!* Followed immediately by *Green Light Go!* No fucker told us about anti-aircraft fire and what it does to a plane. Everyone is scrambling out of the aircraft, it's twisting and swaying and eventually I reach the door and jump. No it's not a

> jump, I have fallen out in a heap. I am clear of our plane and floating
> to earth and not taking any notice of what is happening around me.

Once out, the slipstream hits the face, the shadow of the aircraft passes over, and there is a glimpse of feet and a welcome rush of cold air to replace the previously clammy confines of the aircraft interior. The taut snap of the parachute harness tightening brings with it a frightened exhalation of breath. There is blessed silence after the buffeting slipstream and roaring aircraft now receding in the distance. Corporal E D Weightman with 12 PARA landed in water up to his waist. 'It was pitch black, and I was trying to get myself orientated, I heard the sounds of someone gasping and spluttering.' Private Eric Barley 'took a piece of soil and squeezed it in my hand and thought "this is France." ' Most of them were completely alone in the dark. 'I didn't feel afraid but tensed up,' Barley remembered. Men sought to orientate themselves as in the distance the distinctive ripping sound of German spandau machine-guns sounded through the night.

One hour before, the glider coup de main by five glider-borne platoons of the Ox and Bucks, led by Major John Howard, secured the bridges over the Orne River and Canal. It was perhaps the outstanding glider action of the war, an amazing feat of night navigation and flying, because as Denis Edwards on board emphasised, 'they have to make a one-off decision as they swoop towards the ground at a speed of between 70 and 90 mph.' Most paratroopers feared to land in a glider. *Link arms!* was the call from the senior pilot aboard Denis Edward's glider as they held tight and braced themselves for touch-down.

It began 'with the usual slight bump, a small jerk and a much heavier thump' as the glider careered along, shuddering and bumping up and down at high speed 'like a bucking bronco'. They were taken aback to see the darkness lit by 'a stream of brilliant sparks', mistaken for tracer defensive fire, as the wheels were ripped off and the skids scoured over stony ground. 'There followed a sound like a giant sheet of cloth being viciously ripped apart, then a God Almighty crash like a clap of thunder and my body seemed to be moving in several directions at the same time.' Quite often pilots crashed through cockpit windscreens or the platoon inside was heaped to the front or men ejected through the open door on impact.

Ominous silence followed; 'the peace after all the din was unexpected and quite uncanny,' Edwards recalled, until men began to unstrap themselves and move around the interior. Despite their dazed state of mind they realised the drag parachute that reduced the landing speed to 60 mph had enabled them to plough into the tangled wire emplacements just outside the outermost trenches. Passing the two injured and moaning pilots, still strapped in their seats, who had catapulted beyond the glider, the coup de main force attacked. Within ten minutes the bridges were secured. German sentries had not been alarmed by the succession of crashes and bangs, believing it to be the not too unfamiliar sound of shot-off aircraft bits raining down. Lieutenant Fox, one of the assaulting platoon commanders, was irritably told to 'f—k off' by three German soldiers found sleeping afterwards in an outlying bunker. Surprise was complete.

Few military plans survive crossing the start-line and parachute operations dependent on a myriad of technical, weather-related and enemy variables are no exception. Denis Edwards had a grandstand view of the arrival of the main parachute force. 'The first few planes flew over with little opposition but those that followed ran into heavy flak,' he noticed, 'and at least one was hit, set on fire, and came hurtling down like a comet from about 3,000 feet.' He hoped the paras on board had got out. He then observed 'the para force was getting a hell of a pasting from ack-ack from the now fully alerted ground forces and I was thankful that we had come down first.' BBC war correspondent Guy Byam, having just jumped, looked up and saw: 'The whole sky is a fantastic chimera of lights and flak, and one plane gets hit and disintegrates wholesale in the sky, sprinkling a myriad of burning pieces all over the sky.'

The plan was beginning to unravel. Lieutenant H J Sweeney, one of Howard's platoon commanders watching the arriving reinforcements alongside Edwards, noticed 'one disheartening factor' and that was 'they seemed to be flying in all directions at once, quite unlike the steady stream we had seen on exercises'.

Many paratroopers overshot their drop zones and landed in areas flooded by the Germans in the Dives valley. Men drowned in three feet of water, disorientated and weighed down, panicked by folds of suffocating wet silk. Sapper Tom Barrett overshot his drop zone by thirty miles. His aircraft, evading flak, was flying too fast. 'The slip stream was terrific,' he estimated, pitching out at perhaps 200 mph, nearly twice the permitted drop speed. His overweight container snapped the fastenings on his parachute harness and his kit was torn away, plummeting out of sight.

George O'Connor with 13 PARA came to the aid of a paratrooper who was descending upside down with his feet entangled in his rigging lines. As they moved off the drop zone they passed another paratrooper impaled on one of the anti-glider landing pole obstructions. James Hill descended into four feet of water which subsequently 'entailed five hours cold and very hard work negotiating the numerous underwater obstacles such as farmers fences, Dannert wire, black-thorn hedges and deep submerged irrigation ditches from 10 to 15 feet in width' to get out. Each man was encumbered by some 60lb of equipment. They passed parachute 'blossoms' denoting the submerged remains of men who had drowned, dragged down by their equipment in deep ditches. 'We were able to help each other with the aid of toggle ropes to negotiate the obstacles and swim when it was necessary to do so.' After emerging from the flooded area his group was almost annihilated by a low-flying attack from an Allied fighter bomber. He barely survived with part of his left buttock blown away. They had to leave the mortally wounded survivors behind after administering morphine. The dying men cheered them on, it left an indelible memory with James Hill.

The British 6th Airborne Division assembled with about 40 per cent of its strength that first night, marginally better than the 38 per cent achieved by the 101st US Airborne Division and 33 per cent achieved by the US 82nd. Only 40 per cent of 7 PARA due to relieve Major John Howard at the Orne River bridges turned up during the night. Sixty per cent of 12 and 13 PARA began to establish themselves around the glider landing zones at Ranville, while 8 PARA and the 1st Canadian PARA were widely dispersed, but carried on with their plans as best they were able. 'My advance party dropped at ten minutes to one,' recalled Alastair Pearson the CO of 8 PARA. 'I knew quite well something had happened because instead of the sky being full of parachutes there were singularly few.' He had only 170 men after two hours and one of his soldiers accidentally shot him in the hand. It was a bad start.

When Sid Capon rallied with 9 PARA he remembered, 'Blimey, I thought on arrival, there is no bugger here!' About fifty men were lying around at the alert but only a further hundred filtered in. Lieutenant Colonel Terence Otway the battalion commander had been told by his brigade commander, 'Your attitude of mind must be that you cannot contemplate failure in the direct assault.' Every landed soldier was acutely aware there could be no more Dunkirks. Six hundred para-troopers had been allotted to this task, but fewer than 200 turned up in time. They penetrated the Merville battery shortly before dawn, losing nearly 50 per cent of the assault force. General Montgomery was relying upon three airborne divisions to, at the minimum, restrict the immediate deployment options of the five enemy divisions in situ, in order to guarantee a successful amphibious assault by a further five Allied divisions. All that was on the ground operating in a coherent and directed manner was a conglomeration amounting to one airborne division. Reinforcements would land at dawn and scattered elements of three divisions had at least surmounted the Atlantic Wall, but would it suffice?

FROM THE SEA

At dawn on D–Day ship outlines began to take shape through the early morning haze. 'As full light began to come one saw the ships and planes,' declared Major Iain Macleod with the 50th Northumbrian Division, 'a sight so paralysing that tears came to my eyes.' He reflected: 'It was as if every sea had yielded up her wrecks. It was as if every plane that had ever been built was there, and, so it seemed in fantasy as if dead crews were there too.'

Awestruck by this massive assembly of fighting power, Iain Macleod felt moved 'out of sheer delight at being part of that company in such a place', to quote *Henry V* – 'And gentlemen in England now abed . . .'

D–Day was possibly the final British enterprise to have such a dramatic and decisive impact on the outcome of the war. The United States mounted a similar effort on the right flank, but the British people of this generation regard D–Day as *their* victory. It was conducted from their shores, under their gaze, carried in their ships, and assumed a symbolism like that of the Battle of Britain. Much of the British Army that fought in north-west Europe passed over the Normandy beaches. Many had waited two to four years to return in reconstituted BEF form as the 21st Army Group, to avenge the humiliation of Dunkirk. British ingenuity, largely neglected by the Americans, invented 'the Funnies', specialised armoured vehicles that enabled tanks to land on open beaches to surmount the much vaunted Atlantic Wall. 'Of course we had American officers with us and they worked very closely with us,' explained Captain Goronwy Rees with the D-Day planning staff, 'but the original conception of the plan was a British one and the detailed planning of it was also, I would say, about 90% British.' Swimming Duplex Drive (DD) tanks quickly ashore enabled a considerable lodgement to be achieved within the first twenty-four hours. D-Day was indeed 'the Day'.

The appearance of the fleet was as shocking to the Germans as it was impressive to the Allies. Grenadier Robert Vogt, an infantryman with 726 Regiment atop the Arromanches cliffs opposite the British approach, declared: 'What I saw scared the devil out of me. Even though the weather was so bad, we could see a huge number of ships. Ships as far as the eye could see, an entire fleet, and I thought, "Oh God, we're finished! We're done for now!"'

SS-Obersturmführer (Lieutenant) Peter Hansmann, a reconnaissance commander with the 12th SS Hitlerjugend Division, was driving the same sector of coast when he picked up the mass of shipping through binoculars and saw 'up to the horizon – ships, masts and command bridges'. In the background 'flashes blinked at irregular intervals, but incessantly – naval artillery!' White stripes denoting the wash of approaching landing craft were faintly visible 'extending from the cliffs at Arromanches to the horizon east of the Orne estuary – all coming towards us!' The Germans soon had a nickname for this imaginary township that winked and smoked off the coast, they called it 'the Golden City'.

Sergeant Ian Grant filmed 45 Commando assembling on deck and checking out ammunition and weapons and equipment, 'the special knives they carried inspected with loving attention'. 'We got into the boats,' the landing craft, recalled Lieutenant Hugh Bone with the 2nd East Yorkshire Regiment, 'the padre said some prayers.' They clambered down the grappling nets on ships' sides into violently pitching craft. 'You sat on a little piece of wood, three rows set one behind the other' in Landing Craft Infantry (LCIs) 'and kept our heads down'. Commando Ken Oakly remembered, 'as we boarded the craft we could hear the huge shells being fired by the battleships, it was awe-inspiring.' Men instinctively shrank and ducked as 'they whistled overhead, shells weighing about a ton each'.

The landing craft began to circle their parent ships beyond the range of German guns off-shore as they formed up prior to release. Most were to spend an average of three hours in the square-shaped unwieldy craft that rolled and yawed with every wave. Before long soldiers began to retch from seasickness, becoming so ill they were distracted from the perils ahead. John Russell in the Kings Own Scottish Borderers (KOSB) from Dundee recalled after a breakfast that had turned men green 'many a man was glad to face the Germans rather than stay on the boat'. BBC correspondent Frank Gillard saw the naval commander look at his watch before putting the micro-phone to his face and announce: 'Off you go then – and good luck to you.'

The landing craft set off negotiating the lines of bombarding ships: past battleships with 14-inch guns about seven miles offshore, then the destroyers with 5-inch guns between five and three miles offshore, and finally moving by destroyers at one or two miles, pounding the beaches with direct fire support. One observer saw:

> The squat grey mass of the largest battleship, the *Warspite*, flung swelling clouds of incandescence out of the long trunks of her 15-inch guns. The flames as long as towers, unrolled into clouds of smoke as big as castles. A noise like an express train at speed followed, as the projectile was thrust through the high air into France.

BBC correspondent Robin Duff observed the aerial bombing on land that preceded the assault. 'The beaches shook and seemed to rise into the air, and ships well out to sea quivered with the shock.' Soldiers observing from approaching landing craft could almost tangibly feel the weight of high explosive crashing against the German positions. Duff could see 'some of the tenseness of expectation left the faces of the men who were going into land and was replaced by a smile of the utmost relief'.

It was assessed that it required about 500 ships and craft varying from 100 to 15,000 tons to put a division ashore with its weapons. About seven divisions were coming ashore on D-Day; an intimidating spectacle to the German defenders. The preliminary assault in the British sector was to pit five British brigade groups against six dispersed German companies on the shoreline, with a similar number in depth. Odds were ten to one favouring the attackers at any given point, supported by pulverising naval gunfire. On board B-turret in the battleship *Warspite* eighteen-year-old gunner John Cooper recalled: 'Firing continued. The shock of discharge, hiss of air blasts, rattling of rammers, and banging about of the main gun-loading cages began to deaden the senses.'

It was gruelling work, Cooper remembered, as his filthy blackened gun crew watched their chief gunner taking a gulp of fresh air while remarking, 'as much as I love a whiff of cordite, there is something to be said for the ozone!'

German coastal artillery was almost loath to respond to this paralysing fire. Oberstabsfeldwebel (Sergeant Major) Buskotte attempting to shoot back with two surviving guns directed from his commander's observation post on Franceville plage, received backlashes of fire that churned over the battery position every time they opened a desultory fire. 'It's all very well for the Herr Leutnant to give orders from down there,' [from his beach OP] he shouted into his radio hand-set, 'because it's here where we shall always catch it!'

DD 'swimming' tanks were released at about the three mile point. Many of their flimsy rubberised canvas screens were swamped in choppy water, while others were run over by parent launching craft, pitched forward by uncontrollable swells. 'Being a bloody sailor in a bloody tank was taking patriotism too far,' complained Lieutenant Stuart Hills with the Nottinghamshire Sherwood Rangers Yeomanry. The task of these DD tanks was to land just ahead of the infantry and engage beach pillboxes and provide supporting fire as they attacked. Major General Hobart's 'Funnies' were task-orientated specially landed armoured vehicles. Sherman 'Crab' flail tanks were to beat the beaches with revolving flailing chains to detonate paths through minefields for the assaulting infantry. Crews anticipating a two-thirds casualty rate were unenthusiastic. 'At least 16 of the troop might be wiped out,' recalled Lieutenant Ian Hamilton, leading such a group, and neither were they permitted to stop for the wounded. 'Not very cheering,' he remarked. In order to get over the sea walls, Churchill Armoured Vehicle Royal Engineer (AVREs) were to blast entry points with 290mm mortars ejecting a 40lb projectile nicknamed the 'flying dustbin'. Other AVREs carried fascines to bridge ditches, lay 'Bobbin' non-slip carpets of coarse material to negotiate slippery slopes and trackways to bridge gaps and climb sea walls. The plan depended on these assets arriving in sequential order where required on obstacle-strewn beaches under fire; an ambitious undertaking.

As the landing craft wallowed toward shore navy ratings peering over the top of the rising and falling ramps measured progress and shouted back the information as best they could. Crammed together, cold, violently seasick and lashed by spray each time ramps banged and crested another wave, the soldiers simply endured. Many referring to water-colour map sketches, steered by church spires. Off Juno beach Lieutenant Blois-Brooke aboard a Landing Craft Assault (LCA) was taken aback as it grew light at 'the appalling number of church spires there was on the French shore'. His confidently predicted scheme was beginning to unravel. 'I had already encircled the churches I would use to fix our position,' he recalled, 'but daylight revealed so many I couldn't pick out my selected ones!' Soaked with sea water and retching on the floor of the landing craft, the soldiers could not have cared less. Men were keyed-up; willing it to be 'all right', suppressing a desire to panic and hoping nobody would notice their inner turmoil. 'Everybody had butterflies in their stomachs,' recalled one soldier during the run-in to the beach. 'Everyone was quiet, not their usual jovial selves and I suppose everyone had their own anxieties – as you normally did, realising what a great Armada it was and if we should fail, what a chaos it would be.' Landing craft stank from diesel and stale vomit with sea water sluicing about their feet and knees.

Ahead of the landing craft the DD tanks battled on toward the shore. Lance Corporal Patrick Hennessey with the 13th/18th Hussars had already watched two of his squadron flounder. 'We were buffeted about unmercifully, plunging into the troughs of the waves and somehow wallowing up again to the crests.' They were under way for an hour. 'It was a struggle to keep the tank on course,' he recalled, 'but gradually the shoreline became more distinct and before long we could see the line of houses which were our targets.' Every wave that slapped the flimsy canvas screen reminded the crews of their precarious situation.

As landing craft approached the obstacle belt a desultory fire from the hard-pressed German defenders opened up. 'I heard someone in the craft say "Oh God",' remembered deckhand Marine Neale aboard an LCA. 'Many of the lads had been sick during the journey and the stench in the craft was fairly high,' he recalled, but the sound of firing switched attention to more pressing problems. 'It is strange how emotions transfer themselves.' All were distinctly fearful. 'I heard someone sobbing and felt the urge to do the same, but just then machine guns started to fire and you could hear the bullets whipping by.' The problem was now for the unwieldy shaped rectangular craft to negotiate the fearsome array of jagged metal and poles tipped with mines just protruding from the water ahead of them. John Russell with the KOSB at Sword Beach recalled 'craft weren't coming in close enough and the men were getting drowned because they were hitting them before they could get into shallow water'.

'By now we could hear the enemy machine guns, the explosions of enemy mortars on the beach, we clutched our weapons,' recalled Lieutenant Hugh Bone with the 2nd East Yorks. 'Now was the moment, stuff was falling pretty close to us.' Lieutenant Commander Denis Glover commanding LCI 516 saw the 'lines of bristling stakes' stretched out in rows as they came in towards Sword Beach. They had now to erratically steer through the obstacles under steadily escalating German fire:

> *Whang*, here it comes – those whizzing ones will be mortars and the stuff is falling all around us. Can't avoid them, but the mines and collisions I can avoid. Speed, more speed. Put them off by speed, weave in and out of these bloody spikes, avoid the mines, avoid our friends, avoid the wrecked craft and vehicles in the rising water, and get these troops ashore.

'Some of the men were talking, some smoking, some vomiting quietly into brown bags of grease-proof paper,' recalled another infantryman:

> The wind was bringing to them now the sounds of shells bursting ashore. Each man could feel each thudding detonation somewhere inside him. The talking stopped. Men took up their rifles and machine guns; there was the click of bolts being drawn and rammed home. The slow wallowing motion of the craft eased; they were coming into shallower water.

Pinned inside cramped landing craft bobbing among the beach obstacles, soldiers were helplessly dependent upon coxswains getting them through, while at any moment they may be hit by a shell. Landing craft were engaged by pillboxes on esplanades and at the water's edge. Naval officer Douglas Reeman, observing from a Motor Torpedo Boat off Sword Beach, likened the seaborne landings to a dramatic cavalry charge. 'Shell-bursts hurled towering columns of water all around them.' Desperately striving to ground, 'it was heart-stopping to see them moving steadily through the smoke and falling spray.' Landing craft coming up behind could not only see the punishment being meted out, they could hear it over radio loudspeakers. 'We were listening on the intercom to one of the landing crafts in distress,' recalled Alex Wentworth from West Kilbride. '*We're breaking up, we're going!* This is what we heard, then panic: *We're going, Good luck, lads.*' Boat after boat was hit by 'vivid blobs of tracer licking out from the shore', Reeman observed. Shells shrieked low, skimming the surface in straight lethal lines, 'flat trajectory cannon fire, probably from some antitank guns close to the shore'. These were the bunkers the DD tanks were designed to silence.

Squat grey shapes lurched crab-like on shore as tracks gaining contact with shelving sand pulled tanks out of the water. 'Of course you must understand,' commented Sergeant Leo Gariepy, a Canadian tank commander on Juno Beach, 'that the DD tank in the water looks like a little, very unharmful canvas boat; there's only about 15 inches of rubberised canvas that shows.' Open-mouthed German gunners had not anticipated tanks until well after an initial infantry assault. 'It's only when we're coming out of the water,' Gariepy explained, 'when they realised there were tanks, but by then we were a little too close to their heavy calibre guns on us and they were firing over our heads.' Small explosive charges dropped the water-resistant screens and the tanks were in action; 'Seventy – five, HE, action – Traverse right, steady on. 300 – white fronted house – first floor window, centre. On – Fire!'

'Within a minute of dropping our screen,' Lance Corporal Hennessey recalled, 'we had fired our first shot in anger.' Casualties on the British beaches were completely variable. Troops of the first assault wave ran into a wall of fire in certain areas whereas in others they simply walked ashore. The 2nd East Yorks lost 200 men in the first few minutes, while initially the Lancashires were relatively unscathed.

As landing craft nosed into the beaches soldiers peering through opening ramp doors saw house tops rocking up and down as the breaking surf rose and fell. Motioned through ramp doors by navy ratings, heavily laden troops struggling with equipments and scaling ladders for sea walls clumsily and jerkily shouldered their way through restricted LCA exits. Immediately waist-deep in water, fearful soldiers worked legs through the foaming surf as fast as they were able past twisted girder hedgehog obstacles. Ahead was often a thirty-yard dash to the protection of a sea wall. Diesel and sick smells were dispersed amid a stiff sea breeze tinged with salt spray and the pungent smell of cordite. The staccato crack and thump sounds of incoming machine-gun fire was interspersed with louder body thumping barks of bunkered anti-tank guns. 'There were so many men on the beaches,' recalled Major J Anderson with the Canadian North-Shore Regiment coming ashore at Juno that, 'I think it was like shooting at a flock of birds.' The assault was medieval-like with concrete walls and fortified esplanades needing to be stormed with scaling ladders and grappling hooks after crossing the obstacle-strewn sea moat, while German soldiers hurled stick grenades from above. Corporal Harold Brasier with the Queen's Own Rifles of Canada tried to drag a screaming wounded soldier ashore despite specific orders to stop for no man. Hit in the leg himself he paused the interview as he relived the horror: 'he was just . . . something came in over my shoulder – something really big – and he was just obliterated in front of me.' They were under fire from heavy calibre weapons.

'People were hit, some were dead, others struggling to crawl out of the water,' remembered Hugh Bone with the East Yorks. 'There was some horrible sights, men calling out for help.' Commando Ken Oakly likewise thrashed ashore through cloying water. 'It was very, very bad when we landed.' They had to reach the line of esplanades and fortified houses which provided dubious cover because they were defended. Soldiers under fire have to conduct a basic combat appreciation, the reasoning required to decide what to do in order to achieve their mission and survive. Ken Oakly reasoned: 'When you hear the bullets whizzing through the air, well I've got to get under cover. I've got to do something about this. I've got to find out where it's coming from. Can I attack? Can I reach them with the gun I have?'

'One of the main snags,' recalled Major Mott with B Company the 1st Hampshire Regiment landing at Gold Beach, 'was the weight the men had to carry.' Mott had to wade in knee-deep water for a hundred yards, with surf and equipment weight reducing his desperate efforts to get ashore to a form of slow-motion. 'The first one that went off just disappeared, it was too deep,' declared Bert Mitchell wading ashore with the Gordon Highlanders at Sword Beach. 'He had all his kit on and just disappeared completely.' Every rifleman had fifty rounds of small arms ammunition, Bren magazines, four grenades, two-inch mortar bombs as well as special equipment. There was in addition the helmet, Mae West life-preserver, weapon, entrenching tool and small packs containing clothing, rations and water and further equipment. Small wonder they moved cumbersomely through water and obstacles to reach sea walls, all the time coming to terms with the shock of unfamiliar carnage and din around them. Lieutenant H M Irwin on Gold Beach claimed 'most of us had seen men shot before but nothing like the damage done by spandau fire and 88s'. It was a shock to the system:

Men were blown apart and in the case of machine gun fire, men were hit a dozen times at once – not a chance for them to live. We had been trained in most all aspects and actually pretty well knew what to expect. However, it was not enough to bolster you for this kind of carnage. It took a few minutes on the beach to comprehend, adjust and move forward. Some did not.

The arrival of tanks on the shoreline was decisive and they began to overwhelm the defence by sheer weight of numbers. Major Peter Selerie with the Sherwood Rangers Yeomanry observed the impact a 290mm 'Petard' AVRE had upon a large multi-storey house holding up the advance to Le Hamel off Gold Beach: 'The Petard fired and something like a small dustbin hit the house, just above the front door. It collapsed like a pack of cards, spilling the defenders with their machine guns, anti-tank weapons and an avalanche of bricks into the courtyard.'

Technological surprise, however, worked both ways. 'Do you know, one of the first things I saw was a Sherman tank with three bloody great holes through it,' announced Corporal Herbert Smith arriving at Gold with characteristic soldier-bluntness. 'Crikey, I thought, so old Monty was having us on,' he indignantly reflected. 'He told us at Alamein that the gun hadn't been invented that could pierce a Sherman – well it certainly had now, as we could clearly see.' Flail tanks had however de-mined paths through minefields up to sea walls and other AVRE variants were enabling them to be crossed, but first they needed to be cleared by infantry attacks.

It did not always go according to plan, as Bill Millin with 45 Commando explained, when ten to twelve wounded British soldiers lay across the beach exit road after clearing it. He then heard the noise of a British flail tank coming up from the water's edge to explode the mines. 'The commander couldn't see them and his tank came straight on and crushed its way up this narrow road over the top of the soldiers.'

With momentum born of the desperation to survive, Canadian infantry came to grips with the German bunker positions off Juno Beach. Little tactical flair was demonstrated on the beaches; the only option was to bludgeon through with quarter neither anticipated nor given. Major Charles Dalton with the Queen's Own Rifles of Canada stepped back from the aperture of a pillbox whose machine-gun was shooting up his men and silenced it with his sten. He then blacked out and subsequently discovered, 'it was the man in the pill box, who got up and fired through the ventilator, and the bullet went through my helmet and the back of my head and scalped me, and came out the other side.' 'The thing I hated,' remarked one Canadian soldier, 'was when they'd bring up a carrier with a flame-thrower to burn out one of their pill boxes.' There was no defence against flame, which normally asphyxiated before it did its gruesome work. 'I can still turn sort of green when I think of it,' recalled the witness. They were dealing with a pillbox:

> We could hear the guys inside yelling. We didn't know what they were yelling and I told the Sergeant maybe they wanted to surrender but the door was jammed. I said it might have taken a hit and buckled and they couldn't get out. He said 'Fuck 'em' and yelled at the guy with the flame-thrower to turn on the heat, and you should have heard those Germans in that pill box screaming. God it was awful.

The sea wall at Bernières off Juno Beach was breached by 0915 hours, two hours after the initial assault. Tanks were over the top by 1400. There was similar momentum all along the British beaches as they sought to fight the beach exits clear.

The battle for the shoreline was an anonymous affair for the German defenders, reported at distance from smoked-off strongpoints from which few returned. By the evening of D-Day the Allies had achieved a tenuous lodgement with gaps between the two American landings and between Juno and Sword. These linked up over succeeding days. SS-Obersturmführer Peter Hansmann's reconnaissance ride along the line of the British beaches revealed 'over 400 ships with a wall of barrage balloons along the whole 30 kilometre stretch towards the Orne Estuary'. It was clear that 'coastal defences were knocked out and overran'. He reported the odd appearance of tanks 'that surfaced directly from the sea'. 'Is there such a thing?' he asked. 'At first one saw the cupola, and then they surfaced like some monster from the deep.' He confirmed, 'Infantry in battalion strength moving south towards Bayeux.'

Facing the British landings, 716 Division reported 'only sparse and fragmentary reports are available over the actual conduct of the landings' that were generally cloaked in smoke. Naval bombardment cut communications 'and only a few troops ever returned'. All that was visible at distance were dot-like figures working their way behind bunkers which flashed and smoked, signifying their likely demise.

Hauptmann (Captain) Schimpf, commanding III Battery from Artillery Regiment 1716, peering through his telescope from his Franceville bunker on the east side of the Orne saw 'how assault groups worked their way from bunker to bunker, breaking into dug-outs and working embrasures with flame-throwers and explosive charges'. It was clear the much-hyped Atlantic Wall had been breached, but there remained 337 days of war in Europe still to come.

Home Guard Frank Edwards was asked as he boarded a bus at 0815 that morning: 'Well, have we started or haven't we?' Confusion was caused with the BBC quoting German reports on the eight o'clock news but not confirming until 0932 when the calm authoritative voice of John Snagge announced, 'D-Day has come.' This became apparent as Frank Edwards's bus journey continued. When he returned home that night, 'I saw the biggest queue I have ever seen – it must have been somewhere near 100 strong, single file, of people waiting to buy an evening newspaper.' In contrast to today's more reserved behaviour, D-Day promoted instant bonding among complete strangers in the street. 'How are we doing, mate?' a lorry driver shouted to people in Frank Edwards' bus queue, 'How far in are we?' 'And so it went on,' Edwards recalled. Murial Green remembered a rumour the previous day when her housekeeper confided, 'the Second Front had started and we had landed in northern France,' and a 'sailor's wife had told me that her husband thought it was starting this week,' observing the Americans had disappeared locally. Now it was confirmed. 'D-Day at last! Invasion! Hurrah! God Save the King!' wrote one fifteen-year-old Cheshire schoolgirl in a frenzy of patriotism. 'The Invasion has begun,' wrote Clara Milburn triumphantly in her diary, 'at 1 pm we had a most marvellous broadcast beginning D-Day. *The* Day.' Naval planner Moyra Macleod recalled the emotional vacuum after all the men had gone, 'a complete silence fell and an emptiness, it was still, very still, we'd done all we could.' She and the staff knew the invasion had launched: 'And then we stopped and listened and heard in the distance: boom, boom, boom, the guns beginning to fire over in France.'

The *Daily Mirror* newspaper lead article reminded its readers of the Prime Minister's 'sublime obstinacy' and 'inspiring pessimism', echoing his famous address on achieving office, stating: 'It is blood, tears and sweat that we face again today, but in a very different mood. Then the skies were grey. Now they are ablaze with the lights of triumphs achieved and victory to come.'

The *Mirror* reflected the nation's mood, claiming 'the curtain rises on the closing scene of the greatest human conflict the world has ever known'. Wren Maureen Bolster shared this optimism, feeling 'we've turned the most vital corner of the war – and there – ahead lies peace beyond the immediate battles'.

But it was far from over yet. 'I knew from my husband's letters that the Second Front was imminent, and I really began to worry,' remembered Peggy Rigby, whose husband Raith was a Commando. She 'had a feeling this was going to be some kind of suicide squad and they could not land off those beaches without a terrible loss of life'. She was justifiably concerned because she was pregnant. 'Each soldier, officer, or Marine or whatever had been given this small brown card, which was to be posted when they reached France,' she recalled. 'My card never came,' she explained: 'And as the days sort of dragged on I felt something was amiss. And then it was the 15th of June and I had a bland telegram, telling me that my husband was killed . . . It didn't register really. I couldn't believe it, I was completely stunned. It just said: "Regret your husband killed in action. Letter following." '

Coincidently that same day the fifteen Allied divisions that had managed to get ashore at Normandy virtually equalled the slightly less than sixteen German divisions assembled against them. Bloody stalemate developed among the Normandy hedgerows. Three weeks later Peggy Rigby lost her baby.

Victory did not automatically follow on from D-Day. Both sides anticipating a decisive battle of movement were instead bogged down in the Normandy hedgerow battles. An anaconda-like grip was maintained on the German defence by the Allies who enlarged the lodgement each time the Wehrmacht drew breath, but losses were of 1914–18 proportions. A Blitzkrieg in reverse across France and Belgium followed the spectacular break-out in August. The 'Britishness' of the subsequent conduct of the war in north-west Europe was constrained by these enormous Normandy losses which diluted the manpower needed to sustain the size of the British and Commonwealth formations. Americans appeared to excel in attack and British staying power was again tested during the Arnhem disappointment, the V1 and V2

Flying Bomb attacks against southern England and a totally unexpected German repeat of the Belgian Ardennes offensive as the Allied armies entered Germany during the winter of 1944–5. American strategic muscle inexorably took the lead during the final frustrating months of the war when Germany opted, like the British in 1940, to fight to the last. 'Get it done' reflected the stoicism of this British war-weary generation, providing the will to do whatever it took to finish the war.

Germany surrendered on 8 May 1945 and Japan three months later. It was over.

Servicemen who fought in this war are now in their early eighties. Each year fewer remain, yet they are a unique generation and have attracted the interest of subsequent generations. Why should this be so?

REQUIEM – THE PASSING GENERATION

The final news of VJ (Victory over Japan) Day on 14 August 1945 was as badly handled as the initial declaration of war in September 1939. The Japanese asked for an Armistice on 9 August, after the second atomic bomb was dropped, but it wasn't until five days later at 1145 pm on 14 August that newly elected Prime Minister Clement Attlee finally announced: 'Japan has today surrendered. The last of our enemies is laid low . . .'

Many missed this inspiring speech because they'd gone to bed too early, so most British citizens didn't discover they were at peace until 7 am the next morning when it was re-broadcast. This muddled and unsatisfactory start to a two-day holiday was preceded by rain in many places.

The tortuous sequence of events ending the war reminded many of assurances at the beginning when they were 'sold a pup'. Official statements assured them that the power and influence of the British Empire would see them through. It had not, indeed the war was nearly lost, and informed sectors of British society realised the country would never again dominate world affairs in the same way.

Britain witnessed an immense change in its fortunes between 1939 and 1945. The wartime generation learned to adapt and 'make-do' with less, something that had a huge and enduring impact on those who survived. Sober realisation dawned on the 'island race' that the Atlantic life-line was tenuous and everything imported cost lives. A year after the declaration of war and Dunkirk, Britain had lost her superpower status. The fall of France in 1940 was as shocking as a defeat of the United States would be today. This isolation led to an emotionally charged and symbolic 'stand-alone' attitude. By all accounts this bred more stoicism and individual resourcefulness than had been evident in peacetime.

A notably stoic attitude emerged after the series of startling and successive defeats during the years 1940–2. My father recalled, describing dog-fights over Kent during the Battle of Britain, that 'life actually – it may seem strange to you – went on normally'. Most accepted what needed to be done and that much self-discipline would be required.

People believed they needed to 'pitch in' and make a contribution, if only because the government was unlikely to get it right. Commandos and bomber crews accepted diminished survival chances, consciously prepared to sacrifice themselves for the sake of future generations, as the preceding chapters constantly show. Private George MacDonald Fraser in Burma pointed out: 'Of course media and government felt obliged to present the war in as favourable terms as possible, but that was understood, and nobody was fooled, and no softening was "needed" by the public . . . The British people were not stupid; they had been to war before, and knew all about its realities at first hand.'

Only after 1943, following the Blitz and Baedeker raids, did uniformed casualties outnumber civilian. Life in wartime could be nasty, brutish and short. One ship going down in the Battle of the Atlantic might impact on entire communities alongside the Tyne. Soldiers, sailors and airmen returning on leave from hard fought campaigns across the world could find their homes wrecked and families killed by a chance air-raid. Robert Fife, a Squadron Sergeant Major with the 49th battalion of the Royal Tank Regiment, recalled that during the final six months of the war 'we went into action thirty-six times'. Each time that occurred he assessed his tank crew's chances of surviving were about four to one. This was a hardy generation.

Six years of war created a more cynical, less naïve and less forgiving populace than was the case in peacetime. It was a long haul, unequalled in duration by any national emergency since. My schoolboy father saw the defeated and dishevelled BEF passing by train after Dunkirk, yet was still old enough to fight the campaign from D-Day through north-west Europe. Wren officer Moyra Macleod recalled: 'we'd got used to war and we never thought it was going to end. It was from the time I was 21 to the time I was 27.' She pointed out, 'that's a lot of your life.'

War bred cynicism. One officer observing British soldiers in the 2nd Army advancing on Germany in November 1944 identified that 'Tommy' in 1944 'will not be foozled by facile talk of a land fit for heroes'; he was hard-bitten and pragmatic. 'He wants deeds not words.' He found the typical soldier anticipated 'we shall lose the peace' and be involved in another war within ten or twenty years' time. Korea followed in five. He deeply mistrusted all civilian authority and was convinced business was making a slice out of the war and distrusted the BBC and the daily press. 'In short,' he claimed, 'the British soldier is fighting for the future of the world and does not believe in that future.' My father was embittered at having to officially apply for his individual campaign medals at the end of the war and decided against it. Fifty years later I applied for them when serving as an officer and passed them across.

Cynicism bred unforgiveness in a generation who were not 'politically correct' in their attitudes to the defeated foe after so long a war. The Blitz held bitter memories for many families. Duncan Ferguson with the Argyll and Sutherland Highlanders had a pithy view of his Japanese captors. 'I hate them,' he stated simply. His uncompromising view echoes those of many who served in the Far East, then and now. 'I've got a wee pal, he's forgiven them. He's a true Christian,' he acknowledged, 'but me, I'll never forgive them, never.'

Not only soldiers lacked forgiveness. Two years after the war John Dossett-Davies, who joined the army in 1945, recalled 'even close friends and relatives were rabidly anti-German'. Much less publicised than the US 'Sweet Invasion' and the exodus of GI brides was a second and more clandestine immigration of German and Italian fiancées and wives from 1945 onwards. One of John Dossett-Davies' cousins was a Royal Artillery major who regarded Dossett-Davies' German girlfriend as 'one of the enemy'. He was considering marrying her, but if he had done so his cousin would 'never speak to him again'. He did not go ahead.

My father described what happened when he introduced his young German bride, and their first grandchild to his English family. 'There were no discussions, everything was left unsaid, and the atmosphere was like a dark cloud hanging over us.' Finding lodgings was not easy for such couples, admitted my father. My mother faced similar misgivings in Germany. Her brother Hans, who fought with the SS–Artillery, was killed in Russia when she was seventeen. 'My parents tried to avoid the subject of my going out with an English soldier, they were no doubt thinking about what happened to Hans', to whom she had been very close. 'All I got from my Mum was a stony silence,' she admitted, 'which did make me feel guilty.' Things did not improve on arrival in England. Her new in-laws had friends who were hostile to Germans, having lost a son during an air–raid. 'But I had lost a brother,' she recalled and nobody was listening. It was not a forgiving generation.

This generation is primarily revered because of the unique blend of community spirit and shared compassion it exhibited during the years it stood 'alone' after Dunkirk, an emotional state colloquially referred to as the Blitz spirit. Ironically nobody *felt* alone. The shock of the fall of France and the close call for the BEF at Dunkirk encouraged total strangers to pause and converse in the street. The instinctive need to derive emotional strength from shared compassion bonded this generation like no other. Everybody shared their hopes and disappointments. There was elation at the victory clawed back by the Battle of Britain, the first decisive battle on and above British soil to be witnessed by a large proportion of the population. Gloom and despondency followed with the Blitz and flying bomb raids on London, but there was comfort to be derived in shared adversity and the attempt to regain a foothold on the continent of Europe and win the war. Getting back into Europe acquired such symbolic significance, it was likened to a 'Crusade', realised on D-Day. The Blitz spirit has since spawned a plethora of TV documentaries and feature films that seek to recreate this feeling of community, hard to appreciate for those who did not live through it. Gwyneth Thomas experienced the war as a nurse, serving through the Blitz and what followed: and, explained: 'I don't criticise the young people for saying: "Oh we have heard enough about it." How could you understand what we went through?' she asked. 'How could you be sympathetic? Because you never went through it.'

Did this intangible spirit stem from the fact the majority of people were churchgoers and exhibited a different brand of moral responsibility from the population today? Tank Officer John Mallard with 44 RTR explained: 'Most British young men were happy to fight for their country, because one thought it was worth fighting for; at that time people were generally honest, polite and kind and the standard of morality was high.' He felt this was less the case after 1945. The importance of morality and principle was one reason why Adolf Hitler was surprised the British went to war over Poland, a matter of principle. Parachute Regiment Brigadier James Hill fought the entire duration of the war and explained what sustained him:

> I felt at the time and I have felt afterwards that it was a great relief to me that he [Chamberlain] had gone to Munich or wherever and signed that piece of paper. Now if he hadn't done that I would have felt we hadn't done every damn thing we can to placate that bloody fellow Hitler. That was good and being involved in five years of solid fighting, that meant a great deal to me.

Hill felt fighting for a just cause 'improved our morale', and spiritually underpinned his experience of six years intense war fighting.

But it's important not to over-romanticise this. The Second British Army fighting its way through to Germany in November 1944 did not fight for ideals. 'He hates his enemy,' claimed one correspondent, because the Germans were in the way, 'before he can get home to his family, his football, his beer and his fireside.' Priorities were likely in that order. 'He is frantically tired of the war, because as diaries, letters and interview accounts reveal, he was homesick, misses his family and 'he is willing to do anything to finish it'. It was the same in all theatres of war. Private George MacDonald Fraser disliked the 'Forgotten Army' label applied by the press to the Fourteenth Army in Burma because 'we were not forgotten by those who mattered', he countered, 'our families and our country'. 'When the war ended, everyone was waiting for my father to come back,' recalled Timothy Norton, five years old before his father appeared. 'It was all very mystifying to me, and I was confused for quite a time . . . My nose wasn't in the least put out of joint by my father's arrival,' he admitted, 'it was simply that I didn't need him, or rather, didn't yet feel that I needed him.' Timothy Norton resolved his confusion but there is no way of assessing what impact such homecomings had upon other families and subsequent generations.

'I know we are going to have hell trying to work the peace', reflected one woman, 'we shall probably fail'. The morning after VE-Day.

'Thanksgiving for a great deliverance', declared one leading newspaper.

The wartime generation was extremely conscious of class divisions, and witnessed a degree of social levelling. Churchill's election defeat between VE and VJ Day surprised only the political pundits. When it became clear by 1943 that the Allies were winning on all fronts and were bound to win, questions began to be asked about the future and the need to change. Mass Observation diaries for 1945 indicate the extent to which the war had given British citizens a sense of identity and realisation they were no longer pawns in a political game. They had a voice in public affairs and expressed it during the July landslide victory that brought in the Labour Party under Clement Attlee. Commando Officer Bill Boucher-Myers had already detected the undercurrent of opinion among his men: 'They wanted to get back to their loved ones, and their loved ones were telling them, "You'd better vote Labour because they'll bring you back. Mr Churchill has other things in store for the British Empire."'

War irrevocably changed the domestic status of women, even though there was faltering progress as the soldiers returned home, wanting their old jobs back. Marjorie Herd recalled joining the Wrens and asking her father, long after she married, 'what would have happened to me if there hadn't been a war?' The response was, look after her mother. 'Can you imagine? So thanks to the war I joined the Wrens and got away.' As much as she liked her mother,'I didn't want to be a domestic slave for the rest of my life.' It was going to be difficult to readjust, as Barbara Davies explained:

> When it became obvious that the war was coming to a close work slowed down. After VJ Day we were told we were no longer needed. Within a few weeks all the girls were made redundant. Had we been demobbed from the armed forces we would have been offered retraining or further education but for the 'dilutees' there was nothing at all. The AGU were not helpful. They said their main priority was to give help to the men returning from the war.

'How was I going to get on in civvy life again?' asked Irene Milne from Edinburgh. 'Would I go back to the same job? I was comfortable in the WAAF.' Naomi Milchison from the Mull of Kintyre, describing approaching difficulties for the wartime generation, captured the essence of the situation in her last Mass Observation Diary entry: 'I know we are going to have hell trying to work the peace, trying to give people a worth-while-ness in their peacetime lives comparable with the worth-while-ness of working together during the war. We shall probably fail.'

There was little mediocrity in the lives of this generation. The war was a succession of grim but in the main intensely exciting events. My father remembered looking forward to being called up. 'It was going to be exciting, a complete change, something different.' One highlight was travel, a form of military tourism. Men and women travelled on duty to all parts of the European and imperial globe. However, the benefit was at great physical and emotional cost. Peter Wild from Kelso in Scotland remembered: 'Of all my school friends, not one of them was alive. I counted on my school memorial 98 people of my own age who were killed during the war. They were just the right age, you see.'

One in three of Tank Cavalry officer Michael Trasenster's army and RAF friends with him at Winchester College between 1936–41 were casualties. 'The war left me a more jumpy person,' claimed John Russell who landed with the KOSB on D-Day. 'Because I found with all the action, for long after I'd come home, if a gate banged I was ready to flatten out on my face.' Like so many others, 'I never really got over it.'

It's the truest of clichés to say that the Second World War changed many lives forever. 'My brother was in the Commandos and I think he wasn't happy to be in the glen again,' declared Jean Milchell from Blairgowrie in Scotland. 'He wanted to be where things were moving because he'd seen so much of the world.' 'The war made men out of most of us,' declared Tom Packwood who served as a glider soldier in the Oxfordshire and Buckinghamshire Regiment, 'otherwise 90% of us would probably have never left the villages we were born in.' Apparently directionless youth were conscripted in 1939 and given an aim. Such young people – then as now – often made extremely effective fighting soldiers. When asked what had been the most meaningful influence during his wartime life, Staff Sergeant Glider Pilot John Kingdom answered, 'I don't think the war was, but being in the services was definitely.' Others agreed. 'It gives you a lot of self confidence which I lacked,' he claimed. Captain John Killick, who fought at Arnhem and was later British ambassador to Moscow, believed that: 'People who came out of the forces had something to offer, which the pre-war people did not have. We were all doers' who 'had a talent for organization and getting things done.'

Seventy years after the event it feels even more important to remind ourselves of the debt that we owe this passing generation, my father's generation. 'This is your Victory!' Winston Churchill announced to crowds packing Whitehall on VE Day 1945. All he could offer on assuming the office of Prime Minister five years before was 'Blood, toil, tears and sweat'. The *Daily Telegraph* newspaper lead article on 8 May observed that 'thanksgiving for a great deliverance' is due, because the outcome of the war was about something more than simply 'the fate of the British People', because 'it was recognized that upon our fate depended the survival or the death of what makes life worth living'.

This generation guaranteed the freedoms we enjoy through its 'attitude of never surrender'. This is probably less appreciated today because it is understated – typically throughout every interview and personal account that went into this book.

'Some of the things we were asked to do were crazy, no doubt about that,' declared Commando Ken Oakly. 'The end thing was we couldn't allow Hitler to carry on as he had, otherwise we would all be under the thumb.'

ACKNOWLEDGEMENTS

I am particularly indebted to Cathy Pugh and Simon Braithwaite and the staff of the Second World War Experience Centre at Leeds (LEC) for their generous guidance and providing a plethora of letters, diaries and vivid interview accounts conducted by Peter Liddle and the staff. Alan Brown from the Airborne Assault Museum at Duxford provided some particularly grainy accounts to support the D-Day chapter, as well as generous library support.

I had excellent support from a number of soldiers and civilians of the time, including my mother and father, and have spoken or communicated with a large number of participants, recognised in the notes to sources. I hope I have accurately reflected the private thoughts and emotions they so generously shared. My parents in particular were able to point out the seemingly innocuous occurrences that become so evocative to the general reader. I wish to thank in particular Mary Lloyd, Tony Hibbert, 'Kit' Carson, Harry Chatfield, John Mallard, Michael Trasenster and Eric Allsup.

Every effort has been made to trace the source and copyright of quotations and photographs in the text and these are acknowledged where appropriate. My thanks to those publishers who have permitted quotations and extracts from their books; sources are annotated in the notes that follow the text and the bibliography at the end. My apologies are offered in advance to those who, for any reason, I was unable to establish contact.

My thanks again to my agent Charlie Viney and editor Rupert Lancaster for their astute advice and skilful suggestions as this project came together. Finally, as ever, my love and gratitude to my wife Lynn for her boundless support and tolerance and apologies as I occupy her 'space' in writing this.

NOTES ON SOURCES

CHAPTER 1 THE WORLD THEY LEFT BEHIND

p.6 'leaving Hope . . .', *One of Our Pilots Is Safe*, W. Simpson, pp.7–8 and 10–11.

p.6 'that I had not been alone . . .', Woodroffe BBC broadcast 30 Sep 38, Charlton interview, *Britain at War in Colour,* Binns, Carter and Wood, p.19, Chamberlain's remark attributed to him by his son Frank, reported in BBC interview *In Our Time* 15 Apr 75.

p.6 'these crises really are too tiresome . . .', *August 1939*, S Howarth, p.140.

p.6 'our country . . .', *Dunkirk Diary*, W Saunders, p.7.

p.7 'All the same Chamberlain's broadcast . . .', *From All Sides*, B Willey, p.12.

p.7 'I shall never forget . . .', Cox, *Witness to War*, R Aldrich, p.63.

p.7 'Now, may God bless you all . . .', BBC radio broadcast 3 Sep 39.

p.8 Miss H Sandles the parish clerk . . ., *Lewes at War*, R Ellistone, p.25.

p.8 An audible gasp . . ., *How We Lived Then*, N Longmate, p 27.

p.8 'it's the same time Armistice was declared . . .', *Wartime Women*, ed. D Sheridan, p.49.

p.8 'Although the sun was shining . . .', Interview, BBC *Eyewitness* Series, *The Day the War Broke Out*, broadcast 3 Sep 1998.

p.8 'the whole bottom fell . . .', *Eyewitness* ibid. and interview Josephine Pearce, IWM 000831.

p.9 'Isn't that like Hitler . . .', Aldrich, p.65.

p.9 'They'd seen something . . .', Interview, Ellen Harris, IWM 9820.

p.9 'Where is this 'ere war . . .', Aldrich, p.62.

p.10 'And now I know . . .', *Nella Last's War*, 3 Sep 39, pp.2–3.

p.10 'Our life . . .', *Eyewitness* interview, *The Day the War Broke Out*, BBC broadcast 3 Sep 1998.

p.10 'Get in there and kill 'im!', Ibid. broadcast Oct 39.

p.11 It was her last day . . ., Nella Last, 14 Sep 39, pp.6–7.

p.11 He didn't see him again . . ., Keyzer and McSorley interviews, *Scotland's War*, S Robertson and L Wilson, pp. 10 and 9.

p.11 The 'Battle of Barking Creek' . . ., Barking Creek, *Front Line County*, A Rootes, p.20 and *Battle Over Britain*, F Mason, p.68.

p.12 'The shock to the national system . . .', Interview BBC TV 1989, *The Road to War*, C Wheeler.

p.12 'They would never have another war . . .', Aynsley interview, taken from *Everyman's War*, LEC publication, Autumn/Winter 2002, p.7. Madge Kershaw interview, author, Jun 1984. Hodges interview, *Those Twenty Years*, p.2. Satterthwaite interview, BBC TV 1989.

p.13   'the Germans are the best organized . . .', Interview, *Britain at War in Colour*, Carlton TV 1999.

p.13   Without compromising ideals . . ., *Picture Post* Reader's Letter 16 Sep 39.

p.13   'lost at sea in 1941 due to enemy action', *Articles of War. The Spectator* Magazine, ed. Glass and Smedley, p.3.

p.13   'callous, selfish holders-on . . .', Article *Spectator* Magazine 28 Oct 38, ibid. pp.35–6.

p.14   'We felt that he had betrayed . . .', Interview Willis, *The Road to War*, BBC TV 1989.

p.14   'because there was going to be a war . . .', Lloyd author interview 29 Apr 07, Hibbert author interview 18 Dec 07.

p.15   'the bomb was going to explode one day', Willis, BBC TV, ibid.

p.15   'for I never miss . . .', Diary Entry 24/25 Sep 38, *Wartime Women*, ed. D Sheridan, p.29.

p.15   'Yesterday we broadcast . . .', BBC News 1 Oct 38.

p.15   'The thing was laid out . . .', Thomas interview, *Britain at War in Colour*, Carlton TV 1999.

p.16   'I thought he could not breathe', *In Time of War*, J Leete, p.28.

p.16   'Does one treat wounds first or gas? . . .', Interview, *Britain at War in Colour*, Carlton TV, p.27.

p.17   'the "British" was better than ten foreigners', Interview Tress, *The Road to War*, BBC TV 1989.

p.17   'It may sound trite . . .', *Dilutees from 1942*, LEC doc.

p.17   'has British foreign policy . . .?' Hagglof, Aldrich, p.78.

p.17   'to us, the deferment . . .', Saunders, *Dunkirk Diary*, p.7.

p.18   'I wonder how long . . .?' *August '39*, p.218.

p.18   Red London buses . . ., Figures from *Nella Last's War*, p.2 and Longmate and Whitehead article from LEC pub *Everyman's War*, Aug/Winter 2002, p.49.

p.18   'I wanted to cry . . .', Last, p.9. Addresses, *How We Lived Then*, Longmate, p.63. Reeve, *Everyman's War* art, p.8.

p.19   'All I could see . . .', McSorley, *Scotland's War*, p.16.

p.19   'I remember some poor little girl . . .', Bones, *Everyman's War* art, p.9.

p.19   'I had never felt . . .', Aynesley, ibid. p.9.

p.22   'After she'd left the room . . .', *Eyewitness* BBC, *Let the Children Go*, Radio 4, 2 Sep 69.

p.22   'Dear Mum . . .', Child's postcard, Longmate, p.50.

p.22   'so you two old geezers . . .', Jackson and McSorley, *Scotland's War*, p. 16–17, Oxford boy, Longmate, p.54.

p.22   'the war of nerves . . .', Panter-Downes, Aldrich, p.81–2.

p.23   'I think people . . .', Nella Last, 18 Oct 39, p.12.

p.23   'would be in the inky . . .', Townsend, *From All Sides*, Willey, p.22.

p.23   'It gave me quite a fright . . .', Elephants, Voices from BBC Radio 4, *We Can Take It*, 21 Mar 83.

p.24   'he'd been as quick . . .', RAF pilots, Miss Joan Strange's diary account of *Daily Telegraph* reporting 28 Sep 39, *Britain at War in Colour*, p.31.

p.24   'We had the same machine guns . . .', Ridsdale, interview, *The Road to War*, BBC TV 1989.

p.25   'no foreign nation . . .', Ironside, *Death By Design*, P Beale, p.115.

p.25   'Soon the decks . . .', Gaskin, *Britain at War in Colour*, Carlton TV 1999.

p.25   'Age differences . . .', Medley, *Five Day's to Live*, p.2.

p.26   'it is a proper Granny's knitting . . .', Age averages from a 1992 RCDS paper by Brig K J Drewienkiewicz dealing with the TA early in World War II p.20. Pownall quote, ibid., p.10.

p.26   Two things now dominated . . ., Simpson, *One of Our Pilots is Safe*, pp. 12–15 and 19 and 21–23.

p.27   'we realised that . . .', Lachner, interview, *Die Deutschen im Zweiten Weltkrieg*, Ger TV 1985.

p.27   'There were a couple of German soldiers . . .', David Howarth, *One Family's War*, p.9.

p.27   'by the time the war finished . . .', Brunton, interview, *Wish Me Luck As You Wave Me Goodbye*, J Torday, p.55.

p.27   'no man should be placed . . .', Drewienkiewicz RCDS Paper, p.38.

p.28   'During those eight months . . .', Smedley, *Five Days to Live*, p.11. Officer, *Infantry Officer*, pp. 18–19 and 21.

p.28   'army's mania for uniformity', Mayhew, letter Christmas 1939, *One Family's War*, pp.18–19.

p.29   'many young people . . .', Pushman, *We All Wore Blue*, pp.23 and 27. Tout, *The Culture Bomb: Joining Up in WW II, Everyman's War*, Spring/Summer 2007, p.6. Saunders, BBC TV interview Dec 2004.

p.29   'When we got there . . .', Tonry and Weeks interviews from *Dunkirk – The Soldier's Story*, Dir P Gorden, BBC 2 TV, Dec 2004. Saunders, *Dunkirk Diary*, p.33.

p.30   'We'd never been trained . . .', 18 Div, *Unser Weg Zum Meer*, Hans Georg von Altenstadt, p.9. Seeney, interview, *For Five Shillings a Day*, Begg and Liddle, p.17.

p.30   'A lad of 18 . . .', *Picture Post* Magazine, 16 Sep 1939, p.61.

p.30   'My generation . . .', Brunton, interview, *Wish Me Luck . . .*, p.55.

p.31   'all the time those people . . .', Seeney, interview, *For Five Shillings . . .*, p.21.

CHAPTER 2 THE BLITZKRIEG EXPERIENCE

Naked Soldiers: Norway, April 1940

p.33   'On no account . . .', Hitler and Gerlach, *Hitler's Naval War*, Cajus Bekker, pp.100 and 101.

p.33   'We had to maintain speed . . .', Böttger, *Narvik*, p.13. Hubert, interview, *Die Deutschen im Zweiten Weltkrieg*, BR/SWF/ORF German TV 1985.

p.34   'We were awakened . . .', Recorded interview, *1940*, J B Priestley, BBC TV 1965.

p.35   'They were hard-muscled . . .', Reporter, *Norway. The Commandos. Dieppe*, C Buckley, p.28.

p.36   'I came away disgusted . . .', Ironside Diary 12 Mar 40, *Witness to War*, R Aldrich, p.130.

p.37   'They landed several days . . .', Kynoch, *The Naked Soldiers*, pp. 11–12, 18, 25, 46–7.

p.37   'We south London boys . . .', Parsons, interview, LEC document.

p.38   'None of the other officers . . .', Dalzel-Job, *From Arctic Snow to Dust of Normandy*, p.15.

p.38   'They were completely exposed . . .', Dalzel-Job, p.16 and Parsons, ibid. LEC.

p.38   'paralysed polar bears', Carroll, interview, LEC document. Carton de Wiart, quoted *The War 1939–45* Vol I, ed. Flower and Reeves.

p.39   'A difficult job . . .', Kynoch, *The Naked Soldiers*, pp. 54, Jensen, ibid. p.55, Norwegian officer was Lt Col Ragnvald Roscher Nielson, an officer on Gen Ruge's staff, *Battles for Scandinavia*, J R Elting, Time-Life History WW II p.79.

p.40   'The high pitched scream . . .', Kynoch, p. 71 and 121.

p.41   'I never met . . .', British commander was Sir Adrian de Wiart. Dalzel-Job, *From Arctic Snow to Dust of Normandy*, p. 21.

p.42 'My hands and feet . . .', Kynoch, p.138.

p.42 The battalion traversed . . ., 2 Geb. Div. After-Action Report, Kampf im Gebirge, A Buchner pp.7–25.

p.43 'And all I can remember . . .', Parsons, interview, LEC document.

p.44 'It got rather alarming . . .', Parsons, ibid.

p.44 'Out of nearly 2,000 men . . .', Kynoch, p.141.

p.44 Machine gun fire was splattering . . ., Carroll, interview, LEC document.

p.45 'others with curses . . .', Guy, diary, 22 Apr 40, LEC *The Second World War*, Oct 2005, p.51. Kynoch, pp. 175–6.

Running the Gauntlet: France, May 1940

p.46 Water geysers shot up . . ., Adams, journal 30 Apr–1 May 40, LEC document.

p.47 Had not the French General Staff . . ., Quoted *Witness to War*, R Aldrich, p. 85.

p.50 The war in the West had begun . . ., Stürmabteilung Koch details from R J Kershaw, *Fallschirmjäger*, unpublished ms.

p.50 'I don't know how many . . .', Stubbs, BBC recording, *1940*, J B Priestley documentary, BBC TV 1965. Hodson, *The War 1939–45*, ed. Flower and Reeves, p. 97.

p.51 'The Belgians loved us . . .', Carter, interview, *We Remember Dunkirk* (hereafter *WRD*), F and J Shaw p.21.

p.51 'We were only young lads . . .', Brit soldiers killed in France, *1939:The World We Left Behind*, R Kee, p. 337. Howarth, *One Family's War*, p. 54. Crosson, interview, *Scotland's War*, Robertson and Wilson, p.33.

p.51 'As the lorry columns . . .', Hodson, ibid., p.98.

p.52 'It was mobile war . . .', Bradley, interview, *Dunkirk – The Soldier's Story*, Dir P Gordon, BBC 2 doc 2004. (Hereafter *Soldier's Story*.)

p.53 'We had five rounds . . .', Division movement figures Drewienkiewicz RCDS Paper 1992, Hill and Weeks interviews, *Soldier's Story*.

p.53 'most of us were living on our nerves . . .', Looker, *Scramble*, N Gelb, p.4.

p.54 'I stared at them . . .', Simpson, *One of Our Pilots is Safe*, pp. 54–7, 59–60.

p.54 'It was a lesson . . .', Rosier, *Scramble*, p. 8, Gaynor, p. 9, Bird-Wilson, p.6.

p.55 'This was all wrong . . .', Crockitt, interview, *The Other Side of Dunkirk* (hereafter *OSD*), Dir A. Laurence BBC Bristol 2004.

p.55 'we were in action . . .', Garrett, McLane and Brooks interviews, *Dunkirk – The Final Tribute*, (hereafter *Tribute*) R Dimbleby, BBC TV 2000.

p.55 'Not only were you crying . . .', Weeks, interview, *Soldier's Story*.

p.56 It was his final idealistic diary entry . . ., Steinbrecher, *Wir Stossen Mit Panzern zum Meer*, C. Christophe, Berlin 1941, p.158.

p.56 'I expected my last moments . . .', Pexton, Diary 19–20 May 40, *Private Words*, ed. R Blyth, pp.93–4.

p.58 'you were really getting a bit of an up and down hill feeling . . .', Thorogood, Weeks, Hill and Bradley, interviews, *Soldier's Story*.

p.58 'the mechanised army . . .', Wagstaff, LEC, Kirsty Wagstaff *The Bren Carrier*, World War II, Oct 2005, pp. 40–1. MacLean, interview, *Scotland's War*, p.33. Bowers, *WRD*, p.15.

p.59 'They stunt over our heads . . .', Newbould, interview, *WRD*, p.110. De la Falaise, figures from *Through Hell to Dunkirk*, 7th/12th Lancers Museum pub 1988, quote p.74.

p.59 'When we've lost some ground . . .', Sgt Maj, *Those 20 Years*, G M Hodges, p.93.

p.59 'Turn left . . .', Page, WRD, p.27.

p.60 'Important messages passed . . .', Weeks, interview, *Soldier's Story*. Saunders, Diary 19 May and 27 May 1940, pp. 63 and 66.

p.60 'You could see them . . .', Infantry officer, *Infantry Officer*, pp. 63–5. Weeks and Saunders, interviews, *Soldier's Story*.

p.62 'This stuck in my memory . . .', Rymer, interview ibid., Gunn and Jones, interviews, *WRD*, pp. 1 and 21.

p.62 It could just as easily be in England . . ., Two *BBC Eyewitness* interviews from *Dunkirk 1940*, BBC Radio 4, 20 May 1980.

p.62 'On one grisly occasion . . .', Clapham and Bazeley, interviews *WRD*, pp. 137 and 123.

p.63 'Infantry I saw . . .', Medley, *Five Days to Live*, pp. 31 and 34. Fergusson, *The War 1939–45*, Flower and Reeves, p. 129. Saunders, Diary 18 May 40, p. 62.

p.63 'The equipment we had . . .', MacCuish, interview, *Scotland's War*, p.34.

p.63 'We only knocked down . . .', Author interview 18 Dec 2007.

p.63 'the pillar of smoke . . .', Soldier omen, interview, *BBC Eyewitness, Dunkirk 1940*.

p.64 'It seemed to me that the whole world had suddenly gone mad . . .', Mott, interview, *WRD*, p.101.

p.64 'They seem to be all around us . . .', Saunders, Diary, 27 May 40, p.66.

CHAPTER 3 DELIVERANCE AT DUNKIRK

From the Perimeter to the Beaches

p.66 'A BLACK DAY . . .', Mass Observation (MO) entry, *War-Time Women*, ed. D Sheridan, p. 115.

p.66 'seemed as stunned . . .', Milburn, *Mrs Milburn's Diaries*, 10 May, 17 May and 21 May 40, pp. 36, 38 and 39. Last, *Nella Last's War,* 10 May 40, p. 46.

p.67 'she felt like . . .', Women's reaction, Sheridan, p. 114. Last, 16 May, p.49, 28 May, p. 51. Milburn, 29 May p. 40. MO Diary extract, Sheridan, p.116.

p.67 'We had no idea . . .', Quayle, interview, IWM, 10609/3.

p.68 'All we could do . . .', Hodges, *Those 20 Years*, pp.88, 90–1.

p.68 Survival was dependent on the ability . . ., Crosby, *The Ships That Saved an Army* (hereafter *Ships*), p.209.

p.69 'I thought oh dear . . .', Rymer, interview, *Soldier's Story*.

p.69 'Most of us rinsed our mouth out . . .', Mace, *Spitfire Summer*, M Brown, p. 33.

p.71 'It wasn't long . . .', Cordrey, *Massacre On the Road to Dunkirk*, L Aitken, p.66.

p.71 'To hear this man . . .', Scannell, *Shell Shock*, W Holden, p.76.

p.71 '89 dead Englishmen . . .', Von Imhoff, *Stürm durch Frankreich*, pub 1941, p.141. Von Paar, diary, *Kain, Wo Ist Dein Bruder?,* ed. H Dollinger, pp. 53–4.

p.72 Two days later . . ., *The Leibstandarte* Vol I, R Lehmann, pp.147 and 149.

p.72 'Hans, man they're coming! . . .', Lachman, quoted *Unser Weg Zum Meer*, H G von Altenstadt, 1940 *Wehrmacht* pub, p. 147. Müller quoted, *History of the Panzer Korps Grossdeutschland*, H Spaeter, Vol 1, pp. 102–3.

p.73 'If you are a hunted animal . . .', Saunders, Diary, p.67. Bradley and Fane, interviews, *Soldier's Story*.

p.74 'You're in a ditch . . .', Brown, interview, *OSD*.

p.74 'passing through the outer perimeter . . .', Stonnard, interview, LEC document.

From the Beaches to the Boats

p.75 'Not only did we have the fighters . . .', Rymer, Saunders and Hill interviews, *Soldiers*. Artilleryman, interview, *BBC Eyewitness*: Evacuation voice: *Dunkirk 1940 Part 1*, BBC Radio 4 20 May 1980. Dilley, *WRD*, p.155.

p.78 'I had to lay down . . .', Saunders, Diary May 28, p. 67 and interview *Soldier's Story*. Rymer, interview, ibid. Avon, interview, *Tribute*.

p.78 '*Cur Sir* . . .', Woolett, LEC Peter Liddle interview, Oct 2002.

p.78 Not one single-line brigade . . ., Based on data from the J Drewienkiewicz 1992 RCDS Paper, pp. 52–65.

p.78 'It's not like any other fighting . . .', Quoted *Those 20 years*, G M Hodges, p.93.

p.79 'completely shattered . . .', De Mare and Sargent, *Shell Shock*, W Holden pp. 77–8 and 82. Brown, interview, *OSD*.

p.79 'We were cold . . .', Bazeley and Shearman, *WRD*, pp. 123–4 and 61.

p.80 Following several attempts . . ., Bazeley, Durham and McDonald, *WRD*, pp. 124, 138 and 77.

p.80 'if you stopped . . .', Austin, *Mammoth Book of World War II* (hereafter *WW II*), ed. J E Lewis, p.64.

p.81 'at the time . . .', Bazeley, *WRD*, p.124. Bradley, interview, *Soldier's Story*. Graves, *Ships*, p.196.

p.81 'at the time . . .', Austin, *WW II*, pp.64–5. Saunders, interview, *Soldier's Story*.

From Boats to Home

p.83 As they approached, the whole of Dunkirk . . ., Codd, interview, IWM 9341.

p.83 'He stepped nearer . . .', Deane, quoted *Spitfire Summer*, M Brown, p.39. Ross, ibid. p.41.

p.84 'I never saw Alfa again . . .', Russell, *Ships*, p.201. Fleet Air Arm Lt Charles Lamb, *War in a Stringbag*, p. 67. Lightoller, *Daily Telegraph War Special* article by B Pedley, 3 Jun 2000. Christmas, *Daily Telegraph* article, *Evacuation from Dunkirk*, 27 May 2000.

p.85 Many of the soldiers . . ., Lamb, *War in a Stringbag*, p. 66. Pattrick, *Ships*, p.205.

p.86 'Stuff was coming over . . .', Codd, interview, IWM 9341. Two sailors, interviews, BBC *Eyewitness, Dunkirk 1940*, part 1. Radio 4. 20 May 1980.

p.86 'it was in reality . . .', Crick, *Naval Officer Wounded at Dunkirk*, LEC WW II Magazine. Jul 2000.

p.86 'You're trying to keep an eye . . .', Avon, interview, *Tribute*. Rymer, interview, *Soldier's Story*.

p.86 'They split him down the middle . . .', Jones and Hammond, *WRD*, pp. 22 and 99. Bennett, interview, *Tribute*.

p.88 'I saw him going down like this . . .', Saunders and Avon, interviews, *Tribute*. Crockitt, Bradley and Brown, interviews, *OSD*.

p.88 'All I can remember . . .', Tonry, interview, *Soldier's Story*. Bradley, interview *OSD*.

p.89 'bobbed up and down . . .', *Crested Eagle* observer, quoted *A War of Nerves*, Ben Shephard, p.170. Dally, from *Shell Shock*, W Holden, p.81.

p.89 'I felt a little sick . . .', Adapted from Ross's account in *Spitfire Summer*, M Brown, pp. 49–50.

p.90 'I can remember . . .', Peltz, *Stukas Am Feind*, J Grabler, 1940 article from *Der Adler* Luftwaffe Magazine reproduced in *Der Adler*, S Mayer and M Tokoi, pp. 29–30. Dilley, *WRD*, p. 155.

p.91 'you had maybe ten or fifteen minutes . . .', Jennings, Kingcome and Wallens quoted from *Scramble*, N Gelb, pp. 23, 24–5. Air loss figures, ibid. pp.31 and 19.

p.92 The German Fourth Army admitted . . ., German reports, *Dunkirchen*, Hans-Adolf Jacobsen, p.200. *Die Leibstandarte* Vol 1, R Lehmann, pp. 150–1. *History Panzerkorps Grossdeutschland* Vol 1, H. Spaeter, p.111.

p.92 Wight matched his tenacious prose . . ., Wight and Bisdee, *Scramble*, pp. 26–7 and 28.

p.93 One woman, who watched Dunkirk burn . . ., Hibbert, author interview, 18 Dec 2007. Woman, interview, *Eyewitness, Dunkirk 1940*, part 1. Radio 4. 20 May 1980.

p.94   'Our eyes met . . .', Russell, *Ships*, pp.200–1.

p.94   'We have always spent . . .', Crockitt, interview, *OSD*. Bredin, *Times Obituary*, 9 Mar 2005. Veteran, *Daily Telegraph* article, B Pedley, 3 Jun 2000.

p.95   'Soon people from the town . . .', Bishop, WRD, pp. 11. Dover Harbour, *Front Line County*, A Rootes, pp. 29 and 31. Martin, *WRD*, p. 204.

p.96   'Across the main road ' . . ., Train figures, *Kent at War*, B Ogly, and p.37. Fane, interview, *Soldier's Story*. Lang, WRD, p.54.

p.96   Wrapped in a blanket . . ., Stuka Pilot, contemporary photo.

p.97   'They were superficial . . .', Dennerlein, interview, *Hitler and the Invasion of Britain*, BBC TV Timewatch, dir T Remme. Kumm, *Voices from the Third Reich*, Steinhoff/Pechel/Showalter, p. 56.

CHAPTER 4 CHURCHILL'S MOAT: OPERATION SEA LION

The Beleaguered Army

p.98   'We used to stand . . .', Kershaw, author interview, 18 May 07.

p.98   Normal services for commuters . . ., Figures, *Front Line County*, A. Rootes, pp. 27 and 31–3.

p.98   'every person was notified . . .', Hewett and Morgan, interviews, *We Remember Dunkirk (WRD)*, pp. 13 and 185.

p.99   As each train puffed out . . ., Launders, WRD, p. 65. Headcorn figures, Rootes, p. 30.

p.100   Vital emotional therapy . . ., Crockett, interview *OSD*, Medley, *Five Days to Live*, p. 47, Saunders, *Dunkirk Diary*, p.71.

p.100   'Always one is thinking of him . . .', *Nella Last's War*, 5 Jun 40, p. 54. Thorogood, interview, *Soldier's Story*. Loss figures, Rootes, p.33. Milburn, *Mrs Milburn's Diaries*, 1 Jul 40, p.46. Alan was to spend the rest of the war in a German POW camp.

p.101   'I feel happier now . . .', Currant, Dowding and George VI quoted *Scramble*, N Gelb, p.32.

p.101   'You've only got a riffle . . .', Churchill speech, 18 Jun 40. Bradley, interview, *OSD*.

p.102   'dismayed men . . .', Thomas, quoted from *Spitfire Summer*, M Brown, pp. 56–7.

p.102   'seemed to belong . . .', J B Priestley, *Epic of Dunkirk*, postscript to the BBC News 5 Jun 1940.

p.103   'Therefore the priority . . .', Carpenter, interview, *Hitler and the Invasion of Britain*, BBC *Timewatch* 2000, Dir T Remme (hereafter *BBC Timewatch*). Alan Brooke, *War Diaries 1939–45*, 1 and 2 Jul 40, p.90.

p.103   Their local regiment . . ., Local, *The Battle of Bewdley*, D Birt, p.7.

p.104   'It was degrading . . .', MacInnes, interview, *Scotland's War*, S Robertson/L Wilson, p. 36. MacCuish, ibid., p. 35.

p.104   'people who weren't there . . .', Porton, *Sunday Telegraph* commemorative article, Ian Cobain, 4 Jun 2000.

p.105   'it was by no means a tradition . . .', Churchill speeches, 13 May and 4 Jun 40. Henderson, interview, *Scotland's War*, p. 37.

p.105   'making a plea . . .', Pinner, *A Conscript at War*, Salisbury Wardrobe Museum pub, 1998, pp.16–17.

p.105   'it was an indescribable atmosphere . . .', Dennerlein, interview, BBC *Timewatch*. Teske, quoted from *Invasion of England 1940*, P Schenk, p.1.

Scaling Churchill's Moat

p.106 'a discouragement to them . . .', Hankey, interview BBC *Timewatch*. Johnson, interview P Liddle, LEC Tape 1329.

p.107 'The aim of this operation . . .', Hitler's Directive quoted *Operation Sea Lion*, R Cox, p. 159.

p.107 By September British air reconnaissance . . ., View expressed Alan Brooke, 8 Sep 40, *War Diaries*, p. 105.

p.108 It was up to the Royal Navy and Air Force . . ., Alan Brooke, ibid., 1 Jul 40, p.90. Figures, *The Defence of Britain 1940*, C Barnett, from *Operation Sea Lion*, R Cox, p. 147.

p.108 'There was nothing we desired more . . .', Boat figures, *Front Line County*, A. Rootes, p. 38. Küchle, interview, BBC *Timewatch*.

p.109 'I stand with one eye . . .', Carpenter, interview, BBC *Timewatch*. Howarth, *One Family's War*, ed. P Mayhew, p.86.

p.109 BEF veterans were justifiably suspicious . . ., Medley, *Five Days to Live*, p. 48. Mayhew, *One Family's War*, p. 145.

p.110 'The battle fleet . . .', Elkin, *Hellfire Corner*, R Humphreys, p.42. Pfeiffer, interview, BBC *Timewatch*.

p.110 Freighters were to be assembled . . ., *Herbstreise* details, *Invasion of England 1940*, P Schenk, p. 319.

p.111 Troops were nervous . . ., Angell and Brisley, interviews, *We Remember the Battle of Britain*, F and J Shaw, pp. 1–2 and 103.

p.112 'Forms were literally . . .', Fowler, interview, *Dad's Army*, Dir C Oxley, Channel 4 TV 2001. (Henceforth *Dad's Army*.)

p.113 'I think we were rather proud . . .', Graham, interview, IWM 8337.

p.113 'We had tremendous morale . . .', Finnemore and Shelton, interviews, *Dad's Army*.

p.114 Hauptmann Freiherr von der Heydte's battalion . . ., Goetzel, *Storming Eagles*, J Lucas, pp.34–6. Von der Heydte *Interrogation Report*, SIR 1438, CSDIC (UK) 31 Jan 45, Airborne Forces Museum Aldershot/Duxford.

p.114 'We had boxes of grenades . . .', Yeatman and Storrar, quoted *Scramble*, N Gelb, pp. 68 and 72.

p.115 'in the long talks . . .', Küchle and Dennerlein, interviews, BBC *Timewatch*.

p.116 'Oddly enough we . . . were confident . . .', Pinner, *A Conscript at War*, pp. 23–4. Brunton, interview, *Wish Me Luck As You Wave Me Goodbye*, J Torday, p. 57.

p.116 'it was the opinion . . .', Rebensberg and Pfeiffer, interviews, BBC *Timewatch*.

p.116 'We expected to be invaded . . .', Pinner, ibid., pp. 23–4.

'Stop-Lines' to London

p.117 'When it got to the bend . . .', Johnson, interview, P Liddle, LEC Tape 1329.

p.120 'A tank dangerous at 200 yards . . .', *Picture Post*, 15 Jun 40, pp. 19–21.

p.120 'All of us feel . . .', Fuchs, *Sieg Heil! War Letters of Tank Gunner Karl Fuchs 1937–1941*, Letter 3 Aug 40, p.72.

p.122 'Of course, none of you chaps . . .', Graves, *Scramble*, N Gelb, p. 69.

p.122 Although the Home Guard . . ., Smith and Fowler and figures, *Dad's Army*.

p.123 'Poor boys . . .', Commando unit details, *Invasion of England 1940*, P Schenk, pp. 238–40.

p.123 'We'd never even seen a gun in our lives . . .', Conway, interview, *Dad's Army*.

p.124 English people became aware . . ., Mayhew family, *One Family's War*, p. 95.

p.124 The nation was bonding . . ., Bates, *Articles of War*, ed. F Glass and P Marsden-Smedley, *The Spectator* Magazine 18 Oct 40, pp.138–41. Popular magazine *Women's Own* Oct 40, from *Women in Wartime*, J Waller and M Vaughan-Rees, p.29.

p.125 'the situation is very grave . . .', Briggs, *Wartime Women*, ed. D Sheridan, p. 138. Simon, *Aspects of Life on the British Home Front*, LEC *Everyone's war*, Autumn/winter 2002, p.11. James, interview, *The Battle Remembered*, Dir. G Southcott, Meridian TV 2000.

p.126 German aircraft . . ., Doolittle, D Birt, *The Battle of Bewdley*, p. 13.

p.126 Air reconnaissance . . ., Brooke, *War Diary*, 29 Jul 40, p.96.

p.127 'Who for? . . . for the Germans?', Chennery and Whitfield, interviews, BBC *Eyewitness, The Night the Germans Didn't Come*, BBC Radio 4 7 Sep 71.

p.127 'If the Germans did get across . . .', Tailby, interview, *Dad's Army*. Leedle, interview, *Britain at War in Colour*, S Binns and L Carter, Carlton TV 1999.

p.128 'LDV – air guns – Pansies!', Officer, *The Battle of Bewdley*, p. 28.

p.128 Of twenty-five British divisions . . ., Brooke, *War Diary*, 22 Jul 40, p. 94. Figures, *Operation Sea Lion*, R Cox, p. 51.

p.129 With the Battle of Britain under way . . ., Finnimore, interview, *Dad's Army*. Trigger-happy Home Guards figures from *Time to Kill*, ed. P Addison and A Calder, p.55.

p.129 The guilty Home Guard soldier . . ., HG fatal killings, ibid. Barnard, interview, *Dad's Army*.

p.131 The Sandhurst war-game appraisal . . ., The Operation Sea Lion Sandhurst Exercise is described in R Cox, ed., *Operation Sea Lion*, 1974.

CHAPTER 5 AIR INVASION: THE BATTLE OF BRITAIN

Prelude
p.133 'There's a Spitfire . . .', Gardener, actuality BBC recording 14 Jul 40.

p.133 'If our cause is a just and worthy one . . .', Commentaries, R H Hawkins 17 Jul 40 and C Fisher 19 Jul 40, *Are We At War? Letters to the Times*, ed. A Livesey, pp. 75–6.

p.134 'Does the BBC imagine . . .', Figures from C Barnett article in *Operation Sea Lion*, R Cox, p.150. Hawkins, *Letters to the Times*, p.75.

'Stand By' to 'Scramble!'
p.135 Exhaustion slowed the pace . . ., Neil, interview J Barker, *Sunday Times 50th Anniversary Tribute* (henceforth *Tribute*), 9 Sep 90, p.6. Crook, *Angriff Westland*, D Sarkar, p.89.

p.136 'wear these, . . .', Bartley, Wellum and Wright, interviews, *The Last Few* (henceforth *Last Few*), prod P Thomas, Thames Channel 5 TV, 2000.

p.136 'Only a few hours before . . .', Crook, Sarkar, pp. 40–1.

p.137 'This is us . . .', Wellum, *First Light*, p.141. Currant, *Scramble*, N Gelb, p. 148.

p.137 'I swear that . . .', Bartley, Wellum and Wright interviews, *Last Few*, and Wellum, *First Light*, p. 140.

p.138 'They were everywhere . . .', Priller and speakers from *The Battle of Britain*, R Townshend-Bickers pp.153 and 154–5.

p.138 'Our commanders told us . . .', Henken, *Under Hitler's Banner*, E Blandford, p.98.

p.140 'feeling fine, fresh and fit', Parsons, interview, IWM 9948/6. Duncan, interview, IWM 9995/4. Aitken, interview, *The World at War*, ed. R Holmes, p. 134.

p.140 'I was more scared . . .', Doe and Bamberger, interviews, *The Battle Remembered* (henceforth *Battle Remembered*), Prod/Dir G Southcott, Meridian TV 2000.

p.140 'But jumping up and down . . .', Shipman, *The Saturday Essay* from the *Sunday Times Review* 14 Jul 90, p. 13.

p.141 'So you could never meet them . . .', Brothers and Wright, interviews, *Last Few*.

p.141 'You hadn't time . . .', Bamberger, interview, *Battle Remembered*, Wellum, interview *Last Few* and *First Light*, p. 143.

p.142 'We could hear sirens . . .', Robertson, interview, *Battle Remembered*.

p.143 'and then the next wave . . .', Dyson, Taylor, and Howe Baker, interviews, ibid. Kershaw, author interview 18 May 07.

p.144 'we crossed the Channel . . .', Henken, *Under Hitler's Banner*, p.98. Williams, interview, *Blitz Spirit*, D. Carponen, LWT Grenada TV 2004. Ostermann, *Angriff Westland*, D Sarker. Granz, interview P Crookstan *Sunday Times* Supplement 2 Sep 90.

Interception and Dog-Fight

p.145 'we very often found . . .', Wellum, Wright and Brothers, interviews, *The Few*.

p.146 They always sought to use the advantage . . ., Sanders, interview, ibid. Limmiker, *Under Hitler's Banner*, p.156.

p.146 'is it one of ours . . .', Brothers and Wright, interviews, *The Few*. Adam, *Scramble*, N Gelb, p.113.

p.147 'Almost immediately the clear sky . . .', Beamont, interview, IWM 10128/10129.

p.148 There were men inside . . ., Barham, Gardiner and Bowden, interviews and letters, *We Remember the Battle of Britain*, F and J Shaw, pp.69, 35 and 95.

p.149 'You were pushed way down . . .', Sanders and Wright, interviews, *The Few*. David, *Scramble*, N Gelb, p.124.

p.150 At the end of a mission . . ., Wright and Wellum, interviews, *The Few*.

p.150 Naylor remembered one Canadian pilot . . ., Mills, interview, IWM 11885/3. Legg and Naylor, *Scramble*, N Gelb, pp.185 and 243.

p.151 'I have seen worn-out young men . . .', Clayton, *Sunday Times Battle of Britain Supplement* 9 Sep 90, Article by R Hough, p.2. Henken, *Under Hitler's Banner*, p.101.

p.151 'Never, but never fly straight and level . . .', Wright and Wellum, interviews *The Few* and Wellum, *First Light*, p.165.

p.154 'But once you knew how . . .', Kingcome and Edge, *Scramble*, N Gelb, p.114–15.

Over Target

p.155 'I broke formation . . .', South, *We Remember the Battle of Britain*, p.87. Granz, interview by P Crookston, *Sunday Times* Supplement 2 Sep 90. Mollenbrock, interview, *Blitz Spirit*, D Carpenon, LWT Grenada TV 2004.

p.157 The Germans had destroyed . . ., Mollenbrock, Mooney, Kops, Williams, Cadby and Russell, interviews, *Blitz Spirit*. Wenzel, interview, *Battle Remembered*.

p.158 'He has never got over it . . .', Mooney, *Blitz Spirit*. Wenzel, Stansfield and Piper, interviews, *Battle Remembered*.

p.160 'You're watching . . .', London firemen Holsgrove, Wheeler and Rosoman, interviews, *Blitz: London's Firestorm* (henceforth *Blitz*), L Osmond and J Ware, Discovery channel TV Feb 2008.

p.160 'It's funny they missed the palace . . .', Stansfield, interview, *Battle Remembered*. Cadby, interview, *Blitz Spirit*.

p.161 'blood, toil, tears and sweat', Jacob, interview, *Blitz*. Rescuer was Mr Butler, TV interview, *The World at War*, ed. R Holmes, p.144. Feldon and Wheeler, interviews, *Blitz*.

The Kill and Return to Base

p.162 'You get an oil pipe . . .', Granz, interview with P Crookstan, *Sunday Times* Supplement, 2 Sep 90. Wellum, *First Light*, p. 148. Gray, *The Battle of Britain*, R. Townshend Bickers, p.141. Wright, interview, *Last Few*.

p.163 Perkin got out . . ., Wright, interview, *Last Few*. Perkin, *Scramble*, N Gelb, p.172.

p.164 'Had a row with a German', Gleave, *Scramble*, pp. 169 and 172.

p.164 His wife thought not . . ., Godson, author interview 29 Apr 07. Simpson quote, *The Way of Recovery* from *Forces Sweethearts*, E Taylor, p.47.

p.165 'bucking like a horse . . .', Mollenbrock, interview, *Blitz Spirit*. Wellum, interview, *Last Few*. Zander, *Sunday Times* Supplement article R Hough, p.5, 9 Sep 90.

p.166 'I saw pieces . . .', Bodie, *Scramble*, N Gelb, pp.245–7.

p.166 A secret memorandum . . ., Steinhilper, eye-witness report, *Daily Telegraph* Commemorative Supplement, 18 Jun 1990, p.xxi.

p.167 'I simply couldn't understand . . .', Stevenson, article D Wood, *Daily Telegraph* Commemorative Supplement, 16 Jun 90, p. xxii. Storrar, *Scramble*, N Gelb, p.195.

p.168 'Dusk is mauve and purple . . .', Wright and Wellum, interviews, *Last Few*.

p.169 An infusion of pure oxygen . . ., Wood and Bamburger, interviews, *Battle Remembered*. Webster, *Forces Sweethearts*, J Lumley, p.45. Brothers, interview, *Last Few*.

p.170 'It had happened to Poland and France . . .', Churchill Speech, 20 Aug 40. Deere, *Scramble*, N Gelb, p.265. Godson, author interview 29 Apr 07.

p.171 'East End Faces Hitler With Courage And Humour ' . . ., Kielmansegg, *The Invasion of England* 1940, P Schenk, p.351. Winterbotham, interview, IWM 7462. Correspondent, *Picture Post*, 28 Sep 40, p.18.

CHAPTER 6 COMMANDO RAID

The Commandos

p.173 'It was Christmas . . .', Interview, LEC, Peter Liddle Tape 1329.

p.174 'we must develop . . .', Churchill, 25 Aug 40, quoted *Raiders From the Sea*, Rear Admiral Lepotier, p.18.

p.174 'If you took them by surprise . . .', Durnford-Slater, *Commando*, p. 15. Sherman and Burn, interviews, *The Greatest Raid of All* (henceforth *Raid*), J Clarkson and R Klein, BBC Midlands TV 2006. Young, *Storm From the Sea*, p.12.

p.175 'Our arrival from the sea . . .', Smale, interview, LEC Land Collection. He was to be captured at Dieppe in August 42. Durnford-Slater, *Commando*, p. 34.

p.175 'Though taught the grisly techniques . . .', Gibson, interview, *Scotland's War*, S Robertson and L Wilson, p. 139. Watson, interview, *Raid*. The Commando knife was the emblem visible on the Commando badge later worn on the left arm.

p.176 'a very few of you . . .', Sullivan, interview, *Scotland's War*, p.142–3. Durnford-Slater, *Commando*, pp.16 and 88.

p.177 'Determination is the most important thing . . .', Johnson, interview, LEC tape 1329. Thomson, interview, *Scotland's War*, p.142. Dunning, interview, *Raid*.

p.178 'It seemed that we were *never* going to see a German . . .', Parsons, Liddle interview, LEC, 29 Oct 04. Haydon, quoted *The Commandos*, Time-Life History of World War II, p. 25. Young, *Storm From the Sea*, p. 25.

Raid Planning to Final Approach

p.179 Almost everything possible . . ., Mountbatten, TV interview 1974.

p.180 'shone like diamonds . . .', Arkle, interview, LEC land collection, *The Raid on St Nazaire 28 Mar 42*, (hereafter LEC *Saint-Nazaire*).

p.181 They could continue the momentum . . ., Burn, Sherman and Dunning, interviews, *Raid*.

p.182 'so when we found . . .', Young, *Storm From the Sea*, pp. 35–6. Watson and Purdon interviews, *Raid*.

p.183 'No – my attitude was *I'm coming back!*', De la Torre, Purdon and Gibson, interviews and letter quoted *Raid*.

p.183 'I wondered . . .', Johnson, Liddle interview, LEC tape 1329. Durnford-Slater, *Commando*, p.79. Henriques, *Combined Operations 1940–42*, HMSO, p.55.

H-Hour

p.184 The landing craft . . ., Johnson, interview, ibid. Durnford-Slater, ibid., p. 79.

p.185 Commando raids were short . . ., Woollett, Liddle interview, LEC Oct 2002.

p.186 Totally illuminated . . ., Donitz, quoted B Ralph Lewis article *Saint Nazaire 1942*, Marshall Cavendish War Monthly. Mecke and Dieckmann, The Raid on Saint-Nazaire, *After the Battle Magazine* No 59, p.6.

p.187 'There were tracer bullets . . .', Roderick and Arkle, interviews LEC *Saint-Nazaire*.

p.191 She began to settle . . ., Purdon, Wright and de la Torre, interviews *Raid*. Roderick, interview, LEC *Saint-Nazaire*.

Raid Fight-Through and Demolitions

p.192 'When we were completely stopped . . .', Roderick and Wright, interviews *Raid*. Davidson, interview, LEC *Saint-Nazaire*.

p.193 'Once they got cracking . . .', Arkle, interview, LEC *Saint-Nazaire*. De la Torre, interview, *Raid*. Naval rating, *Combined Operations 1940–42*, HMSO, p.83.

p.193 'It was as much as we could do . . .', Roderick, interview, LEC *Saint-Nazaire*.

p.194 They would have to fight . . ., De la Torre, Purdon and Wright, interviews, *Raid*.

p.195 'You know Captain Giles . . .', Johnson, Liddle interview, LEC tape 1329. Radio operator Eric de la Torre, p. Liddle and C. Pugh article, *Raiders, Everyone's War*, Autumn/Winter 2007.

p.195 'We set fire . . .', Johnson, Liddle LEC interview, tape 1329. Durnford-Slater, *Commando*, p.84.

p.196 The Vaagso Boxing Day raid . . ., Woollett, LEC Liddle interview, Oct 2002. Johnson, interview, ibid., tape 1329. De la Torre, LEC interview, *Raiders, Everyone's War*, Autumn/Winter 2007, p.61.

Aftermath

p.198 'The *Campbeltown* . . .', Arkle and Davidson, interviews, LEC *Saint-Nazaire*. De la Torre, interview, *Raid*.

p.198 'He discovered . . .', Beattie interviewed in 1974 and de la Torre, interviews, *Raid*.

p.198 'Jerry doesn't like these blokes . . .', Movietone News Clip, *Scotland's War*. p. 144.

p.199 'he was becoming very uneasy . . .', Carrington quoted, *Dieppe Through the Lens*, H G Henry, *After The Battle* publication, p.60. Von Below, *At Hitler's Side*, p. 155.

p.200 'some of our men . . .', Milburn, *Mrs Milburn's Diaries*, ed. P Donnelly, 30 Dec 42, p.121 and 31 Mar 42, p.132. Durnford-Slater, *Commando*, p.54.

p.201 'It was very moving . . .', Williamson, interview, *Scotland's War*, p.144. Young, *Storm*

From the Sea, p.23. Paton, Ian Speller article, *Raiders, Everyone's War*, Autumn/ Winter. De la Torre, Liddle/Pugh article, ibid., p. 62.

CHAPTER 7 NORTH ATLANTIC CONVOY

'For those in peril on the sea': Merchant Seamen

p.203 '*Eternal Father strong to save. . .*', Bagot, quoted from *War Under the Red Ensign*, D Hay, pp.40–1.

p.203 'it was a family affair', Dykes, *Voices From the Battle of the Atlantic*, K Tildesley, from *Everyone's War. Maritime Issue*, published by the Leeds Second World War Experience Centre, Spring/Summer 2003, p.13. (Henceforth *LEC Maritime Issue*.)

p.204 'Hey Dad . . .', Crawford letter, quoted *Britain At War in Colour*, S Binns and L Carter, Carlton TV 1999. Manning, interview, *Forgotten Heroes: Merchant Seamen*, producer A Dodds and directed T Roberts, BBC *Timewatch* 2004. (Henceforth *Forgotten Heroes.*)

p.204 'We were terrified . . .', Smith, interview, *Scotland's War*, S Robertson and L Wilson, p.131.

p.205 'I'm not sure . . .', Figures, *The Merchant Seaman's War*, T Lane, p.12 and 8 and *The War at Sea*, J Thompson, IWM publication, p.76. Dormer, Diary, LEC doc, p.8. Paterson, interview, *Scotland's War*, p.131.

p.206 'It was a damn nuisance . . .', Carroll and Keese interviews, *Forgotten Heroes*. Figures, Lane, pp.12–13.

p.206 'Professional seamen . . . took less kindly . . .', 'Pansy RN' from *The Battle of the Atlantic*, J Costello and T Hughes, p.45. Smith, interview, *Scotland's War*, p.131. Harding-Dennis, *War Under the Red Ensign*, D Hay, p. 73.

p.207 'uphold discipline . . .', Miner, interview, *The World At War*, TV Series, ed. R. Holmes, p.85. Convoy Commodore Rear Admiral Kenelm Creighton, Costello and Hughes, p.45.

p.207 'Sometimes you slept . . .', Foster, Kease and Carroll, interviews, *Forgotten Heroes*.

p.208 Many merchant seamen . . ., Foster and Othman, interviews, ibid.

p.208 German success peaked . . ., Churchill, *Their Finest Hour*, 1949, p.529. Pound, 5 Mar 42, quoted *Engage the Enemy More Closely*, C Barnett 1991, p.460. U–Boat figures, Tildesley, *LEC Maritime Issue*, pp.6–7 and 10.

p.209 'So it then developed . . .', Goldman, interview, *Forgotten Heroes*. Baker-Cresswell, interview, *Wish Me Luck As You Wave Me Goodbye*, J Torday, p.42. Ohrsen, interview, *Die Deutschen Im Zweiten Weltkrieg*, J Hess and H Wuermeling, SWF ORF German TV 1985.

Convoy Under Sail

p.210 It was the equivalent . . ., Dormer, LEC account and Diary of experiences: *Prelude* and HM trawler *Cape Argona*, Breen, *Lt Derric Breen RNVR*, LEC doc.

p.210 'no real rules to follow', MacLean, interview, *Scotland's War*, p.132. Chevasse, *The War At Sea*, J Thompson, p.146. Baker-Cresswell, interview, J Torday, p.37.

p.211 'When you sign on a ship . . .', Harding-Dennis, *War Under the Red Ensign*, p. 70. Dormer, *First Days in the Navy*, LEC doc, p. 6. Othman, interview, *Forgotten Heroes*.

p.211 German U-boat wolf-packs . . ., Clarke and Foster, interviews, ibid. Chevasse, *The War At Sea*, p.147.

p.211 Smaller corvette crews . . ., Macdonald-Hastings, *In A Destroyer, Picture Post* wartime magazine, Vol 8 No 3, 20 Jul 40, p. 12. Destroyer/Corvette figures A Hague article on Russian Convoys, *LEC Maritime Issue*, p.36.

p.212 'still makes me feel sick . . .', Goldman and Clarke interviews, *Forgotten Heroes*. Harrison, Diary 12 Aug 40, from T Lane, p.74. Collision details Notes, ibid. p. 94. Cutcliffe, *World War II Reminiscences of J D Cutcliffe*. LEC E003123.

p.214 'You would get chaps . . .', Breen, LEC doc. Butler, interview, *Wolf-pack: U-Boats in the Atlantic 1939–44, World At War*, Thames TV 1973. (Henceforth *World at War*.)

p.214 'We were not so much worried . . .', Bathie, Kerslake, Short and Carroll interviews, *Forgotten Heroes*.

p.215 Discipline in these . . .,Anderson and U-Boat detail, *Wolf-Packs At War*, J Showell, pp.8–14.

U-Boat Strike to Abandon Ship

p.218 Atlantic veterans . . .,Smith, *Scotland's War*, p.132. Butler, interview, *World At War*, Baker-Cresswell, J Torday, p.38.

p.219 'those squeaks . . .', Elfe, *The Battle of the Atlantic*, A Williams, 2002, p.71. Kronenberg, article by K Orth, *LEC Maritime Issue*, p.24.

p.220 'Well, the torpedo . . .', March, Goldman and Clarke, interviews, *Forgotten Heroes*.

p.220 Confusion was thereby highest . . .,Figures of sinkings and deaths T Lane chart, p. 228.

p.221 'The ship didn't last . . .', Clarke and March, interviews, *Forgotten Heroes*.

p.221 'in nine cases out of ten . . . due to the incompetence . . .', *Journal of Commerce* correspondence, 11 Jan 40, T Lane, p.224.

p.222 Crew deaths as a percentage . . ., Manning, interview, *Forgotten Heroes*. Page, T Lane, p.231. Mortality percentage figures, ibid., pp.230 and 227.

p.223 'Britain's survival depended . . .', Breen, LEC account. Harding-Dennis, *Under the Red Ensign*, D Hay, p.72.

p.224 'It was *us* or *them* . . .', Hart, *World at War*. Börner and Schunk, *LEC Maritime Issue*, p.25.

Surviving

p.225 'I could see him . . .', Thomas, interview, *World at War*. Kerslake, interview, *Forgotten Heroes*.

p.225 Sea temperature . . ., Mortality figures, T Lane, p.229.

p.226 Survival was a question . . .,*Shillong* experience, ibid., p.246.

p.226 'Big men screaming . . .', Harding-Dennis, D Hay, p.72. Smith, T Lane pp.237–8. Manning, interview, *Forgotten Heroes*.

p.227 'The sort of thing . . .', Goldman and Clarke, interviews, *Forgotten Heroes*.

p.227 'Cheerio, good bye and good luck', Gibb, interview 1 Sep 42, *Shipping Casualties Section – Trade Section*. LEC Doc.

p.228 'We just watched ourselves shivering . . .', Franklin, *Diary PH Franklin. Third Radio Officer Richmond Castle. 4–13 Aug 42*. LEC Doc.

p.228 'I just cried . . .', Lunde and Short, interviews, *Forgotten Heroes*.

p.229 'there are two men . . .', Lunde and Short, interviews, ibid. Cutcliffe, *World War II Reminiscences. J.D. Cutcliffe*. LEC E003123.

p.230 'Eh – and p'raps they thought . . .', Short, interview, *Forgotten Heroes*. Franklin, Diary. Thomas, interview, *World at War*.

p.231 Likewise a Merseysider . . ., Kease, interview, *Forgotten Heroes*. Franklin, Diary, LEC Doc. Ceramic figures, T Lane, pp.25–6.

p.232 Fighting for the Empire . . ., Franklin, Diary. Voyage figures, T Lane, p.13.

NOTES ON SOURCES

CHAPTER 8 DESERT AND JUNGLE

Desert Tank Men

p.234 'to get back into the bustle . . .' Rendell, interview, *The Rendell Story*, Bovington Tank Museum (BTM), 1996. Ling, BTM account, p.14. Flatow, *A Personal Narrative of El Alamein*, BTM Doc.

p.234 'I sat on deck . . .', Wardrop, *Tanks Across the Desert*, ed. G Forty, p.17, Sutton 2003.

p.235. 'I'd like to get it to the BBC . . ., Rendell, BTM, p.25. Watson, *A Corporal's Story*, BTM doc, p.3.

p.236 'In fact desert seems . . .' Roach, *The 0815 to War*, Leo Cooper 1982, p.42. D'Arcy Clark, letter to parents 15 Feb 43, LEC Doc.

p.237 These had to be reached . . ., Ling and Flatow BTM accounts. Routine details based on *Notes from Theatres of War. No 10. Cyrenaica and Western Desert Jan–Jun 42*. War Office pub 1942, p.2.

p.238 'Of course the flies . . .' Rollins, interview S Wheeler and L Hill, BTM Jun 2006. McGinlay, *7 RTR in the Desert*, BTM Aug 2001. Penn, *World at War*, ed. R Holmes, pp.271–2.

p.238 The desert was cold . . ., Ling, BTM account, p.1.

p.239 'I know the names . . .', Rendell, BTM account, p.17. Flatow, BTM narrative, p.17. Allsup, *Tank Men*, R J Kershaw, p.404.

p.240 'When the heat . . .', Halm, *Der Jahrhundertkrieg*, G Knopp, Ullstein 2003, p.162.

p.242 'I stretched my arm . . .', Watson, BTM doc. Grant Tank Commander, *Tank Magazine*, Vol. 38 Mar 56, p.243. Ling, BTM doc, pp.29–30 and 3. Flatow, BTM narrative, p.21.

p.243 'and he was right . . .', Watson, BTM account, p.4.

p.243 'Under such conditions . . .', Report, *Notes from Theatres of War. No 10. Cyrenaica and Western Desert Jan–Jun 42*. War Office pub Oct 42, p.16.

Jungle Infantry

p.246 They trickled along . . ., Kameyama, *Tales by Japanese Soldiers* (henceforth *Tales*), K Tamayama and J Nunneley, Cassell 2000, p.157.

p.247 They were proven completely wrong . . ., Reed, interview, *World at War*, p.272. Hogan, interview, ibid., p.504.

p.247 'They DO NOT KNOW their jobs . . .', Bennett, quoted *The Jungle, the Japanese and the British Commonwealth Armies at War 1941–45*, p.35, figures p.52. Alexander letter, ibid., p.44. McKenzie, interview, *Scotland's War*, S Robertson and L Wilson, p.98.

p.248 'It was the eeriness . . .', Marshall, interview, *World at War*, based on examination of a British soldier's diary retrieved from the jungle, p. 214. Okada, interview, ibid., pp. 213, 214 and 215. British commander, quoted T R Moreman, p.23.

p.249 It was to prove . . ., Cooper, *'B' Company*, Dobson 1978, pp.26 and 29–30. Lowry, *Fighting Through to Kohima*, Leo Cooper, 2003, pp.16–17 and 21. MacDonald Fraser, *Quartered Safe Out Here*, pp.38–9.

p.250 'The pin-up dream girl . . .', Cooper, ibid., p.50. White, quoted T R Morehouse, p.3.

p.251 'There are the first huge drops . . .', Horner, quoted *War in Burma 1942–45*, J Thompson. Imperial War Museum pub, p.170. Hammersley, *World at War*, p.499. MacDonald Fraser, p.232.

p.251 'this ain't fighting . . .', Lowry, pp.71–2. MacDonald Fraser, p.244. Officer, quoted T R Moreman, p.4.

p.252 'At that time the soldiers . . .', Cooper, pp. 35 and 110. Sugita, interview, *World at War*, p.507.

p.254 'I remember every step . . .', MacDonald Fraser, pp.87–8 and xviii. Cooper, pp. 124–5, 74 and 79–80.

p.255 'But it wasn't a major big battle . . .', MacDonald Fraser, pp.3 and 89. Cooper, pp. 77, 87–8. Lowry, p. 124. New, interview, *World at War*, pp.502 and 504.

p.256 'was his military family . . .', Calvert, interview, *World at War*, p.503. Okada, interview, ibid., p.503. MacDonald Fraser, pp.16–17.

p.257 'During those nights . . .', MacDonald Fraser, p.58. Cooper, p.60. Lowry, p.172.

p.259 Bodies were later recovered . . ., Lowry, pp.105–6. Hammersley, interview, *World at War*, p.509. Boshell, *The Battle of Kohima*, 60th Anniversary of the Second World War, Crown Copyright, pub 2005, p.6.

p.260 'we watched them . . .', Edwards, Diary 12 Aug 43, quoted *Mass Observation*, ed. S Koa Wing, Folio 2007, pp.190–91.

CHAPTER 9 RAF BOMBER RAID

'You're on Tonight': Take-Off

p.262 'They didn't want anybody . . .', Bayes, quoted *Scramble*, M Bowman, pp.183–4. Moffat, interview quoted *The Valour and the Horror*, M Weisbord and M Simonds Mohr, p.92.

p.263 'You get a feeling . . .', Butler, interview, LEC, tape LEEWW/2003–2111.

p.263 A 4,000 lb 'Cookie' exploded . . ., Harvey, interview, *The Valour and the Horror*, p.79. Currie, *Lancaster Target*, p.71.

p.264 'On landing back at base . . .', Harris, interview, *The World at War*, ed., R Holmes, p.297. Rae, Bowman, p.69.

p.264 'Good food . . .', Wallace and Raymond, Bowman, pp.231 and 226.

p.265 'This for me was the worst part . . .', Read, Bowman, p.226. Favreau, interview, *The Valour and the Horror*, p.93.

p.265 'They used to take away . . .', Yorkshire man, ibid., pp.75–6.

p.265 'I did my best . . .', Rutherford, Diary 16 Mar 44 and 7 Sep 43, *Mass Observation – Britain in the Second World War* (henceforth *Mass Observation*), ed. S Koa Wing, Folio Society 2007, pp. 215 and 193–4.

p.266 'I think it was the manners . . .', Edwards, Diary 12 Feb 44, ibid., p.211. Gould, interview, *Britain at War in Colour*, S Binns and L Carter, Carlton TV 1999.

p.267 'Suddenly one day . . .', Ruherford, Diary 12 Dec 43, *Mass Observation*, p.202.

p.268 'Our experiences had changed us for ever . . .', Davies, *Dilutees from 1942*, LEC document. Gibson and McLean, interviews, *Scotland's War*, pp.71 and 73.

p.268 'It made me quite ill . . .', Rutherford, Diary 9 Mar 44, *Mass Observation*, p.215.

p.268 'As soon as the Wing Commander . . .', Sutherland, interview, *Dambusters*, Dir I Duncan, Windfall Films 2002. (Henceforth *Dambusters*.) Butler, LEC tape.

p.269 'He didn't know . . .', Hockaday, Bowman, p.111. Harvey, interview, *The Valour and the Horror*, p.79. Harris, *The World at War*, p.308.

p.270 'Bollocks I'm coming back . . .', Currie, *Lancaster Target*, p.44.

p.271 'Normally when you were . . .', Fragment of poem quoted Bowman, p.105. Brown, interview, *Dambusters*.

p.271 'One was just as likely . . .', Chop rate statistics and material based upon *Letters From a Bomber Pilot*, D Hodgson, pp.8 and 29. Harvey and Dyson, interviews, *The Valour and the Horror*, p.108 and quote p. 95. Masters, Bowman, p.80.

p.272 'Wood explained . . .', Johnson, interview, *Dambusters*. Wood, Bowman, p.80.

p.272 Canadian Doug Harvey witnessed . . ., D'Ath–Weston, Bowman, p.111. Price, ibid., p.110. Read, ibid., p.116. Harvey, interview, *The Valour and the Horror*, p.94.

p.273 As the heavy bomber . . ., Currie, *Lancaster Target*, p.34. Hodson, *Spectator* Magazine article 27 Oct 44, quoted from *Articles of War*, ed. P Marsden–Smedley, p.347.

p.276 'The most dangerous part . . .', Harvey and Moffat, interviews, *The Valour and the Horror*, pp. 88 and 82.

Flight and Target Approach

p.277 'He assessed one pilot . . .', Allen, quoted *Round the Clock*, P Kaplan and J Currie, Cassell 1993, p.158.

p.279 'Your mind said . . .', Harvey and Favreau, interviews, *The Valour and the Horror*, pp.82–3.

p.280 'It was the most incredible . . .', Gray, quoted *Ghosts of Targets Past*, Grub Street 2005, pp.134, 88 and 132. Murrow, quoted *Round the Clock*, pp.198–201. Peto-Shepherd, War in the Air, LEC extract from privately published *The Devil Take the Hindmost*.

p.281 'There were things taking place . . .', Brown, interview, *Dambusters*. Currie, *Lancaster Target*, pp.72 and 91. Thom, quoted *Hell on Earth*, M Rolfe, Grubb Street 2001, p.21. Gray, *Ghosts of Targets Past*, p.88.

p.281 When the bomb-aimer . . ., Butler, LEC tape.

p.282 'Above the city . . .', Phripp, *The Valour and the Horror*, p.84. Raymond, Bowman, p.194. Forsdike, interview, *The World at War*, pp.189–90.

p.283 It would take twice as long . . ., Doubleday and Price, Bowman, pp.66 and 102. Rutherford, Diary 27 Nov 43, *Mass Observation*, p.200. Butler, LEC tape.

From Target to Home Base

p.285 Other flaming torches . . ., Wheeler, Bowman, p.77. Drewes intercept taken from *The Luftwaffe War Diaries*, C Bekker, Macdonald 1966, p.337.

p.285 'Neither of our upper or rear gunners . . .', Johnston, Bowman, p.90. Pestridge, LEC document *RAF Pestridge*.

p.286 'At that time . . .', Currie, *Lancaster Target*, p.70. Herget, interview, *The World at War*, p.310.

p.286 'Eye witnesses told him . . .', Thom, *Hell on Earth*, M Rolfe, p.32.

p.287 The jolt . . ., Dyson, *Observer Magazine* article 28 Oct 77. Rackley incident taken from *Lancaster at War*, M Garbett and B Goulding, Ian Allan 1971, p.100.

p.288 There were rarely survivors . . ., Lee, quoted *Round the Clock*, pp.123–4. Brown, *Report by RAF PJI Sgt L.W.Brown. 3.10.44*. AB Mus. Document.

p.288 'Dawn had broken . . .', Hodson, *Spectator* article 27 Oct 44, *Bomber's Life*, taken from *Articles of War*, p.347.

p.289 Four of the six targets . . ., Brown, interview, *Dambusters*.

p.289 'the little anxiety . . .', Hodson article, ibid. Currie, *Lancaster Target*, p.144.

p.289 'the sweetest smell of all . . .', Birch, Bowman, p.184. Wheeler, ibid., p.77.

p.290 'One night you'd be . . .', Brown, interview, *The Valour and the Horror*, p.84. Waldridge, Bowman, p.68.

CHAPTER 10 THE D-DAY EXPERIENCE

The Eve of 'The Day'

p.293 'That dreadful bombing . . .', Macleod, interview, *Britain at War in Colour*, Carlton TV 2000 (henceforth *Britain at War*). Milburn, Diary 14 Jul 42, 27 Jan and 24 Feb 44, *Mrs Milburn's Diaries*, pp.146, 200 and 204. Chelsea man quoted Tom Pocock article, *Daily Telegraph* Supplement, 3 Jan 94, P.D2.

p.293 'We were being conditioned . . .', Sweeney, *Ham and Jam*, Battlefield Tour pub 5th (V) Bn RGJ 1 Jun 96, AB Mus doc, p.96. Reid, LEC interview by B. Atkinson, tape 2316.

p.294 Anti-tank ditches and minefields . . ., Köhler, *Wehrmacht* Magazine, *Gepanzerte Kuste*, Heft (issue) 5, 1944.

p.294 'Many of you will not survive . . .', Grant, *Cameraman at War*, p.43. Minogue, interview, *The World At War*, p.464. Oakly, interview, *Britain at War*.

p.294 'we'd have to tell lies . . .', Pearson and Wild, interviews, *Scotland's War*, pp.158 and 157.

p.295 The Allied D-Day plan . . ., Figures from *D-Day – Piercing the Atlantic Wall* (henceforth *D-Day*), RJ Kershaw, Ian Allan 1994, pp. 25, 27, 34 and 237.

p.296 'nerves were taut . . .', Andrews, interview, taken from *Op Overlord. The News Portsmouth 1944/1984*, p.12. Norton, interview, ibid. Gould, interview, *Britain at War*. Grant, *Cameraman at War*, pp. 39 and 42. Edwards, *Normandy Diary* 4/5 Jun 44, AB Mus account.

p.297 Some of the fleet . . ., Capon, manuscript, *3 Sep 39* section *Merville*, p.20, AB Mus doc. Reid, interview, LEC tape 2316.

p.297 'It didn't honestly dawn on her . . .', Grant, *Cameraman at War*, p. 41. McBryde, *A Nurse's War*, Hogarth Press 1986, p.71. Pearson, interview, *Scotland's War*, p.162.

From the Sky

p.298 'By this time . . .', Edwards, Diary 5 Jun, AB Mus. Reid, LEC interview, tape 2316. Barrett, AB Mus manuscript.

p.299 'either in innocence . . .', Hill, taken from address given at the Royal Hospital Chelsea, 12 May 94, AB Mus doc. Weightman, taken from *Para Memories. The 12th Yorks Para Bn.*, (henceforth *Para Memories*), E Barley and Y Fohlen, Para Press 1996, p.17.

p.299 With his parachute . . ., Edwards, Diary 5 Jun. Clarke, Kershaw *D-Day*, p.55.

p.300 'So all six hundred . . .', Pead, personal account, p.2, AB Mus. O'Connor, *To France Without a Passport*, unpub ms, p.47, AB Mus. Clarke, Kershaw *D-Day*, p.57.

p.301 The second adrenalin rush . . ., Pead, AB Mus. Edwards, Diary 5 Jun, AB Mus. Hill, LEC interview by P Liddle, Feb 2001.

p.304 By the time the aircraft . . ., Edwards, Diary 5 Jun and O'Connor ms p. 48, both AB mus.

p.304 'the vibration in the air . . .', Oelze and Steiner, quoted Kershaw *D-Day*, pp.68, 80 and 82.

p.304 'If I live through this . . .', Pead, AB mus doc. O'Connor, unpublished ms, p.50, AB Mus docs.

p.305 It took them nearly forty minutes . . ., Edwards, Diary, 5 Jun, AB Mus. Lough, taken from *5 Para Bde Post Ops Report, Appendix A*, AB Mus.

p.305 'Shortly before we made landfall . . .', Bristow, quoted Kershaw *D-Day*, p.70.

p.306 They were thundering . . ., Todd, article *Daily Telegraph Supplement*, 3 Jun 94, P.D5. Buckley, *Para Memories*, p.26.

p.306 All eyes were on . . ., Clarke, Kershaw *D-Day*, pp.70–1. Pead, AB Mus account.

p.307 'What an example . . .', O'Connor, unpub ms., AB Mus pp.50–1. Hill, Address, Chelsea, 12 May 94.

p.308 'The amber glows . . .', Pead, AB Mus acc p.3. Capon, unpub ms, AB Mus, p.21.

p.308 Men sought to orientate themselves . . ., Weightman and Barley, *Para Memories*, p.25.

p.309 Surprise was complete, Edwards, Diary 6 Jun, AB Mus. German soldiers, Kershaw *D-Day*, p.66.

p.309 'they seemed to be flying . . .'; Edwards, Diary 6 Jun, AB Mus. Byam, *War Report. D-Day to VE Day*, ed. D Hawkins, BBC 1946, p.60. Sweeney, *Normandy. A Personal Account of 5th and 6th Jun 1944.* AB Mus acc.

p.310 The dying men . . ., Barret, O'Connor and Hill, personal accounts AB mus unpublished accounts, and Hill conversation with author 1994.

p.311 Reinforcements would land . . ., Capon, account, AB mus. Pearson, interview, *Scotland's War*, p.159. Otway, Hill's remarks, Kershaw *D-Day*, p.77.

From the Sea

p.312 'the Day', Macleod, from *Spectator* article 5 Jun 1964, from *Articles of War*, ed. F Glass and P Marsden-Smedley, p.308. Rees, interview, *The World at War*, p.365.

p.312 'the Golden City', Vogt, interview, *Deutsche Im Zweiten Weltkrieg-Zeitzeugen Sprechen*, Steinhoff, Pechel and Showalter, Gustav Lubbe Verlag, 1989, p.362. Hansmann, *Kriegsgeschichte der 12 SS Pz Div Hitlerjugend*, H.Meyer, Manin Verlag 1982, pp. 57–9.

p.313 'Off you go then . . .', Grant, *Cameraman at War*, p.45. Bone and Oakly, interviews, *Britain at War*. Gillard, *War Report*, p. 58.

p.314 'some of the tenseness . . .', *Warspite* observer, D Holbrook from *Flesh Wounds*, Buchan and Enright 1987, p.119. Duff, *War Report*, p.63.

p.314 'It's all very well . . .', Cooper, *Op Overlord 1944/1984, The News*, Portsmouth, p.33. Buskotte, Kershaw *D-Day*, p.102.

p.315 The plan depended . . ., Hills and Hamilton quoted, *Tank Men*, R J Kershaw, Hodder and Stoughton 2008, pp.313–14.

p.315 Landing craft stank . . ., Blois-Brooke, quoted *The D-Day Landings*, P Warner, Kimber 1990, p.75. Soldier, interview, *D-Day Plus 40*, ITN TV 1984.

p.316 'craft weren't coming in . . .', Hennessey, *Young Man in a Tank*, BTM pub, pp.57–8. Neale, Warner, p.82. Russell. Russell, interview, *Scotland's War*, p.163.

p.317 These were the bunkers . . ., Reeman, *D-Day. A Personal Reminiscence*, Arrow 1984. Wentworth, interview, *Scotland's War*, p.162.

p.318 'Within a minute . . . we had fired our first shot in anger', Gariepy, interview, *The World at War*, p.472. Hennessey, *Young Man in a Tank*, p.58.

p.319 'When you hear the bullets . . .', Anderson and Brasier, interviews, *Nan Red*, Dir. G Hurley, ITN TV 1984. Oakly, interview, *Britain at War*.

p.319 'Men were blown apart . . .', Mott, Warner, p. 199. Mitchell, interview, *Scotland's War*, p.163. Irwin, Warner, p.265.

p.320 'The commander couldn't see them . . .', Selery and Smith, Warner, pp. 151–2 and 146. Millin, interview, *Scotland's War*, p.161.

p.321 'We could hear . . .', Dalton, interview, *D-Day Plus Forty*, ITN TV 1984. Flame-thrower witness quoted from *Six War Years 1939–45*, B Broadfoot, Doubleday 1974, pp.337–8.

p.322 It was clear . . ., Hansmann, Meyer, pp.59–61. Schimpf, *Gefectsbericht über die Kampfe im Abschnitt der 716 Div. am 6.6.44*, pp. 6 and 10–11.

p.322 'And then we stopped . . .', Edwards, Diary 6 Jun 44, *Mass Observation*, pp.223–5. Green, Diary 5 Jun 44, ibid., p.223. Schoolgirl, quoted *How We Lived Then*, N Longmate, p.489. Milburn, Diary 6 Jun 44, *Mrs Milburn's Diaries*, p.214. *Daily Mirror* Newspaper, Wed 7 Jun 44. MacLeod, interview, *Britain's War*.

REQUIEM

p.326 'life actually . . . went on normally', Author interview, 18 May 07.

p.326 'Of course media and government . . .', MacDonald Fraser, *Quartered Safe Out Here*, Introd, p.xxi.

p.326 This was a hardy generation , Fife, interview, *Wish Me Luck As You Wave Me Goodbye*, J Torday, pp.70 and 72.

p.326 'we'd got used to war . . .', Macleod, interview, *Britain's War in Colour*, Carlton TV 2000.

p.327 Fifty years later . . ., Officer, Capt B L A, based on *Spectator* article *What the Soldier Thinks*, 24 Nov 44, from *Articles of War*, pp.348–9.

p.327 'I've got a wee pal . . .', Ferguson, interview, *Scotland's War*, p.182.

p.328 'But I'd lost a brother . . .', Dossett-Davies, *Forces Sweethearts*, J Lumley, Bloomsbury 1993, pp.116–20. Leslie and Charlotte Kershaw, author interviews, 4 Dec 2006 and Unpub Ms, *The War Years*, author's collection.

p.328 'How could you be sympathetic . . .', Thomas, interview, *Britain at War in Colour*, Carlton TV 2000.

p.329 'Most British young men . . .', Mallard, author interview and notes 4 Oct 2006.

p.329 'Hill felt fighting . . .', Hill, LEC P Liddle interview, Feb 2001.

p.329 Timothy Norton resolved his confusion , 2nd British Army Soldier, *Articles of War*, p.349. MacDonald-Fraser, *Quartered Safe Out Here*, HarperCollins 2000, p.39. Norton, interview, J.Torday, p.110–11.

p.332 'They wanted to get back . . .', Boucher-Myers, interview, *Scotland's War*, p.189.

p.333 'I know we are going . . .', Herd, interview, *Scotland's War*, p.185. Milchison, Diary 12 Aug 45, p.190. Davies, *Dilutees 1942*, LEC Document.

p.333 'Because I found . . .', Kershaw, author interview, 18 May 07. Wild and Russell, interviews, *Scotland's War*, p.186. Trasenster, author interview, 25 Sep 2006.

p.334 'had a talent . . .', Milchell, interview, *Scotland's War*, p.185. Packwood, LEC interview by P Liddle, Oct 2000. Kingdon, interview, ibid., Sept 2000. Killick 89 para Fd Security Sqn, interview, ibid., Oct 2001.

p.334. 'The end thing . . .', Oakly, interview, *Britain at War in Colour*, Carlton TV 2000.

BIBLIOGRAPHY

GENERAL PUBLISHED SOURCES

Addison, P and Calder, A *The Soldier's Experience of War in the West*, Pimlico 1997.

Bekker, C *Hitler's Naval War*, Corgi 1976.

– *The Luftwaffe War Diaries*, Macdonald 1964.

Bickers, R T *The Battle of Britain*, Salamander 1990.

Birt, D *The Battle of Bewdley*, Peter Huxtable Designs 1988.

Brown, M *Spitfire Summer*, Carlton Books 2000.

Bucher, A *Kampf im Gebirge*, Schild Verlag 1957.

Buckley, C *Norway, The Commandos, Dieppe*, HMSO 1977.

Costello, J and Hughes, T *The Battle of the Atlantic*, Collins 1977.

Cox, R, ed. *Operation Sea Lion*, Thornton Cox 1974.

Elliston, R A *Lewes At War 1939–45*, Alma Cott 1995.

Garbett, M and Goulding, B *The Lancaster at War*, Ian Allan 1971.

Glass, F and Marsden-Smedley, P *Articles of War*, Paladin 1990.

Hay, D *War Under the Red Ensign*, Jane 1982.

HMSO *Combined Operations 1940–2*, HMSO 1943.

Holden, W *Shell Shock*, Channel 4 Books 1998.

Holmes, R *Battlefields of the Second World War*, BBC 2001.

Howarth, S *August '39*, Hodder and Stoughton 1989.

Imhoff, C von *Stürm durch Frankreich*, Hans von Hugo Verlag 1941.

Jacobsen, H-A *Dunkirchen*, Scharnhorst Buchkameradenschaft 1958.

Kaplan P and Currie, J *Round the Clock*, Cassell 1993.

Kee, R *1939 The World We Left Behind*, Cardinal 1984.

Kershaw, R J *D-Day*, Ian Allan 1994.

– *Tank Men*, Hodder and Stoughton 2008.

Lane, T *The Merchant Seaman's War*, Bluecoat Press 1990.

Lehmann, R *The Leibstandarte*, Vol I, Fedorowicz 1987.

Lepotier *Raiders From the Sea*, William Kimber 1954.

Livesey, A, ed. *Are We At War?* Times Books 1989.

Longmate, N *How We Lived Then*, Arrow Books Ltd 1973.

Lucas, J *Storming Eagles*, Arms and Armour 1998.

Lumley, J *Forces Sweethearts*, Bloomsbury 1993.

Mayer, S and Tokoi, M *Der Adler*, Bison Books 1977.

Moreman, T R *The Jungle, The Japanese and the British Commonwealth Armies At War 1941–45*, Frank Cass 2005.
Ogley, B *Kent At War*, Froglets Pub 1994.
Ramsey, W G *The Battle of Britain. Then and Now*, After the Battle Pub 1980.
Rolfe, M *Hell on Earth*, Grubb Street 1999.
Rootes, A *Front Line County*, Robert Hale 1980.
Sanders, HS-G *The Green Beret*, Four Square 1959.
Sarkar, D *Angriff Westland*, Ramrod Pub 1994.
Schenk, P *Invasion of England 1940*, Conway Maritime Press 1990.
Showell J M *Wolfpacks at War*, Ian Allan 2001.
Spaeter, H *Grossdeutschland*, Vol I, Fedorowicz 1992.
Taylor, E *Forces Sweethearts*, Robert Hale 1990.
Thomas, D *An Underground At War*, John Murray 2004.
Thompson, J *The War at Sea*, Sidgwick and Jackson 1996.
– *War in Burma 1942–5*, Pan 2002.
Waller, J and Vaughan-Rees, M: *Women in Wartime*, Optima 1987.
Wheeler, M *1939–1945 Langton Green*, private pub.
Williams, A *The Battle of the Atlantic*, BBC 2002.
Young, P *The Fighting Man*, Orbis 1981.

MEMOIRS AND PERSONAL ACCOUNTS

Aitken, L *Massacre on the Road to Dunkirk*, Purnell 1977.
Aldrich, R J *Witness to War*, Corgi 2005.
Altenstadt, HG von *Unser Weg Zum Meer*, Wehrmacht 1940.
Anonymous: *Infantry Officer*, Batsford 1943.
Barley, E and Fohlen, Y *PARA Memories*, Para Press 1996.
Binns, S, Carter, L and Wood, A *Britain at War in Colour*, Carlton 2000.
Blandford, E *Under Hitler's Banner*, Motorbooks 1996.
Blythe, R, ed. *Private Words*, Penguin 1991.
Bowman, MW *Scramble*, Tempus 2006.
Campbell Begg, R and Liddle, P *For Five Shillings a Day*, HarperCollins 2000.
Cooper, R *B Company*, Dobson Books 1978.
Currie, J *Lancaster Target*, Goodall Pub 1981.
Dalzel-Job, P *From Arctic Snow to Dust of Normandy*, Nead-an Eoin 1991.
Danchev, A and Todman, D, ed. *Alanbrooke War Diaries*, Weidenfeld and Nicolson 2001.
Dollinger, H *Kain, wo ist dein Bruder?*, Fischer Taschenbuch Verlag 1987.
Donnelly, P, ed. *Mrs Milburn's Diaries*, Futura 1979.
Durant, N *Experiences of the Second World War in Burma*, George Mann 1995.
Durnford-Slater, J *Commando*, Greenhill 2002.
Flower, D and Reeves, J *The War 1939–45*, Panther 1967.
Fountain, N, ed. *The Battle of Britain and the Blitz*, Michael O'Mara Books 2002.

Fuchs, H, ed. *Sieg Heil. Letters of Tank Gunner Karl Fuchs 1937–1941*, Archon Books 1987.

Gelb, N *Scramble*, Pan 1986.

Grant, I *A Cameraman at War*, Patrick Stephens 1980.

Gray, P *Ghosts of Targets Past*, Grubb Street 2000.

Hawkins, D *War Report*, Ariel Books BBC 1985.

Hodges, G M *Those 20 Years*, Private Pub 1981.

Hodgson, D *Letters from a Bomber Pilot*, Thames Methuen 1985.

Holmes, R, ed. *The World At War*, Ebury Press 2007.

Humphreys, R *Hellfire Corner*, Budding Books 1994.

Knopp, G *Der Jahrhunderte Krieg*, Ullstein, 2003.

Koa Wing, S *Mass Observation*, Folio 2007.

Kynoch, J *The Naked Soldiers*, Charnwood Pub 1995.

Lamb, C *War in a Stringbag*, Cassell 2001.

Last, N *Nella Last's War*, Profile Books 2006.

Lewis, J E, ed. *World War II*, Robinson 2002.

Lowry, M *Fighting Through to Kohima*, Leo Cooper 2003.

MacDonald Fraser, G *Quartered Safe out Here*, HarperCollins 2000.

Mayhew, P, ed. *One Family's War*, Spellmount 1985.

McBryde, B *A Nurse's War*, Hogarth Press 1986.

Medley, R H *Five Days to Live*, Dover and Co, private pub 1990.

Pinner, L *A Conscript at War*, Wiltshire Regiment Pub 1998.

Plummer, R *The Ships that Saved an Army*, Patrick Stephens 1990.

Pushman, M G *We All Wore Blue*, Futura 1989.

Roach, P *The 0815 to War*, Leo Cooper 1982.

Robertson, S and Wilson, L *Scotland's War*, Mainstream 1995.

Saunders, W *Dunkirk Diary*, Birmingham City Library 1989.

Shaw, F and J *We Remember Dunkirk*, Echo Press 1983.

– *We Remember the Home Guard*, Echo Press 1983.

– *We Remember the Battle of Britain* Echo Press 1983.

Sheridan, D *Wartime Women*, Mandarin 1991.

Simpson, W *One of Our Pilots is Safe*, Hamish Hamilton 1942.

Tamayama, K and Nunnely J *Tales by Japanese Soldiers*, Cassell 2000.

Torday, J *Wish Me Luck as You Wave Me Goodbye*, Spreddon Press 1989.

Weisbord, M and Simonds Mohr, M *The Valour and the Horror*, HarperCollins 1991.

Willey, B *From All Sides*, Alan Sutton 1989.

Young, P *Storm From the Sea*, Greenhill 1989.

FILM, AUDIO AND TV

Britain At War in Colour: Binns, S, Carter L, Carlton TV 1999.

Eyewitness 1930–1939, 1940–1949: Bourke, J, BBC Radio Collection.

Blitz Spirit: Carpanen, D, LWT Grenada TV 2004.

The World at War — Wolf Pack, dir. Childs, T, Thames TV 1973.
Night Bombers: Cozens, H I, Crown Copyright Film.
Dambusters: Dir Duncan, I, Windfall Films 2002.
Dunkirk — the Soldier's Story, dir. Gordon, P, BBC 2 TV Dec 2004.
Die Deutschen Im Zweiten Weltkrieg: Hess, J and Wuermeling, H L, German SWF ORF TV 1985.
Things To Come: Korda, A, 1936.
Dad's Army, dir. Oxley C, Secret History Series, Laurel Productions Channel 4 TV 2001.
Dunkirk — The Final Tribute, introd. Richard Dimbleby, Potter, S and Reid, A, BBC TV 2000.
The Greatest Raid of All: introd. Jeremy Clarkson, Pearson, R, BBC Midlands 2006.
Hitler and the Invasion of Britain, dir. Remme, T, BBC TV *Timewatch* 2000.
Forgotten Heroes, dir. Roberts, T G, BBC TV *Timewatch* 2004.
Time Team — Blitzkrieg on Shooter's Hill Robinson, T, Series 15 Episode 8, Channel 4 TV Feb 2008.
Blitz: London's Firestorm, prod. Osmond, L, Discovery Channel 2008. *1940* Priestly, J B, BBC TV 1965.
The Battle Remembered, prod. Southcott, G, Meridian TV 2000.
The Last Few: Thomas, P, Channel 5 TV 2000.
The Road to War, Great Britain: Wheeler, C, BBC TV 1989.

PERIODICALS

Allan, T B 'Untold Stories of D-Day', *National Geographic* Jun 2002.
Gill, A A 'The Last of the Few', *Sunday Times* Magazine, 2 Dec 2007.
Liddle, P and Pugh, C, 'British Army Commandos', *Everyone's War*, LEC Pub, Autumn/Winter 2007.
Musgrove, F 'A Bomber Command Navigator Remembers and Considers', *Everyone's War*, LEC Pub, Autumn/Winter 2004.
Orth K 'The U-Boat Experience', *Everyone's War*, LEC Pub, Spring/Summer 2003.
Pallud, J-P 'The Norwegian Campaign', *After the Battle* Magazine 2004, Issue 126.
Price, A 'Nachtjagd', *War Monthly*, Marshall Cavendish.
Sanders, H S-G 'The Raid on Vaagso', *After the Battle* Magazine 2000, Issue 109.
Speller I 'Hell Has Many Different Names: The Raids on Saint-Nazaire and Dieppe 1942', *Everyone's War*, LEC Pub, Autumn/Winter 2007.
Tildesley, K 'Voices from the Battle of the Atlantic', *Everyone's War*, LEC Pub, Spring/Summer 2003.
Tout, K 'The Culture Bomb: Joining up in the Second World War', *Everyone's War*, LEC Pub, Spring/Summer 2007.
Whitehead, I 'Aspects of Life on the British Home Front', *Everyone's War*, LEC Pub, Autumn/Winter 2002.
Wartime Magazines: various issues of *Picture Post, Wehrmacht, Der Adler*.

BIBLIOGRAPHY

UNPUBLISHED ACCOUNTS AND MEMOIRS

Adams, J RN Sub Lt on destroyer HMS *Walker*, Narvik campaign, Diary 13 Apr–6 Jun 1940. LEC Doc.

Arkle, F First-Lt RNVR on *ML 177*, experiences of Saint-Nazaire Raid 28 Mar 1942, LEC Doc.

Barrett, T Parachute Royal Engineer soldier, *Tom – His War*, unpub ms AB Mus.

Breen, D Naval Signalman/Telegraphist HMS *Egret* RN escort destroyer during the Battle of the Atlantic, LEC Doc.

Brown, L W RAF Parachute Jump Instructor report of ditching at sea of Stirling aircraft 9 Aug 44, AB Mus Doc.

Butler, L Flt Sgt Bomber Command, 467 Sqn, LEC tape LECLEE/2003–2111.

Capon, S Paratrooper, 9 PARA, *3rd September 1939*, AB Mus unpub ms.

Carroll, T Pte, 2nd Bn Irish Guards, 1940 Norway campaign, LEC Doc.

Cutcliffe, J D MV *Richmond Castle* survivor, nine days in open boat, LEC Doc.

Davidson, G RN rating aboard ML *192*, Saint-Nazaire Raid of 28 Mar 1942, LEC Doc.

Davies, B Female worker aircraft factory, *Dilutees from 1942*, unpub. LEC Account.

Dormer, G RN Sub Lt on armed Trawler HMS *Cape Argona*, Diary account early part of the Battle of the Atlantic, LEC Doc.

Drewienkiewicz, K J 'Early Training and Employment of Territorial Army in Build Up and Early Days of World War II'. MA Thesis, RCDS 1992.

Edwards, D Pte, 2nd Bn Oxfordshire and Buckinghamshire Regiment, *Normandy Diary*, glider-infantry D-Day experiences, AB Mus.

Flatow, A F Major tank officer, 45 RTR, *A Personal Narrative of El Alamein*, BTM Doc.

Franklin, P H Third Radio Officer MV *Richmond Castle* torpedoed 4 Aug 42, lifeboat diary 4–13 Aug, LEC Doc.

Gibb, W Chief Officer MV *Richmond Castle* torpedoed 4 Aug 42, interview report, LEC Doc.

Heydte, von der German Fallschirmjäger Officer, *Interrogation Report* SIR 1438, CSDIC (UK) 31 Jan 45, AB Mus.

Hill, J Brig, Comd 3rd PARA Bde, Address Royal Hospital Chelsea 12 May 1994. AB Mus doc.

– Personal Account Normandy experiences. AB Mus.draft Doc.

Kershaw, L Pte, AA Royal Artillery, *The War Years*, unpub Ms author's collection.

Killick, J Captain, 89 Parachute Field Security Sqn, LEC P. Liddle interview Oct 2001.

Kingdom, J Staff Sgt Glider Pilot Regt, LEC P. Liddle interview Sep 2000.

Ling, D Capt tank officer 44RTR, Diary and papers of the Desert War 2000, BTM.

Lough, E S Major HQ 5th Para Bde, Normandy experiences D-Day, AB Mus.

O'Connor, G Pte 13 PARA, *To France Without a Passport*, D-Day parachute experience, unpub ms, AB Mus.

Packwood, T Glider Infantry Normandy and N.W. Europe, LEC P. Liddle interview Oct 2002.

Parsons, G Pte, No 5 Independent Company 1940 Norway campaign, LEC Doc.

Pead, R A Sgt 9 PARA mortar platoon, unpub account Normandy parachute experiences, AB mus.

Pestridge, J RAF, shot down 9/10 Aug 43 on return from Mannheim bombing mission, *The Last Trip*, unpub LEC account.

Peto-Shepherd, D Bomber pilot, *The Devil Take the Hindmost*, LEC unpub doc.

Pye, F J Second Officer MV *Richmond Castle* torpedoed 4 Aug 42, interview report, LEC Doc.

Read, H Parachute signaller, 3 PARA Bde, 6th Airborne Div, D-Day experiences, LEC B Atkinson interview, Tape 2316.

Rendell, B Tank Sgt 1 RTR, interview, *The Rendell Story*, 1996, BTM Doc.

Roderick, J Lt Commando, Saint-Nazaire Raid account 28 Mar 1942, LEC Doc.

Rollins, P Tank Tpr 40RTR, interview S Wheeler and L Hill Jun 2006, BTM.

Sampson, E Pte RASC experiences Norway campaign, LEC Doc.

Stonard, E Pte, 72nd Field Regt Royal Artillery, account of experiences during retreat from France and Dunkirk 1940, LEC Doc.

War Office. Notes From Theatres of War, Western Desert and North Africa, 1942–3, author's collection.

Watson, P Tank Cpl, 2RTR, *A Corporal's Story*, BTM Doc.

INTERVIEWS

Allsup, E Lt Tank Comd 8RTR, author interview 6 Dec 2006.

Carson, K Flt Sgt, Navigator 512 Sqn RAF. Author interview 22 Sep 2007.

Chatfield, H Flt Lt 512 Sqn RAF. Glider tug pilot. Author interview 22 Sep 2007.

Hibbert, A Lt Royal Artillery experiences France and Dunkirk 1940. Author interview 18 Dec 2007.

Hill, J LEC Interview P. Liddle Feb 2001.

Johnson, A Commando on Vlaagso raid Dec 1942, LEC Tape 1329, P. Liddle interview 29 Oct 2004.

Kershaw L and Kershaw C Wartime experiences of father, schoolboy, Home Guard, Royal Artillery D-Day and north-west Europe 1944–5, and mother wartime and Germany 1945, author interviews 18 May 2007.

Lloyd, M Nursing Sister Princess Mary's Nursing Service, treated RAF 'Guinea Pig' burns' victims 1940, author interview 29 Apr 2007.

Mallard, J M Tank Officer 44 RTR author interview 4 Oct 2006.

Trasenster, M Lt Tank Officer 4/7 RDG experiences in Normandy. Author interview 25 Sep 2006.

PICTURE ACKNOWLEDGEMENTS

Author's collection: 244 above. From *World War II: The Battle of Britain*, Time-Life, 1977: 20, 118 above (William Vandivert). From *Picture Post*, vol. 7, no. 13, 29 June 1940: 20 above. From *Picture Post*, vol. 7, no. 8, 25 May 1940: 49 above. From *Picture Post*, vol. 7, no. 10, 8 June 1940: 49 below. From *Picture Post*, vol. 7, no. 10, 8 June 1940: 76 above. From *Picture Post*, vol. 7, no. 12, 22 June 1940: 76 below. Fom *Picture Post*, vol. 7, no. 11, 15 June 1940: 118 below. From *Picture Post*, vol. 16, no. 2, 11 July 1942: 152 above. From *Picture Post*, vol. 17, no. 5, 31 October 1942: 152 below. From *World War II: The Commandos*, Time-Life, 1981: 188 below. From *The Raid on Saint-Nazaire, After the Battle* magazine, no. 59: 189 below. From *World war II: The Battle of the Atlantic*, Time-Life, 1977: 216. From *Signal* magazine, 2 April 1943: 217 above. From *Picture Post*, vol. 11, no. 1, 5 April 1941: 217 below. From *Der Zweite Weltkrieg, Band 1*, F. Burda, Burda druck und Verlag, 1952: 244 below. From *Picture Post*, vol 25, no. 9, 25 November 1945: 245 above. From *Lancaster at War*: 275 above.

Corbis: 331 (Keystone). Getty Images: 21 (Central Press), 77 (Keystone), 119 below (Stephenson), 153 (Bert Hardy), 189 above (Popperfoto), 275 below (Bert Hardy), 302 below (Haywood Magee), 330 (Picture Post). Imperial War Museum: 48 (A26184), 119 above (D22946), 188 above (N479), 274 (C4552), 302 above (H38992), 303 (FLM2571).

Every reasonable effort has been made to contact the copyright holders, but if there are any errors or omissions, Hodder & Stoughton will be pleased to insert the appropriate acknowledgement in any subsequent printing of this publication.

INDEX

Figures in italics indicate captions.